Striving for Better Jobs

DIRECTIONS IN DEVELOPMENT
Human Development

Striving for Better Jobs

The Challenge of Informality in the Middle East and North Africa

Roberta Gatti, Diego F. Angel-Urdinola,
Joana Silva, and András Bodor

WORLD BANK GROUP

ISBN (paper): 978-0-8213-9535-6
ISBN (electronic): 978-0-8213-9536-3
DOI: 10.1596/978-0-8213-9535-6

Cover photo: © Toufik Berramdane. Used with permission. Further permission required for reuse.
Cover design: Naylor Design

Library of Congress Cataloging-in-Publication Data

Striving for better jobs : the challenge of informality in the Middle East and North Africa / Roberta Gatti . . . [et al.].
     p. cm. — (Directions in development)
     Includes bibliographical references.
  ISBN 978-0-8213-9535-6 (alk. paper) — ISBN 978-0-8213-9536-3
     1. Informal sector (Economics)—Africa, North. 2. Informal sector (Economics)—Middle East.
3. Labor market—Africa, North. 4. Labor market—Middle East. I. Gatti, Roberta.
II. World Bank.
   HD2346.A56S77 2012
   331—dc23
                                  2012011909

Contents

Boxes

Figures

Tables

Preface

Throughout the Arab World, many are striving for the opportunity to realize their potential and aspirations in a region that is rich in both human and physical capital. Although in several countries in the region economic growth has been sustained for several decades, this process has failed to create enough opportunities in the form of good jobs. This report addresses one of these potential margins of exclusion: informal employment and the vulnerabilities and lack of opportunity associated with it.

This report has two main objectives. The first is to provide an understanding of the extent, determinants, and challenges posed by informal employment, bringing together new evidence, data, and country-specific analyses.

The second objective is to open up and inform a debate on feasible policy options to better manage vulnerability through social security coverage extension, promote fulfilling work, and support an inclusive development process. The informality phenomenon in the Middle East and North Africa (MENA) region involves the vast majority of workers in the private sector, and so the evidence in this report suggests the need to rethink policy making, especially concerning labor markets and social security reform, because many of the intended beneficiaries operate beyond the reach of legislative reform. The observed patterns in MENA indicate that informal employment is consistently associated with overall worse conditions, lower pay, and lower productivity than formal employment. This report analyzes the constraints that underpin the formal-informal divide and discusses policy options that can support a broad-based development process.

This report was completed in the aftermath of the Arab Spring. The region is undergoing important institutional transitions—including continuous instability in some countries—that are complex and outside the scope of this report. This report focuses primarily on options for technical reform.

At the same time it stresses the importance of an inclusive social dialogue open to a broader set of actors, including those whose voices were traditionally not heard, such as youth, women, the unemployed, and informal workers.

A widely accepted definition describes informality as an activity that is unregulated by formal institutions such as labor laws, registration, and taxation. Although many angles to informality can be identified, this report looks at informality through the human development lens and focuses particularly on *informal employment*. As such, the working definition adopted herein defines informality as a lack of social security coverage (usually understood as pensions, or if a pension system is not existent, as health insurance). The report aims to characterize the magnitude of the informality phenomenon in the MENA region compared to other regions of the world and, to the extent possible, its evolution over time and macroeconomic determinants. This is discussed in chapter 1. Regional and cross-country comparisons are useful, but a more country-specific analysis is needed to explain the ample heterogeneity observed. Thus the analysis in chapter 2 uses all available household-level datasets to create a detailed profile of informal workers. Informality among firms matters for job quality and workers' access to risk-sharing mechanisms and is a key piece of this puzzle. An in-depth study of the dynamics of firms is beyond the scope of this work. However, data from firm-level surveys are used to describe the characteristics of informality in firms, both in micro-firms that operate outside the regulatory framework as well as in larger formal firms that do not fully comply with social security contributions and taxes (chapter 3). Data on earnings, job mobility patterns, attitudes, and self-rated job satisfaction are used to provide a full characterization of the quality of informal jobs (chapter 4). The resulting evidence corroborates the view that important segmentations exist across formal and informal job sectors, and that much of the observed informality is likely due to segmentation and exclusion factors, which in some countries are linked to the prominent role of the public sector as employer. Chapter 5 discusses determinants of informality and links them to options for reform. Although a "one size fits all" approach is clearly not suitable to address the heterogeneity of informality in the region, policy options in five complementary areas emerge as the key to promoting social security coverage extension, better job quality, and overall a more inclusive development process: (1) creating a level playing field for small and large firms to compete; (2) addressing regulatory barriers in labor

markets; (3) realigning incentives, pay, and benefit packages in the public sector; (4) redesigning key features of pension systems and extending
social security coverage; and (5) increasing access to skills-upgrading
instruments for informal workers.

Data availability defined the geographic scope of this report. With the
exception of the evidence presented in chapter 1, which relies in part on
standardized International Labour Organization data and thus allows for
full coverage, this report focuses on the countries in the MENA region
for which household-level data with information on social security coverage were available: the Arab Republic of Egypt, Iraq, Jordan, Lebanon,
Morocco, the Syrian Arab Republic, and the Republic of Yemen. With the
exception of household data for Egypt and administrative data kindly
provided by the Jordan Social Security Corporation, none of these surveys' data track individuals over time. As a result, the scope to draw broad
inferences at the regional level about the dynamics of informality as well
as to identify causal determinants is limited. Moreover, some of the diagnostics are based on data that are a few years old. However, the behavioral patterns identified are likely to continue to be valid, especially if
linked to slow-changing institutional determinants. Additionally, with the
exception of Egypt, only cross-sectional data were available for firms. The
large majority of firm-level data are drawn from cross-sectional Investment
Climate Surveys, which sample only registered firms. Data surveying
informal/micro-firms were available only for Egypt and Morocco.

To overcome these constraints, this project cosponsored four new surveys that were fielded in 2009 and 2010: the Egypt and Morocco youth
surveys, the Lebanon Labor Force Survey, and the Syria matched
employer-employee module. In these four surveys, questions were
included about social security coverage, job characteristics, workers' attitudes, willingness to contribute to social security, and the like. The
Lebanon and Syria surveys also included innovative modules reporting
the results of direct cognitive and noncognitive skills tests, which are
linked to informality for the first time in this literature. Notwithstanding
these important additions to the database for the report, data availability
and access presented a considerable constraint. An important message
emerging from this work is that generating more and better data, promoting open access to them, and especially investing in longitudinal surveys
are likely to have large payoffs in terms of a deeper understanding of labor
markets in this region. The lack of experimental evidence on how firms
and individuals respond to incentives to formalize also imposes a limit on
the ability to make inferences about the possible impact of different

intervention in the context of MENA. This is another area in which investments can have high returns.

This report builds on and adds to the growing body of literature addressing the question of informality worldwide and in the MENA region. With its broad country coverage and intensive use of all regional household- and firm-level data accessible to the World Bank, this study provides a unique source for cross-country comparisons and benchmarking of informal employment in MENA. The use of newly collected information on workers' attitudes, benefit structure, and working conditions provides a full characterization of the quality and features of informal jobs. Moreover, introducing direct measures of cognitive and noncognitive ability allows researchers, for the first time, to reduce much of the usually unexplained variation in determinants and returns to informality. By linking this systematic and innovative empirical analysis with a detailed description of constraints and regulatory barriers, especially those associated with labor markets and pension institutions, the report provides a framework for policy options that can be adapted to the different country contexts. Because of the multifaceted nature of informality, this report touches upon many agendas, including labor market regulation, public sector reform, social insurance design, private sector dynamics, and skills upgrading. Although their in-depth treatment is clearly beyond the scope of this work, these issues are explored from the specific angle of their effect on informality. As such, this report complements numerous recent and ongoing analytical efforts, including the World Bank MENA Private Sector Flagship Report, *From Privilege to Competition*; the MENA Flagship Report, *Jobs for Shared Prosperity: Time for Action in the Middle East and North Africa*; Country Economic Memorandums; and country-specific labor market studies in the region.

Acknowledgments

This report is the product of the collaborative effort of a core team led by Roberta Gatti and comprising Diego Angel-Urdinola, Joana Silva, and András Bodor (principal authors); Kimie Tanabe (data management); and May Wazzan, with important contributions from Mohamad Alloush, Carole Abi Nahed Chartouni, Anne Hilger, Arvo Kuddo, and Matteo Morgandi.

Many colleagues have provided useful inputs at different stages of this report, including Surani Abeysekera, Rita Almeida, Luca Etter, Alvaro Forteza, Maros Ivanic, David McKenzie, Jaime Saenz, Amina Semlali, and Andrew Stone. Background papers were written for this report by Mohamad Alloush, Diego Angel-Urdinola, Mehdi Benyagoub, András Bodor, Carole Abi Nahed Chartouni, Yoonyoung Cho, Yohana Dukham, Mario di Filippo, Norman Loayza, Daniela Marotta, Shaumik Paul, Amina Semlali, Joana Silva, Kimie Tanabe, Tomoko Wada, and George Wellner. Amy Gautam edited the report.

We are grateful to the participants of the consultations held in Cairo (September 2010), at the International Labour Organization (ILO)–World Bank labor market course in Turin (October 2010), and in Tunis (March 2011) for their insights into the nature of informal employment in the Middle East and North Africa region. We thank our peer reviewers, Ahmed Galal, William Maloney, and Milan Vodopivec, for their guidance; Gordon Betcherman and William Maloney for useful discussions; and Jean-Pierre Chauffour, Prof. Alia Abdel Monem El Mahdi, Sherine El-Shawarby, Caroline Freund, Santiago Herrera, Robert Holzmann, Ruslan Yemtsov, and the participants of the brainstorming workshops that were held at the World Bank and at the International Monetary Fund in Washington, DC, in October 2009, October 2010, and May 2011, for their valuable comments. Through this report, four new surveys were cosponsored (Egypt youth, Morocco youth, Lebanon Labor Force Survey, Syria employer-employee matched module). We acknowledge the productive collaboration to structure the questionnaires with Gloria La Cava, Yaa Oppong, David Robalino, Haneen Sayed, and Tara Vishvanath. We are grateful to the Social Security Corporation of Jordan for sharing data on social security contributions.

This work was supported by the Arab World Initiative. We thank Shamshad Akhtar and Steen Jorgensen for their strategic guidance.

Contributors

The authors of the chapters are as follows:

Preface and Overview	Roberta Gatti
Chapter 1	Diego F. Angel-Urdinola with Anne Hilger and Surani Abeysekera
Chapter 2	Diego F. Angel-Urdinola with Kimie Tanabe and Anne Hilger
Chapter 3	Joana Silva
Chapter 4	Roberta Gatti
Chapter 5	András Bodor and May Wazzan with Arvo Kuddo and Roberta Gatti

Abbreviations

ALMP	active labor market program
CAPMAS	Central Agency for Public Mobilization and Statistics
DB	defined benefit
DC	defined contribution
ECA	Europe and Central Asia
EPL	employment protection legislation
ERF	Economic Research Forum
GCC	Gulf Cooperation Council
GDP	gross domestic product
ICA	Investment Climate Assessment
ID	identification
ILCS	International Conference of Labor Statisticians
ILO	International Labour Organization
IRA	individual retirement account
IV	instrumental variable
LAC	Latin America and the Caribbean
MDC	matching defined contribution
MEAS	Micro- and Small Enterprises Survey
MENA	Middle East and North Africa
MIMIC	Multiple Indicator–Multiple Cause
MSE	micro- and small enterprise
NDC	notional defined contribution
NGO	nongovernmental organization
NPS	New Pension Scheme
NSSF	National Social Security Fund

OECD	Organisation for Economic Co-operation and Development
OLS	ordinary least squares
PAYG	pay-as-you-go
PF	provident fund
PMT	proxy means testing
RSBY	Rashtriya Swasthya Bima Yojana
SA	South Asia
SEA	Southeast Asia
SME	small and medium enterprise
SSA	Sub-Saharan Africa
SSC	Social Security Corporation
TPI	third-party insurer
UI	unemployment insurance
UN	United Nations
WAP	working-age population

Currency values are given in U.S. dollars unless otherwise indicated.

Overview

Informality is a complex phenomenon, encompassing unpaid workers and workers without pension or health insurance coverage, small or micro-firms that operate outside the regulatory framework, and large registered firms that might decide to partially evade corporate taxes and social security contributions. The report looks at informality through a human development angle and focuses specifically on informal employment. In line with this approach, the working definition for informality adopted in the report is "lack of social security coverage" (usually understood as pensions, or if a pension system does not exist, as health insurance), which captures well the vulnerability associated with informal employment. Although a great deal of heterogeneity is seen across countries, informality is widespread, and some Middle East and North Africa (MENA) countries are among the most informal economies in the world. Evidence from this and other studies indicates that informal workers in most MENA countries are engaged in low-productivity jobs, more so than in comparator countries. Informal workers in the region are generally paid less for otherwise similar work in the formal sector, and their self-reported work satisfaction is low. Moreover, the data underscore the presence of important mobility barriers between formal and informal employment. Although extending social security coverage is likely to bring about welfare improvements in and of itself, countries will find it necessary to remove existing barriers to the creation of high-quality jobs to promote long-term inclusive growth and, thus, formality. Policies that can support this process include those that

1) Create a level playing field for small and large firms to compete
2) Move toward labor regulations that promote labor mobility and provide support to workers in periods of transition

3) Realign incentives, pay, and benefit packages in the public sector
4) Reform pension and existing social insurance systems and introduce new instruments for coverage extension and
5) Enhance the productivity of informal workers through training and skills upgrading.

Background

Economic growth has been sustained for many years precrisis in the region, but this has not resulted in the creation of an adequate number of jobs and has succeeded, at best, in generating low-quality, informal jobs. The report addresses one margin of exclusion: informal employment and the vulnerabilities and lack of opportunities associated with it.

Informality in the MENA region involves the vast majority of workers outside of the public sector, and because many of the intended beneficiaries operate outside the reach of existing systems, the report's findings point to the need to rethink policy making, especially with regard to those policies pertaining to labor market and social security reform. The report analyzes the constraints that prevent informal workers from becoming formal and discusses policy options to effectively address these constraints. The current transitions in MENA are accompanied by important challenges, but they also provide new opportunities to improve living standards and equity. Achieving this will require, above all, a new and inclusive social dialogue open to a broader set of actors, particularly to those whose voices have traditionally not been heard, such as youth, women, the unemployed, and informal workers.

This Overview first describes the magnitude of the informality phenomenon in the MENA region relative to other regions of the world, its macroeconomic determinants, and, to the extent possible, its evolution over time. The first section provides a detailed profile of informal workers in the region. The next section describes the characteristics of informality in micro-firms that operate outside the regulatory framework and in larger firms that do not fully comply with social security contribution requirements and tax obligations. This Overview then discusses earnings, job mobility patterns, attitudes, and workers' self-rated job satisfaction to provide a better understanding of the quality of jobs in the informal sector. The evidence corroborates that important segmentations exist between formal and informal jobs, and that much of the observed informality is likely due to barriers to mobility into better jobs. In some countries, these barriers are linked to the prominent role of the public sector as the main employer in the formal sector. The last section discusses policy options for effectively expanding coverage of health insurance and pension systems and promoting the creation of better quality jobs.

Understanding Informality

This report looks at informality through a human development angle and focuses particularly on *informal employment*. Informality is a complex phenomenon, comprising unpaid workers and workers without social security or health insurance coverage, small or micro-firms that operate outside the regulatory framework, and large registered firms that might partially evade corporate taxes and social security contributions. Three indices are commonly used to measure informality: (1) the Schneider Index,[1] which uses a broad set of country correlates to estimate the share of production not declared to tax and regulatory authorities, (2) the share of employed workers without social security coverage, and (3) the prevalence of self-employment. Defining informality as "lack of social security coverage" captures well the vulnerability associated with informal employment and, as such, is the working definition in this analysis.

Informality is a fundamental characteristic of underdevelopment and has costs and benefits. As depicted in figure O.1, a larger informal sector is often associated with lower gross domestic product (GDP) per capita. For most countries in the region, the share of informal to total employment is broadly aligned with the level that their economic development would predict. Informal employment is associated with costs and negative externalities that may be a source of economic slowdown. For example, a large informal sector implies that a heftier tax burden will fall on the formal sector. This may hold back new and productive firms, precisely those firms that have the potential for driving growth in a dynamic economy. In addition, informal activities use and congest public infrastructure without contributing to the tax revenues necessary to maintain them. Moreover, workers involved in the informal sector often lack a written contract regulating their work relationship and/or pension and health insurance coverage. This exposes them to significant occupational risks, including a potentially less safe and decent work environment, as well as insufficient mechanisms to cope with risks related to

Figure O.1 Informality and Economic Development

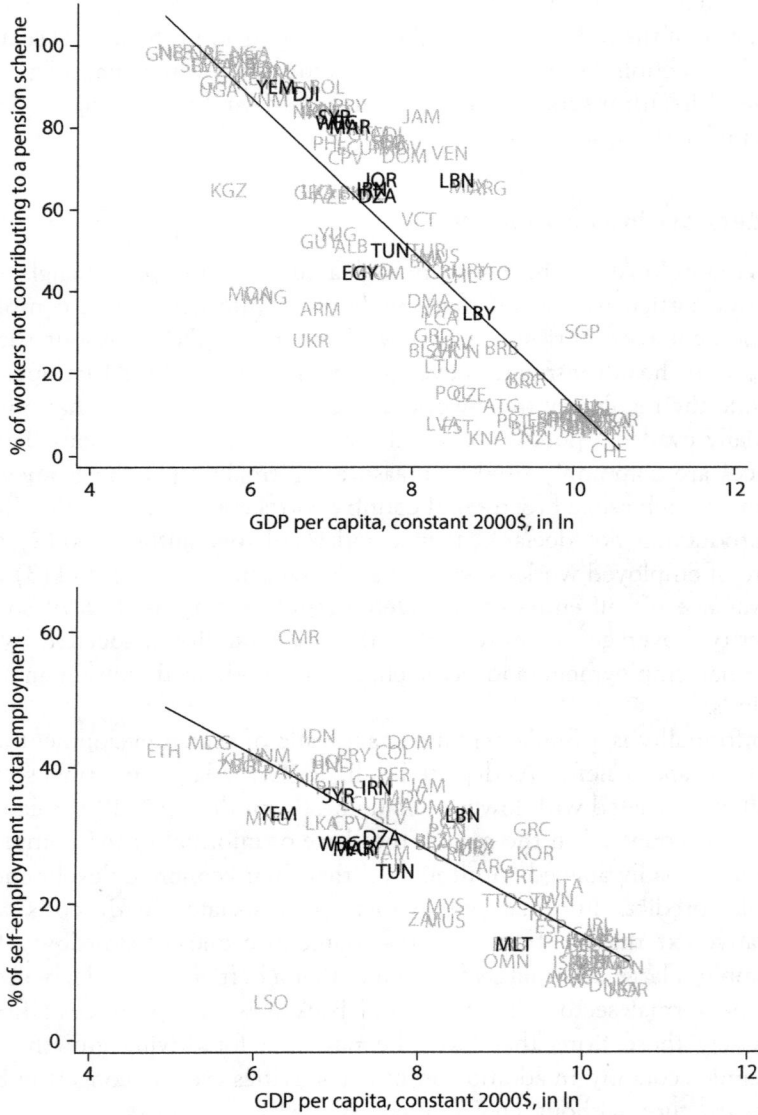

% of workers not contributing to a pension scheme
100
80
60
40
20
0
4
6
8
10
12
GDP per capita, constant 2000$, in ln
YEM
DJI
JAM
VEN
KGZ
JOR
LBN
DZA
VCT
TUN
EGY
ARM
LBY
UKR
SGP
LTU
ATG
KNA
NZL
CHE
% of self-employment in total employment
60
40
20
0
4
6
8
10
12
GDP per capita, constant 2000$, in ln
CMR
ETH
IDN
DOM
IRN
SYR
YEM
LBN
GRC
DZA
KOR
TUN
PRT
MYS
MLT
OMN
LSO

Source: Loayza and Wada 2010.
Note: GDP = gross domestic product.

old-age and health problems. Nevertheless, informal employment has benefits for the labor market and population, because it provides employment to a significant portion of the population, may be a source of innovation and entrepreneurship (many firms start operating informally when they are small and formalize as they grow), and serves as a safety net in periods of transition (such as during times of economic downturn).

Informality can be the result of exclusion or of a rational choice by entrepreneurs or workers who decide to opt out of the formal labor market. Traditionally informality has been considered the result of involuntary exclusion of workers due to high and distortive regulation (De Soto 1989). Other factors can also affect workers' and firms' decisions to work informally, including myopia (that is, lack of awareness about retirement needs and health risks) and limited information, both of which might be associated with exclusion margins, such as geographic location and low human capital (that is, poor people in remote areas and/or uneducated agricultural workers may not have access to social security systems but would join them if they could). Some workers and firms decide to opt out of the formal economy as a result of a rational cost-benefit evaluation (Perry and others 2007). These reasons for informality are not mutually exclusive and likely coexist in a continuum. In all cases, widespread informality implies high vulnerability, and so a clear rationale for government intervention can be found. On the one hand, when involuntary exclusion from formal employment is predominant (for example, small firms can survive only if they avoid paying taxes, or salaried workers would like access to social security but cannot find jobs with coverage), then policies that reduce existing barriers are needed to improve welfare. Such policies might include rationalizing regulations to create a level playing field for small and large firms to compete fairly, as well as tackling labor market reform. On the other hand, when more workers and firms voluntarily opt out of the regulatory system, policy interventions that rebalance the perceived costs and benefits of participating in the formal sector are needed. Such policies can focus on improving the quality and outreach of key public services, enhancing communication and transparency about social services, and redesigning and extending instruments for better management of health- and age-related risks.

Informality in MENA: Levels and Trends

The MENA region displays lower employment and higher unemployment rates than any other region in the world. Although economic growth was sustained in the years before the 2008 financial crisis and employment growth was positive (and particularly high for women), high population growth has continued to put pressure on labor markets to absorb an increasing number of new entrants. Moreover, in the last decade, jobs were created mainly in low value-added service sectors, most of which are associated with high rates of informal employment, such as construction, commerce, and transport. This process may have prevented the benefits of economic growth from being shared fully among poorer segments of the population and has led to increasing informality.

A typical country in MENA produces about one-third of its GDP and employs 65 percent of its labor force informally. This means that around two-thirds of all workers in the region may not have access to health insurance and/or are not contributing to a pension system that would provide them with income security after retirement. From a fiscal per-spective, about one-third of total economic output in the region remains undeclared, with considerable implications for government revenue. As illustrated by figure O.2, the typical MENA country is more informal than the typical developed country and countries in Europe and Central Asia (ECA) when considering the percentage of labor for not contribut-ing to social security and self-employment. It is, however, less informal than the typical country in Latin America and the Caribbean (LAC), East Asia and Pacific (EAP), South Asia (SA), and Sub-Saharan Africa (SSA).

Important variations are found in the prevalence of informality across non-GCC countries, depending, among other factors, on the availability of natural resources and labor and on the size of the public sector. Non-GCC countries are quite heterogeneous in terms of size, availability of resources and labor, economic development, and demographic structure, all factors that influence the size of the informal economy, which, as a result, varies significantly (see figure O.3 and chapter 2 for a more thorough discus-sion). In general, resource-rich/labor-abundant economies (such as the Islamic Republic of Iran and the Syrian Arab Republic) tend to display high informality rates in the region as proxied by the share of the labor force not contributing to social security (between 66 and 73 percent) and by the share of self-employment to total employment (between 32 and 54 percent). However, their share of undeclared output to total GDP (at around 20 percent) is comparable to that of GCC countries. This occurs because these countries generally have few, but large, formal firms (many in the energy sector) that are capital intensive, resulting in lower informal-ity in production than in labor (Loayza and Wada 2010). On the contrary,

Figure O.2   Informality in MENA Compared to Other Regions

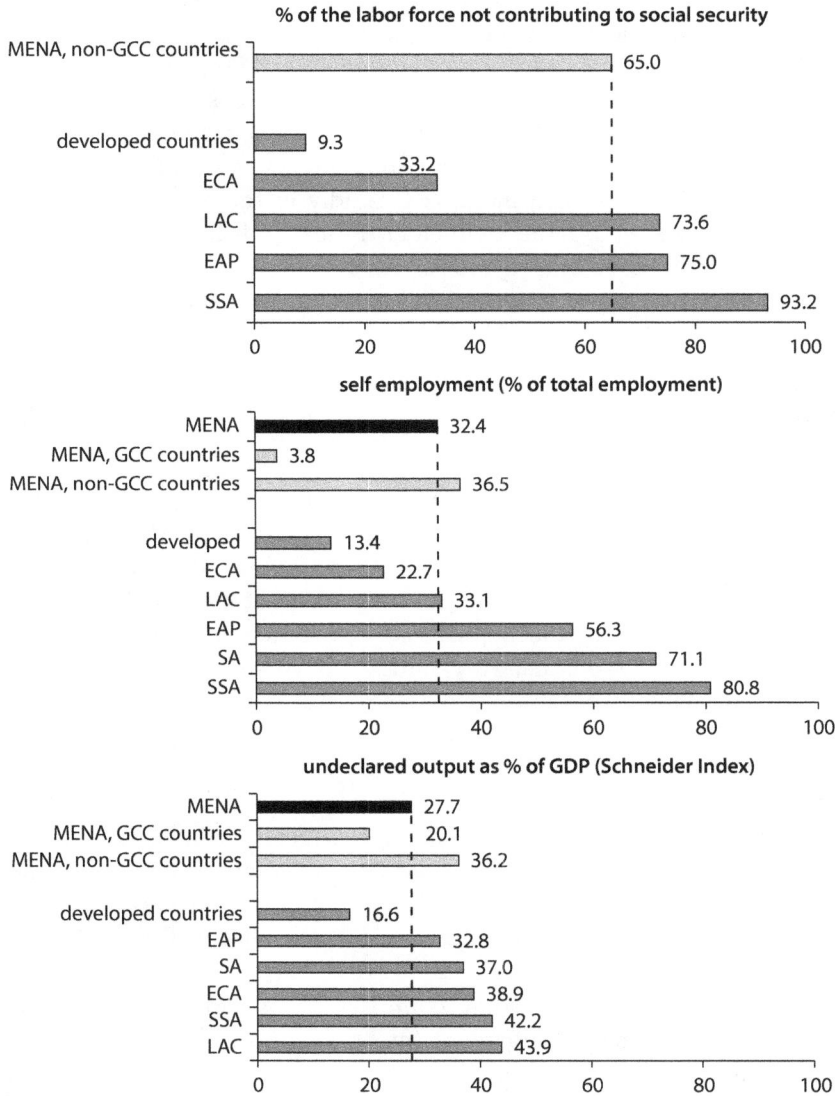

% of the labor force not contributing to social security

MENA, non-GCC countries — 65.0

developed countries — 9.3
ECA — 33.2
LAC — 73.6
EAP — 75.0
SSA — 93.2

(x-axis: 0, 20, 40, 60, 80, 100)

self employment (% of total employment)

MENA — 32.4
MENA, GCC countries — 3.8
MENA, non-GCC countries — 36.5

developed — 13.4
ECA — 22.7
LAC — 33.1
EAP — 56.3
SA — 71.1
SSA — 80.8

(x-axis: 0, 20, 40, 60, 80, 100)

undeclared output as % of GDP (Schneider Index)

MENA — 27.7
MENA, GCC countries — 20.1
MENA, non-GCC countries — 36.2

developed countries — 16.6
EAP — 32.8
SA — 37.0
ECA — 38.9
SSA — 42.2
LAC — 43.9

(x-axis: 0, 20, 40, 60, 80, 100)

Source: Schneider et al., 2010 for Schneider Index; WDI for self employment and pension scheme.
Note: EAP = East Asia and Pacific; ECA = Europe and Central Asia; GCC = Gulf Cooperation Council; LAC = Latin America and the Caribbean; SA = South America; SSA = Sub-Saharan Africa. The periods covered are the latest years in 2000–10 for pension scheme, 2000–11 for self- employment, and 1999–2007 for the Schneider index, respectively. Data on social security contributions in GCC countries are only available for Bahrain, 2007 (20 percent), and Qatar, 2008 (4.4 percent) (Palleres-Miralles, Romero, and Whitehouse 2012).

resource-poor/labor abundant economies (such as the Arab Republic of Egypt, Tunisia, and Morocco) display a high share of undeclared output (between 35 and 40 percent of GDP) and a lower share of the workforce not contributing to social security (between 45 and 76 percent), which is consistent with a higher share of medium-size (and semiformal) labor-intensive firms and, in some cases, significant public sector employment.

Informality in MENA has been rising in recent years. Data indicate that informality has been increasing rapidly in the entire developing world, as proxied by the Schneider Index and the share of self-employment to total employment. The increase in the share of unde-clared/informal output to total GDP in recent years has been a global trend (figure O.4).

Who Are Informal Workers?

Informality is highest among the working poor. Overall, in MENA informality decreases as wealth increases. In countries such as Lebanon, the share of informal employment is significantly lower among the wealthiest segments of the population. Nevertheless, in some MENA countries, informality is so widespread that it remains significant even among the wealthier segments of the population. In the Republic of Yemen and Syria, for instance, more than two-thirds of all workers who belong to the richest households work informally (figure O.5). In the Arab Republic of Egypt, the Republic of Yemen, and, to a lesser extent, Morocco, an interesting pattern emerges, whereby informality decreases with income/wealth but unemployment increases with income/wealth. This correlation suggests that in these countries, programs targeted at informal workers would be addressing the working poor, but interventions targeted at the unemployed (although a clearly visible and often vocal category) would reach those who can afford to be unemployed, that is, those who are relatively better off.

Over the life cycle, in some countries an important transition is made from informal employment into public sector employment as young individuals reach prime-age adulthood. Figure O.6 illustrates employment patterns by age for urban workers in a selected group of countries. Informality rates are very high among youth between the ages of 15 and 24. After age 24, informality decreases rapidly until individuals reach 40 to 45 years of age. After age 45, informality rates fall to between 20 and 30 percent. This rapid decrease in informality rates goes hand in hand with a rapid rise in public employment,

Figure O.3   Informality Rates for Selected Non–Gulf Cooperation Council Members

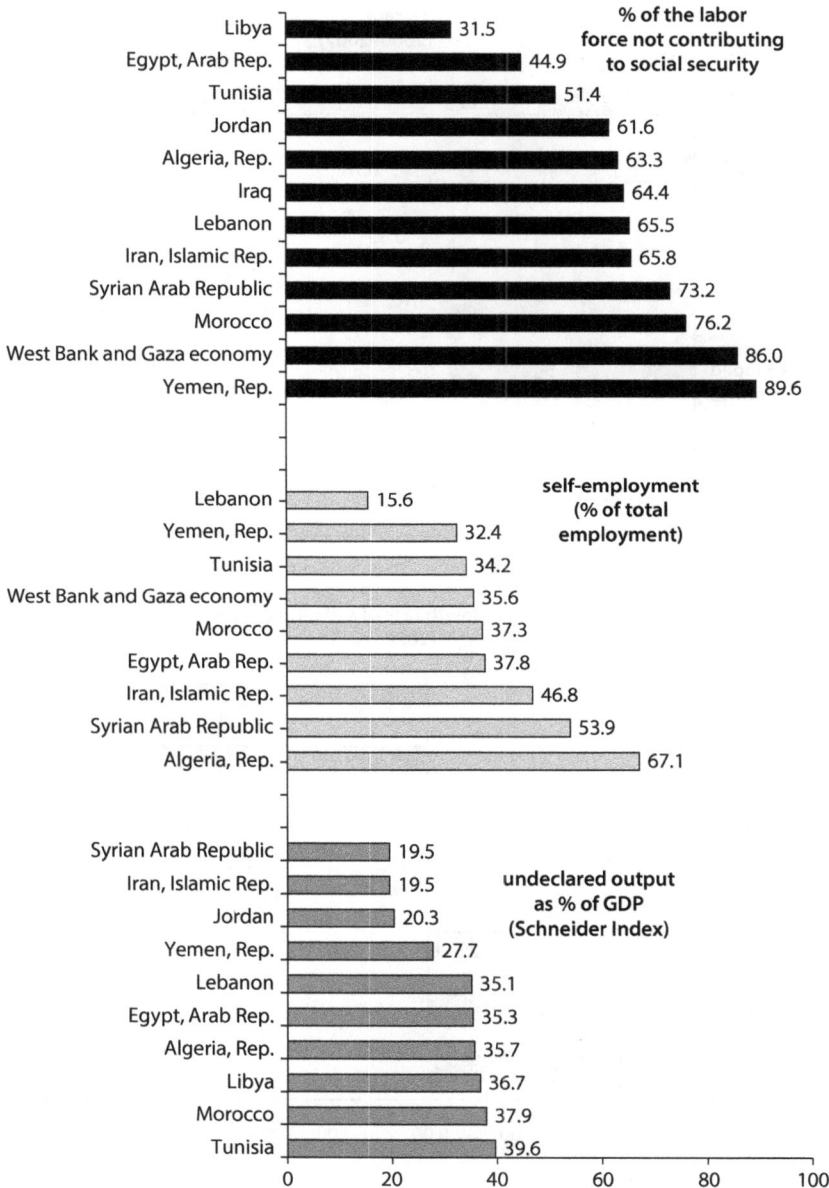

% of the labor force not contributing to social security

Libya	31.5
Egypt, Arab Rep.	44.9
Tunisia	51.4
Jordan	61.6
Algeria, Rep.	63.3
Iraq	64.4
Lebanon	65.5
Iran, Islamic Rep.	65.8
Syrian Arab Republic	73.2
Morocco	76.2
West Bank and Gaza economy	86.0
Yemen, Rep.	89.6

self-employment (% of total employment)

Lebanon	15.6
Yemen, Rep.	32.4
Tunisia	34.2
West Bank and Gaza economy	35.6
Morocco	37.3
Egypt, Arab Rep.	37.8
Iran, Islamic Rep.	46.8
Syrian Arab Republic	53.9
Algeria, Rep.	67.1

undeclared output as % of GDP (Schneider Index)

Syrian Arab Republic	19.5
Iran, Islamic Rep.	19.5
Jordan	20.3
Yemen, Rep.	27.7
Lebanon	35.1
Egypt, Arab Rep.	35.3
Algeria, Rep.	35.7
Libya	36.7
Morocco	37.9
Tunisia	39.6

Source: Processed from Loayza and Wada 2010.
Note: Time periods are as follows: Schneider Index, average 1999–2007; self-employment, 1999–2007; not contributing to social security (S.S.), 2000–2007.

Striving for Better Jobs • http://dx.doi.org/10.1596/978-0-8213-9535-6

Figure O.4   Annual Growth Rates of Informality

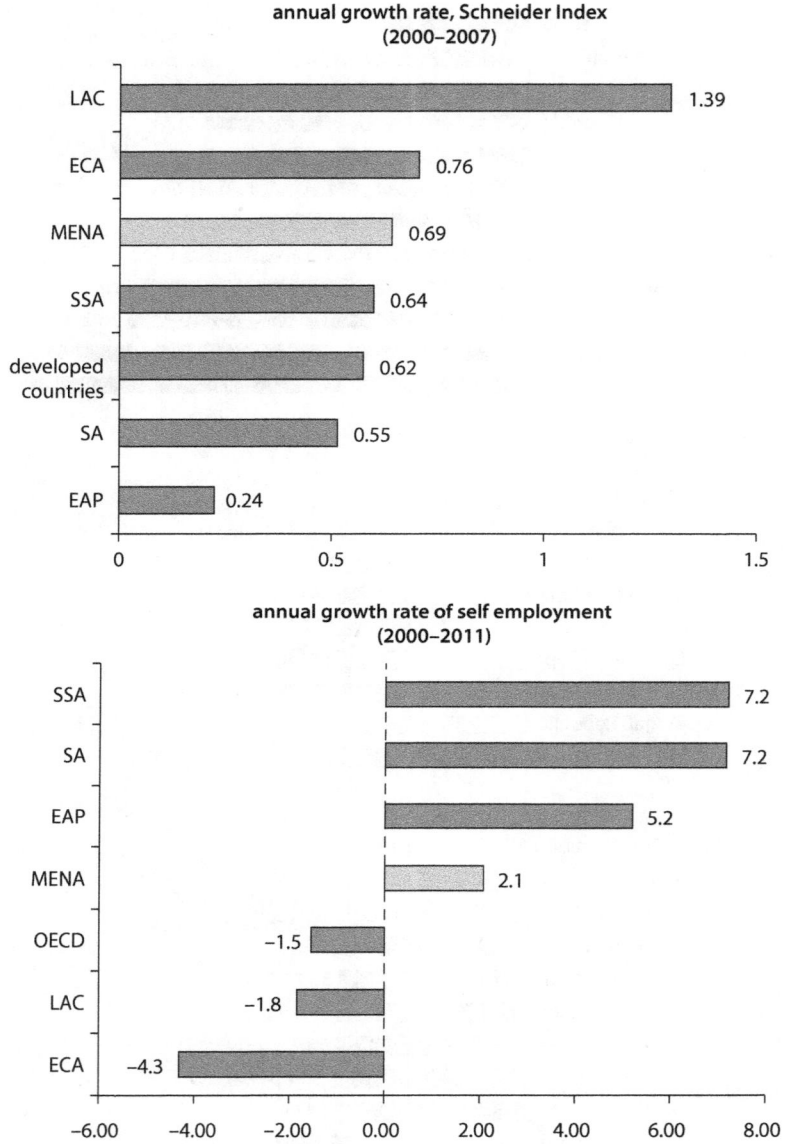

**annual growth rate, Schneider Index
(2000–2007)**

LAC	1.39
ECA	0.76
MENA	0.69
SSA	0.64
developed countries	0.62
SA	0.55
EAP	0.24

**annual growth rate of self employment
(2000–2011)**

SSA	7.2
SA	7.2
EAP	5.2
MENA	2.1
OECD	−1.5
LAC	−1.8
ECA	−4.3

Source: Processed from Loayza and Wada 2010.
Note: EAP = East Asia and Pacific; ECA = Europe and Central Asia; LAC = Latin America and the Caribbean;
SA = South America; SSA = Sub-Saharan Africa.

Figure O.5   Informality Rates by Quintile of Per Capita Consumption for Selected Countries

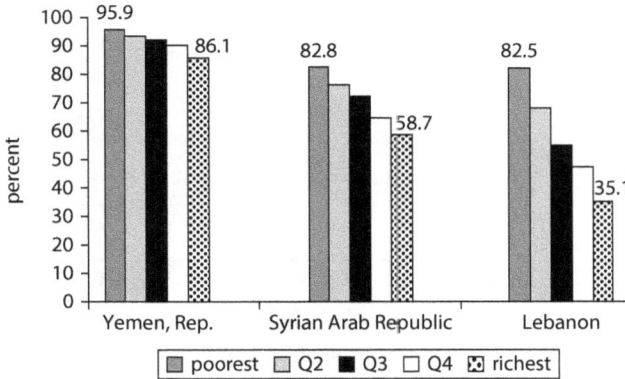

Source: Angel-Urdinola and Tanabe 2011.
Note: Q = quintile.

suggesting that a large portion of younger informal workers enter into public sector jobs as they become adults. These trends are very different from those observed in Latin America. Still, one has to be cautious in interpreting these results as they are likely to reflect vintage effects since, especially in countries such as Egypt, more public sector jobs were available to earlier cohorts of workers. For example, in countries such as Mexico, although informality rates also decrease with age, the observed transition occurs not between informality and public employment, but between informality and self-employment, with many young individuals becoming entrepreneurs and thus contributing to a more dynamic creation of employment in the private sector (Perry and others 2007).

Lower levels of education are strongly and linearly associated with higher rates of informality in most countries, an association that seems to be driven primarily by more educated workers joining the public sector (particularly in Egypt, Jordan, Morocco, and Syria). Informality rates among workers who completed primary and/or basic education (accounting for at least 50 percent of all the employed in most countries in the region) are generally much higher than among those workers who completed secondary and/or tertiary education. Consistent with the transitions depicted in figure O.6, differences in informality rates by age and education are mainly due to the life-cycle movement of older and more

Figure O.6 Employment Status by Age for Selected Countries, Urban Areas Only

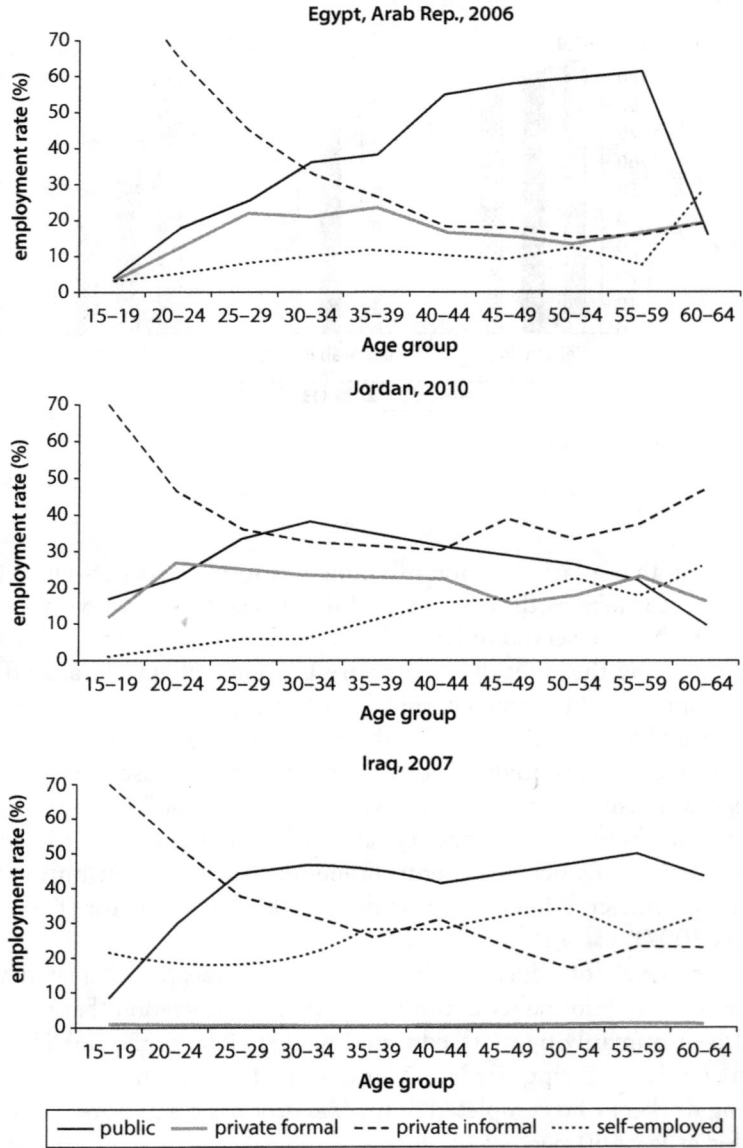

Egypt, Arab Rep., 2006

Jordan, 2010

Iraq, 2007

—— public   —— private formal   - - - private informal   ······ self-employed

figure continues next page

Striving for Better Jobs • http://dx.doi.org/10.1596/978-0-8213-9535-6

Figure O.6 Employment Status by Age for Selected Countries, Urban Areas Only *(continued)*

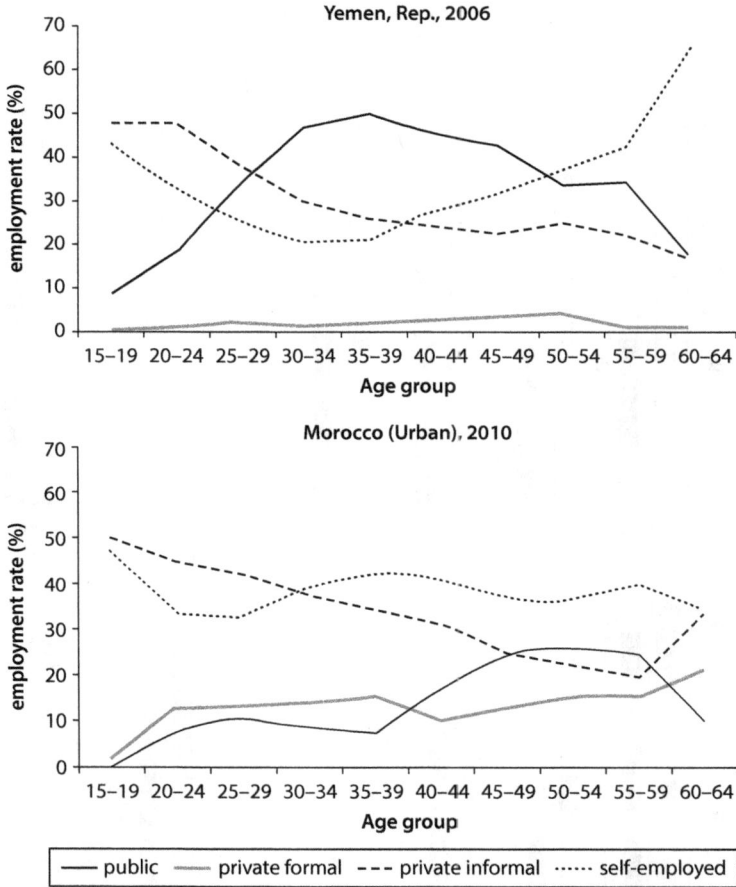

Yemen, Rep., 2006

Morocco (Urban), 2010

— public   — private formal   - - - private informal   ······ self-employed

Source: Angel-Urdinola and Tanabe 2011.

educated workers from informal employment to public sector employment. In countries where the bulk of formal jobs are in the public sector (such as the Republic of Yemen and Iraq), differences in informality rates across education levels in the private sector are negligible (figure O.7).

Informality is more prevalent among workers in small firms. In the private sector, informal workers are mostly employed in small firms, with a distribution that is particularly skewed toward firms with fewer than five workers and that are most likely engaged in low-productivity activities (figure O.8). Controlling for other observable characteristics, workers in medium-size (10 to 50 workers) and large-size (more than

Figure O.7   Informality Rates by Highest Educational Level Completed

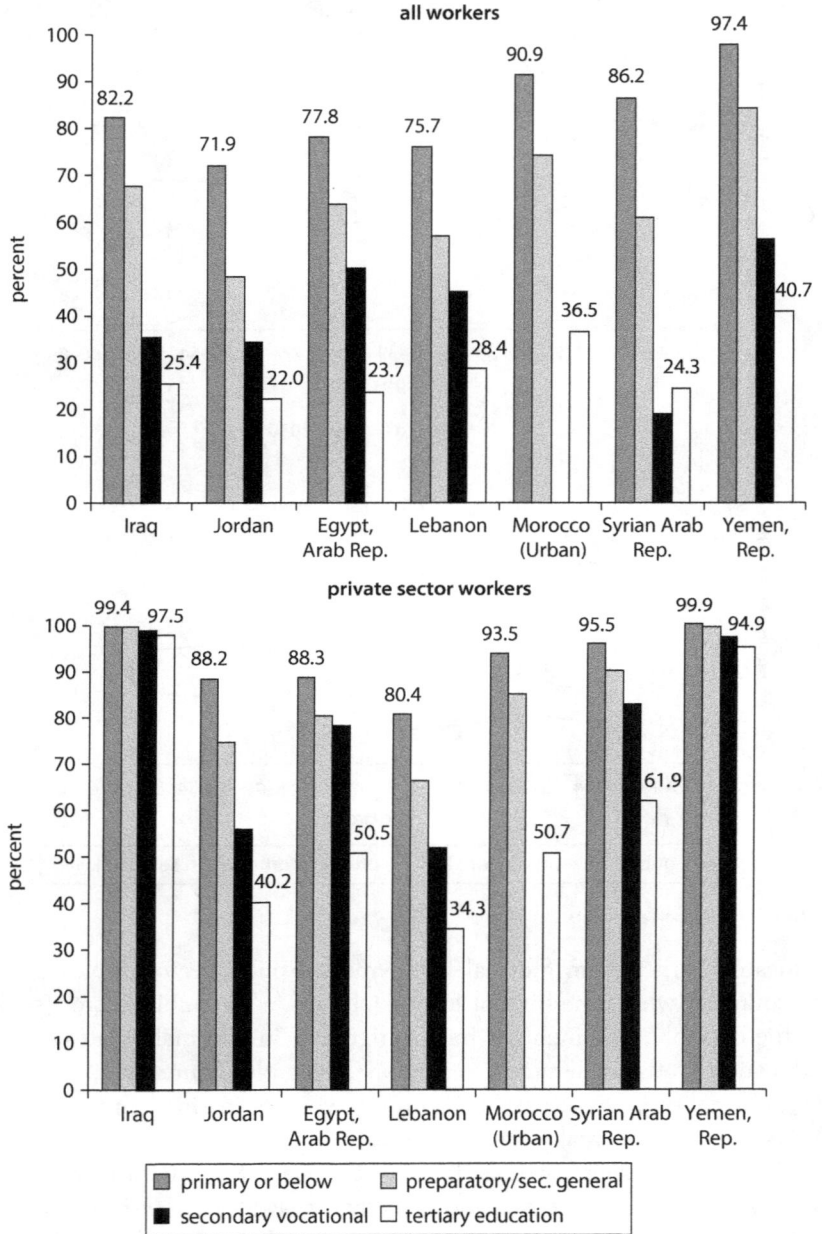

all workers

private sector workers

primary or below   preparatory/sec. general
secondary vocational   tertiary education

Source: Angel-Urdinola and Tanabe 2011.

Figure O.8 Informality and Firm Size

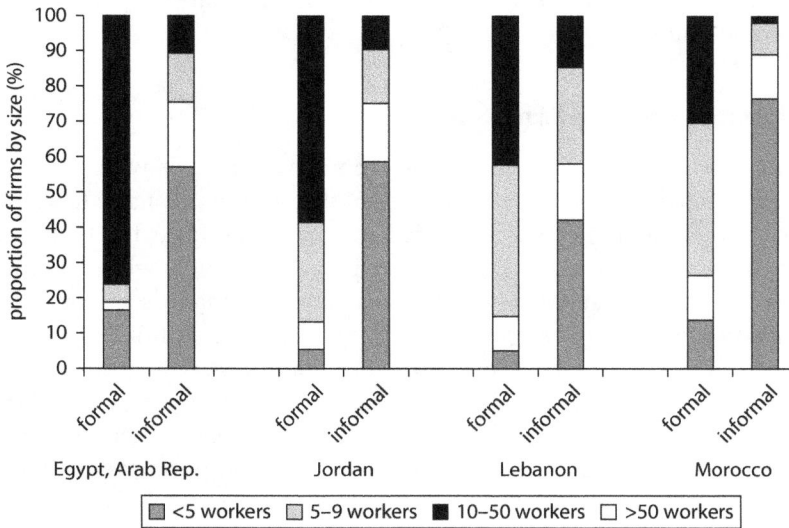

Sources: Lebanon Labor Force Survey 2010; Morocco Youth Survey 2010; Egypt Labor Market Panel Survey (ELMPS) 2006.
Note: In Morocco 10–50 workers actually incorporates 10–100 workers, and >50 captures firms with 100+ employees only.

50 workers) firms are, respectively, 16 to 21 and 17 to 53 percent less likely to work without social security coverage than workers in small-size (five to nine workers) firms.

The relationship between gender and informality is quite complex. It should be noted that despite positive improvement in female employment rates in the last decade, labor force participation among women in the MENA region remains the lowest in the world, and among women who participate, unemployment is quite high, especially among the most educated. In countries such as the Republic of Yemen and Morocco, where agricultural employment constitutes an important share of overall employment, being a woman—other things being equal—is associated with a higher probability of working in the informal sector, because women are often employed in unpaid or subsistence agriculture. When public employment constitutes a significant share of overall employment, as in Egypt, Iraq, and Syria, being a woman is associated with a lower probability of working in the informal sector, because women who participate in the labor forces in these countries (generally those with higher levels of education) self-select into public sector jobs, which have working hours, benefits, and overall safety characteristics that are perceived as more desirable.

Informality among Firms

Firms can operate informally along various margins. For wage workers, working informally is the result of factors that go beyond individual skills and attitudes and relates to labor demand features such as the types and availability of jobs and workers' relative bargaining power with the hiring firm. Hence, understanding why firms operate informally is an important dimension of informal employment. In particular, small firms might not register their activity to avoid paying taxes and/or to avoid paying social security contributions for their workers (in full or in part). Registered firms (usually larger firms) might only partially report their sales and underreport workers and/or workers' wages to avoid paying taxes and/or social security contributions.

Informality is prevalent among firms in MENA. In the region many firms never formalize, and even those that formally register still operate informally for a significant amount of time. Among existing formal firms, MENA has the highest share of firms starting up in the informal sector (25 percent compared to less than 10 percent in the LAC and ECA regions). Also, firms in the region have, on average, a longer operating period without formalization than other developing regions (four years versus less than one year in the LAC and ECA regions; see figure O.9). Small enterprises, which account for a large share of all private sector jobs, are mostly unregistered and often employ workers informally. Among larger registered firms (with 10 or more employees), about one-fifth of sales and workers are not reported. A great deal of heterogeneity exists in the region, but high taxes are consistently identified by entre-preneurs as the top constraint to formalization, together with the cost of registration, bureaucratic complexity, and administrative requirements. In many economies, including Algeria, Djibouti, Iraq, and the West Bank and Gaza economy, there seems to be ample room for simplification of business entry regulations and procedures.

A strong association emerges between informality and low productiv-ity among firms. When firm informality is measured as the share of workers and sales that are underreported for social security and tax purposes, respectively, firm size, low productivity, and a manager's education seem to be its key determinants. Although the available data

Figure O.9   Unregistered Firms, by Region

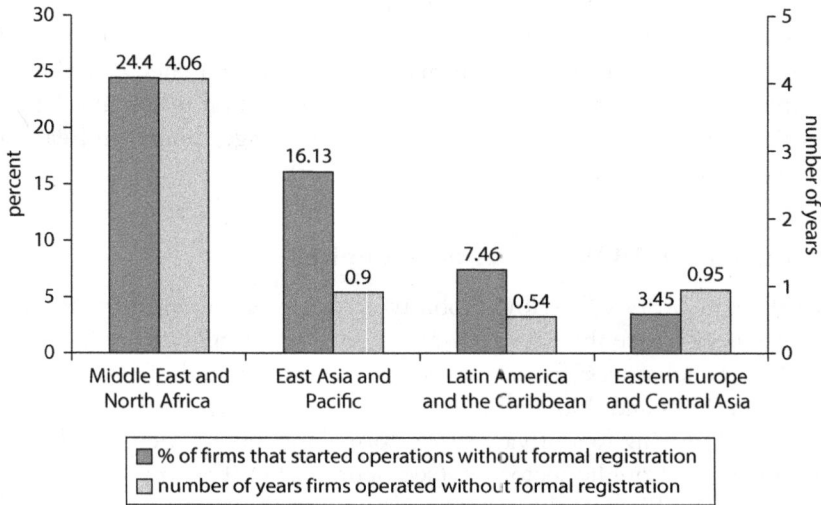

Source: World Development Indicators Dataset.

do not allow identification of a causal relationship between firm informality and the aforementioned determinants, these patterns are observed consistently in other regions. For instance, firm size has a significant association with informality and productivity: In Morocco, data suggest that labor productivity in smaller firms (nine employees or less) is one-half the productivity of firms with more than 100 employees. In addition to affecting productivity, firm size is strongly associated with underreporting wages to the social security administration. Specifically, among otherwise similar firms (for example, similar sector, product, or years in operation) doubling firm size is associated with a significant reduction in worker underreporting (such as by 10 percent in the Republic of Yemen and by 35 percent in Jordan). The education level of managers and workers is also a strong predictor of underreporting workers to social security and/or tax authorities.

A large education gap exists between managers of informal and formal firms. Consistent with patterns in other countries, informal micro-firms in MENA typically have managers and a workforce with lower levels of education. For instance, among small firms in Egypt, the share of managers who have completed secondary school or have attained university education is about 45 percent in informal firms versus

85 percent in formal firms (figure O.10). Workers in informal firms also
tend to be less educated. Indeed, insufficient skills and education of the
working force are perceived as serious constraints to employment and
output growth in informal firms. Data from matched employer-
employees surveys for small informal firms show that informal salaried
workers are younger, are more likely to work longer hours, and earn a
relatively lower hourly wage than formal workers.

Informality in MENA: Exclusion or Choice?

Workers in MENA face low mobility across informal and formal jobs.
In instances where the data allowed for analysis, mobility from informal
to formal jobs was found to be extremely limited. For example,
between 2008 and 2009, an informal worker in Egypt had a 4 percent
chance of moving to a private sector formal job and a 5 percent chance
of moving to a public sector job (see figure O.11). The implied average
job duration of informal salaried work is about three years in Egypt and

**Figure O.10   Highest Level of Education of Managers in Formal and Informal
Manufacturing Firms in Egypt, 2009**

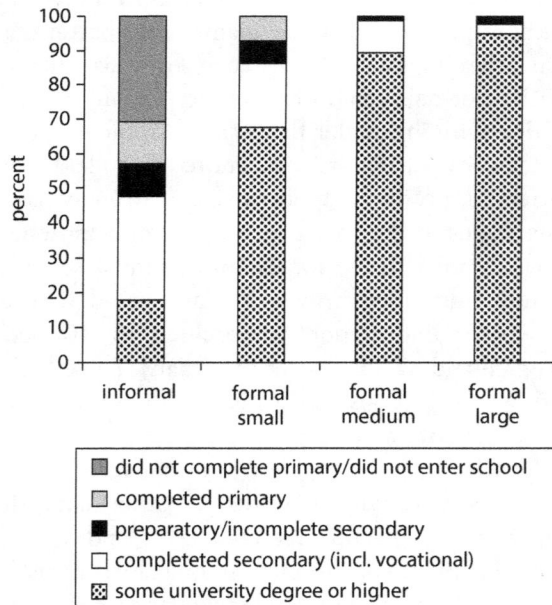

Source: World Bank 2010.

Figure O.11   Transitions of Originally Informal Salaried Private Sector Male Workers

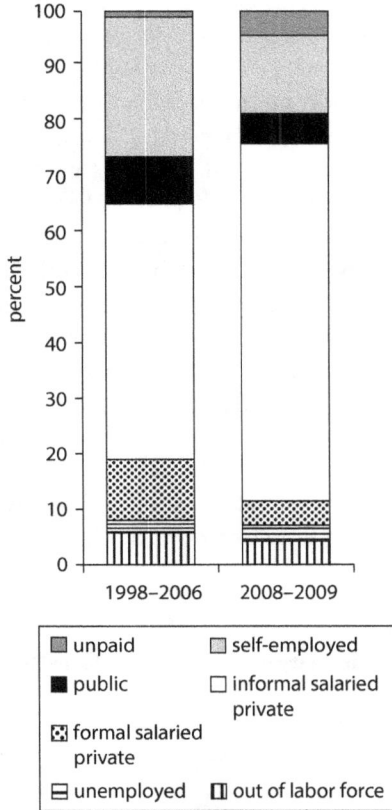

Source: Silva and others 2010.

is reported to be about four and one-half years in Lebanon and Syria, both longer than the duration observed in countries such as Mexico, where workers move out of informal salaried jobs within two years (see Maloney 1999).

Monetary returns to skills differ substantially across informal and formal wage employment. Informal workers earn lower salaries than formal workers with similar skills: The estimated premium associated with formal jobs varies from 10 percent for all workers (15 to 65 years of age) in Syria to more than 50 percent among Moroccan youth (15 to 34 years of age). The formality wage gap persists even when differences in individual characteristics (for instance, age, education, and measured ability) and firm type are explicitly accounted for (see figure O.12). Most measures of job quality, including amount of annual leave and other benefits as well as access to training, suggest poorer working conditions in informal jobs. This is also reflected in direct and indirect measures of job satisfaction. For example, Moroccan youth working in informal jobs reported being significantly less satisfied than youth working in formal jobs. In Egypt and Lebanon, informal workers are uniformly more likely than formal workers to want to change jobs or to be searching for a new job.

In the absence of well-developed public and private formal labor intermediation systems, social networks matter for finding jobs. More than 70 percent of workers in Lebanon and Syria reported having found jobs predominantly through personal connections. This is even more common in the informal sector. Such a strong reliance on personal social networks (which are often formed within homogenous socioeconomic strata) is likely to limit the size of the talent pool from which firms can select their workforce. There is also evidence that networks matter intergenerationally for finding employment. All else being equal, the chance

Figure O.12   Estimated Formality Premium by Gender in Different Countries

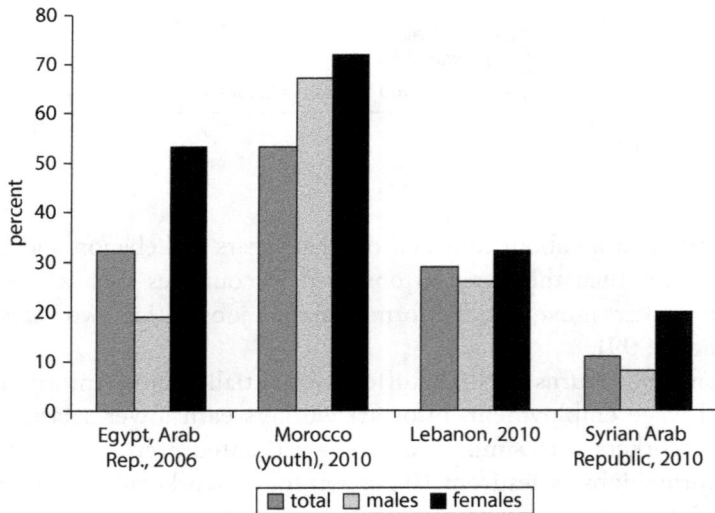

Sources: Angel-Urdinola and Tanabe 2010; Alloush and others 2011.

of a worker holding a formal job in Morocco increases significantly if his or her father also has a formal job.

Low mobility across informal and formal jobs, persistent wage gaps, and low self-reported satisfaction in informal jobs all suggest the presence of labor market segmentations.[2] These patterns dispel the notion that informal jobs in MENA primarily reduce asymmetric information for new entrants to the labor market. Instead, they support the view that segmentations and important margins of exclusion exist along the formal and informal sectors, implying that relevant labor market outcomes (including unemployment rates and earnings) are not arbitraged across the two sectors. In some countries, such as Egypt, these differences are predominantly driven by the public/private sector employment divide.

Barriers to Coverage and Policy Options

The observed patterns indicate that economies in the MENA region generate a limited number of good jobs, with a large and growing informal sector characterized by overall worse working conditions and lower productivity than in the formal private sector. A complex set of institutional barriers and distorted incentives account for this disequilibrium. As a result, promoting a more inclusive growth process, with the creation of decent jobs and reduced vulnerabilities, will require a set of coordinated policies spanning the business environment, labor market regulations, civil service reform, pension system design, and skills-upgrading interventions. Importantly, the observed high prevalence of informality indicates a need to rethink policy making. A vast majority of economic agents operate outside the realm of regulation, and until recently in many countries, those outsiders (including the unemployed, youth, women, and informal workers) may not have been adequately represented in the social dialogue and consensus-building process around reform.

Five key distinct and complementary policy options, each linked to the drivers of informality in the MENA region, are identified: (1) creating a level playing field for small and large firms to compete, (2) moving toward labor regulations that promote labor mobility and provide income support to workers in periods of employment transition, (3) realigning incentives, pay, and benefit packages in the public sector, (4) reforming pension and existing social insurance systems and introducing new instruments for coverage extension, and (5) enhancing the productivity of informal workers through training and skills upgrading.

Designing Reforms that Foster Competition

Although MENA countries have moved progressively away from state-led growth, their private sectors, with few exceptions, still suffer from limited dynamism and stagnating private investments. Even if private sector reforms have accelerated in recent years (as measured by *Doing Business* indicators; International Finance Corporation and World Bank 2012), policy gaps still remain. In particular, high taxes and compliance costs are consistently seen as binding constraints to firms' growth and formalization. Importantly, policy uncertainty and discretion in implementing the law constrain investment and reinforce the role of existing firms, who have a vested interest in protecting their rents and limiting competition (World Bank 2009). In such an environment, the costs of joining the formal economy are often prohibitively high for small enterprises that opt to operate "below the radar" and consequently face limited opportunities to grow, exploit economies of scale, or connect to larger markets and access know-how.

Informality appears to be intertwined with the development process and can be largely explained as the private sector's response to restrictive regulation. It should be noted that informality is preferable to a fully formal economy where firms or workers are unable to comply with or are able to circumvent regulations. Policies solely based on strict enforcement of regulations are likely to increase formalization in the short term but are also likely to increase unemployment and could eventually reduce growth. Instead, formalization would be better achieved as the result of a development process whereby growth becomes more inclusive, incentives to create more good jobs are fostered, and rents are more evenly distributed among the outsiders (informal workers and the unemployed). This process can begin by improving the regulatory framework for businesses, including simplifying regulations, decreasing barriers to entry (such as business registration and high corporate taxes), and consistently enforcing regulations to induce firms to compete fairly.

Reforms to entry regulations have been shown to have positive, albeit moderate, effects on formalization. Possible reforms options include (1) reducing the costs of registration and the number of procedures and minimum capital requirements, (2) providing information on procedures and benefits of becoming a formal business and training entrepreneurs (for example, on filling forms), and (3) facilitating registration by establishing one-stop shops for registration. Although no evidence is at hand on the likely impact of these reforms in the MENA region, relevant international data are available. For example, in Mexico, simplifying the process of business registration had a moderate impact on formalization of existing firms, but formalization was substantially increased by creation of new businesses by former wage earners. Overall, the evidence suggests that it might be difficult to promote formalization for a large number of existing informal firms without a change in the associated benefits or without reducing other compliance costs such as taxation.

Small firms in Egypt and Morocco identify taxation as a significant constraint to formalization. Lowering the corporate tax rate can impact tax revenue through three main channels: (1) existing formal firms may invest more and earn more income on which they pay taxes, (2) existing informal firms may be induced to formalize and start paying taxes, and (3) new firms may be induced to operate formally. Evidence from other regions suggests that the net effect on tax revenue is likely to depend on whether a reduction in the tax rate is accompanied by additional enforcement and a reduction in exceptions.

In many MENA countries, investment climate reforms have accelerated in recent years. However, consistent implementation of reforms matters greatly for their success. According to recent evidence (World Bank 2009), as a consequence of reforms related to the investment climate, private investment in the MENA region increased by only 2 percent of GDP, compared to between 5 and 10 percent in Asia, Eastern Europe, and Latin America. The same report estimates that the number of registered businesses per 1,000 people in MENA is less than one-third of that reported in Eastern Europe and Central Asia, and the average business in MENA is 10 years older than that found in East Asia or Eastern Europe (suggesting slower firm entry and exit). Close to 60 percent of business managers surveyed did not think that the rules and regulations were applied consistently and predictably, and policy uncertainty, unfair competition, and corruption were identified as major concerns for investors. Reforms are unlikely to produce the expected results without a credible commitment to more transparency and fairness in the relationship between businesses and the government. Discretionary enforcement of regulation acts as a strong deterrent to small entrepreneurs who start their businesses informally but are then forced to stay small to escape controls. Staying small may, in turn, make it prohibitively costly to formalize over time.

Realigning Incentives, Pay, and Benefits in the Public Sector
In some countries the public sector continues to employ a large share of workers. For example, in Egypt, Iraq, and Syria, up to one of every three

workers is employed by the public sector. Public sector jobs often offer higher wages than private sector jobs, as well as more job security and generous social security coverage (Bodor, Robalino, and Rutkowski 2008). Such advantageous conditions are, not surprisingly, very attractive to workers. In a recent survey, 70 percent of youth in Egypt indicated that "it is best to work in the public sector." In Syria, only a quarter of those officially in the queue for public employment accepted a recent offer of training and private sector placement, because registering in social security rosters would imply removal from the public sector queue. Many of these workers then enter into informal employment as a means of supporting themselves while waiting for a public sector job. The generosity of public sector employment conditions (including pay, benefits, and job security) thus contributes to higher informality and important segmentations, making the need for civil service reform even more pressing. Moreover, the prospect of obtaining stable and remunerative employment in the public sector distorts skills formation, because a number of workers acquire education (especially in the humanities) that is not necessarily in line with private sector demands.

Reforming the civil service is a key priority. In the short run, eliminating institutionalized queuing for public sector employment can reduce the segmentation between public and private employment and foster labor mobility. Queuing for public sector jobs contributes decisively to unemployment among graduates in the region and fosters informality. Moreover, wage scales in the public sector currently reward education level and tenure, but not performance. In several MENA countries, placement depends on connections and is virtually irreversible, because dismissing a civil servant is a difficult and complex process. Linking the public sector wage scale to competence and performance and easing the rigidity of civil service contracts may reduce the gap between public and private sector employment, thus limiting the incentive to work informally while queuing.

Moving toward Labor Regulations That Promote Labor Mobility and Provide Support to Workers in Periods of Employment Transition

Labor market regulation is perceived as an important constraint by more than one-third of employers in MENA, the highest share among all regions in the developing world. Employment protection legislation (EPL) includes a wide array of regulatory items, such as minimum wage, hiring and firing regulations, and provisions for fixed-term contracts. In MENA, legislated minimum wages are generally low, are not well enforced, and do not constrain employment outcomes significantly. However, in some countries, such as Tunisia, a centralized and rigid wage-setting process may significantly contribute to informality and higher unemployment. Moreover, in some countries in the region, firing regulations are extremely restrictive, requiring notification and approval of a third party for a single worker's dismissal. In parallel, severance pay is often generous. Such strict EPL reinforces segmentations between insiders (workers with formal, protected jobs) and outsiders (the unemployed and informal or fixed-term workers), because many firms circumvent regulations and resort to employing informal workers to fulfill their business needs.

MENA countries might improve compliance and employment outcomes by easing some labor legislation provisions. Although certain provisions in labor legislation in some MENA countries might be rigid in theory, in reality they are widely evaded. A shift toward a richer and more flexible set of labor contracts (including more fixed-term contracts and fewer open-ended contracts) would provide opportunities for young workers and new entrants to join the formal sector through flexible working arrangements with social insurance coverage. Policy reforms that ease regulations and make them more realistic to comply with should be supplemented with social protection system reforms that better protect the income position of workers and their employment transitions.[3] For example, recent experience shows that moderately strict EPL, when combined with a well-designed system of unemployment benefits and a strong emphasis on active labor market programs, can help create a dynamic labor market while also providing adequate employment security to workers (OECD 2008). Adequate safety nets could also play an important role in protecting workers from sudden job loss, helping workers transition between jobs, and preventing more people from slipping into poverty. The newly legislated unemployment insurance schemes in Jordan and Egypt provide an example of reforms that should be considered by other countries in the MENA region.

Keeping the cost of labor at a realistic level via affordable social security contributions and relaxing wage rigidities are likely to reduce informality. In general, institutionalized minimum wages in the MENA region are neither high (with the exception of Morocco) nor binding. Yet centralized wage-setting mechanisms, as in the case of Tunisia, contribute to informality by setting artificially high wage floors for certain occupations and skill levels. In addition to keeping minimum wages at low levels that can be realistically enforced, wage-setting mechanisms in the MENA region should be anchored to changes in productivity. In countries where minimum wages are high (whether economy wide or sector specific), and where it is not politically feasible to reduce them, governments could consider reducing the minimum wage for youth to improve transitions of new labor market entrants into formal employment, while maintaining higher minimum wages to protect well-established workers. Similarly, labor taxes in MENA are not high by international standards, with the exception of Morocco and Egypt. The wedge between the employer's labor cost and the worker's take-home pay (that is, the tax wedge) could be further reduced through social insurance reforms that lower the social security contribution rates or by shifting a portion of the labor taxes toward other general revenue sources, such as consumption or property taxes.

Engaging in a more inclusive social dialogue is key to sustaining these reforms. There are important political economy aspects to labor market reform. In particular, the traditional tripartite structure that convenes government actors, trade unions, and employer representatives is likely to favor the status quo of protective regulation for employed, unionized workers. Including representation from outsiders would likely shift the dialogue toward facilitating entry into labor markets, improving mobility, and promoting a more equitable distribution of returns across less favored segments of the population.

Enhancing the Productivity of Informal Workers through Training and Skills Upgrading

The low-productivity dimension of informality is especially notable in MENA's poorer countries and rural areas, where workers with limited literacy and education are engaged in micro-entrepreneurship and low-yield agricultural work. Effectively increasing productivity in the informal sector, particularly in rural areas, is a complex undertaking that requires creating opportunities that promote human capital and connect people to markets. Well-designed programs aimed at increasing productivity in the informal sector through training and skills upgrading are a potentially important intervention to promote inclusive growth in the medium term. Privately and publicly provided training programs intended to increase workers' employability are abundant in the region. However, these programs tend to be delivered through in-class trainings targeted to urban, unemployed workers and rarely reach informal workers (overwhelmingly the working poor), especially in rural areas. With limited access to these types of training opportunities, many informal workers are unable to enhance their skills and thus remain in low-paying, low-productivity jobs.

Emerging evidence from skills upgrading interventions sheds light on several success factors for informal, rural employment. How training is delivered matters. For example, programs such as the Barefoot College in India and the Agriculture and Fishing Fund in the Republic of Yemen suggest that the very modalities with which training is delivered (such as hands-on, community-based, or combining learning with earnings) are key factors for success. Training might be most effective if provided with placement services such as job search assistance and soft skills training. Low levels of literacy, scarce information, inflexible program schedules, traveling restrictions, and language barriers all limit access to and usefulness of traditional, class-based training programs for informal workers, especially in rural areas (World Bank forthcoming).

Facilitating the setup of training cooperatives might allow small firms to overcome the high fixed costs of structuring and delivering on-the-job training. Because informal workers are overwhelmingly employed in small enterprises or hold less stable jobs in larger companies, they are less likely to receive on-the-job training than formal workers. Providing incentives to firms (such as through training cooperatives) and workers (such as by providing vouchers) to engage in training could promote skills upgrading. To make these interventions more effective, reorienting and tailoring the delivery and design of training toward the particular needs of informal workers is necessary. Second-chance programs, traditional apprenticeships, and training specifically designed for the self-employed and micro-entrepreneurs are examples of interventions likely to be effective in the MENA region.

Reforming Existing Social Insurance Systems and Introducing New Instruments for Coverage Extension

Coverage extension through social insurance systems is an important yet complex undertaking. In MENA expansion of social insurance schemes, particularly pensions, beyond the civil service has been achieved in all countries, but it has happened in a fragmented manner, and coverage remains limited. For example, in many countries, including Djibouti, Iraq, Morocco, and Syria, and in the West Bank and Gaza economy, no legal coverage instruments are available for self-employed and agricultural workers. No pension schemes exist for agricultural workers in Algeria, the Islamic Republic of Iran, Iraq, Libya, the West Bank and Gaza economy, and the Republic of Yemen. Although the existing pension

Striving for Better Jobs • http://dx.doi.org/10.1596/978-0-8213-9535-6

systems in the MENA region have limited coverage, they are quite generous. Internal rate-of-return computations indicate returns of between 6
and 17 percent, significantly higher than alternative investment instruments. Workers with information about these returns indicate that they
want to participate in the pension system; this suggests that lack of participation in social security might be largely driven by constraints to
accessing the system (that is, exclusion). Given the generosity of existing
pension systems, policy makers might be reluctant to extend coverage at
these favorable conditions beyond the current (limited) set of beneficiaries, to avoid amplifying the implicit pension debt. This justifies sequenc-
ing coverage extension, where reforms aimed at improving the
sustainability of current systems will need to precede coverage extension.
Consequently, coverage extension can take different forms, including
extending provisions of current mandatory systems, improving the design
of existing social insurance schemes to promote coverage, or extending
coverage beyond existing mandatory social insurance systems and traditional professions through new instruments. The latter, depending on
country parameters and social preferences, could be based on providing
universal or targeted benefits (that is, adopting a noncontributory and/or
a contributory approach).

Important links are found between coverage outcomes and the design
of social insurance schemes in the MENA region, particularly for pensions. Many countries in the region have defined benefit pension systems
with design elements that are not in line with international best practices.
Often these features contribute to low participation (coverage) rates;
they include limited legal coverage, short minimum vesting periods that
promote gaming of the system, generous early retirement provisions that
distort incentives to participation, and the use of average wages in the last
few years of service as a basis for calculating benefit amounts, which
makes these schemes more expensive. Addressing these issues through
reforms to ensure adequate, affordable, and sustainable benefits appears
to be an important precondition for effective coverage extension to a
large and increasing share of the population. Moving toward a defined
contribution system is likely to achieve some of these objectives.
Moreover, defined contribution systems are more useful for providing a
platform to integrate different risk management instruments to cover
risks such as disability, unemployment, and work injury, in addition to
those associated with old age.

Adequate coverage extension in MENA is not likely to be achieved if
efforts do not go beyond providing traditional social insurance and do not

specifically target informal workers and those outside the labor force. Though this notion might be considered controversial, access to social insurance coverage could be designed to be unconditional on a formal employment relationship for some workers, particularly for the self-employed or those with irregular earnings and working patterns. Moreover, some workers might have too limited a savings capacity to contribute meaningfully to social security. Governments that opt to extend social insurance coverage beyond the existing mandatory social insurance system by targeting groups of informal workers are faced with a set of decisions related to strategy, design, and implementation. Key decisions pertaining to coverage extension strategies should be informed by an assessment of the relative appropriateness of contributory or non-contributory programs (in the light of existing country conditions), fiscal sustainability, and an evaluation of universal versus targeted subsidies. Matching defined contribution schemes are one promising option for extending coverage. These schemes are voluntary defined contribution savings mechanisms offering old-age or other social insurance benefits, where the government or employer provides incentives to enroll by matching individual contributions at a given rate and threshold. Piloting these schemes targeted to informal workers with limited but positive savings capacity could provide policy makers with important insights on effective levers to increase coverage. In the short run, noncontributory schemes (such as social pensions) are still likely to play an important supplemental role. Middle-income countries such as Lebanon, Syria, and Jordan, where poverty-based targeting systems are emerging, might consider targeted contributory interventions. In poorer countries such as Djibouti and the Republic of Yemen, means-tested noncontributory strategies may be more appropriate, because contributory schemes are not yet feasible given current country conditions.

Going beyond the traditional assumptions of agent rationality is important for promoting voluntary participation of informal workers in social insurance schemes, especially where contributions are required. Many of the observed behaviors in experimental settings contradict the standard economic models' predictions based on the assumption of agent rationality. In particular, behaviors such as procrastination and loss aversion could deter voluntary participation in savings schemes. Therefore, program features such as auto-enrollment, default options, and auto-escalation of savings could induce participation. Addressing the particular needs of informal workers in the design of programs could also mean allowing for flexible contribution schedules, amounts, and withdrawal conditions.

Moreover, implementation arrangements that aim at minimizing transaction costs can also increase participation in these programs. Finally, complementary financial literacy and general interventions to raise awareness of the benefits of social insurance schemes should be considered.

Notes

1. Schneider (2004) developed a Multiple Indicator-Multiple Cause (MIMIC) model to quantify the size of the informal economy as a percentage of GDP.
2. A labor market is considered segmented if it consists of various subgroups with little or no crossover capability.
3. The International Labour Organization, European Union, and Organisation for Economic Co-operation and Development have embraced the concept of "flexicurity," combining flexible regulation, safety nets (such as unemployment insurance), and active social policies. One component of flexicurity policies is flexible and reliable contractual arrangements (from the perspective of the employer and the employee, of "insiders" and "outsiders") through modern labor laws, collective agreements, and work organization.

References

Alloush, M., C. Chartouni, R. Gatti, and J. Silva. 2011. "Informality and Exclusion: Evidence from Lebanon and Syria." Mimeo. Washington, DC: World Bank.

Angel-Urdinola, D., and K. Tanabe. 2011. "Micro-Determinants of Informal Employment in the Middle East and North Africa Region." Mimeo. Washington, DC: World Bank.

Bodor, A., D. Robalino, and M. Rutkowski. 2008. "How Mandatory Pensions Affect Labor Supply Decisions and Human Capital Accumulations: Options to Bridge the Gap between Economic Theory and Policy Analysis." Washington, DC: World Bank.

De Soto, H. 1989. *The Other Path: The Invisible Revolution in the Third World.* New York: HarperCollins.

Elbadawi, I., and N. Loayza. 2008. "Informality, Employment and Economic Development in the Arab World." *Journal of Development and Economic Policies* 10 (2): 25–75.

International Finance Corporation and World Bank. 2012. *Doing Business.* http://www.doingbusiness.org.

Loayza, N., and T. Wada. 2010. "Informal Labor in the Middle East and North Africa: Basic Measures and Determinants." Mimeo. Washington, DC: World Bank.

Maloney, W. F. 1999. "Does Informality Imply Segmentation in Urban Labor Markets? Evidence from Sectoral Transitions in Mexico." *World Bank Economic Review* 13 (2): 275–302.

OECD (Organisation for Economic Co-operation and Development). 2008. *Employment Outlook.* Paris: OECD.

Perry, G., W. Maloney, O. Arias, P. Fajnzylber, A. Mason, and J. Saavedra-Chanduvi. 2007. *Informality: Exit and Exclusion.* Washington, DC: World Bank.

Radwan, S. 2007. "Good Jobs, Bad Jobs, and Economic Performance: A View from the Middle East and North Africa Region, Employment and Shared Growth." In *Employment and Shared Growth: Rethinking the Role of Labor Mobility for Development,* ed. Pierella Paci and Pieter Serneels, 37–51. Washington, DC: World Bank.

Schneider, F. 2004. "The Size of the Shadow Economies of 145 Countries All over the World: First Results over the Period 1999 to 2003." DP 1431. Bonn: IZA.

World Bank. 2009. "From Privilege to Competition: Unlocking Private-Led Growth in Middle East and North Africa." Washington, DC: World Bank.

———. 2010. "Egypt Investment Climate Assessment 2009: Accelerating Private Enterprise-Led Growth." Washington, DC: World Bank.

———. Forthcoming. "Challenges to Enterprise Performance in the Face of the Financial Crisis-Eastern European and Central Asia." Washington, DC: World Bank.

CHAPTER 1

How Large Is Informality and Why Do We Care?

SUMMARY: This chapter provides general background on the basic measures of the prevalence of informal employment in the Middle East and North Africa (MENA). Informality is best understood as a complex, multi-faceted phenomenon, which is determined by the relationship that the state establishes with private agents through regulation, monitoring, and provision of public services. Results indicate that some countries in the MENA region are among the most informal economies in the world. A typical country in MENA produces about one-third of its GDP and employs 65 percent of its labor force informally (using the Schneider Index and the share of the labor force without social security coverage, respectively). These stylized facts indicate that more than two-thirds of all workers in the region may not have access to health insurance and/or are not contributing to a pension system that would provide income security after retirement. At the same time, from a fiscal perspective, these results indicate that about one-third of total economic output in the region remains undeclared and, therefore, not registered for tax purposes.

What Is Informality?

There are many angles to informality. In his classic study, De Soto (1989) defines informality as the collection of firms, workers, and activities that operate outside the legal and regulatory framework. Overall informality can be studied through three main lenses: a firm-based productivity perspective, an employment perspective (workers), and a fiscal perspective (untaxed activities). Informality is a heterogeneous concept, comprising different situations such as the unregistered small firm, the street vendor, and the large registered (and hence "formal") firm that employs some of its workers without offering written contracts or access to social security benefits:

- *Firms*: A generally accepted definition of "firm" informality was proposed by the Delhi Group in 1997. According to their definition, the informal sector includes private unincorporated enterprises (or quasi-unincorporated), which produce at least some of their goods and services for sale or barter, have fewer than five paid employees, are not registered, and are engaged in nonagricultural activities (ILO 2002). Studies generally measure informality at the firm level through a direct (micro-) measurement based on individual surveys, such as the World Bank's Enterprise Surveys, that explicitly ask the firm's owner or manager for information on the years in which the firm started its operations and legally registered. A discrepancy between the two is typically considered the period during which the firm operated informally (Angel-Urdinola, Reis, and Quijada 2009).

- *Workers*: According to this definition, the informal sector is proxied by informal employment in either formal (small unregistered or unincorporated firms) or informal enterprises, with "informal employment" refereeing to the absence of benefit from or registration to social security or the absence of a written contract (see box 1.1. for more details on defining informality). Hence, informal sector employment includes *informal employment* in *formal sector enterprises* comprising (1) contributing family members and (2) employees; *informal employment* in *informal sector enterprises* comprising (1) own-account workers,[1] (2) employers, (3) contributing family workers, (4) employees, and (5) members of producers cooperatives; and *informal employment* in *households* producing goods exclusively for their own final use and households employing paid domestic workers comprising (1) own-account workers and (2) employees.

- *Untaxed Activities*: From a fiscal point of view, a large informal sector constitutes a set of activities that are "hidden" for tax purposes. The United Nations System of National Accounts (EC and others 2008) distinguishes between four types of such activities: (1) informal activities, which are undertaken "to meet basic needs"; (2) underground activities, which are deliberately concealed from public authorities to avoid either

---

Box 1.1   Defining Informality

The concept "informal employment" was adopted by the 17th International Conference of Labor Statisticians (ILCS) in 2003. Hart (1973) was the first author to make the distinction between formal and informal employment based on the difference between wage-earning employment (formal) and self-employment on a permanent and regular basis, either alone or in a partnership (informal). The guidelines of the definition refer to the characteristics of the job, and the criteria are absence of benefit from or registration for social security or, more strictly, the absence of a written contract. The guidelines provide more detailed criteria that are to be determined "in accordance with national circumstances and data availability." Although informal employment is a job-based concept, the category of "informal sector employment" is an enterprise-based concept as defined by the 15th ICLS in 1993. A set of characteristics of the economic units is used: (1) legal status (unincorporated individual enterprises owned by households) and (2) nonregistration of the unit or nonregistration of its employees or size of the unit (fewer than 5 or 10 permanent employees). Because this enterprise-based definition was missing the dramatic increase of informal jobs outside the traditional enterprises (especially the flexible and unprotected jobs directly or indirectly created by formal enterprises confronted with strong competition), the broader concept of informal employment was adopted. "Self-employment" comprises own-account workers, employers, and contributing family workers, as defined in the International Classification of Status in Employment. Although it includes categories such as professionals, self-employment can be used as a proxy for the main component of informal employment, especially as it has been collected in household surveys and population censuses, and data are available.

Source: World Bank 2009.

---

the payment of taxes or compliance with certain regulations (for example, most cases of tax evasion and benefit fraud); (3) illegal activities, which generate goods and services forbidden by the law or which are unlawful when carried out by unauthorized producers; and (4) household activities, which produce goods and services for own-consumption.

How to Measure Informality

If defining informality is a complex task, its measurement is even more daunting. Given that it is identified by working outside the legal and regulatory frameworks, informality is best described as a hidden, unob-served variable. Hence, accurate and complete measurement is not feasi-ble, but an approximation is possible using indicators that reflect its various aspects. To provide an estimate of the magnitude of informality in a country, it is better to use a variety of different indicators that, taken together, can provide a more robust approximation to informality. Several direct and indirect methods are used to measure informality (Angel-Urdinola, Reis, and Quijada 2009):

- *Survey methods*: Informality could be measured directly using individual surveys, such as the World Bank's Enterprise Surveys, which explicitly ask the firm's owner or manager for information on the years in which the firm started its operations and was legally registered. A discrepancy between the two is typically considered as the time when the firm oper-ated informally. In some household or labor force surveys, interviewees are asked whether they have signed a formal contract in their current employment, or whether they are affiliated with the social security administration (meaning that they, or their employer, are contributing to a pension plan or another social protection program). A potential problem with direct measures is that the interviewee's answer depends heavily on the phrasing of the question, and many interviewees might be reluctant to reveal their behavior (for example, in the case of firms).

- *Tax audits*: Tax-audit data can be used to determine the percentage of firms audited that evade taxes and to quantify the amount of tax under-reporting as informal activity (as well as a firm's legal status). The short-coming is that tax audits are not conducted randomly typically, and hence the information is not representative of the population of firms (Perry and others 2007).

- *National Accounts*: An indirect method commonly used to estimate the size of the informal economy is the difference between aggregate income and aggregate expenditures from the National Accounts. This measure has the advantage of being conceptually simple. However, it has been used mainly in developed countries, because it requires inde-pendent calculations of aggregate income and expenditure.

- *Multiple Indicator-Multiple Cause model:* Another method that has been used recently is the Multiple Indicator-Multiple Cause (MIMIC) model, popularized by Schneider (2004), who applied it for 145 countries. This model assumes that although informal activity is not observable, its magnitude can be represented by a latent variable (in index form), and both its causes and effects can be observed and measured. This latent variable is then used in a set of two equations: First, the latent variable is the dependent variable, and its causes are the explanatory variables; second, the effects of informality are modeled as a function of the latent variable. The set of equations is then simultaneously estimated, and the fitted values of the latent variable are used to compute an estimate of the size of the informal sector as a share of GDP. This technique has been criticized because of the lack of theoretical support for the equations that are supposed to capture the causes and effects of informal activity. Nevertheless, its use remains widespread, probably as a consequence of the aforementioned difficulties to obtain broad estimates of informality.

Three indicators are commonly used to measure informality: the Schneider Index, lack of social security coverage, and prevalence of self-employment (Loayza and Wada 2010). The Schneider Index combines the MIMIC method, the physical input (electricity) method, and the excess currency-demand approach for the estimation of the share of production that is not declared to tax and regulatory authorities.[2] Lack of social security coverage is often estimated as the fraction of the labor force (or employment) that does not contribute to a retirement pension scheme, as reported in the World Bank's *World Development Indicators*. The prevalence of self-employment is often computed as the ratio of self-employment to total employment (as reported by the ILO). Additional measures, such as the share of total employment without health insurance and the share of unpaid workers in total employment, are also commonly used proxies of informality (Angel-Urdinola and Tanabe 2011). Table 1.1 and box 1.2 present the different definitions used for MENA countries included in the study.

Although each indicator has its own conceptual and statistical shortcomings as a proxy for informality, taken together they provide a robust approximation to the issue. Cross-country scatter plots of the three measures of informality against each other provide evidence for the significant correlation among the three indicators, with correlation coefficients ranging from 0.10 to 0.91 (which are high enough to represent the same phenomenon but not so high as to make them mutually redundant) (figure 1.1).[3]

This report addresses informality from a worker's perspective and focuses specifically on informal employment. Informal employment can be captured in many ways. Informal employment is often proxied as (1) the share of unpaid employment, (2) the share of self-employment,

Table 1.1 Summary of Data and Definitions Used in This Report

	Algeria	Djibouti	Egypt, Arab Rep.	Iran, Islamic Rep.	Iraq	Jordan	Lebanon	Libya	Malta	Morocco	Syrian Arab Republic	Tunisia	West Bank and Gaza economy	Yemen, Rep.
Not contributing to social security	X	X	X	X	X	X	X	X	X	X	X	X	X	X
Percentage of self-employed	X		X	X	X		X		X	X	X	X	X	X
Schneider Index	X		X	X		X	X	X		X	X	X		X
Share of employment without access to health insurance					X		X			X				
Share of unpaid workers (to total employment)			X		X		X			X	X			

Source: See annex table 1A.2 for information on data sources.

Note: For a detailed description of the micro-surveys used in this study, see the annex in chapter 2.

Box 1.2   Main Definitions of Relevant Variables and Survey Questions from Data Available in MENA

Working-age population (WAP) is composed of individuals in the age group 15 to 64 years old.

Employed are those individuals in the WAP who satisfy any of the following conditions: (1) the person did any work for at least one hour during the previous week (with a remuneration that could have been monetary or in-kind); (2) the person was "temporarily absent" from work because of holidays, illness, paid absence for education or training, maternity leave, strike, work dispute, seasonal work, and the like.

Informal workers as defined in this report are those individuals in the WAP (or, in the ILO dataset, participate in the labor force) who are employed and do not make contributions to social security. In different countries, depending on data availability, different questions were used to define informal workers: **Iraq**: *Is this job included in retirement systems and social security?* (social security includes pension and medical benefits); **Morocco**: *What is your status as regards the social and medical security?* 1 = member; 2 = beneficiary; 3 = not covered (social security and medical insurance comes together); **Egypt**: *Do you have social security?* (Almost all people who have social security are covered by health insurance); **the Republic of Yemen**: *Benefit offered for this job? (Pension)* (Among those covered by pension systems, only 29 percent have health insurance); **Syria**: *Covered by social security or insurance and salaries?* (Social security includes pension and medical benefits); **Lebanon**: *Is worker benefiting from health insurance? Yes* (1 = national security fund; 2 = government employees; 3 = army and security forces; 4 = municipality; 5 = private insurance at employer's expense; 6 = mutual fund; 7 = private through an institution, syndicate, or committee).

Indicator	Calculation			Description
Labor force participation rate (%)	LF (U+E)	÷	WAP	Share of WAP in the labor market
Employment rate (%)	E	÷	WAP	Share of employed in the WAP
Unemployment rate (%)	U	÷	LF (U+E)	Share of unemployed in the labor force

Source: Based on Labor Force Surveys.
Note: E = employed population; LF = population in the labor force (employed and unemployed); U = unemployed population; WAP = population between 15 and 64 years old.

Striving for Better Jobs • http://dx.doi.org/10.1596/978-0-8213-9535-6

Figure 1.1   Correlation among Most-Used Informality Indicators

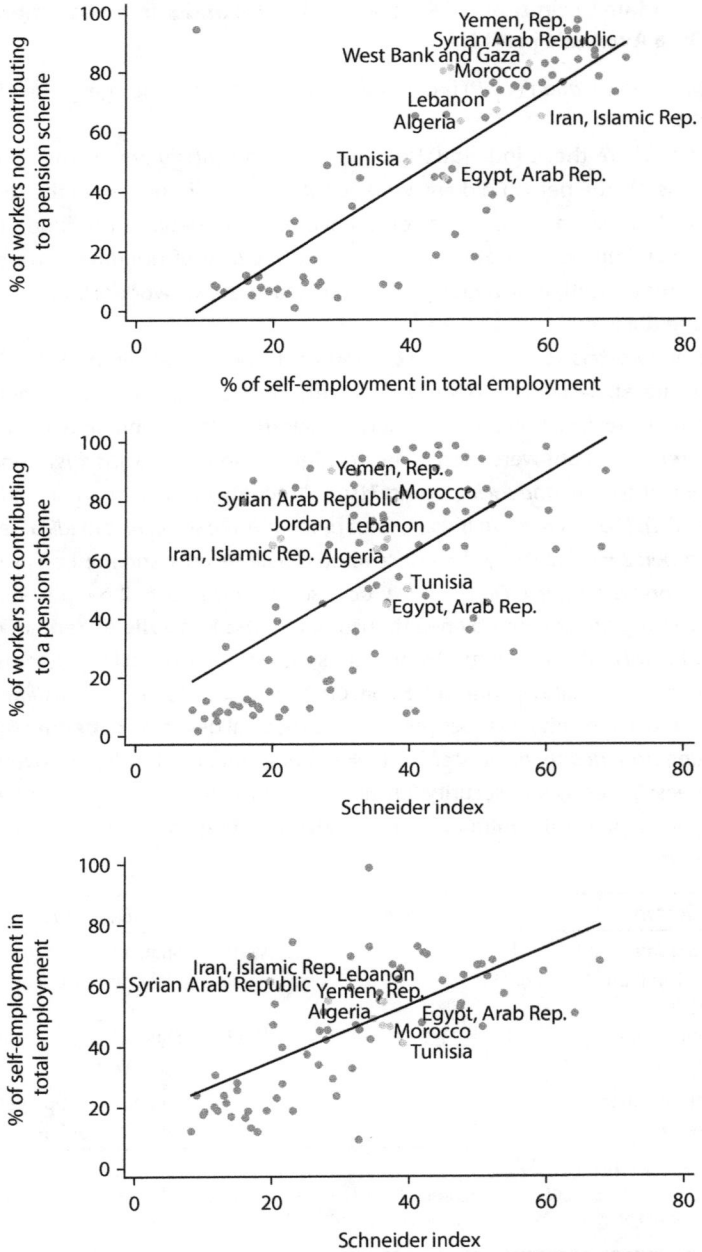

Source: Processed from Loayza and Wada 2010.

(3) the share of total employment not contributing to social security (Gasparini and Tornarolli 2006; Loayza and Rigolini 2006; World Bank 2009), and (4) the share of employees without a contract. Figure 1.2 displays the correlations among these different measures for countries where data are available. As illustrated by the correlations, not having access to social security is positively correlated with all other measures (and especially with not having access to health insurance), although the magnitude of the correlation varies by country and by strata (urban or rural). The strong and positive association between contributing to social security and having access to health insurance (in most cases both come bundled in the social security package) suggests also that informal workers are generally not covered against health risks.[4] As seen in figure 1.2, unpaid work and self-employment are negatively correlated. This indicates that some features of informality among the self-employed are quite unique from those of unpaid workers. However, both of the aforementioned definitions are positively correlated with not having access to social security, indicating that the "share of overall employment not contributing to social security" is able to capture some of the features of informality inherent to these two different groups.

In the context of this report, the standard definition of informality will be the share of the labor force/employment that does not contribute to social security. In characterizing informal employment from the worker/ social protection perspective, one core definition relates to the absence of workers' coverage by traditional social security programs, most notably health insurance and pensions, but often also other benefits available to workers by virtue of their labor contract (Perry and others 2007). To ensure comparability across countries, and based on data availability, informal employment is defined herein as the share of overall labor force/employment not contributing to social security (and therefore not covered by a pension system and, in most cases, not covered by health insurance). Various advantages are found by selecting this definition. The first is data availability. As presented in table 1.1, data used to proxy alternative definitions of workers' informality, such as health insurance coverage, lack of contract, and unpaid employment, are not available for many countries in the MENA region. Second, the lack of social security coverage captures well different aspects of informal employment and thus is more likely to portray the common features of informal employment. In particular, as seen in figure 1.2, unpaid work and self-employment are negatively correlated, suggesting that some features of informality among the self-employed are quite different when compared with those of unpaid workers. However, both of these

**Figure 1.2   Correlations among Different Definitions of Labor Informality
(Worker's Side)**

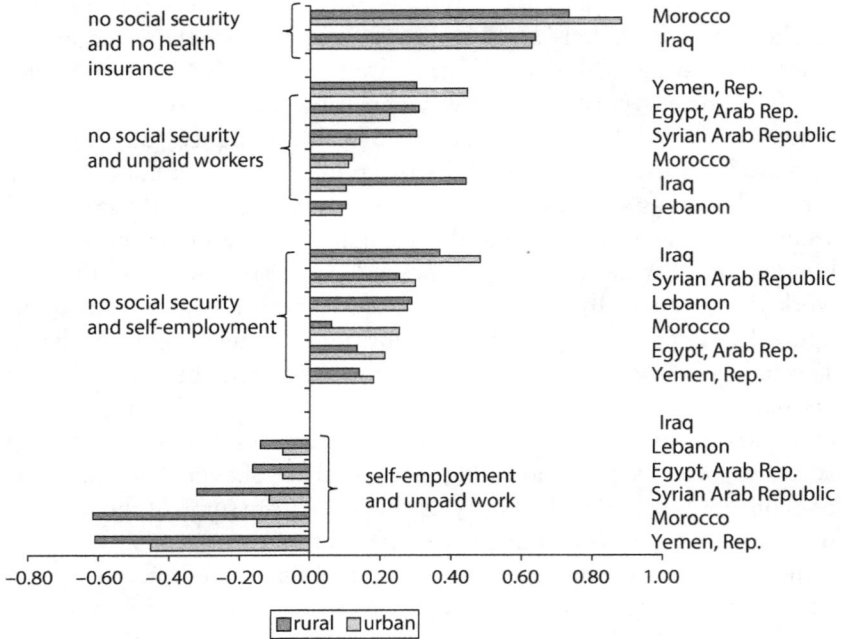

Source: Angel-Urdinola and Tanabe 2011.

definitions are positively correlated with not having access to social security,
indicating that this definition is able to capture some of the features of
informality inherent to these two very different groups. Finally, the definition has been used often in other regional studies on informality, which
allows for comparability between MENA and other world regions (ILO
2002; Perry and others 2007; World Bank 2009).

Why Does Informality Matter?

There are costs and benefits to informality. In many countries the
informal sector often represents a very resourceful part of the economy
and is a source of creativity and dynamism. However, important costs
are associated with informality, such as unprotected work, low firm
productivity, and tax evasion. A traditional view of informality argues
that, in general, workers and firms in the informal sector would prefer
to be formal (such as by registering with the state, paying taxes, or

being affiliated with social security), but regulatory and administrative barriers prevent them from doing so. As argued by Perry and others (2007), however, considerable evidence in Latin America suggests that the informal sector is fairly heterogeneous, with workers and firms that have been excluded from the formal economy coexisting with others that have opted out on the basis of implicit cost-benefit analyses. This latter concept of "exit" posits that at least some of those in the informal sector are there as a matter of choice. Specifically, some workers and firms, upon making some implicit or explicit assessment of the benefits and costs of formality, actually prefer operating informally. A wide range of degrees to which exit or exclusion holds in any economy are found. Hence, these two perspectives are complementary characterizations rather than competing hypotheses.

Informality is a fundamental characteristic of underdevelopment. As depicted in figure 1.3, a larger informal sector is often associated with lower GDP per capita. For most countries in the region, the share of informal to total employment is mostly aligned where it should be given the level of economic development. A two-way relationship can explain the strong and negative association between informality and economic development. On the one hand, widespread informality induces firms to remain suboptimally small, use irregular procurement and distribution channels, and constantly divert resources to mask their activities or bribe officials. As such, informality may be a source of economic retardation because it is associated with misallocation of resources and loss of the advantages of legality (such as police and judicial protection, access to formal credit institutions, and participation in international markets) (Loayza and Wada 2010). On the other hand, low levels of economic development affect the capacity and quality of institutions to enforce regulation, collect taxes, and provide services that firms deem worth paying for through taxation (such as social security and infrastructure). At the same time, a powerful spurious effect could drive this association, because informality and low income could result from policies and institutions that affect negatively both. Measurement issues might also affect this correlation, because in countries with higher informality more GDP escapes formal measurement. Informality also has positive implications for the labor market, because it provides employment to a significant share of the population, may be a source of innovation and entrepreneurship (many firms start operating informally when they are small and formalize as they grow), and serves as a safety net in periods of transition. As such, at a given level of distortion, it is preferable to a fully formal

Figure 1.3   Informality and Economic Development

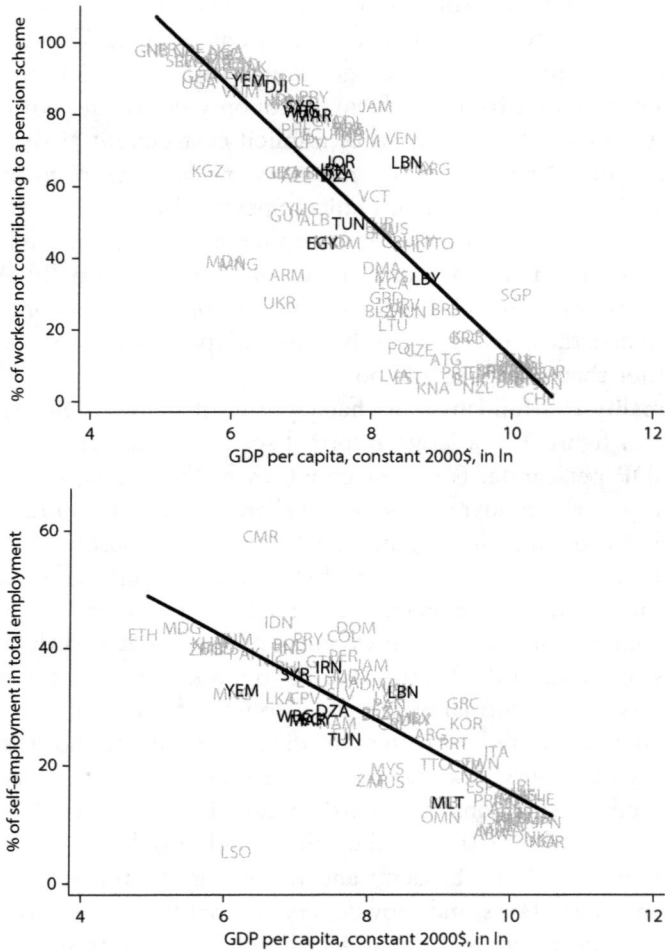

Source: Loayza and Wada 2010.
Note: GDP = gross domestic product.

economy where agents are unable to circumvent regulation-induced rigidities and would not otherwise be able to exist without the flexibility provided by the informal sector.

The evidence suggests that higher levels of informality are associated with lower levels of economic growth. Loayza and Wada (2010) conducted a simple regression analysis of the association between informality and growth for all countries for which data are available (that is, using the

Schneider Index, self-employment as a share of total employment, and share of the labor force not contributing to social security). Using all available informality proxies, the authors find that higher informality is associated with lower economic growth. The dependent variable is the average growth of GDP per capita over 1985–2005. Loayza and Wada (2010) consider a period of about 20 years for the measure of average growth to achieve a compromise between merely cyclical, short-run growth (which would be unaffected by informality) and very long-run growth (which could be confused with the sources, rather than consequences, of informality). They include a proxy for the overall capacity of the state as a control variable (level of GDP per capita and initial ratio of government expenditures to GDP) in the regression. The explanatory variables of interest are the three informality indicators, considered one at a time. Regression analysis uses both ordinary least-squares (OLS) and instrumental-variable (IV) methods. It should be noted, however, that results from cross-country regressions often encounter skepticism because of the many potential sources of spurious correlation. The authors' estimates indicate that controlling for the country's initial level of expenditures and GDP, an increase of one standard deviation in any of the informality indicators leads to a decline of 0.7–1 percentage points in the rate of GDP per capita growth (figure 1.4). Loayza, Oviedo, and Serven (2005) identify informality as one

Figure 1.4 Effect of Informality on Growth
(Decline in GDP growth per standard deviation increase of each indicator)

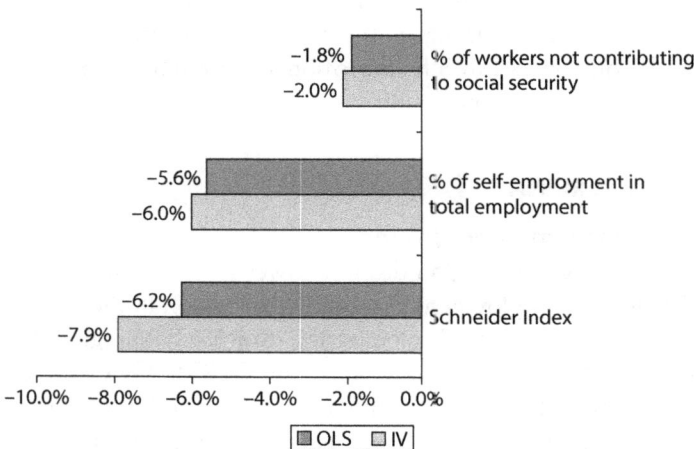

Source: Processed from Loayza and Wada 2010.
Note: IV = instrumental variable; OLS = ordinary least-squares.

of the main channels through which regulation affects growth, with a heavier regulation burden reducing growth and inducing higher informality.

Important adverse consequences of labor informality on other human development outcomes are seen, such as less protection at old age, lower access to and affordability of "quality" health care, and reduced employment quality (high working hours, unsafe conditions, and low pay). Social insurance systems in most MENA countries are historically based on Bismarckian principles, whereby pension, health, and disability benefits are linked to employment in the formal sector. As a result, formal sector actors (public and private sectors, employers and employees) have contributed to social security programs and in return have been covered by relatively generous, multidimensional benefit packages. Those outside the formal sector, in both urban and rural areas, have traditionally had limited or no access to formal risk management instruments or other government benefits. At the same time, noncontributory antipoverty and social protection programs developed recently in MENA remain limited in scope and reach, in most cases, a very narrow portion of society. In this sense, nearly all MENA countries are characterized by "truncated welfare systems." Informal workers in MENA are likely to use inadequate mechanisms to cope with social risks, such as informal and less effective social safety net arrangements or by selling assets or withdrawing children from school (which can have long-term adverse consequences). Emerging evidence also finds that informality is associated with lower life expectancy and health outcomes. Using data from the Republic of Yemen, Cho (2011) finds that, controlling for other factors, individuals living in households having a head working in the formal sector are associated with better health outcomes: lower malnutrition for children, low out-of-pocket expenses, and low adult morbidity.

Informality in MENA

Brief Macroeconomic Background

On average, the MENA region displays lower levels of employment and higher levels of unemployment than any other region in the world. Some basic macroeconomic trends comparing the MENA region to other regions in the world and, within MENA, non-GCC to GCC members are presented to provide context to the analysis that follows.[5] The level of economic development and other macroeconomic variables, such as recent economic growth and employment composition, are likely to be important factors for understanding a country's profile and determinants

Figure 1.5 Employment and Unemployment Rates in MENA

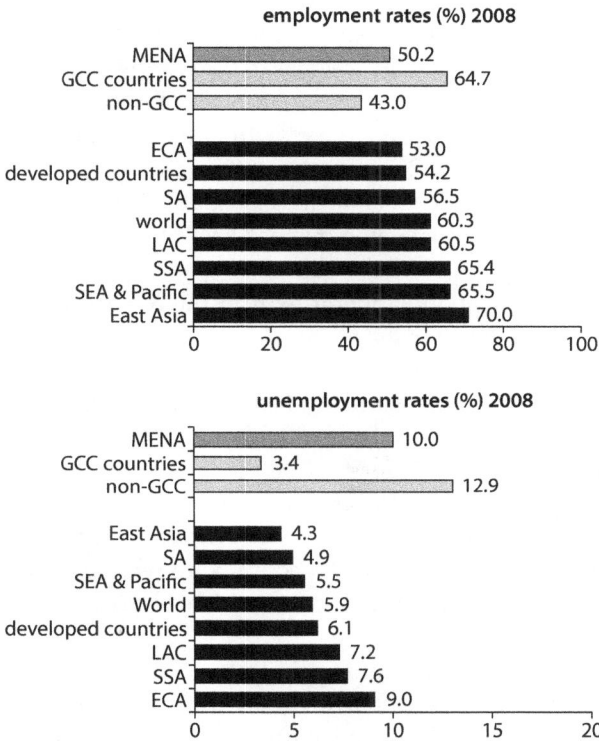

employment rates (%) 2008

MENA	50.2
GCC countries	64.7
non-GCC	43.0
ECA	53.0
developed countries	54.2
SA	56.5
world	60.3
LAC	60.5
SSA	65.4
SEA & Pacific	65.5
East Asia	70.0

unemployment rates (%) 2008

MENA	10.0
GCC countries	3.4
non-GCC	12.9
East Asia	4.3
SA	4.9
SEA & Pacific	5.5
World	5.9
developed countries	6.1
LAC	7.2
SSA	7.6
ECA	9.0

Source: World Development Indicators dataset.
Note: ECA = Europe and Central Asia; GCC = Gulf Cooperation Council countries; LAC = Latin America and the Caribbean; SA = South Asia; SEA = Southeast Asia; SSA = Sub-Saharan Africa.

of informality. Figure 1.5 illustrates the patterns of employment in MENA (subdivided into non-GCC and GCC countries) versus other regions. Differences between GCC and non-GCC countries are notable. GCC countries display high employment rates and low unemployment rates in comparison to the rest of the world. On the other hand, non-GCC countries show low employment rates (mainly because of low levels of female employment) and by far the highest unemployment rates in the world (at 13 percent in 2008).

In recent years, MENA countries have displayed positive economic growth and rapid employment growth, especially for women. Although annual GDP per capita growth rates among GCC and non-GCC countries have been rather similar in recent years and generally above the world average, annual employment growth rates have been significantly larger for GCC than for non-GCC countries (suggesting that GCC countries show higher employment elasticities to growth) (figure 1.6). In the MENA region, as in many other regions in the world, employment growth rates for the period 1998–2008 have been higher for women than for men. In particular, during this period, the growth rate of female (male) employment was 6.4 percent (4.2 percent) in GCC countries and 3.8 percent (2.9 percent) in non-GCC countries. Despite such rapid increases in female employment, female employment levels in the region remain the lowest in the world.

At the same time, population growth in the MENA region has been faster than in other regions. Annual population growth of 1.9 and 2.7 percent per year in GCC and non-GCC countries, respectively (figure 1.7), is among the highest in the world (and equivalent to those in Sub-Saharan Africa). While MENA countries created jobs at a higher pace than other countries in the world, the level of employment creation did not keep pace with population growth. Unemployment rates in GCC countries remain low at the time this report was written, but rapid population growth (especially if these countries continue to receive flows of international migrants) poses important potential risks for increasing unemployment and informality.

MENA countries differ significantly from other middle-income countries in the composition of employment generation (World Bank 2011). In the typical country in MENA, agriculture contributes to a larger extent to employment growth than in other middle-income countries. In other regions, there was a shift of labor away from agriculture towards services. In the typical MENA country, the contribution of manufacturing and private services, especially the trade, tourism, logistics and communication sectors (figure 1.8) is low. These sectors were the main contributors to employment growth in comparable middle income countries (such as Malaysia or Indonesia). Hence, jobs created in the typical MENA country were low-quality jobs, skewed toward low value-added sectors, which reflects the lack of structural transformation. In GCC countries, employment growth took place largely in the construction sector (jobs taken up by expatriates) and the creation of higher paid public sector jobs directed to nationals.

Informality Levels and Trends

A typical country in MENA produces about 28 percent of its GDP and employs 65 percent of its labor force informally. Using available data, Loayza and Wada (2010) assess the prevalence of informality in MENA

Figure 1.6 Economic Growth and Employment Growth

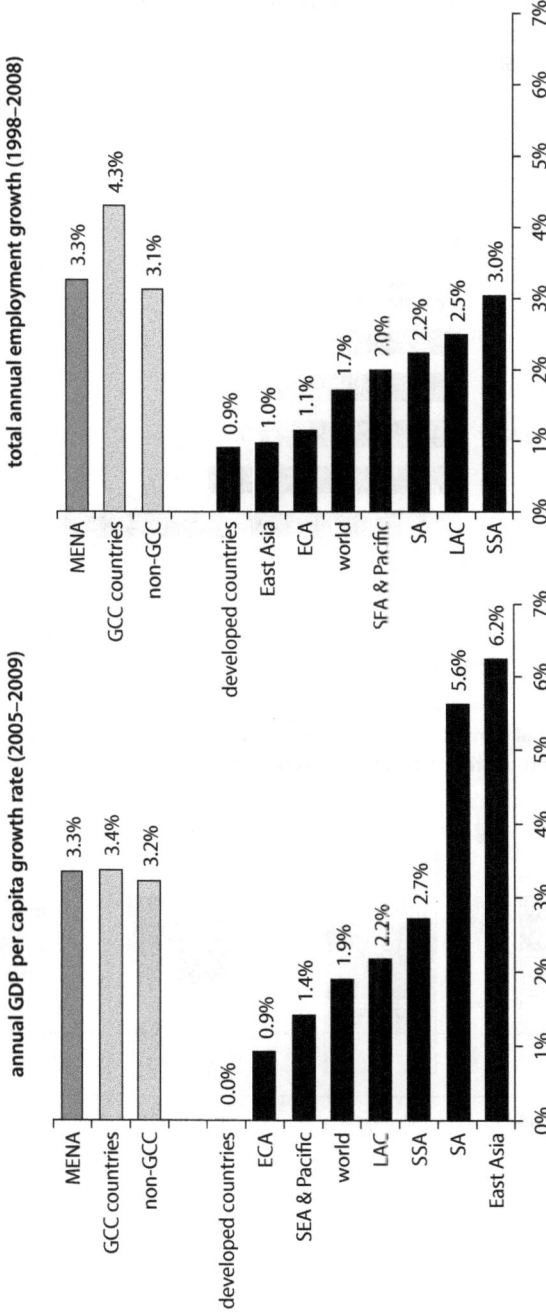

annual GDP per capita growth rate (2005–2009)

MENA	3.3%
GCC countries	3.4%
non-GCC	3.2%
developed countries	0.0%
ECA	0.9%
SEA & Pacific	1.4%
world	1.9%
LAC	2.2%
SSA	2.7%
SA	5.6%
East Asia	6.2%

total annual employment growth (1998–2008)

MENA	3.3%
GCC countries	4.3%
non-GCC	3.1%
developed countries	0.9%
East Asia	1.0%
ECA	1.1%
world	1.7%
SEA & Pacific	2.0%
SA	2.2%
LAC	2.5%
SSA	3.0%

Source: World Development Indicators dataset.

Note: ECA = Europe and Central Asia; GCC = Gulf Cooperation Council; LAC = Latin America and the Caribbean; SA = South Asia; SEA = Southeast Asia; SSA = Sub-Saharan Africa.

Figure 1.7   Annual Population Growth Rates (%) (2005–2009)

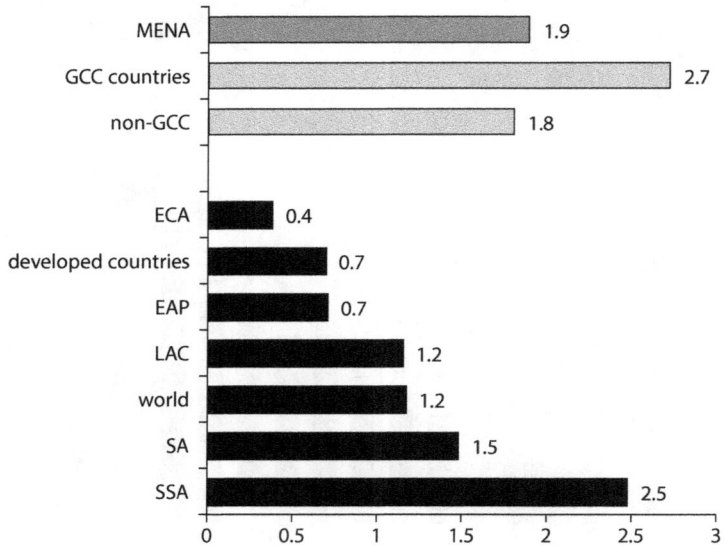

Source: World Development Indicators dataset.
Note: ECA = Europe and Central Asia; GCC = Gulf Cooperation Council; LAC = Latin America and the Caribbean;
SA = South Asia; SSA = Sub-Saharan Africa.

Figure 1.8   Sectoral Contribution to Annual Employment Growth in Typical MENA Country and Selected Other Countries, Average for 2000s

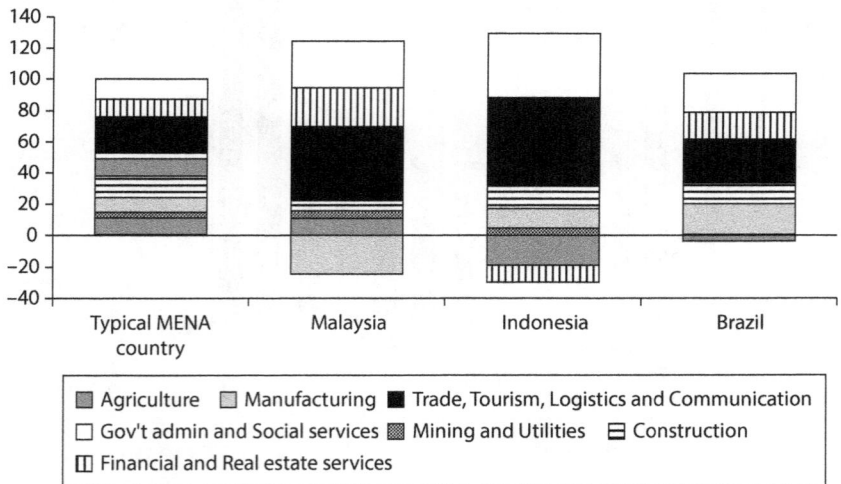

Source: World Bank 2013.

using three commonly used proxies of informality: (1) the Schneider Shadow Economy Index, (2) the share of the labor force not contributing to social security, and (3) the share of self-employment to total employment (figure 1.9). These stylized facts indicate that more than two-thirds of all workers in the region may not have access to health insurance and/or are not contributing to a pension system that provides income security after retirement age. At the same time, from a fiscal perspective, these results indicate that about one-third of total economic output in the region remains undeclared and therefore, not registered for tax purposes.

The degree of informality in the median country in MENA is lower than that of most developing countries, but much higher than that of the median developed country. As illustrated by figure 1.9 and using the lack of coverage measure, the typical MENA country has a labor informality rate larger than ECA, and lower than LAC, EAP, SA, and SSA. Using the Schneider Index, the median country in MENA has a lower informal production than the other developing regions. Using the share of self-employed, a typical MENA country is as informal as a typical country in LAC, more informal than a typical country in ECA, and less informal than a typical country in EAP, SA, and SSA.

Important variations are found in the prevalence of informality across non-GCC countries, depending, among other factors, on the availability of natural resources and labor. Non-GCC countries are quite heterogeneous in terms of size, availability of resources and labor, economic development, and demographic structure, all factors that influence the size of the informal economy (see chapter 2 for a more thorough discussion). The prevalence of informality varies significantly across countries in this group (figure 1.10). In general, resource-rich/labor-abundant economies (such as the Islamic Republic of Iran and the Syrian Arab Republic) tend to display high informality rates in the region as proxied by the share of the labor force not contributing to social security (between 66 and 73 percent) and by the share of self-employment to total employment (between 32 and 54 percent). However, their share of undeclared output to total GDP (at around 20 percent) is comparable to that of GCC countries. This occurs because this group of countries generally has few, but large, formal firms (many in the energy sector) that are capital intensive, thus rendering lower informality in production than in labor (Loayza and Wada 2010). On the contrary, resource-poor/labor-abundant economies (such as Egypt, Tunisia, and Morocco) display a high share of undeclared output (between 35 and 40 percent of GDP) and a lower share of the workforce not contributing to social security (between 45 and

Figure 1.9   Prevalence of Informality in MENA versus Other Regions

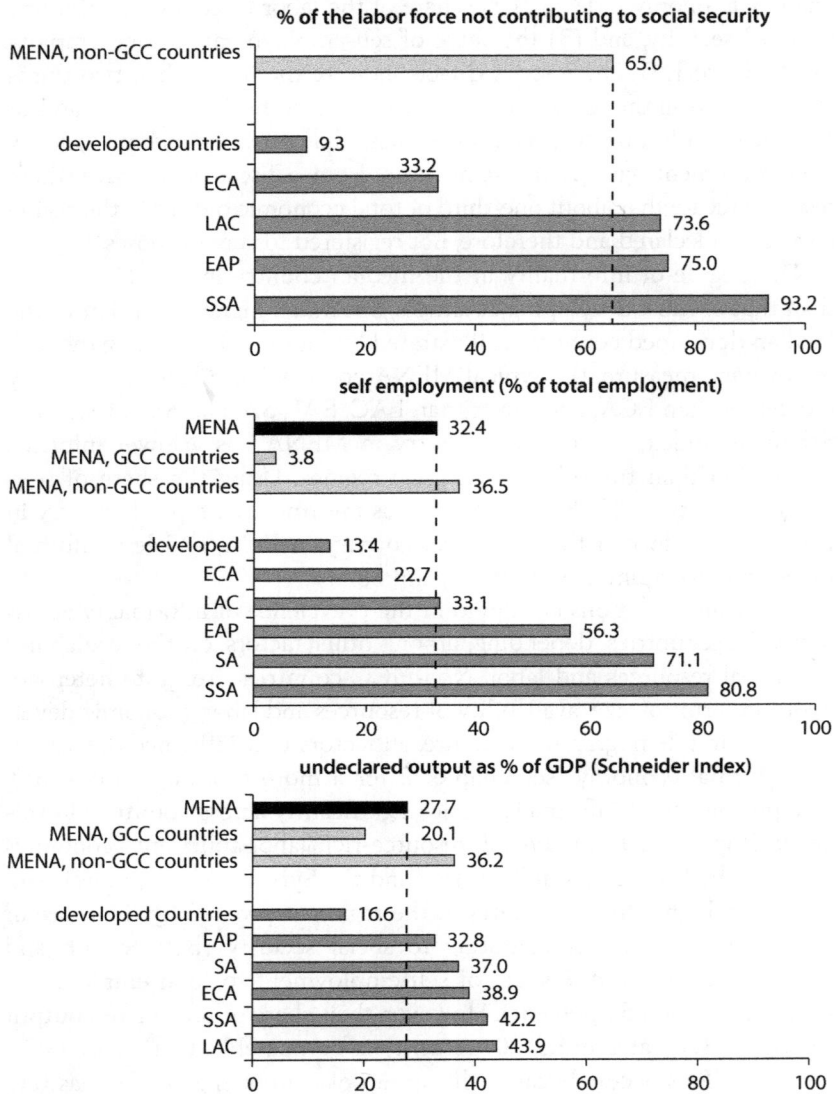

% of the labor force not contributing to social security

Region	Value
MENA, non-GCC countries	65.0
developed countries	9.3
ECA	33.2
LAC	73.6
EAP	75.0
SSA	93.2

self employment (% of total employment)

Region	Value
MENA	32.4
MENA, GCC countries	3.8
MENA, non-GCC countries	36.5
developed	13.4
ECA	22.7
LAC	33.1
EAP	56.3
SA	71.1
SSA	80.8

undeclared output as % of GDP (Schneider Index)

Region	Value
MENA	27.7
MENA, GCC countries	20.1
MENA, non-GCC countries	36.2
developed countries	16.6
EAP	32.8
SA	37.0
ECA	38.9
SSA	42.2
LAC	43.9

Source: Schneider et al., 2010 for Schneider Index; WDI for self employment and pension scheme.
Note: EAP = East Asia and Pacific; ECA = Europe and Central Asia; GCC = Gulf Cooperation Council; LAC = Latin America and the Caribbean; SA = South Asia; SSA = Sub-Saharan Africa. The periods covered are the latest years in 2000–10 for pension scheme, 2000–11 for self- employment, and 1999–2007 for the Schneider index, respectively. Data on social security contributions in GCC countries are only available for Bahrain, 2007 (20 percent), and Qatar, 2008 (4.4 percent) (Palleres-Miralles, Romero, and Whitehouse 2012).

Figure 1.10   Informality Rates for Selected Non-GCC Economies

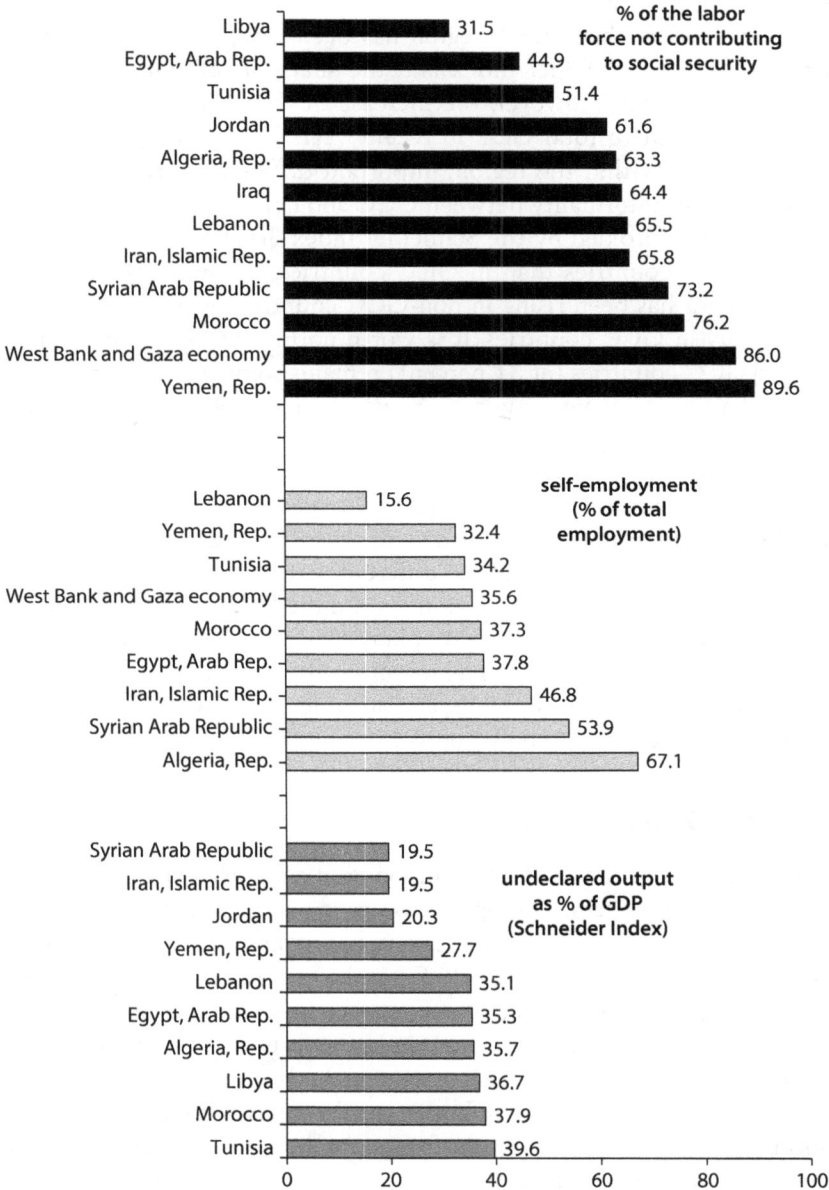

% of the labor force not contributing to social security

Libya	31.5
Egypt, Arab Rep.	44.9
Tunisia	51.4
Jordan	61.6
Algeria, Rep.	63.3
Iraq	64.4
Lebanon	65.5
Iran, Islamic Rep.	65.8
Syrian Arab Republic	73.2
Morocco	76.2
West Bank and Gaza economy	86.0
Yemen, Rep.	89.6

self-employment (% of total employment)

Lebanon	15.6
Yemen, Rep.	32.4
Tunisia	34.2
West Bank and Gaza economy	35.6
Morocco	37.3
Egypt, Arab Rep.	37.8
Iran, Islamic Rep.	46.8
Syrian Arab Republic	53.9
Algeria, Rep.	67.1

undeclared output as % of GDP (Schneider Index)

Syrian Arab Republic	19.5
Iran, Islamic Rep.	19.5
Jordan	20.3
Yemen, Rep.	27.7
Lebanon	35.1
Egypt, Arab Rep.	35.3
Algeria, Rep.	35.7
Libya	36.7
Morocco	37.9
Tunisia	39.6

Source: Processed from Loayza and Wada 2010.
Note: Time periods are as follows: Schneider Index, average 1999–2007; self-employment, 1999–2007; not contributing to social security (S.S.), 2000–2007.

76 percent), which is consistent with a higher share of medium size (and semiformal) labor-intensive firms.

Informality in the MENA region has been rising in recent years, as proxied by the Schneider Index and the share of self-employment to total employment. However, the increase in the share of undeclared/informal output to total GDP in recent years has been a global trend (figure 1.11). Within the region, important differences are seen in the growth rate of informality between GCC and non-GCC countries. First, informality, as proxied by the Schneider Index, has been growing faster in non-GCC countries than in GCC countries. Second, although self-employment has been rising in non-GCC countries, it has been declining rapidly in GCC countries. It is worth noting that self-employment in non-GCC countries (at 37 percent) remains somewhat lower than in other developing regions such as South Asia and Sub-Saharan Africa (71 and 81 percent, respectively) (Loayza and Wada 2010).

This report focuses its analysis and discussion on non-GCC MENA countries. A discussion of the aggregate trends in GCC and non-GCC countries is important to provide a comprehensive overview of informality throughout the region, but the different dynamics in labor markets in GCC and non-GCC MENA economies and the lack of micro-data make in-depth analysis of the informality phenomenon in GCC countries outside the scope of this report. Hence, all results from this point forward focus only on non-GCC countries, and any references to "MENA" need to be understood to refer to only non-GCC countries.

What Causes Informality?

Informality can be the result of exclusion or of a rational exit in opting out of the coverage system. The option to participate in the informal sector reflects cost and benefit considerations but is not always voluntary or desirable (Loayza and Wada 2010). From the perspective of a worker or a firm, joining the informal sector can be seen as either "exiting" the legal framework or "being excluded" from it. In the former case the informality option implies a voluntary decision, whereas in the latter it is derived from segmentation or segregation. In both cases, however, what matters is that informality in the economy results from a combination of factors affecting the potential gains, costs, and restrictions related to legally established firms and workers. Formality entails costs of entry (in the form of lengthy, expensive, and complicated registration procedures) and costs of permanence (including payment of taxes, compliance with mandated labor

Figure 1.11   Annual Growth Rates of Informality

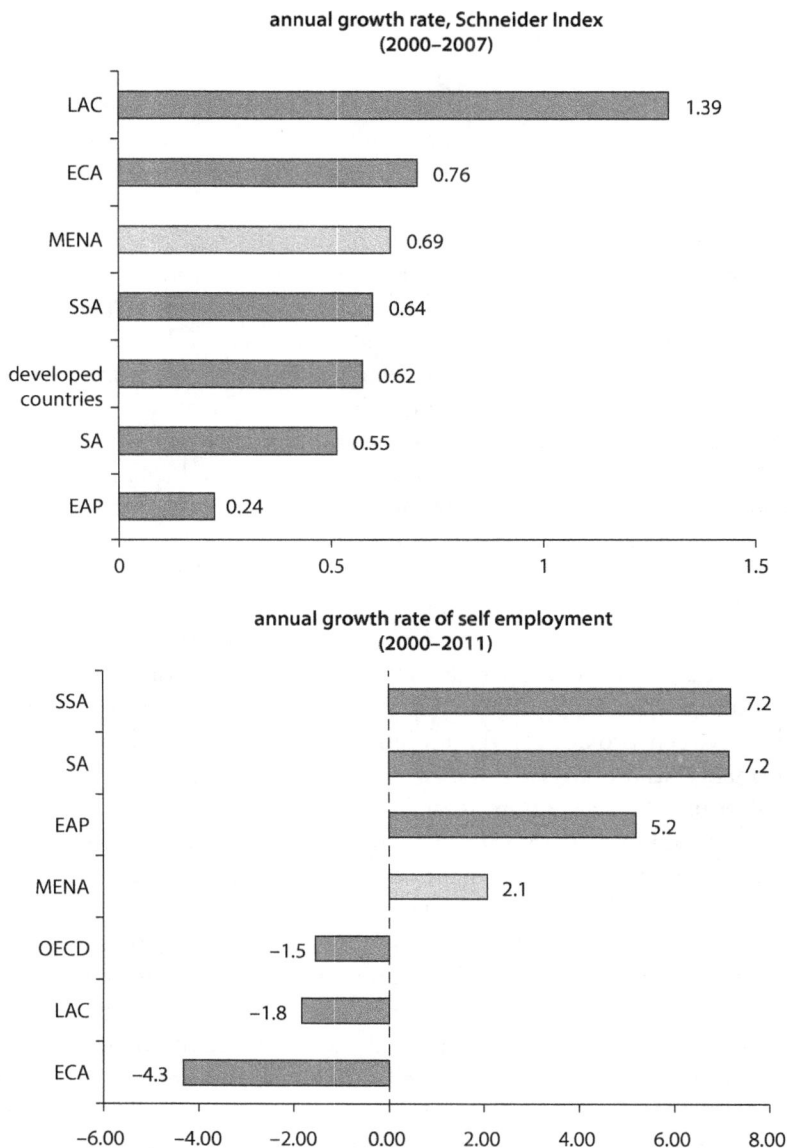

**annual growth rate, Schneider Index
(2000–2007)**

**annual growth rate of self employment
(2000–2011)**

Source: Processed from Loayza and Wada 2010.
Note: EAP = East Asia and Pacific; ECA = Europe and Central Asia; LAC = Latin America and the Caribbean;
SA = South Asia; SSA = Sub-Saharan Africa.

benefits and remunerations, and observance of environmental, health, and other regulations). The benefits of formality potentially consist of police protection against crime and abuse, recourse to the judicial system for conflict resolution and contract enforcement, access to legal financial institutions for credit provision and risk diversification, and, more generally, the possibility of expanding markets both domestically and internationally. At least in principle, formality also reduces the need to pay bribes and prevents incurrence of penalties and fees to which informal firms are likely subjected. Informality is more prevalent when the regulatory framework is burdensome, the quality of government services to formal firms is low, and the state's monitoring and enforcement power is weak (Friedman and others 2000; Johnson and others 1997; Loayza and Rigolini 2009; Schneider and Enste 2000). According to Galal (2005), the current regulatory framework in Egypt, for instance, discourages formality, leading to an annual loss in tax revenues equivalent to 1 percent of GDP.

The prevalence of informality depends on structural characteristics of countries, such as governance, productivity, and economic composition. Loayza and Wada (2010) analyze the structural factors that influence informality: (1) a country's governance structure and regulatory framework (which will affect the opportunity cost of informality), (2) labor productivity, demographics, and employment composition, and (3) the size of the public sector. To illustrate the relative importance of these determinants, Loayza and Wada (2010) first calculate a series of correlations between proxies for the aforementioned factors and the level of informality (as proxied by the share of the labor force not contributing to social security) for all countries where data are available. The authors find that, remarkably, the majority of correlation coefficients between these structural factors and informality are statistically significant, ranging between 0.29 and 0.83. Second, the authors use cross-country regression analysis to evaluate the importance of each proposed explanation regarding the causes of informality. The authors' regression results indicate that law and order, business regulatory freedom, education, and sociodemographic factors are all remarkably robust determinants of informality, with informality decreasing as these factors improve. Similarly, informality decreases when the production structure shifts away from agriculture and when demographic pressures from youth and rural populations decline. The main results are summarized as follows:

- *Governance and regulation*: A country's governance structure will directly affect the opportunity cost of informality. The prevalence of informality is influenced by the extent to which countries enforce law and regulation (more enforcement is associated with more compliance, especially if penalties are costly) and by the level of labor market regulatory freedom (more regulation/higher labor costs provide incentives for firms to bypass regulation) (figure 1.12).[6] Controlling for other factors, Loayza and Wada (2010) find that a 1 percent increase in the index of business regulatory freedom (index of law and order) is associated with 5 to 6 (2 to 3) percent lower informality worldwide.

Figure 1.12 Correlation between Informality and Governance/Regulation

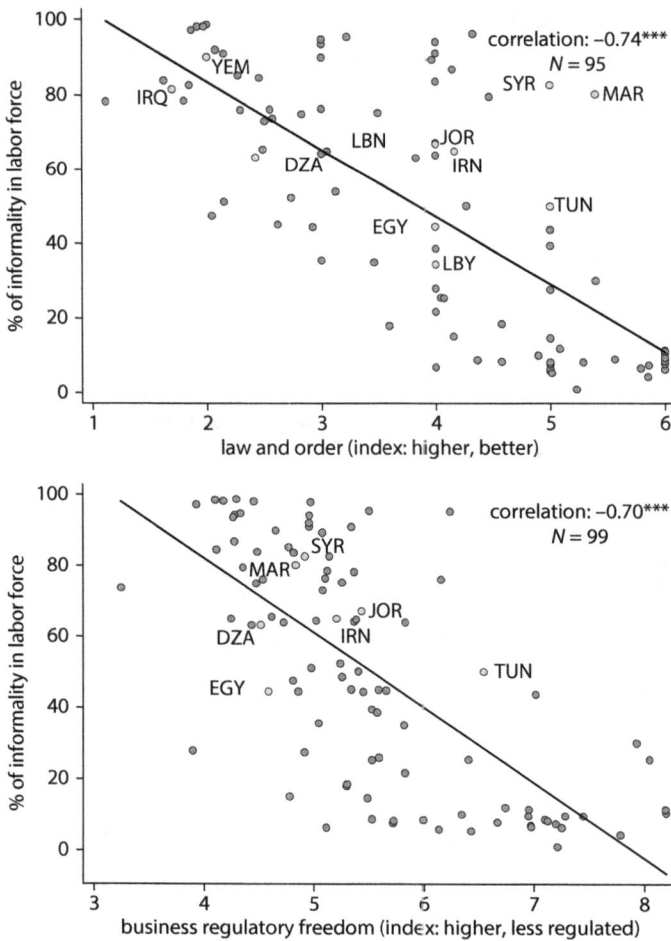

Source: Processed from Loayza and Wada 2010.

Striving for Better Jobs • http://dx.doi.org/10.1596/978-0-8213-9535-6

- *Productivity, demographics, and employment composition*: A higher level of education is associated with lower informality because investments in human capital increase productivity and hence make business regulations less onerous and formal returns potentially larger. Other things equal, Loayza and Wada (2010) find that an additional year of education of the labor force is associated with a 5 to 6 percent lower level of informality worldwide (figure 1.13). Furthermore, a production

Figure 1.13   Correlation between Informality and Education/Demographic Factors

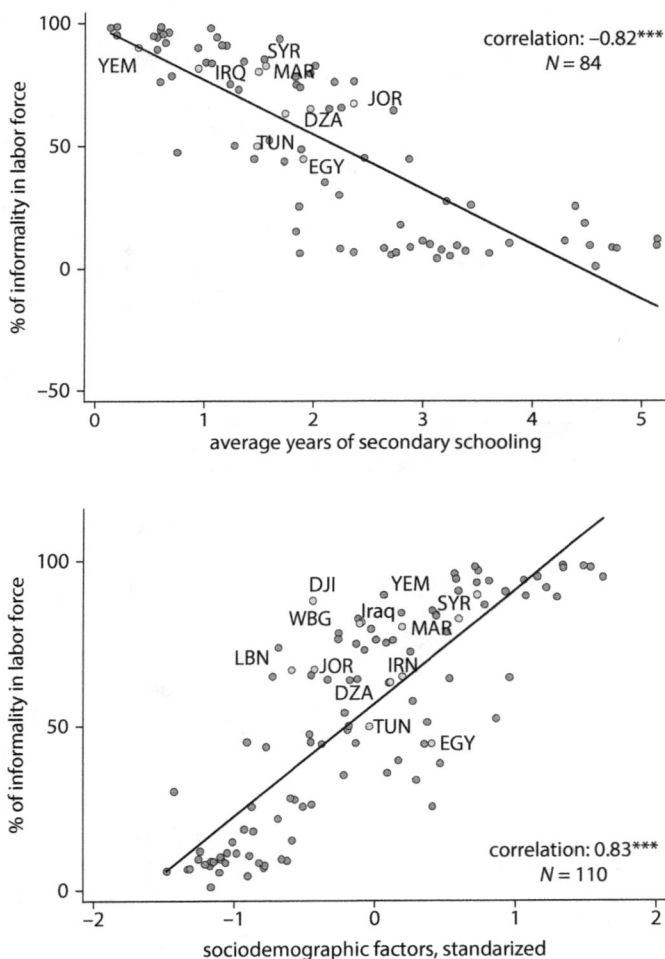

Source: Processed from Loayza and Wada 2010.

structure tilted toward agriculture, rather than toward the more complex processes of industry, favors informality by making legal protection and contract enforcement less relevant and valuable. Finally, a demographic composition with larger shares of youth or rural populations is likely to increase informality by making monitoring more difficult and expensive, by placing bigger demands on resources for training and acquisition of abilities, by creating bottlenecks in the initial school-to-work transition, and by making the expansion of formal public services more problematic (Fields 1990; ILO 2004; Schneider and Enste 2000).[7]

- *Size of the public sector*: Informality may also be affected by the size of public sector. Informality tends to be less prevalent in economies with a larger state presence (figure 1.14). In fact, in economies heavily dominated by the state, informality is practically nonexistent, as in the former Soviet Union and other communist countries in Eastern Europe. The influence of the state on informal employment can be direct, through the absorption of labor and economic production. This is especially important for the MENA region, given the state's traditionally important role as source of formal employment. The influence can also be indirect, through the links that the government establishes with private firms, by requiring them to register officially and comply with its regulations. Furthermore, given a sufficient level of quality, the size of the government can affect the state's ability to monitor and enforce formal taxes and regulations.[8]

- *Labor costs:* Demand for formal employment will be determined by direct and indirect labor costs relative to informal workers. Higher indirect costs of labor, generally in the form of stricter employment protection legislation and/or high labor taxes, are associated with higher levels of informality (Botero and others 2004; Djankov and Ramalho 2009; Grubb and Wells 1993). This is likely to be important in MENA, where, compared with international benchmarks, firing regulations are rather strict and labor taxes are rather high (Angel-Urdinola and Kuddo 2010). Figure 1.15 illustrates proxies for indirect labor costs (labor taxes and severance pay for redundancy dismissals) using available data from the *Doing Business* 2011 dataset and compares a selected group of non-GCC countries with respect to the world median (represented by the horizontal and vertical lines in the figure). Some economies in the region that display high levels of informality (such as Morocco, Syria, Lebanon,

Figure 1.14 Correlation between Informality and Government Size

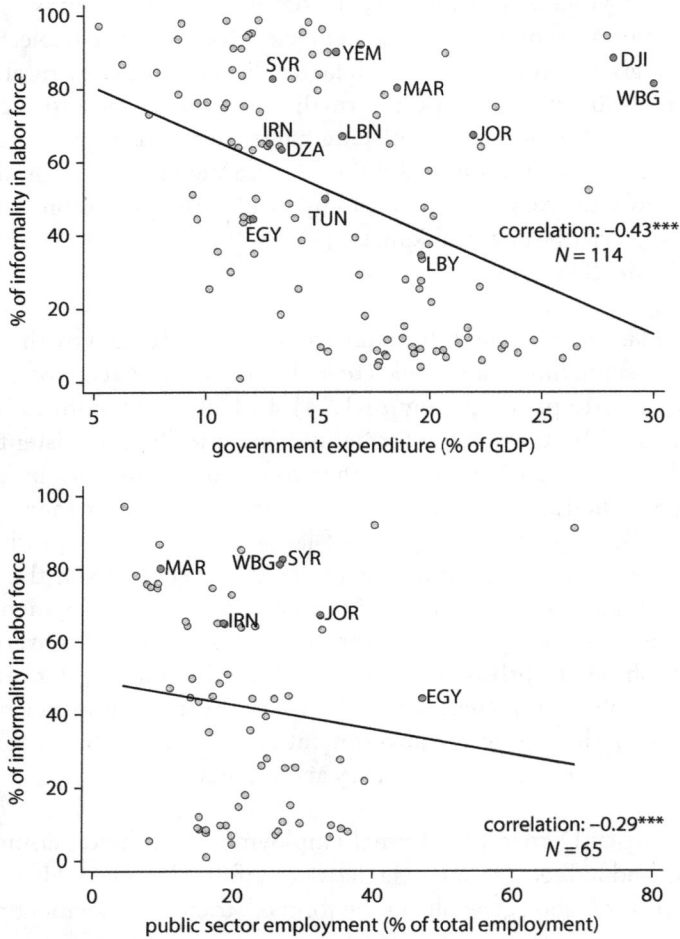

correlation: −0.43***
N = 114

correlation: −0.29***
N = 65

Source: Processed from Loayza and Wada 2010.

West Bank and Gaza economy, and Algeria) are also associated with high levels of labor taxes and with high severance payment schemes. Although some authors find a positive and significant relationship between the generosity of severance pay schemes and informality, the relationship between labor taxes and informality is inconclusive here (that is, some countries from ECA and OECD display high levels of labor taxes and low levels of informality).

Figure 1.15 Correlation between Informality and Indirect Labor Costs

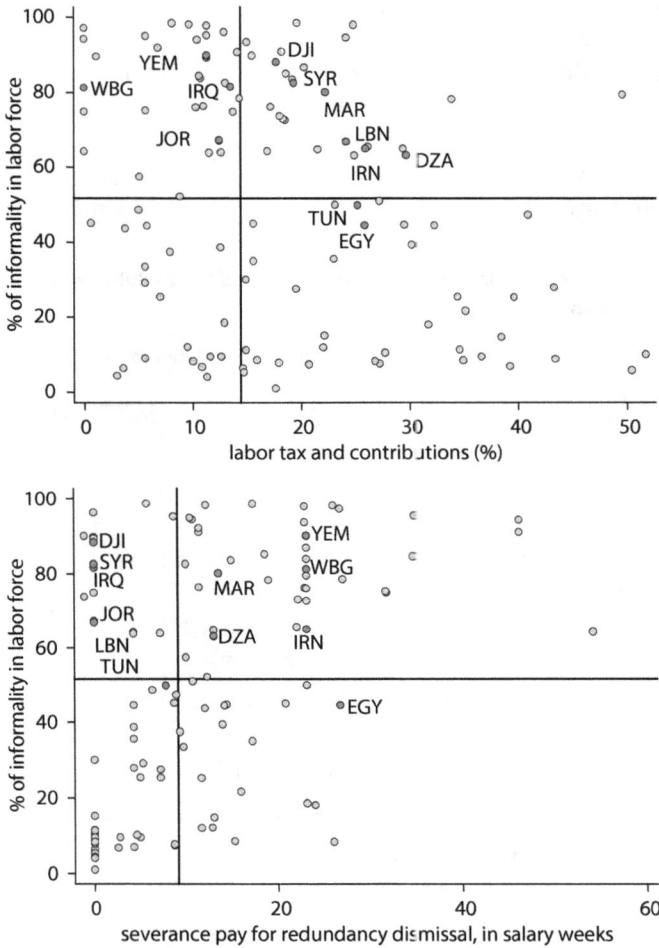

Source: Based on *Doing Business* 2011 data.
Note: Lines inside figures represent world medians.

Structural Characteristics in MENA Countries

MENA's large youth bulge and educational deficit has important implications for the region's prevalence of informality. Loayza and Wada
(2010) illustrate the importance of structural factors on informality for
a selected group of countries in the MENA region where data are available. The authors find that MENA countries, while being quite heterogeneous, have characteristics that are associated with higher prevalence

of informality. In particular, MENA countries have a large youth bulge and still display important education deficits. As mentioned before, countries with a larger youth to total population ratio are associated with higher informality levels. The right-hand panel of figure 1.16 illustrates the percentage difference between the youth bulge in MENA versus the world's median for a selected group of countries. Results indicate that with the exception of Lebanon, the youth bulge for all other countries in the region is larger than the world's median (ranging

Figure 1.16   Percentage Difference in Education and Youth Bulge with Respect to the World Median

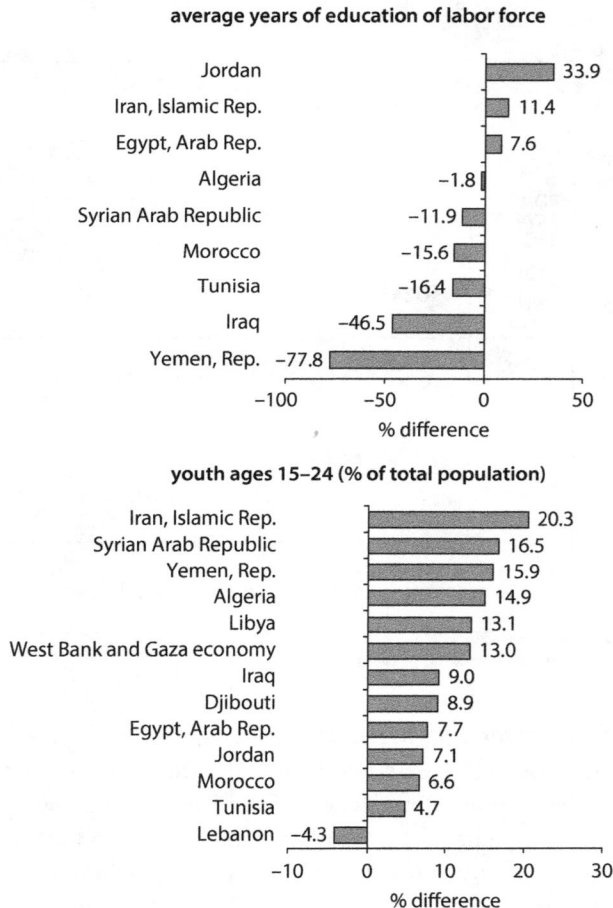

average years of education of labor force

Country	% difference
Jordan	33.9
Iran, Islamic Rep.	11.4
Egypt, Arab Rep.	7.6
Algeria	−1.8
Syrian Arab Republic	−11.9
Morocco	−15.6
Tunisia	−16.4
Iraq	−46.5
Yemen, Rep.	−77.8

youth ages 15–24 (% of total population)

Country	% difference
Iran, Islamic Rep.	20.3
Syrian Arab Republic	16.5
Yemen, Rep.	15.9
Algeria	14.9
Libya	13.1
West Bank and Gaza economy	13.0
Iraq	9.0
Djibouti	8.9
Egypt, Arab Rep.	7.7
Jordan	7.1
Morocco	6.6
Tunisia	4.7
Lebanon	−4.3

Source: Processed from Loayza and Wada 2010.

from 5 percent in Tunisia to 20 percent in the Islamic Republic of Iran). At the same time, some countries in the region, such as Iraq and the Republic of Yemen, display important education deficits, which are associated with lower levels of productivity (and thus higher levels of informality).

Some countries in the region remain very rural by world standards. As illustrated by figure 1.17, the share of total population living in rural areas in countries such as the Republic of Yemen, Syria, Egypt, and Morocco is high by world standards. Not surprisingly, in these economies

Figure 1.17 Percentage Difference in Rural Population and Agricultural Output with Respect to the World Median

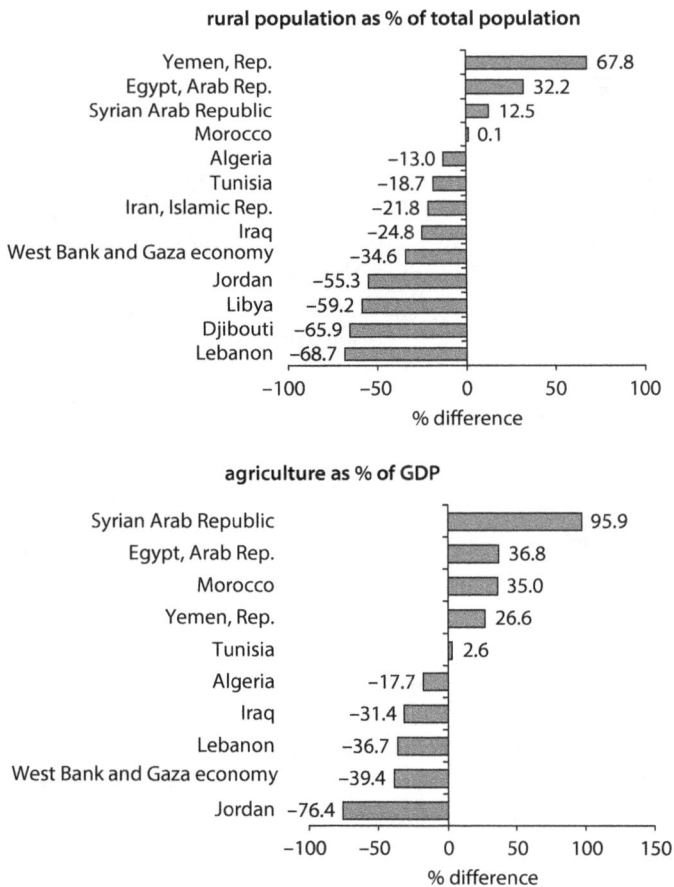

rural population as % of total population

Country	% difference
Yemen, Rep.	67.8
Egypt, Arab Rep.	32.2
Syrian Arab Republic	12.5
Morocco	0.1
Algeria	−13.0
Tunisia	−18.7
Iran, Islamic Rep.	−21.8
Iraq	−24.8
West Bank and Gaza economy	−34.6
Jordan	−55.3
Libya	−59.2
Djibouti	−65.9
Lebanon	−68.7

agriculture as % of GDP

Country	% difference
Syrian Arab Republic	95.9
Egypt, Arab Rep.	36.8
Morocco	35.0
Yemen, Rep.	26.6
Tunisia	2.6
Algeria	−17.7
Iraq	−31.4
Lebanon	−36.7
West Bank and Gaza economy	−39.4
Jordan	−76.4

Source: Processed from Loayza and Wada 2010.

Striving for Better Jobs • http://dx.doi.org/10.1596/978-0-8213-9535-6

the share of agricultural to total economic output tends to be a larger component of the total economy. Because the agricultural sector remains largely informal in developing countries, countries with relatively large agricultural sectors will likely display higher informality rates than countries with relatively small agricultural sectors (such as Jordan and Lebanon).

Finally, the public sector still plays a major employment and economic role in many countries in the region. Almost by definition, the large majority of employment in the public sector is formal. As such, controlling for other factors, countries with relatively larger public sectors are likely to be associated with lower prevalence of informality. Figure 1.18 indicates that some countries in the region (such as Egypt, Jordan, and Syria) have public sectors that are quite large by international standards.

Conclusions

Informality is a fundamental characteristic of underdevelopment. Higher levels of informality are associated with lower levels of economic growth. Widespread informality implies that a large number of people and economic activities operate outside the legal-institutional framework. International evidence indicates that widespread informality induces firms to remain suboptimally small, use irregular procurement and distribution channels, and constantly divert resources to mask their activities or bribe officials. Conversely, formal firms will be able to use resources with less regulatory restrictions, which enables them to be less labor intensive compared with their country's labor endowments. Informality may also be a source of further economic retardation because it is associated with misallocation of resources and entails losing the advantages of legality, such as police and judicial protection, access to formal credit institutions, and participation in international markets. At the same time, informality constitutes an important source of employment growth and of dynamism in many economies.

Important adverse consequences of labor informality on human development outcomes are found. Informal workers in MENA have limited or no access to formal risk management instruments to cope with social risks. Social insurance systems in most MENA countries historically have been based on Bismarckian principles, in which formal sector actors (public and private sectors, employers and employees) contributed to social security programs, in return for relatively generous, multidimensional benefit packages, often including health insurance,

Figure 1.18   Percentage Difference in Public Employment with Respect to the World Median

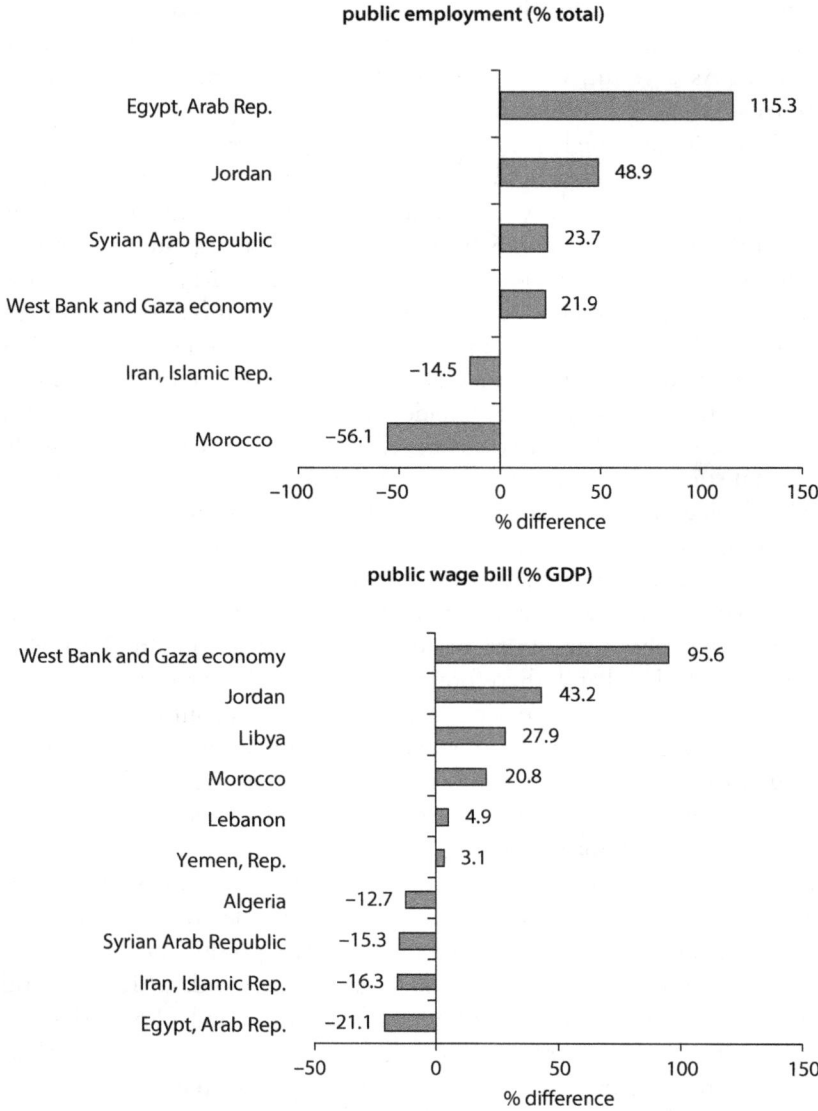

public employment (% total)

public wage bill (% GDP)

Source: Processed from Loayza and Wada 2010 and WDI dataset.

old-age pension, disability and workers' insurance, and, in some cases, housing, child care, and sports and recreation benefits. Those outside the formal sector, in both urban and rural areas, have had limited or no access to formal risk management instruments or other government benefits. As a result, informal workers cope with many risks though informal safety net arrangements.

Although not as high as in other developing regions, informal employment is rather prevalent in most MENA countries. Moreover, in some of them, informality is nearly as high as in the most informal countries in the world. This observation is important because a large informal sector denotes misallocation of resources (labor in particular) and inefficient utilization of government services, which can jeopardize the countries' growth and poverty-alleviation prospects. A typical country in MENA produces about one-third of its GDP and employs 65 percent of its labor force informally (using the Schneider Index and the share of the labor force without social security coverage, respectively). These are remarkable statistics, especially from a human development perspective. These stylized facts indicate that more than two-thirds of all workers in the region may not have access to health insurance and/or are not contributing to a pension system that would provide income security after retirement age. At the same time, from a fiscal perspective, these results indicate that about one-third of total economic output in the region remains undeclared and, therefore, not registered for tax purposes.

Important variations are seen in the prevalence of informality across non-GCC MENA countries, depending on the availability of natural resources and labor. Resource-rich/labor-abundant economies (such as the Islamic Republic of Iran, Syria, and the Republic of Yemen) tend to display the highest labor informality rates in the region (as proxied by the share of the labor force not contributing to social security and the share of self-employment to total employment) but low undeclared output to total GDP (explained by the capital intensity of their production). Resource-poor/labor-abundant economies (such as Egypt, Jordan, Tunisia, and Morocco) display a high share of undeclared output and a lower share of the workforce not contributing to social security, likely reflecting their higher share of medium size (and semiformal) labor-intensive firms.

Still, not all is negative about informality: The informal sector is likely to be an important mechanism for employment transition, especially among youth. Given that informality entails misallocation of resources and lower growth, should it be reduced at all costs? The answer to this important policy question is "no." Although informality is suboptimal with respect to a situation of streamlined regulations and adequate provision of public services, it is indeed preferable to a fully formal economy that is unable to circumvent its regulation-induced rigidities. Also, the informal sector could be an important source of economic dynamism and may provide some needed flexibility for small firms to grow and operate productively. The crucial policy implication is that the mechanism of formalization matters greatly for its effects on employment, efficiency, and growth. If formalization is based purely on enforcement, it will likely lead to unemployment and low growth. On the other hand, if it is based on improvements in both the regulatory framework and the quality and availability of public services, it will bring about more efficient use of resources and higher growth. Also, the informal sector is a mechanism for workers to cope with unemployment risks and/or a sector of employment transition, especially for youth as they acquire experience.

Annex

Annex Table 1A.1   Sample Economies in the Informality Regression

Country code	Economy	Non-contributor to pension scheme (74 economies)	Self-employment (62 economies)	Schneider Shadow Economy Index (93 economies)
DZA	Algeria	√	√	√
ARG	Argentina	√	√	√
AUS	Australia	√	√	√
AUT	Austria	√	√	√
BGD	Bangladesh	√	√	√
BEL	Belgium	√	√	√
BOL	Bolivia	√	√	√
BWA	Botswana			√
BRA	Brazil	√	√	√
BGR	Bulgaria			√
BFA	Burkina Faso		√	√
CMR	Cameroon		√	√
CAN	Canada	√	√	√
CHL	Chile	√	√	√
CHN	China	√	√	√
COL	Colombia			√
ZAR	Congo, Dem. Rep.	√	√	√
COG	Congo, Rep.			√
CRI	Costa Rica	√	√	√
CIV	Côte d'Ivoire			√

(table continues next page)

Annex Table 1A.1   Sample Economies in the Informality Regression (continued)

Country code	Economy	Non-contributor to pension scheme (74 economies)	Self-employment (62 economies)	Schneider Shadow Economy Index (93 economies)
HRV	Croatia	√		√
DNK	Denmark	√	√	√
DOM	Dominican Rep.	√	√	√
ECU	Ecuador	√	√	√
EGY	Egypt, Arab Rep.	√	√	√
SLV	El Salvador	√	√	√
EST	Estonia	√		√
ETH	Ethiopia		√	√
FIN	Finland	√		√
FRA	France	√	√	√
DEU	Germany	√	√	√
GHA	Ghana	√		√
GRC	Greece	√	√	√
GTM	Guatemala	√	√	√
GNB	Guinea-Bissau	√		
GUY	Guyana	√		
HTI	Haiti			√
HND	Honduras	√	√	√
HKG	Hong Kong SAR, China		√	√
HUN	Hungary	√		√
ISL	Iceland	√	√	
IND	India	√		√
IDN	Indonesia	√	√	√
IRN	Iran, Islamic Rep.	√	√	√
IRL	Ireland	√	√	√
ITA	Italy	√	√	√
JAM	Jamaica	√	√	√
JPN	Japan	√	√	√
JOR	Jordan	√		√
KEN	Kenya	√		√
KOR	Korea, Rep.	√	√	√
KWT	Kuwait			√
MDG	Madagascar		√	√
MWI	Malawi			√
MYS	Malaysia	√	√	√
MLI	Mali			√
MEX	Mexico	√	√	√
MAR	Morocco	√	√	√
MOZ	Mozambique			√
NAM	Namibia		√	√

(table continues next page)

Annex Table 1A.1   Sample Economies in the Informality Regression *(continued)*

Country code	Economy	Non-contributor to pension scheme (74 economies)	Self-employment (62 economies)	Schneider Shadow Economy Index (93 economies)
NLD	Netherlands	√	√	√
NZL	New Zealand	√	√	√
NIC	Nicaragua	√	√	√
NER	Niger	√	√	√
NOR	Norway	√	√	√
PAK	Pakistan	√	√	√
PAN	Panama		√	√
PNG	Papua New Guinea			√
PRY	Paraguay	√	√	√
PER	Peru	√	√	√
PHL	Philippines	√	√	√
POL	Poland	√		√
PRT	Portugal	√		√
SEN	Senegal	√		√
SLE	Sierra Leone	√	√	√
SGP	Singapore	√	√	√
SVK	Slovak Republic	√		√
SVN	Slovenia			√
ZAF	South Africa		√	√
ESP	Spain	√	√	√
LKA	Sri Lanka	√	√	√
SWE	Sweden	√		√
CHE	Switzerland	√	√	√
SYR	Syrian Arab Rep.	√	√	√
TZA	Tanzania	√		√
THA	Thailand	√	√	√
TGO	Togo			√
TTO	Trinidad and Tobago	√	√	
TUN	Tunisia	√	√	√
TUR	Turkey	√		√
UGA	Uganda	√		√
GBR	United Kingdom	√	√	√
USA	United States	√	√	√
URY	Uruguay	√	√	√
VEN	Venezuela, RB	√	√	√
ZMB	Zambia	√	√	√
ZWE	Zimbabwe			√

Annex Table 1A.2   Definitions and Sources of Variables Used in Regression Analysis

Variable	Definition and construction	Source
Noncontributor to pension scheme	Labor force not contributing to a pension scheme as the percentage of total labor force. Average of 2000–2007 by country.	World Development Indicators, various years
Self-employment	Self-employed workers as percentage of total employment. Country averages but periods to compute the averages vary by country. Average of 1999–2007 by country. ECA countries are excluded (Loayza and Rigolini 2006).	ILO, data retrieved from laborsta.ilo.org
Schneider Shadow Economy index	Estimated shadow economy as a percentage of official GDP. Average of 1999–2007 by country.	Schneider 2007; Schneider, Buehn, and Montenegro 2010
Law and Order	An index ranging 0 to 6 with higher values indicating better governance. Law and Order are assessed separately, with each subcomponent comprising 0 to 3 points. Assessment of Law focuses on the legal systems, and Order is rated by popular observance of the law. Average of 2000–2007 by country.	PRS group, data retrieved from https://www.prsgroup.com
Business Regulatory Freedom	An index ranging 0 to 10 with higher values indicating less regulated. It is composed of following indicators: (1) price controls; (2) administrative requirements; (3) bureaucracy costs; (4) starting a business; (5) extra payments/bribes; (6) licensing restrictions; and (7) cost of tax compliance. Average of 2000–2007 by country.	Gwartney, Lawson, and Norton 2008, the Fraser Institute. Data retrieved from www.freetheworld.com
Labor Regulatory Freedom	An index ranging 0 to 10 with higher values indicating less regulation. It is composed of following indicators: (1) minimum wage; (2) hiring and firing regulations; (3) centralized collective bargaining; (4) mandated cost of hiring; (5) mandated cost of worker dismissal; and (6) conscription. Average of 2000–2007 by country.	Gwartney, Lawson, and Norton 2008, Fraser Institute, data retrieved from www.freetheworld.com

(table continues next page)

Annex Table 1A.2   Definitions and Sources of Variables Used in Regression Analysis *(continued)*

Variable	Definition and construction	Source
Average years of secondary schooling	Average years of secondary schooling in the population aged 15 and over. The most recent score in each country is used.	Barro and Lee 1993, 2001, and calculations
Sociodemographic factors	Simple average of following three variables: (1) youth (aged 10–24) population as a percentage of total population; (2) rural population as a percentage of total population; (3) agriculture as a percentage of GDP. All three variables are standardized before the average is taken. Average of 2000–2007 by country.	Calculations with data from World Development Indicators, ILO, and the UN
Public sector employment	Public sector employment as a percentage of total employment. Country averages but periods to compute the averages vary by country. Average of 2000–2007 by country.	ILO, data retrieved from laborsta.ilo.org
Government expenditure	General government final consumption expenditure as a percentage of GDP. Country averages but periods to compute the averages vary by country. Average of 2000–2007 by country.	World Development Indicators, various years

Note: ECA = Europe and Central Asia; GDP = gross domestic product; ILO = International Labour Organization; UN = United Nations.

Notes

1. Own-account workers are workers working on their own account or with one or more partners, holding a job defined as a self-employed job, and not having engaged on a continuous basis any employees to work for them during the reference period (ILO 1993).

2. The currency demand method was developed by Tanzi (1980, 1983) who assumes that transactions in the informal economy take place in the form of cash payments, which are most easily hidden from authorities. Hence, an increase in informality is likely to go hand in hand with an increase in currency demand. The excess demand for currency is estimated econometrically, controlling for factors traditionally associated with currency demand (such as income and interest rates) as well as factors associated with an increase of activity in the informal economy (such as direct/indirect tax burden, government regulation). The physical input (electricity consumption) method takes electricity consumption as a proxy for overall economic activity. Kaufmann and Kaliberda (1996) estimate the growth of the informal economy as the difference between the growth rate of official GDP and the growth rate of electricity consumption.

3. Additional descriptive statistics on these three informality indicators for countries in MENA are presented in the annex.

4. In all countries included in the analysis there is a positive correlation (ranging from 0.17 in the Republic of Yemen and 0.45 in Iraq) between being self-employed and not contributing to social security and a positive correlation (from 0.10 in Lebanon to 0.40 in the Republic of Yemen) between being an unpaid worker and not contributing to social security. At the same time, in all countries included in the sample, there is a negative correlation between being an unpaid worker and being self-employed (from −0.11 in Lebanon to −0.51 in the Republic of Yemen). This indicates that not contributing to social security captures some of the aspects of informality faced by both unpaid workers and self-employed, which are two very different groups. Correlations are available upon request.

5. Economies that belong to the non-GCC MENA group are Algeria, the Arab Republic of Egypt, the Islamic Republic of Iran, Iraq, Jordan, Lebanon, Libya, Morocco, Syrian Arab Republic, Tunisia, and the Republic of Yemen as well as the West Bank and Gaza economy. Countries that belong to the GCC MENA group are Bahrain, Kuwait, Oman, Qatar, Saudi Arabia, and the United Arab Emirates.

6. Law enforcement is measured by the Index on the Prevalence of Law and Order obtained from *The International Country Risk Guide*. The index is a proxy for both the quality of formal public services and the government's enforcement strength. To measure labor regulation, the Index of Business

Regulatory Freedom and Labor Market Regulatory Freedom is used, taken from Fraser Foundation's *Economic Freedom of the World* report.

7. Labor productivity is proxied by (1) the average years of secondary schooling of the adult labor force (from Barro and Lee 2001) and (2) an index of sociodemographic factors composed of the share of youth in the population, the share of rural population, and the share of agriculture in GDP, obtained from the WDI dataset.

8. Government size is proxied by (1) the share of employment in the public sector to total employment (from ILO's LABORSTA dataset) and (2) government consumption expenditure as a percentage of GDP (from WDI).

References

Angel-Urdinola, D., and A. Kuddo. 2010. "Key Characteristics of Employment Regulation in the Middle East and North Africa." SP Discussion Paper 1006. Washington, DC: World Bank.

Angel-Urdinola, D., J. G. Reis, and C. Quijada. 2009. "Informality in Turkey: Size, Trends, Determinants and Consequences." Mimeo. Washington, DC: World Bank.

Angel-Urdinola, D., and K. Tanabe. 2011. "Micro-Determinants of Informal Employment in the Middle East and North Africa Region." Mimeo. Washington, DC: World Bank.

Barro, R. W., and J.-W. Lee. 1993. "International Comparisons of Educational Attainment." *Journal of Monetary Economics* 32 (3): 363–394.

———. 2001. "International Data on Educational Attainment: Updates and Implications." *Oxford Economic Papers* 53 (3): 541–563.

Botero, J. C., S. Djankov, R. La Porta, F. Lopez-de-Silanes, and A. Shleifer. 2004. "The Regulation of Labor." *Quarterly Journal of Economics* 119 (4): 1339–1382.

Cho, Y. 2011. "Informality and Protection from Health Shocks: Lessons from Yemen." Unpublished manuscript. Washington, DC: World Bank.

De Soto, H. 1989. *The Other Path: The Invisible Revolution in the Third World.* New York: HarperCollins.

Djankov, S., and R. Ramalho. 2009. "Employment Laws in Developing Countries." *Journal of Comparative Economics* 37 (1): 3–13.

EC, IMF, OECD, UN, and World Bank. 2008. *System of National Accounts 2008.* European Commission, International Monetary Fund, Organisation for Economic Co-operation and Development, United Nations, and World Bank, New York.

Fields, G. 1990. "Labour Market Modeling and the Urban Informal Sector: Theory and Evidence." In *The Informal Sector Revisited*, ed. David Turnham, Bernard Salomé, and Antoine Schwarz, 49–69. Paris: OECD.

Friedman, E., S. Johnson, D. Kaufmann, and P. Zoido-Lobaton. 2000. "Dodging the Grabbing Hand: The Determinants of Unofficial Activity in 69 Countries." *Journal of Public Economics* 76 (3): 459–493.

Galal, A. 2005. "The Economics of Formalization: Potential Winners and Losers from Formalization in Egypt." In *Investment Climate, Growth, and Poverty*, ed. Gudrun Kochendorfer-Lucius and Boris Pleskovic. Washington, DC: World Bank.

Gasparini, L., and L. Tornarolli. 2006. "Labor Informality in Latin America and Caribbean: Patterns and Trends from Household Survey and Micro-data." Mimeo. Washington, DC: World Bank.

Grubb, D., and W. Wells. 1993. "Employment Regulation and Patterns of Work in EC Countries." Economic Studies 21. Paris: OECD.

Gwartney, J. D., and R. Lawson, with S. Norton. 2008. *Economic Freedom of the World: 2008 Annual Report*. Vancouver: Economic Freedom Network.

Hart, K. 1973. "Informal Income Opportunities and Urban Employment in Ghana." *Journal of Modern African Studies* 11 (1): 61–89.

ILO (International Labour Organization). 1993. "Resolutions Concerning International Classification of Status in Employment." Adopted by the 15th International Conference of Labour Statisticians. Geneva: ILO.

———. 2002. "Decent Work and the Informal Economy: Sixth Item on the Agenda." 90th International Labour Conference: 2002. Report VII (2A). Geneva: ILO. http://www.ilo.org/public/english/standards/relm/ilc/ilc90/pdf /rep-vi.pdf.

———. 2004. *Global Employment Trends for Youth*. Geneva: ILO.

Johnson, S., D. Kaufmann, A. Shleifer, M. I. Goldman, and M. L. Weitzman. 1997. "The Unofficial Economy in Transition." *Brookings Papers on Economic Activity* 2: 159–239.

Kaufmann, D., and A. Kaliberda. 1996. "Integrating the Unofficial Economy into the Dynamics of Post Socialist Economies: A Framework of Analyses and Evidence." Policy Research Working Paper 1691. Washington, DC: World Bank.

Loayza, N., A. M. Oviedo, and L. Serven. 2005. "The Impact of Regulation on Growth and Informality Cross-Country Evidence." Policy Research Working Paper 3623. Washington, DC: World Bank.

Loayza, N., and J. Rigolini. 2006. "Informality Trends and Cycles." Policy Research Working Paper 4078. Washington, DC: World Bank.

———. 2009. "Informal Employment: Safety Net or Growth Engine?" Mimeo. Washington, DC: World Bank.

Loayza, N., and T. Wada. 2010. "Informal Labor in the Middle East and North Africa: Basic Measures and Determinants." Mimeo. Washington, DC: World Bank.

Pallares-Miralles, M., C. Romero, and E. Whitehouse. 2012. "International Patterns of Pension Provision II: A Worldwide Overview of Facts and Figures." Social Protection and Labor Discussion Paper 1211. World Bank, Washington, DC.

Perry, G., W. Maloney, O. Arias, P. Fajnzylber, A. Mason, and J. Saavedra-Chanduvi. 2007. *Informality: Exit and Exclusion.* Washington, DC: World Bank.

Schneider, F. 2004. "The Size of the Shadow Economies of 145 Countries All over the World: First Results over the Period 1999 to 2003." DP 1431. Bonn: IZA.

Schneider, F., A. Buehn, and C. E. Montenegro. 2010. "Shadow Economies All over the World : New Estimates for 162 Countries from 1999 to 2007." Policy Research Working Paper Series 5356. World Bank, Washington, DC.

Schneider, F., and D. Enste. 2000. "Shadow Economies: Size, Causes, and Consequences." *Journal of Economic Literature* 38 (1): 77–114.

Tanzi, V. 1980. "The Underground Economy in the United States: Estimates and Implications." Banca Nazionale des Lavoro 135:4.

———. 1983. "The Underground Economy in the United States: Annual Estimates, 1930–1980." IMF Staff Papers 30:2.

World Bank. 2009. "Turkey Country Economic Memorandum: Informality: Causes, Consequences, Policies." Report 48523-TR. Washington, DC: World Bank.

———. 2013. *Jobs for Shared Prosperity: Time for Action in the Middle East and North Africa.* Washington, DC: World Bank.

CHAPTER 2

Profile and Micro-Determinants of Informality

SUMMARY: This chapter assesses the main micro-determinants of informal employment in MENA. Analysis in the chapter quantifies the patterns of labor informality (defined as the share of all employment with no access to social security) according to age, gender, educational level, employment sector, profession, marital status, employment status, and geographic area in a selected group of non-GCC MENA countries. Countries in the MENA region are quite heterogeneous in terms of size, economic development, and demographic structure. Results indicate that the sizes of the public and agricultural sectors are perhaps the main correlates of informality in the MENA region. Countries where agricultural employment still constitutes a large share of overall employment (such as Morocco and the Republic of Yemen) display higher levels of overall informality. On the other hand, informality is lower in countries with larger public sectors and more urbanization, such as Egypt and Lebanon. The existence of a large public sector, which is still associated with generous benefits and better employment quality, creates an important segmentation between public and private employment in many MENA countries. Age, education, and firm size also represent important determinants of informality. Informality rates are generally highest among youth between ages 15 and 24, a group that accounts for 24 to 35 percent of total employment in most MENA countries, and among workers in small firms, whereas informality is generally lower among workers who have attained a university education and who work in the public administration.

Introduction

Chapter 2 aims to understand the key micro-determinants of informal employment in MENA. The behavior of informal employment in MENA differs widely between GCC countries and non-GCC countries. Informal employment in GCC countries, as proxied by the share of the labor force not contributing to social security, is rather low (at 6.4 percent) and prevalent mainly among the self-employed. In non-GCC countries, using the same proxy, the share of the labor force not contributing to social security is high (at 67.2 percent) and prevalent mainly among wage earners (Angel-Urdinola and Tanabe 2011). The main purpose of the chapter is to quantify the patterns of informal employment according to age, gender, educational level, employment sector, profession, marital status, employment status, and strata (that is, urban or rural). Based on availability of micro-data and given the general focus of the report on addressing informality from a human development standpoint, analysis in this chapter is limited to a selected group of non-GCC countries for which the relevant data are available: Egypt, Iraq, Jordan, Lebanon, Morocco, Syria, and the Republic of Yemen. This chapter consists of three main sections. The first section provides a brief macroeconomic background for these selected countries, focusing on patterns of economic and employment growth. The second section presents the profile of informality, composed of a set of statistics describing the share of workers in the informal sector according to various socioeconomic characteristics. The third section presents the main determinants (or correlates) of informality through regression analysis.

Countries in the region are quite heterogeneous in terms of size, economic development, demographic structure, and employment composition. Each of the countries included in the analysis has important economic and demographic factors that are likely to affect the level and characteristics of informal employment, such as the size of the agricultural sector compared with the secondary and tertiary sectors (higher levels of agricultural employment are associated with higher labor informality), size of the public sector (a larger public sector is associated with lower levels of labor informality), educational level of the labor force (a better educated labor force is associated with lower levels of labor informality), and age composition of the labor force (countries with younger populations are associated with higher levels of labor informality), among others (table 2.1 and figure 2.1). Important variations are found: Some of the countries are still very rural, and agricultural

Table 2.1 Economic and Demographic Factors for Selected Non-GCC Countries

	GDP per capita (2000$ constant)[a]	Agriculture, value added (% of GDP)[a]	% employment age 15–24[a]	% employment in the public sector	% employment with university education	% unemployment[a]
Egypt, Arab Rep.	1,785.83	13.22	23.1	30.0	16.8	8.7
Iraq	730.79	8.57	23.2	36.9	12.8	17.5
Jordan	2,244.83	2.58	21.5	35.6	25.8	12.7
Lebanon	5,858.76	6.94	28.7	13.5	17.2	9.0
Morocco	1,718.14	14.64	34.7	11.1	6.6[b]	9.6
Syria Arab Republic	1,329.85	16.99	32.3	26.8	7.4	8.4
Yemen, Rep.	559.97	14.34	21.9	38.6	5.4	15.0

Source: Household surveys for available years.

a. World Development Indicators (WDI) dataset, last available year 1999–2008.

b. WDI for 2006.

Figure 2.1   Employment Composition by Sector (Using Latest Available Year)

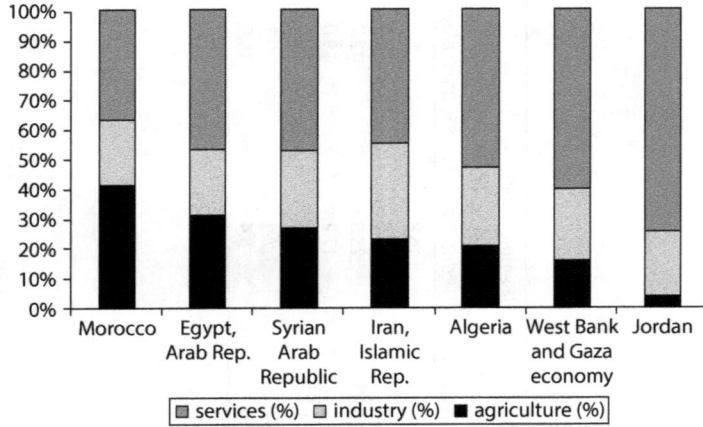

Source: World Development Indicators (all available non-Gulf Cooperation Council economies).
Note: Latest year available in the period 2003–2007.

employment constitutes almost half of overall employment (such as the Republic of Yemen and Morocco); others have better educated workers (such as Jordan, Egypt, and Lebanon); and in some countries, the public sector still accounts for a significant share of overall employment (such as Jordan, Egypt, the Republic of Yemen, Iraq, and Syria).

Macroeconomic Context

Countries in the region have displayed favorable economic growth in recent years. Some basic macroeconomic trends for the countries included in the analysis are presented to provide context to the analysis that follows. As discussed in chapter 1, the level of economic development and other macroeconomic variables, such as recent economic growth and employment composition, are likely to be important factors to understand a country's profile and determinants of informality. This is particularly relevant in MENA, given the social, economic, and cultural heterogeneity of countries in the region. Figure 2.2 illustrates the average yearly economic growth rate of GDP per capita in a selected group of non-GCC countries for the periods 2000 to 2005 and 2005 to 2009. The region's economic performance was above the world's average in both time periods. Between 2005 and 2009, annual per capita growth rates showed important variation across countries, with some displaying rapid

Figure 2.2 Yearly GDP Per Capita Growth Rate

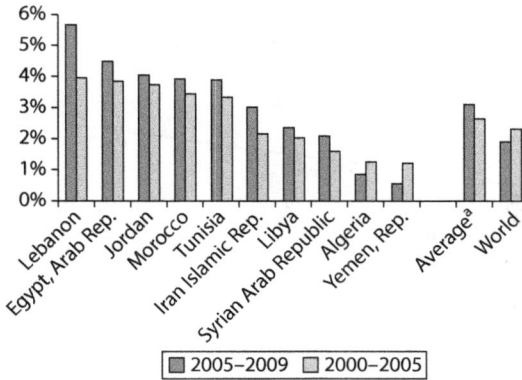

Source: World Development Indicators.
a. Unweighted average (selected countries).

growth (such as Lebanon, Egypt, Jordan, Morocco, and Tunisia), others moderate growth (such as the Islamic Republic of Iran, Libya, and Syria), and some poor growth (such as the Republic of Yemen and Algeria). Some countries performed much better between 2005 and 2009 compared with 2000 to 2005 (mainly Lebanon and the Islamic Republic of Iran), whereas in others, the opposite occurred (such as Algeria and the Republic of Yemen).

While employment growth in the region has been among the highest in the world in the past decade, the level of employment creation has been unable to keep up with population growth (see discussion in chapter 1 and figure 2.3). This demographic dynamic contributed to high unemployment rates, especially among youth, and a difficult school-to-work transition.

Joblessness in many MENA countries remains notable, especially among women. School-to-work transition patterns highlight the incidence of joblessness and the disadvantaged position of women in MENA. Figure 2.4 illustrates the patterns of school-to-work transition in selected countries. This transition is measured by the length of time between when 50 percent of the population is enrolled in school and when 50 percent is employed. It takes as little as one year in the Republic of Yemen to up to approximately 18 years in Iraq. In developed countries, a comparable process takes on average 1.4 years (Angel-Urdinola and Semlali 2010). Large differences exist in school-to-work

Figure 2.3   Growth in Employed and Working-Age Population in Non-GCC MENA Countries, 1998–2009

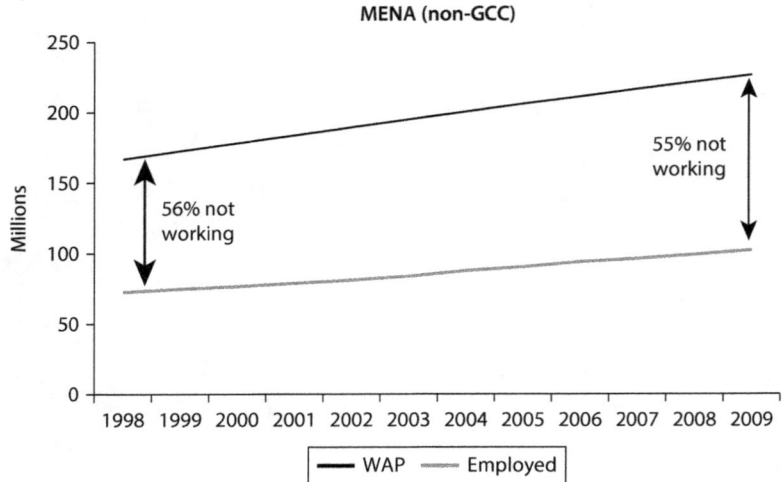

MENA (non-GCC)

Source: World Bank, based on the ILO's EAPEP (Economically Active Population, Estimates and Projections) database.
Note: GCC - Gulf Cooperation; MENA - Middle East and North Africa.

transition patterns by gender. Upon exiting the school system, the majority of women in the countries considered (except for the Republic of Yemen) enter into joblessness (that is, unemployment and/or inactivity), and only a small proportion successfully move into employment. According to the definition used, the school-to-work transition never fully occurs for women in most of the countries. This has important implications for the region's economic growth potential. First, international experience indicates that greater economic equality between women and men is associated with poverty reduction, higher GDP, and better governance (Klasen 1999). Recent studies indicate that many economies in MENA display lower participation rates than those predicted given their age and education structures. If female labor force participation in these countries rose to the level predicted by women's age and education structure, household earnings could increase substantially (World Bank 2003).

The service sector has been an important source of employment growth in recent years, with crucial implications for informality. A closer look at available data on employment growth by country

Figure 2.4 School-to-Work Transition (for Ages 15–35) in MENA

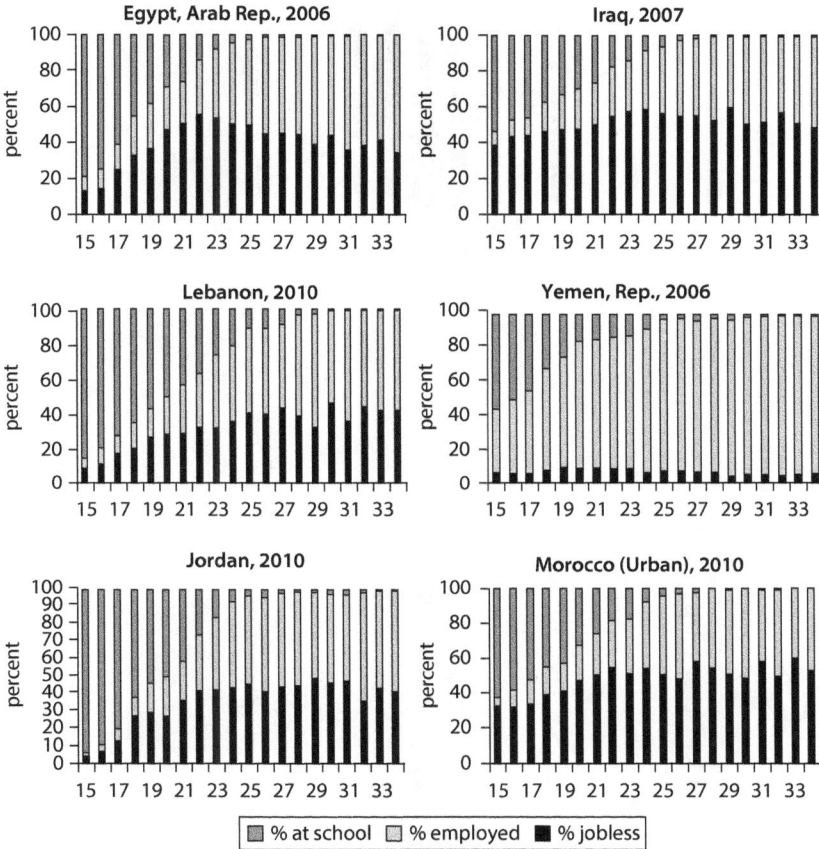

between 2000 and 2007 reveals several interesting patterns. Data indicate important variation in annual employment growth across countries in the region, from an increase of almost 8 percent per year in Algeria to a decrease of almost 3 percent per year in Syria (left-hand panel of figure 2.5). As illustrated by the right-hand panel of figure 2.5, in many countries, the service sector (mainly commerce and construction) has been an important engine of employment growth, generally followed by the industrial sector. The contribution of agriculture to total employment growth has been important in some economies such as Egypt and the West Bank and Gaza economy, but it has also

Figure 2.5   Employment Growth between 2000 and 2007 for Selected Countries

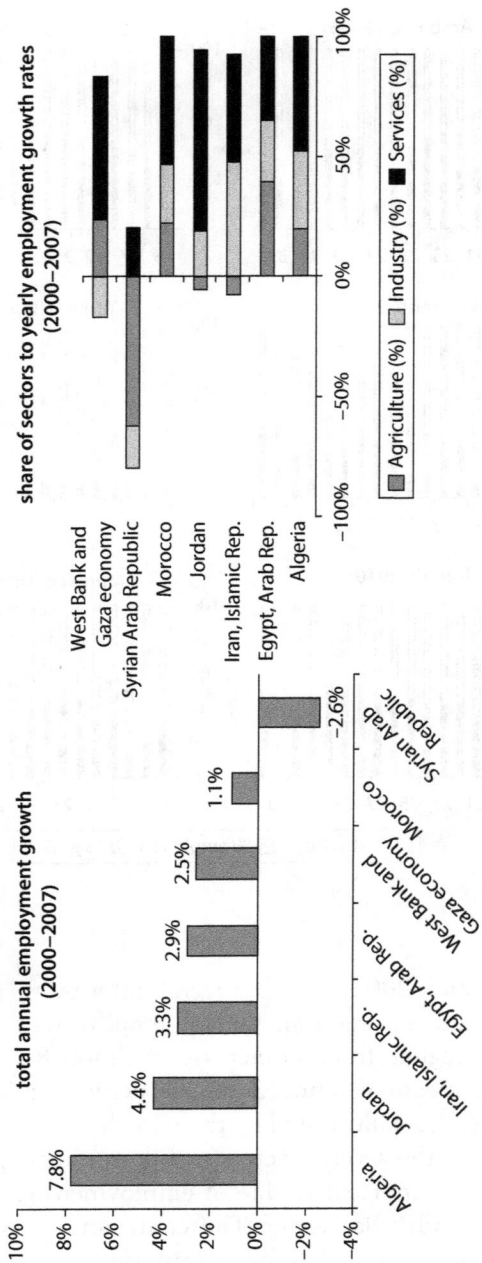

total annual employment growth
(2000–2007)

share of sectors to yearly employment growth rates
(2000–2007)

■ Agriculture (%)   ■ Industry (%)   ■ Services (%)

Source: ILO's KILM dataset.

Table 2.2   Composition of Employment Growth in the Services Sector for Selected Countries, 2000–2007
percent

	Algeria	Egypt, Arab Rep.	Iran, Islamic Rep.	Jordan
Construction	29.7	28.3	42.8	6.2
Commerce and personal services	44.2	31.0	21.5	35.0
Transport	9.5	19.4	19.2	13.9
Value added/social services	16.7	21.4	16.4	44.8

Source: World Development Indicators and ILO's KILM dataset.

contributed to negative growth in employment (that is, to employment destruction) in countries such as Syria, Jordan, and the Islamic Republic of Iran. In Syria, for instance, the negative growth in employment between 2000 and 2007 is largely explained by a rapid decrease in agricultural employment.

The expansion of the service sector (mainly construction and commerce) has gone hand in hand with an increase in informality and self-employment in the region. The expansion of employment in the service sector has been an important feature of many economies in MENA in recent years. As presented in table 2.2, the construction and commerce sectors account together for 40 to 70 percent of all employment growth in the service sectors recently. In Morocco, employment growth was 5.1 percent in transport and 3.7 percent in construction for the period 1998 to 2003 (World Bank 2009). These results are likely to have key implications for informality trends because construction and commerce are sectors often associated with high rates of informal employment. Indeed, as illustrated in figure 2.6, informality (as proxied by the Schneider Index and by the share of self-employment of total employment) has increased in recent years, at a time when employment in the construction and commerce sectors has been expanding.

Informality Profile

This section presents the profile of informality for the countries included in the analysis.[1] The profile consists of a set of statistics describing workers in the informal sector according to various characteristics, such as socioeconomic status, educational level, age, gender, strata (urban or rural), marital status, and occupation, among others. The informality profile is presented for all workers in the sample (including the public sector), and separately for private sector workers. The analysis includes urban

Figure 2.6   Annual Growth of Informality for Selected Economies

Annual growth rate 2000–2007

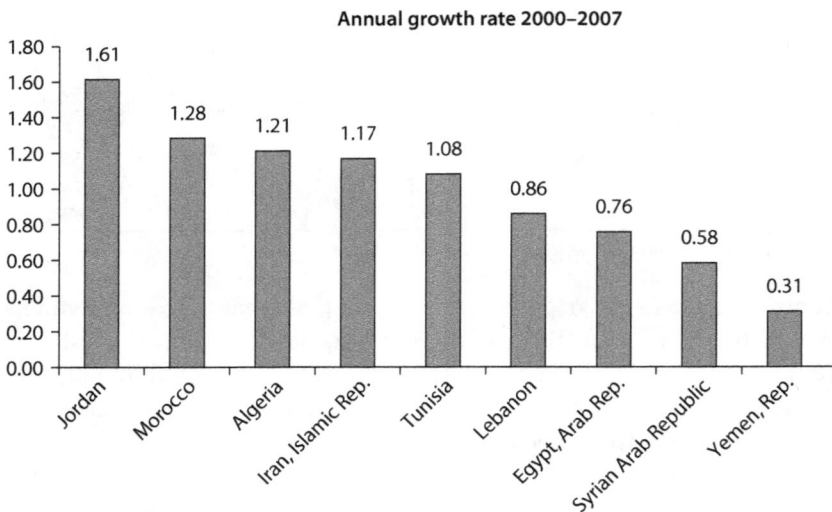

Source: World Development Indicators and ILO's KILM dataset.

Table 2.3   Informality Rates for Selected Countries

percent

	All workers	Urban workers	Rural workers
Egypt, Arab Rep., 2006	58.3	42.6	70.0
Iraq, 2007	66.9	63.5	76.1
Jordan, 2010	44.2	47.5	28.3
Lebanon, 2010	56.2	48.3	66.7
Morocco, 2010	—	72.7	—
Syrian Arab Republic, 2011	71.0	65.9	76.3
Yemen, Rep., 2006	91.4	84.7	94.0

Source: Angel-Urdinola and Tanabe 2011.
Note: — = Data not reliable.

and rural workers. Many informality studies (Perry and others 2007) exclude rural employment from the analysis because in other regions it is predominantly informal. In MENA countries, this is not necessarily the case because of an important public sector presence (and, thus, formal employment) in rural areas. Although rural employment remains more informal than urban employment (except in Jordan), informality rates in both rural and urban areas are more comparable than in other regions of the world (table 2.3).

Informality is a more persistent phenomenon among the poor. As expected, informality generally decreases as wealth increases. Nevertheless,

Box 2.1 Informality in Tunisia 2005–2009

Because of data availability, informality in Tunisia is proxied as the share of overall employment working in the private sector without a contract. Also, analysis could be conducted for urban areas only. Therefore, results for Tunisia cannot be compared with other countries in the region. As suggested by the table below, urban informality increased by 6 percent (from 50.5 percent to 53.5 percent) between 2005 and 2009. The increase was more pronounced among men (8 percent increase) and among workers with university education (34 percent increase). Not surprisingly, men account for the majority of all informal workers (73.5 percent in 2009) and informality rates are higher among men than women, because many women generally self-select themselves into public sector/formal jobs (Angel-Urdinola and Tanabe 2011). Informality rates are increasing rapidly among young adults (25–34) and adults (35–54).

Informality Rates in Urban Areas, 2005–2009

percent

	% total informal workers, 2009	Informality rate, 2005	Informality rate, 2009	% change
Total urban	100.0	50.5	53.5	6.1
Gender				
Male	73.5	53.7	57.9	7.8
Female	26.5	41.2	41.4	0.3
Age group				
15–24	10.8	67.9	70.9	4.4
25–34	32.2	50.4	54.7	8.5
35–54	50.5	45.3	49.3	8.8
55–64	6.5	53.1	52.0	−2.1
Education				
Primary or below	38.5	69.4	72.6	4.6
Basic	39.0	44.9	50.5	12.5
Secondary	0.8			
vocational		53.1	46.0	−13.3
Tertiary	21.8	15.4	20.6	33.5

Source: Angel Urdinola, Brodmann, and Hilger 2011.
Note: Results based on 2005–2009 averages.

in some MENA countries, informality remains significant even among the wealthier segments of the population. In the Republic of Yemen for instance, more than two-thirds of all workers who belong to the richest households work in the informal sector. Yet, in other countries such as Lebanon, informality rates are significantly lower for the wealthiest segments of the population (figure 2.7).

In most countries in the region, the vast majority of formal workers are employed in the public sector. Labor markets in many MENA countries are still influenced by the legacy of a large public sector, which accounts for about 29 percent of overall employment in the Arab world (Elbadawi and Loayza 2008), and civil service in many MENA countries is larger than in other countries with similar levels of income and economic structure. Historically, in countries such as Egypt, the growth in the civil service was the result of a social contract in the 1970s and 1980s whereby the government effectively offered employment guarantees to university graduates and to graduates of vocational secondary schools and training institutes. Despite the fact that employment growth in the public sector has slowed dramatically in recent years, public sector employment (government and public enterprises) in most countries still accounts for more than 60 percent of all formal sector employment in MENA

Figure 2.7   Informality Rates by Quintile of Per Capita Consumption for Selected Countries

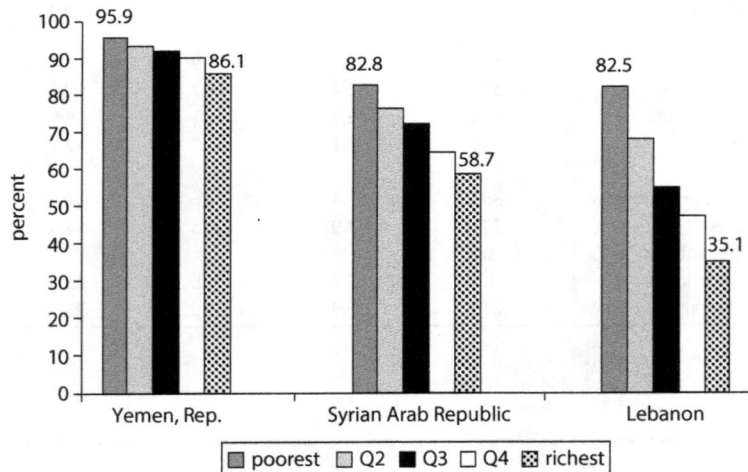

Source: Angel-Urdinola and Tanabe 2011.
Note: Q = quintile.

(figure 2.8). In some countries, such as the Republic of Yemen and Iraq, formal employment is almost entirely associated with public employment. The public sector remains the main engine of formal employment: In Egypt about 45 percent of all new formal jobs (about 260,000) created in the economy between 1998 and 2006 were in the public sector (Angel-Urdinola and Semlali 2010).

Given the weight of the public sector in overall formal employment (figure 2.9), changes in the size of the public sector are likely to affect overall informality trends, especially given that formal private employment growth remains limited. In particular, the creation of formal private sector jobs has not been sufficient to offset the downsizing of the public sector in many countries (Radwan 2007). Radwan argues that formal businesses in many MENA countries face important challenges that restrain their capacity to grow, such as dealing with complex bureaucratic procedures; access to poor infrastructure, credit, and technologies; and high labor taxes. A recent assessment of the private sector in Morocco reveals that excessive regulation of the labor market has pushed much of the economic activity into the informal sector (World Bank 1999). At the same time, the private sector in many MENA countries is primarily composed of small and medium enterprises (SMEs), which represent about 95 percent of all registered enterprises. The great majority of SMEs in MENA have fewer than five workers and are characterized by high levels

Figure 2.8   Size of Private Salaried Formal Sector versus Other Sectors

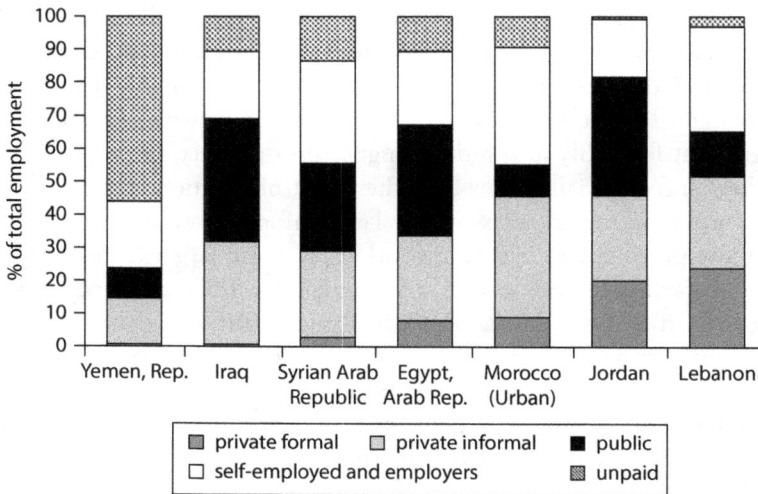

Figure 2.9   Distribution of Formal Employment for Selected MENA Countries

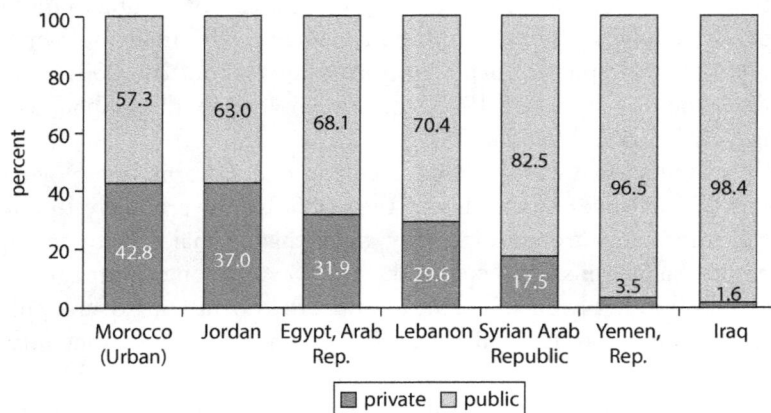

of informality; low participation of women; concentration in low-growth sectors; low use of modern technologies; and a low level of product quality, competitiveness, diversification, and innovation. Overall, a large public sector and restrictive regulations contribute to squeeze the formal private sector and limit its dynamics (see chapter 5, part 1).

The private formal sector in the region is still nascent. Employment in the formal private sector is almost nonexistent in the Republic of Yemen and Iraq, and below 10 percent of total employment in Syria, Egypt, and Morocco, although it is somewhat larger in Jordan and Lebanon. As seen earlier, this reflects a number of factors, including the country's production structure, the large size of the public sector, which effectively competes for resources and talent with the private formal sector, and the design of pension systems (which in the Republic of Yemen and Iraq do not extend in reality to the private sector). To the extent that formality also reflects higher productivity, more productive workers and especially firms bear the brunt of taxation. This small private formal sector coexists with a large informal sector that includes both low-productivity firms and workers, but also larger firms that have secured favorable application of regulations through rent seeking. Especially if compared with the latter, one might argue that the small formal private sector bears disproportionately the taxation burden.

An important transition is made from informal employment into public sector employment as young people reach prime age adulthood. Figure 2.10 illustrates employment patterns by age for urban workers in a selected group of countries. Informality rates are very high among youth

Figure 2.10   Employment Status by Age for Selected Countries, Urban Areas Only

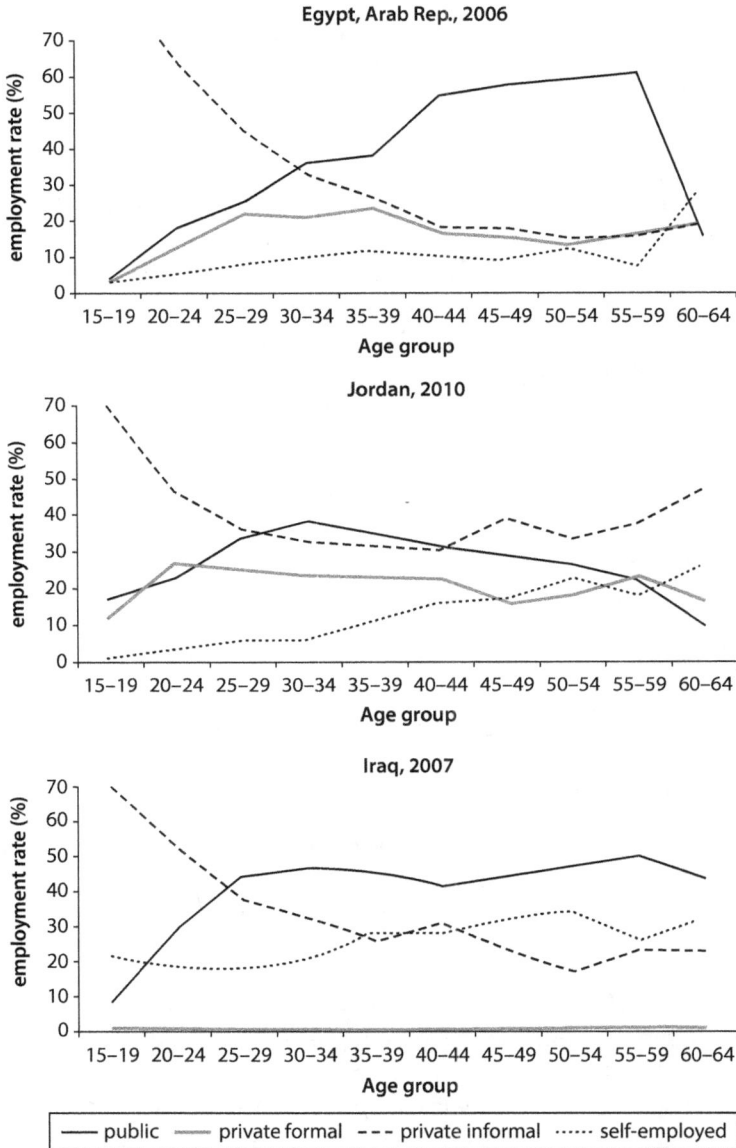

Egypt, Arab Rep., 2006

Jordan, 2010

Iraq, 2007

—— public   —— private formal   - - - private informal   ⋯⋯ self-employed

figure continues next page

Figure 2.10   Employment Status by Age for Selected Countries, Urban Areas Only
(continued)

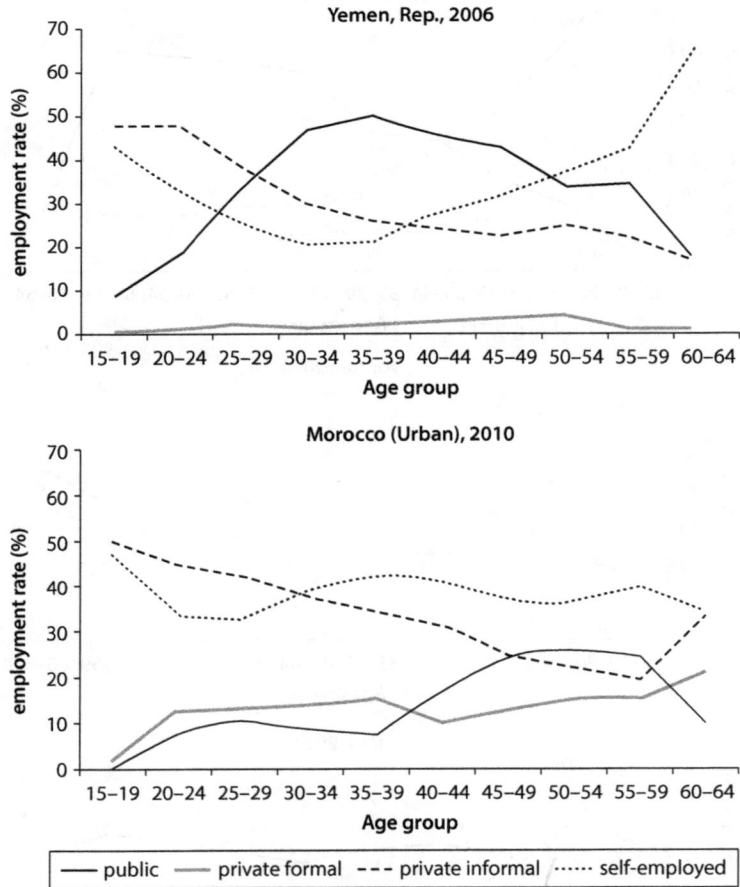

Yemen, Rep., 2006

Morocco (Urban), 2010

Legend: —— public   —— private formal   - - - private informal   ······ self-employed

Source: Angel-Urdinola and Tanabe 2011.

between ages 15 and 24. After age 24, informality decreases rapidly until individuals reach prime working age (40 to 45 years). After age 40, informality rates are lower (20 to 30 percent). This rapid decrease in informality rates goes hand in hand with a rapid increase in public employment, which suggests that informal workers enter into public sector jobs as they move from youth into adulthood. Not surprisingly, many individuals in the region queue in the informal sector until they find a job in the public administration. Still, one has to be cautious in interpreting these results as they are likely to reflect vintage effects since, especially in countries like Egypt, more public sector jobs were available to earlier cohorts of workers. These trends are very different from those observed in Latin America. In Mexico, for instance, although informality rates also decrease by age, the observed transition occurs not between informality and public employment, but between informality and self-employment (Perry and others 2007).

Self-employment is low among youth and young adults but increases rapidly after individuals reach age 50, suggesting a transition from public employment into self-employment as individuals retire from the public administration. As illustrated by figure 2.10, the share of individuals who work in the formal private sector remains almost nonexistent in countries such as the Republic of Yemen and Iraq (at all age groups), which suggests a very limited formal private sector. Even in more dynamic and diversified economies, such as Egypt, Jordan, and Morocco, formal private sector employment accounts for a maximum of 25 percent of overall employment at all age groups. Finally, interesting patterns are seen in the trend in self-employment by age. Although overall rates of self-employment remain low, especially among youth, the share of self-employment to overall employment increases steadily as people reach retirement age, suggesting that workers (especially those who decide to retire early) transition from public employment into self-employment.

Informality rates are generally higher for wage earners outside the public administration and the self-employed. Results indicate that informality rates among wage earners (who account for 50 percent of overall employment for most countries in the analysis) range between 40 and 60 percent. Informality rates among the self-employed (who account for 15 to 36 percent of all employment for most countries in the analysis) are even higher, from 80 percent in Lebanon to almost 100 percent in Iraq and the Republic of Yemen (table 2.4). The promotion of self-employment/micro-entrepreneurship continues to be a core strategy to boost employment, and so creation of new, flexible, and innovative mechanisms to ensure pension and social security coverage for the self-employed should be developed and implemented (see chapter 5).

Self-employed individuals have somewhat different profiles than informal wage earners. As mentioned earlier, self-employed workers in MENA are generally informal because they rarely participate in social security contributing schemes. Nevertheless, this group of workers displays somewhat different characteristics as compared with other informal workers (mainly wage earners). Table 2.5 presents a set of descriptive

Table 2.4 Informality Rates by Employment Status

Employment status	Iraq, 2007		Jordan, 2010		Egypt, Arab Rep., 2006		Lebanon, 2010		Morocco (Urban), 2010		Syrian Arab Republic, 2011		Yemen, Rep., 2006	
	Pop. share	% Inf.	Pop. share	% Inf.	Pop. share	% Inf.	Pop. share	% Inf.	Pop. share	% Inf.	Pop. share	% Inf.	Pop. share	% Inf.
Wage worker	68.9	51.7	71.7	56.5	64.3	42.6	65.4	43.1	51.4	67.1	55.6	52.2	23.9	63.7
Employer	—	—	11.2	94.6	13.2	78.4	4.8	84.0	3.9	98.4	6.7	89.4	—	—
Self-employed	20.5	100.0	15.4	98.5	9.9	82.1	27.2	80.1	29.6	98.1	24.0	93.4	20.3	100.0

Source: Angel-Urdinola and Tanabe 2011.

Note: Inf. = informality; Pop. = population; — = not available.

Table 2.5   Self-Employed versus Informal Wage Earners (Basic Characteristics)

	Egypt, Arab Rep.		Lebanon	
	Informal wage earners	Self-employed	Informal wage earners	Self-employed
Average age (in years)	31.8	38.3	31.9	41.8
Average years of education				
(in years)	6.9	6.3	11.4	9.5
Average wage rate (in LC)	2.4	—	4.55	6.01
Time at job	—	—	5.12	14.1
Gender				
Men	78.6	71.6	66.1	85.7
Women	21.4	28.4	33.9	14.3
Age group				
15–24	32.5	8.8	34.2	7.2
25–34	32.7	31.5	33.9	26.5
35–54	27.5	49.5	25.9	48.7
55–64	7.3	10.1	5.9	17.6
Education				
Primary or below	56.4	61.3	19.0	33.1
Preparatory/secondary				
general	7.3	6.6	22.4	30.0
Secondary vocational	30.2	25.5	27.0	23.3
Tertiary education	6.1	6.7	31.6	13.4

Note: LC = local currency; — = not available.

statistics for Lebanon and Egypt highlighting important differences in the characteristics of workers in these two groups:

- *Self-employed are generally older and less educated.* Results in table 2.5 indicate that in Egypt and Lebanon, self-employed workers are older than informal wage earners (6 years older in Egypt and about 10 years older in Lebanon, on average). In both countries, the majority of self-employed (almost half) is between 35 and 54 years of age. The share of youth (15–24) who work as self-employed is very low (9 percent in Egypt and 7 percent in Lebanon). Self-employed workers are less educated than informal wage earners. On average, self-employed workers in Egypt (Lebanon) have attained one (two) years of education fewer than informal wage earners. In Lebanon, only 13.4 percent of all self-employed have attained tertiary education compared with 31.6 percent among wage earners.

- *In Lebanon, self-employed workers have more stable jobs and earn relatively higher wages.* Despite being less educated, self-employed workers in Lebanon (which account for about 33 percent of all employment) earn on average wages that are 30 percent higher than those among informal wage earners, which could reflect experience. Also, self-employed workers claim to have worked in the same job for 14 years (on average) as compared with 5 years among informal wage earners.

Age, gender, and education also constitute important correlates of informality. Figure 2.11 presents a basic set of correlations between informal employment and individual characteristics such as age, gender, and years of education. Not surprisingly, results indicate that age and education are negatively correlated with informality (that is, higher age and more education are associated with less informality). The size of the correlation between years of education and informality is large for all countries (from −0.35 in Lebanon to −0.47 in Syria), suggesting an important negative relationship between education and informal employment. Nevertheless, the magnitude of the correlation between age and informality varies across countries and strata. For instance, the negative association between age and informality seems to be larger in Egypt, Syria, and Iraq than in Morocco, the Republic of Yemen, and Lebanon, and generally stronger in urban than in rural areas (figure 2.11 shows results only for urban areas).

Being a woman is associated with higher informality rates in some countries and with lower informality rates in others, mainly depending on the overall structure the country's employment (figure 2.11). In countries where agricultural employment constitutes an important share of overall employment, such as Egypt and the Republic of Yemen, being a woman is associated with higher levels of informality because women are often employed in unpaid/subsistence agriculture. In countries where public employment represents a significant share of overall employment, such as Iraq, and Syria, being a woman is associated with lower levels of informality. Given low overall levels of female labor force participation in these countries, women who participate in the labor force (generally those with higher levels of education) self-select into public sector jobs. Hence, as illustrated in figure 2.12, informality rates are higher among men than among women in Iraq, Syria, Lebanon, Morocco, and Jordan, and higher among women than among men in the Republic of Yemen. However, once the sample is restricted to private sector workers, informality rates between men and women are equally high in most countries.

Figure 2.11   Basic Correlations by Strata (Informality and Individual's Characteristics)

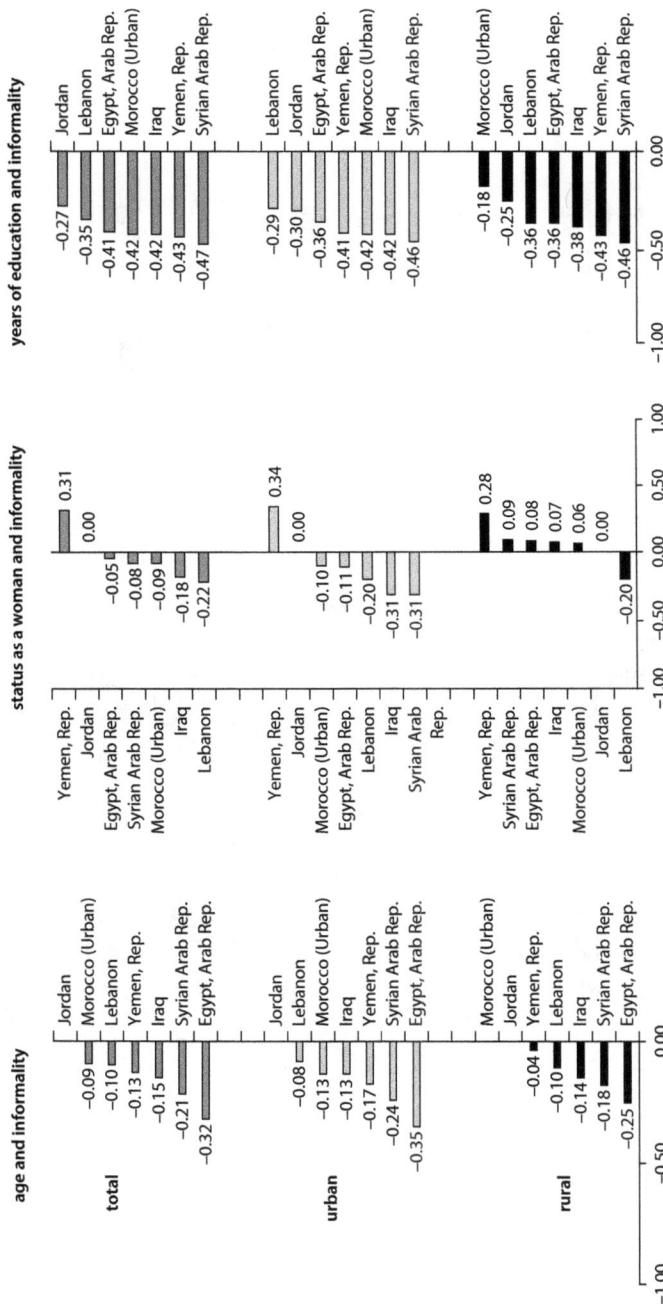

Source: Angel-Urdinola and Tanabe 2011.

Figure 2.12   Informality Rates by Gender

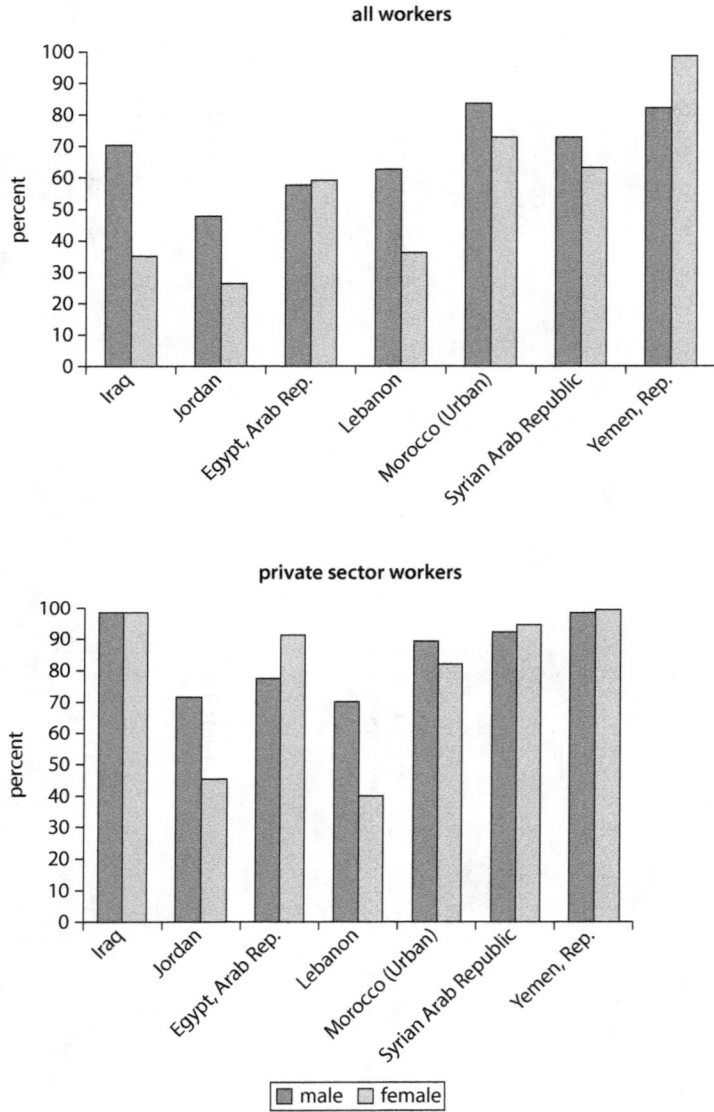

Over workers' life cycles, an increase in employment in the public sector mirrors the decline in informal salaried employment. A closer look at informality rates by age group and educational attainment indicates important differences for workers in the private sector. Informality rates are generally highest among young people between the ages of 15 and 24, a group that in most countries in the sample accounts for 24 to 35 percent of total employment. Above age 25, informality rates decrease rapidly up to age 54 in most countries. Informality rates increase again for workers between ages 55 and 64 (which make up 5 to 8 percent of total employment in most countries) as some workers find employment in the informal sector after they retire from their formal jobs. Informality rates among workers who attained primary and/or basic education (who account for at least 50 percent of overall employment in most countries in the region) are generally much higher than among workers who attained secondary vocational and/or tertiary education. Differences in informality rates by age and education are less pronounced for workers in the private sector. Indeed, in some countries such as the Republic of Yemen and Morocco, differences in informality rates by age and educational attainment for workers in the private sector are negligible (figures 2.13 and 2.14).

Informality is generally higher in the primary sector, with important implications for countries with a large agriculture sector. Results suggest that the great majority of workers in agriculture and mining activities (which account for as little as 5 percent of employment in Iraq and as much as 30 percent in Morocco) work in the informal sector (table 2.6). In the tertiary sectors (that is, services), informality rates vary among countries, ranging from 46 percent in Lebanon to 93 percent in the Republic of Yemen. Among workers employed in the public administration/social services (which in countries such as Egypt, Iraq, and Syria account for as much as one-third of total employment), informality rates are below 20 percent. This is probably explained by the existence (in some countries) of fixed-term contracts in the public sector.

Determinants of Informality

Although a profile of informality is informative, the main drawback is that it cannot be used to disentangle its determinants. For example, the fact that a group of workers (such as agricultural workers) displays high rates of informality may be due in large part to other characteristics of the group (such as the educational level of the group's members).

Striving for Better Jobs • http://dx.doi.org/10.1596/978-0-8213-9535-6

Figure 2.13   Informality Rates by Age Groups

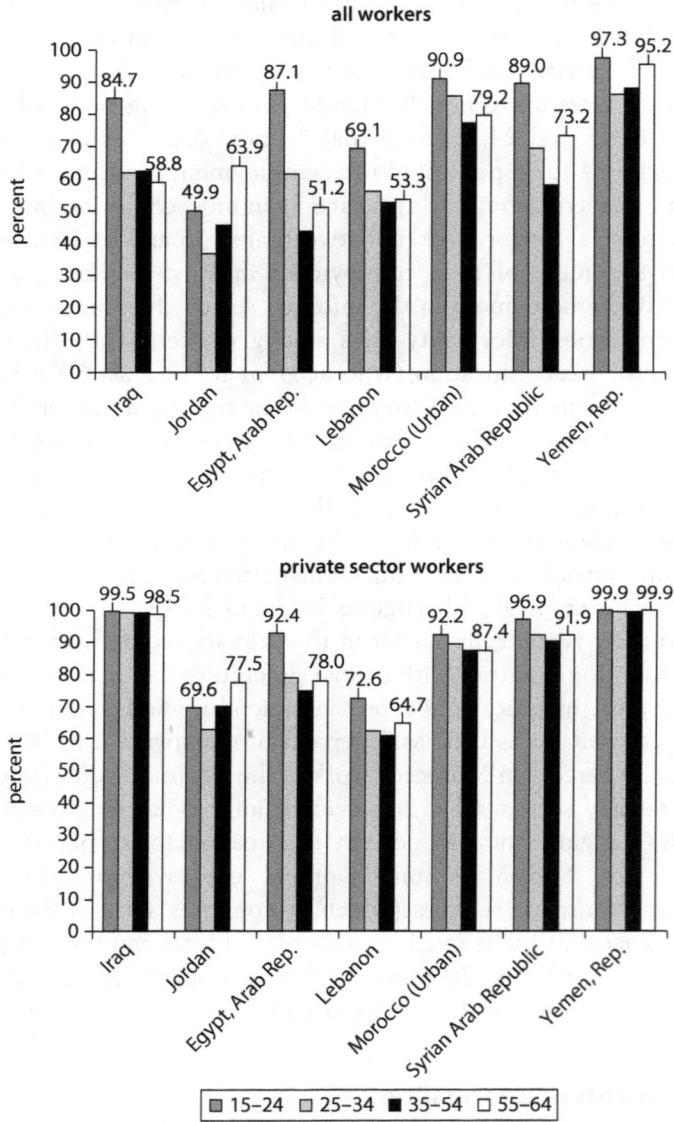

all workers

private sector workers

☐ 15–24   ☐ 25–34   ■ 35–54   ☐ 55–64

Source: Processed from Angel-Urdinola and Tanabe 2011.

Figure 2.14   Informality Rates by Highest Educational Level Completed

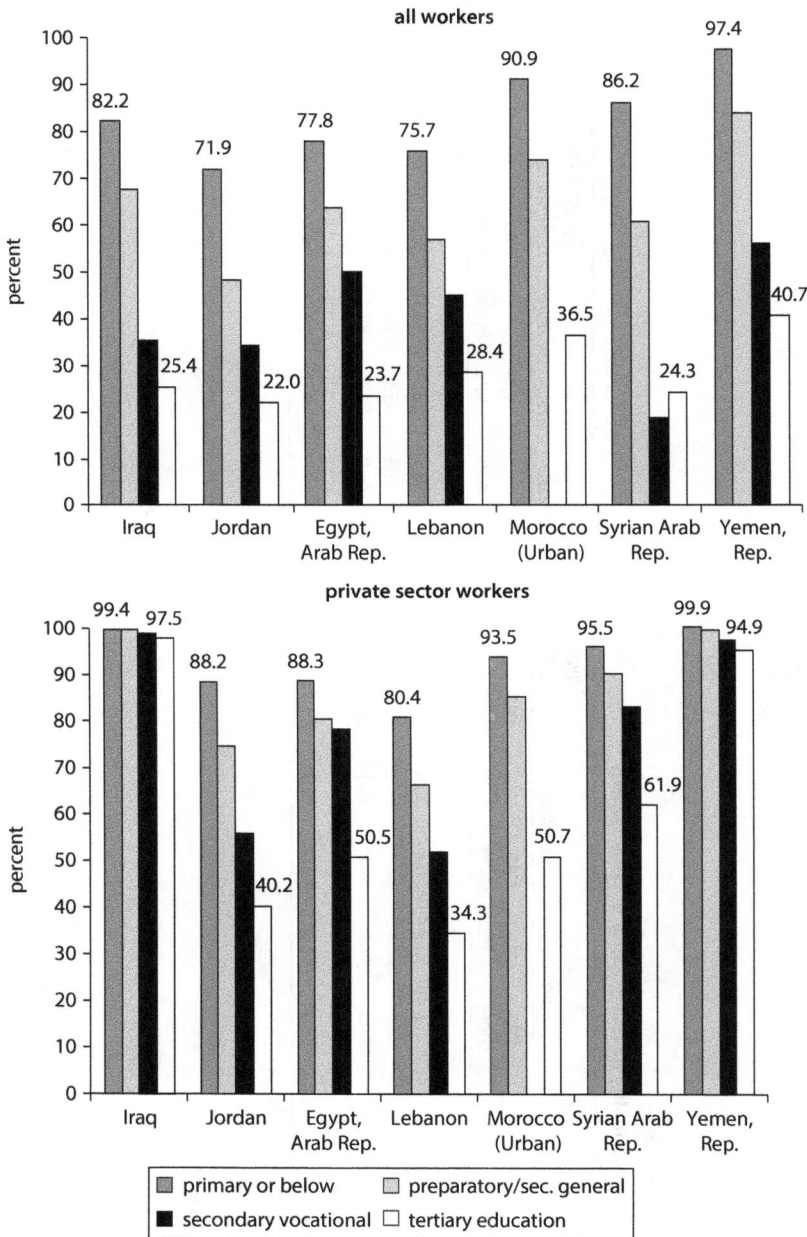

all workers

private sector workers

- ■ primary or below   ▫ preparatory/sec. general
- ■ secondary vocational   □ tertiary education

Source: Angel-Urdinola and Tanabe 2011.

Table 2.6 Informality Rates by Sector of Employment

Sector[a]	Iraq		Jordan		Egypt, Arab Rep.		Lebanon		Morocco (Urban)		Syrian Arab Republic		Yemen, Rep.	
	Pop. share	% Inf.	Pop. share	% Inf.	Pop. share	% Inf.	Pop. share	% Inf.	Pop. share	% Inf.	Pop. share	% Inf.	Pop. share	% Inf.
Industry														
Primary sector	4.6	52.2	6.4	92.6	25.5	94.1	6.6	94.4	28.4	94.1	31.6	92.4	18.4	95.6
Secondary sector	30.7	78.7	32.7	63.1	21.3	65.8	24.5	75.3	12.6	78.9	6.1	75.5	3.4	86.0
Tertiary sector	27.5	71.8	49.0	75.1	28.0	62.7	68.9	46.0	54.5	82.2	37.7	87.2	40.0	93.3
Public administration/ social services	37.2	12.2	12.0	30.7	25.3	11.0	—	—	4.5	18.5	24.6	17.6	38.2	11.7

Source: Angel-Urdinola and Tanabe 2011.

Note: Inf. = informality; Pop. = population; — = not available.

a. Primary sector (agriculture); secondary sector (manufacturing and construction); tertiary sector (wholesale, transport, services), public administration, and social services (including education and health).

To provide more insights about the determinants or correlates of informality, this section assesses informality through regression analysis using a simple probit regression model. The dependent variable of the regression model is a binary variable that takes a value of one if the worker is employed in the informal sector (that is, if the worker does not contribute to social security) and zero otherwise. Separate regressions are provided for the full sample and for workers in the nonagricultural sector.[2] The main independent variables used include (1) strata (an urban dummy), (2) demographic characteristics of the worker (a male dummy, a married dummy, and the worker's age group), (3) the highest educational level attained by the worker, (4) employment status and sector of the worker, and (5) ownership of the firm where the worker is employed (using a dummy for publicly owned firms). As these are cross-sectional regressions, results should not be interpreted causally.

The main results are summarized as follows:

- *Strata*: In many countries, especially in Latin America (Perry and others 2007), rural employment is mainly associated with agricultural activities and mainly informal. In MENA countries, this is not necessarily the case, because of an important public sector presence (and, thus, of formal employment) in rural areas. Controlling for other factors, urban workers are only 3 to 12 percent less likely to be employed informally than otherwise similar workers in rural areas in Egypt and Lebanon. Although rural employment remains more informal than urban employment, informality rates in both rural and urban areas are comparable. Indeed, in some countries such as Iraq, Morocco, and the Republic of Yemen, the difference in the probability of workers' formality between urban and rural areas is small and/or not statistically significant (table 2.7).

- *Gender*: The effect of being male on the probability of working in a formal job varies across countries (figure 2.15 and table 2.7). In Egypt and Morocco, controlling for other factors, being a male worker is associated with a 4 to 12 percent lower probability of being employed informally, as is generally the case in many developing countries (see Perry and others 2007 for estimates from Latin America). On the other hand, in Iraq, Lebanon, Jordan, and Syria, being male is actually associated with a 6 to 17 percent higher probability of working in the informal sector. This result is probably due to female workers (generally educated ones) participating in the labor force who tend to queue for

Table 2.7 Marginal Increase in the Probability of Being "Informal" according to the Characteristics of the Worker (Nonagricultural Employment Only)

Dependent variable: informal employment	Egypt, Arab Rep. All	Egypt, Arab Rep. Priv.	Iraq All	Iraq Priv.	Yemen, Rep. All	Yemen, Rep. Priv.	Lebanon All	Lebanon Priv.	Syrian Arab Republic All	Syrian Arab Republic Priv.	Morocco (Urban) All	Morocco (Urban) Priv.	Jordan All	Jordan Priv.
Urban dummy	−9.5	−8.0	N.S.	N.S.	N.S.	−1.8	−13.5	−12.1	4.1	1.8	−2.3	−1.5	N.S.	N.S.
Male dummy	−12.0	−9.7	17.1	5.5	N.S.	N.S.	13.3	16.0	11.9	3.2	−3.7	−3.4	3.8	13.9
Married	−13.9	−11.3	N.S.	N.S.	−8.0	N.S.	−11.5	−10.1	−5.9	−0.9	−1.2	−1.1	N.S.	N.S.
Age group														
25–34	−12.9	−10.3	−7.6	N.S.	−16.1	−1.7	−5.7	−6.2	−26.9	−4.8	−2.6	−1.9	−4.7	N.S.
35–54	−29.2	−23.3	−12.7	−1.5	−26.2	−4.7	−12.4	−12.5	−33.8	−7.4	−3.3	−2.3	N.S.	N.S.
55–64	−30.3	−35.9	−24.3	N.S.	−20.2	N.S.	−15.3	−15.4	−36.4	−9.6	−3.2	−2.1	N.S.	15.5
Education														
Middle school	−11.0	−10.4	−8.8	N.S.	−17.5	−2.5	−14.6	−12.2	−12.1	−4.5	N.S.	N.S.	−10.0	−16.7
High school	−17.1	−15.0	−22.7	−2.1	−26.7	N.S.	−25.7	−25.4	−27.4	−7.9	−14.4	−11.5	−15.4	−36.9
Tertiary	−25.2	−33.7	−25.3	N.S.	−19.9	−6.6	−33.2	−37.2	−31.8	−17.7	−21.6	−20.6	−17.9	−46.6
Sector														
Tertiary sector[a]	−4.6	−3.8	N.S.	N.S.	25.1	3.7	−13.1	−10.7	23.9	11.8	4.7	4.0	12.4	18.2
Public administration and social services versus[b]	−11.1	−11.1	−14.2	−7.7	N.S.	N.S.	—	—	—	—	−5.8	−6.4	−9.7	−11.7
Ownership														
Public firm	−59.4	—	−82.4	—	−80.7	—	−52.8	—	−74.6	—	−33.3	—	−48.8	—
Observations	8,752	5,244	12,362	4,361	8,500	3,939	13,373	11,254	32,461	20,471	6,500	6,252	4,441	2,237

Source: Angel-Urdinola and Tanabe 2011.

Note: All = all workers; Priv. = private sector workers. All coefficients are multiplied by 100. Coefficients that are not statistically significant are denoted by N.S. Underlined coefficients are significant at a 10 percent confidence level. Other coefficients are significant at a 5 percent confidence level. Omitted categories: Age group: 15–25; Education: primary education or below. Employment sector: secondary sector (manufacturing and construction); Ownership: private firms. — = not available.

a. Tertiary sector (wholesale, transport, services).

b. Public administration and social services (including education and health).

Figure 2.15 Marginal Increase in the Probability of Being "Informal" according to Gender and Marital Status
percent

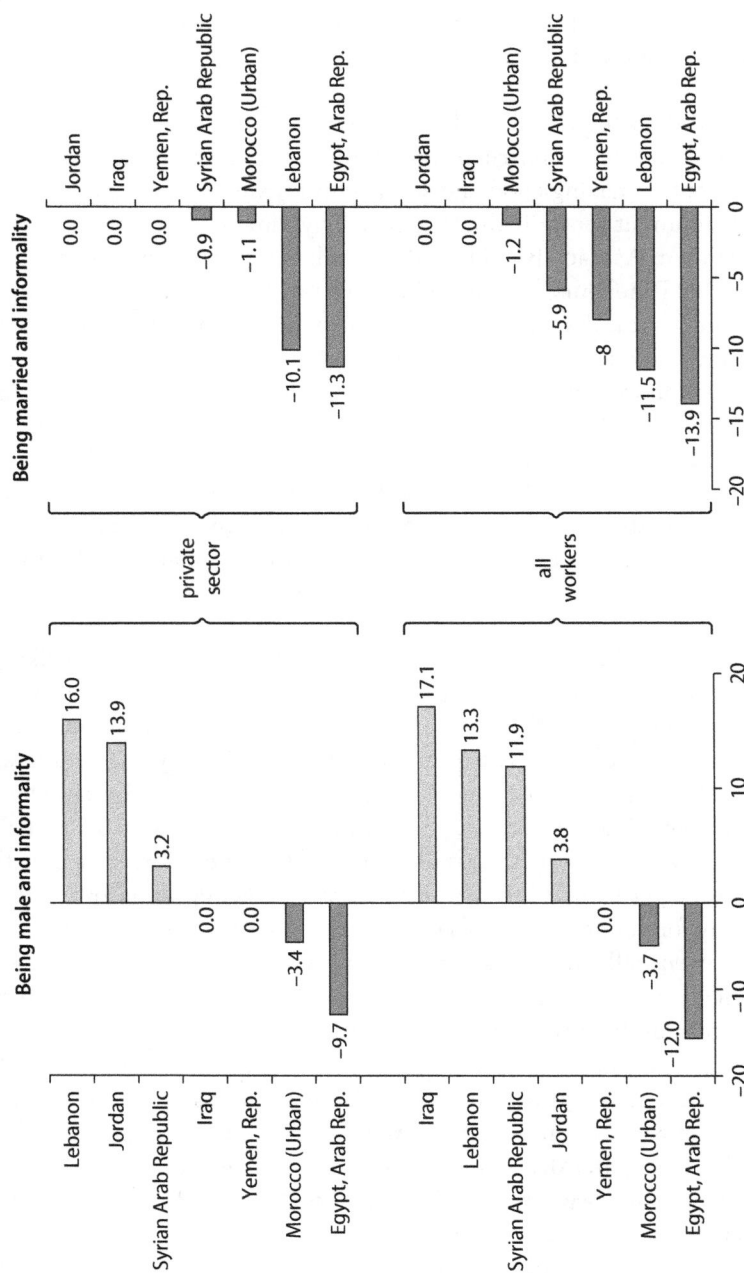

Being male and informality

Being married and informality

private sector

all workers

Source: Angel-Urdinola and Tanabe 2011 (see table 2.7 for more details).

105

formal jobs in the public sector (Angel-Urdinola and Semlali 2010). In the Republic of Yemen, gender does not seem to be an important determinant of informality.

- *Marital status:* In the MENA region, important associations are found between marriage and labor outcomes. Recent literature shows that having good and stable employment is an important social requirement for individuals, especially young men, to get married. For instance, Assaad, Binzel, and Gadallah (2010) use Egypt's Labor Market Panel Survey of 2006 (ELMPS 06) to study the role of employment (that is, having a good, fair, or poor job) on the timing of marriage. The authors find that having a better job leads men to a faster transition into marriage. These results are consistent with the findings herein, as being married, controlling for other factors, is associated with a 10 to 14 percent lower probability of working in the informal sector in Egypt and Lebanon, and a 2 to 8 percent lower probability in Morocco, the Republic of Yemen, and Syria (figure 2.15 and table 2.7). In Jordan, marital status is not significantly associated with informal employment.

- *Age:* Controlling for other factors, younger workers are more likely to work in the informal sector (table 2.7). Results from Egypt, the Republic of Yemen, and Syria indicate that adults aged 35 and older are 13 to 34 percent less likely to work in the informal sector than youth aged 15 to 24. In Iraq, Lebanon, Jordan, and Morocco, the association between age and informality is less strong, because adults 25 and older are only 2 to 8 percent less likely to work in the informal sector than youth aged 15 to 24. It is worth noting that acquiring informal jobs is a way for young individuals to enter the labor market, gain experience, and eventually move into formal employment, as informality decreases quickly with age. The effect of age on informality is generally lower in magnitude for private sector workers. This is expected since the private sector in MENA remains largely informal. To better illustrate this phenomenon, figure 2.16 shows informality rates by age for men and women for Syria and Egypt. Results in the left-hand panel show that informality rates decrease rapidly as age increases up to ages 40 to 45 and increases again thereafter as individuals retire. Results also indicate that early retirement is quite common, especially among women. In the private sector (shown in the right-hand panel of figure 2.16), informality rates by age are rather flat and high, especially for women,

Figure 2.16 Informality Rates by Age Group (Syrian Arab Republic and the Arab Republic of Egypt)

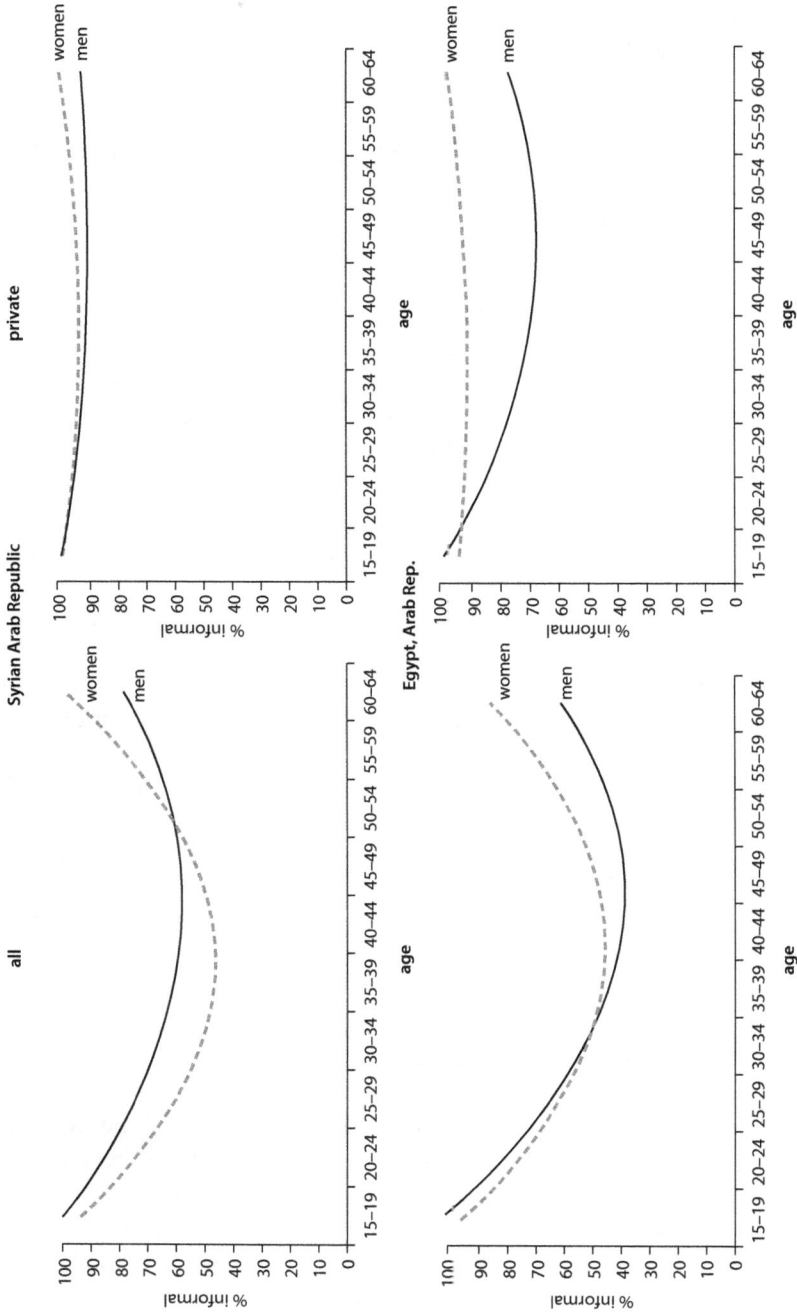

Source: Angel-Urdinola and Tanabe 2011.

suggesting that the negative slope between age and informality is driven by workers entering public sector employment as they reach prime working age.

- *Highest educational level attained:* Controlling for other factors, more education is associated with a lower probability of being employed in the informal sector. The negative relationship between attaining higher education and having a lower probability of being employed informally is much lower for private sector workers (confirming the results presented in the profile of informality). Controlling for other characteristics, attaining middle school (high school) is associated with a 5 to 18 (12 to 37) percent lower probability of working in the informal sector compared with otherwise similar workers who attained at most primary school. Attaining tertiary education is associated with up to a 47 percent lower probability of being employed informally compared with otherwise similar workers who attained at most primary school. In some countries (for example, Iraq, Syria, and the Republic of Yemen), having completed high school decreases the probability of workers being employed informally as much as (or even more than) having attained tertiary education. Generally, one would expect the opposite result (as in Egypt, Jordan, and Lebanon), namely, a lower probability of being employed informally for workers with tertiary education. Finally, to control for heterogeneity in skills beyond educational attainment, quintile dummies (omitting the lowest quintile) representing the results of a cognitive nonverbal test (measuring workers' logical and analytical skills) in Lebanon and Syria are included. Interestingly, this factor was not a significant determinant of informality (results are available upon request).[3]

- *Sector of employment*: Controlling for other factors, the association between informality and sector of employment varies across countries. In countries where the tertiary sector is more developed toward high value-added services such as financial services, transport, tourism, and communications (such as in Egypt and Lebanon), workers in the tertiary sector are associated with a 4 to 13 percent lower probability of working informally compared with workers in the secondary sector (manufacturing and construction). On the other hand, in countries where the tertiary sector is mainly geared toward low value-added personal services and wholesale or retail (such as in the Republic of Yemen and Syria) workers in the tertiary sector are associated with a 4 to 25 percent higher probability of working infor- mally compared with workers in the secondary sector. Workers in public administration and social services are associated with 6 to 14 percent lower informality rates than otherwise similar workers in the secondary sector.

- *Public sector employment*: Controlling for other factors, this variable is perhaps the most important determinant of informality. In all countries where information about firm ownership is available, workers in the public sector are associated with a 30 to 85 percent higher probability of working formally compared with otherwise similar workers in the private sectors. Indeed, as illustrated in figure 2.9, the public sector hosts a significant share of all formal employment. As such, changes in the size of the public sector relative to the private sector will likely be important determinants of informality dynamics (box 2.2).

- *Firm size:* Data on firm size were only available for a few countries in the region (Egypt, Iraq, Jordan, and Morocco). For these countries, firm size dummy variables are included in the regression analysis (small-size firm dummy, fewer than 10 workers; medium-size firm dummy, 10 to 50 workers; and large-size firm dummy, more than 50 workers). Regression coefficients are shown in figure 2.17; the results indicate an important association between informality and firm size. Workers in medium-size (large-size) firms are 16 to 21 (17 to 53) percent less likely to work in the informal sector compared with workers in small-size firms.

Conclusions

Socioeconomic conditions in the region are quite heterogeneous, which has important implications for informality. Each country included in the analysis has important economic and demographic factors that are likely to affect the level and characteristics of informal employment, such as the size of the agricultural sector compared with the secondary and ter- tiary sectors (higher levels of agricultural employment are associated with higher labor informality), the size of the public sector (a larger public sector is associated with lower levels of informality), the educa- tional level of the labor force (a more educated labor force is associated with lower levels of labor informality), and the age composition of the labor force (countries with younger populations are associated with

Box 2.2 Informality Trends and the Size of the Public Sector (Egypt, 1998–2006)

Informality dynamics: Informality in Egypt, as proxied by the share of all employment not contributing to social security according to data from the Egypt Labor Market Panel Survey, increased rapidly from 49.0 percent in 1998 to 58.3 percent in 2006. This result holds true using other proxies for informality such as the share of workers without a contract, share of all employment in small firms, share of unpaid to total employment, and share of self-employed to total employment. These dynamics are consistent with Assaad (2009), who finds that informality, as proxied by the share of workers without a contract, increased from 57 percent in 1998 to 61 percent in 2006.

Informality Rates in the Arab Republic of Egypt, for 1998 and 2006 (urban and rural areas)

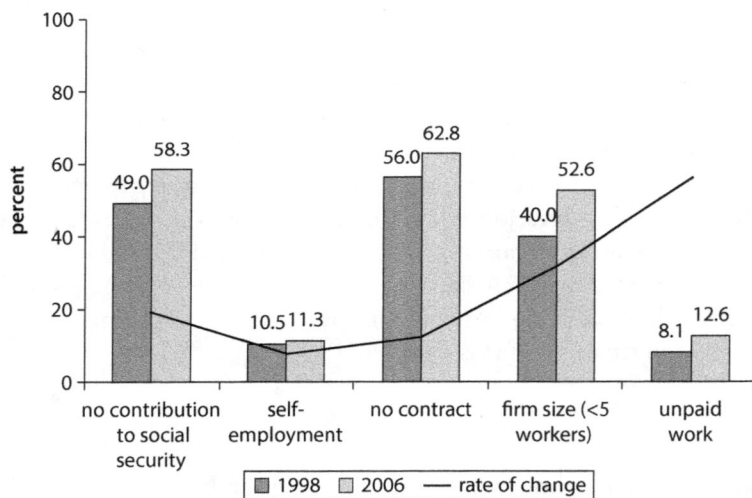

Source: Angel-Urdinola and Tanabe 2011.

As suggested by the table below, the increase in informality is largely explained by the fact that the public sector contracted as a share of total employment (from 47 percent in 1998 to 39 percent in 2006). Indeed, informality within the public and private sectors displayed only a slight increase during the period of study. These results are also consistent with previous work by Radwan (2007), who argues that one of main

box continues next page

Box 2.2 Informality Trends and the Size of the Public Sector (Egypt, 1998–2006)
(continued)

reasons for the rise of informal employment in MENA has been the decline in public sector employment as a share of total employment.

Informality Rates and Employment Shares by Sector (Egypt, Arab Rep., 1998 and 2006)

	1998		2006	
	Pop. share	% informal	Pop. share	% informal
Private	53.3	60.8	60.9	67.3
Public	46.8	2.5	39.1	4.3

Source: Angel-Urdinola and Semlali 2010; Angel-Urdinola and Tanabe 2011.
Note: Inf. = informal; Pop. = population.

Figure 2.17 Marginal Increase in the Probability of Being "Informal" according to Firm Size (Omitted Category, Small Firms, 2–9 Workers)
percent

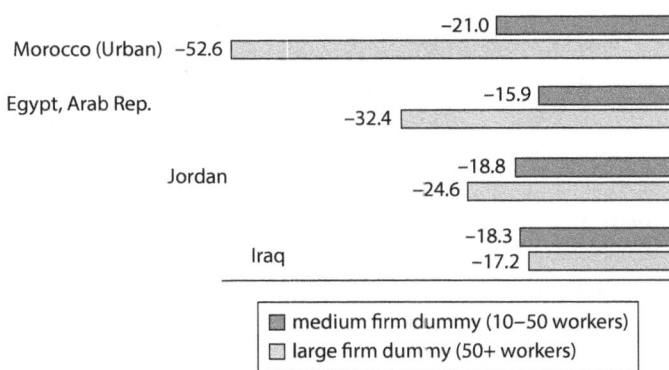

- medium firm dummy (10–50 workers)
- large firm dummy (50+ workers)

Source: Angel-Urdinola and Tanabe 2011.

higher levels of labor informality), among others. There are important variations across countries: Some of them are still very rural, and agricultural employment constitutes almost half of overall employment (the Republic of Yemen and Morocco); some countries have more educated workers (Egypt, Jordan, and Lebanon); and in some, the public sector still represents a significant share of overall employment (Egypt, the Republic of Yemen, Iraq, Jordan, and Syria).

Several factors make informality in the MENA region a persistent phenomenon that may continue to rise in the years to come. The current demographic transition, the reduced importance of public employment, and the increase in private low-productivity employment are all likely to contribute to an increase in informality in the near future. Declining fertility and mortality rates, coupled with an increasing share of young people who attain tertiary education (notably women), are important factors contributing to the expansion of the informal sector. Informal employment is increasingly becoming (even for some educated individuals) a permanent state of employment associated with low pay, poor working conditions, and limited mobility to the formal sector. One of the main reasons for the increase of informal employment in MENA is the decline in public sector employment as a share of total employment. The creation of formal private sector jobs has not been sufficient to offset the downsizing of the public sector in many countries. Formal businesses in many MENA countries face important challenges that restrain their capacity to grow, such as dealing with complex bureaucratic procedures; access to poor infrastructure, credit, and technologies; and high labor taxes. Overall, the formal private sector is very small in most MENA countries, and some might argue that this sector might also unfairly bear the brunt of paying all taxes.

Informality is a more pronounced phenomenon among the poor. Informality rates among workers generally decrease as their household wealth increases. Nevertheless, in some countries informality remains significant even among the wealthier segments of the population. In the Republic of Yemen and Morocco, for instance, more than two-thirds of all workers who belong to the richest households work in the informal sector. This result has important implications. As indicated in chapter 1, informal employment in non-GCC countries, albeit large, produces little output relative to its employment share, suggesting very low levels of worker productivity. This generally occurs when informal workers are constrained in access to credit, services (such as utilities), and/or technology.

Contrary to other developing regions, patterns of urban and rural informality in MENA are somewhat similar, because of the presence of the public sector in rural areas. Urban workers are only 5 to 12 percent less likely to be employed in the informal sector than otherwise similar workers in rural areas. Controlling for age and education, in countries such as Iraq, Morocco, and the Republic of Yemen, the probability of being employed in the informal sector does not vary across urban and rural workers.

The size of the public sector and the size of the agricultural sector are perhaps the main determinants of informality in the MENA region. Countries in the MENA region are quite heterogeneous in terms of size, economic development, and demographic structure. Countries where agricultural employment still constitutes a large share of overall employment (such as Morocco and the Republic of Yemen) are associated with higher levels of overall informality. On the other hand, countries with larger public sectors and more urbanization such as Egypt, Syria, Jordan, and Lebanon are associated with lower levels of overall informality. The existence of a large public sector, which is still associated with generous benefits and better employment quality, creates an important segmentation between public and private employment in many MENA countries. At the same time, the private sector in many MENA countries is primarily composed of small and medium enterprises, which account for about 95 percent of all registered enterprises. In all countries where information about firm ownership is available, workers in the public sector are associated with a 45 to 80 percent lower probability of working informally as compared with otherwise similar workers in the private sector. Self-employed and agricultural workers in most MENA countries are associated with a 10 to 20 percent higher likelihood of being employed informally compared with otherwise similar workers employed as wage earners.

Age, gender, firm size, and education also constitute important determinants of informality. Informality rates are generally highest among young people between ages 15 and 24, a group that in most countries in the sample accounts for 24 to 35 percent of total employment. Above age 25, informality rates decrease rapidly in most countries. Attaining secondary technical and tertiary education is associated with a 40 percent higher probability of being employed formally compared with otherwise similar workers who attained at most a primary education. The relationship between gender and informality varies across countries. In Egypt and Morocco, controlling for other factors, being a male worker is associated with a 4 to 12 percent lower probability of being employed informally, as women generally queue for formal sector jobs. On the other hand, in Iraq, Jordan, and Lebanon, being a male is actually associated with a higher probability of working in the informal sector as is generally the case in many developing countries. Finally, results indicate an important association between informality and firm size. Workers in medium and large firms are 16 to 53 percent less likely to work in the informal sector compared with workers in small firms.

Striving for Better Jobs · http://dx.doi.org/10.1596/978-0-8213-9535-6

Annex

Annex Table 2A.1   Description of the Data Used for the Micro-Analysis

Country	Survey	Year	Description
Egypt, Arab Rep.	Labor Market Panel Survey (ELMPS)	2006	ELMPS was conducted by the Population Council and the Central Agency for Public Mobilization and Statistics (CAPMAS) with support of USAID Egypt and the Ford Foundation. ELMPS 06 is designed as a panel survey in the sense that it follows the same households and individuals that were interviewed in the Egypt Labor Market Survey of 1998 and reinterviews them. Individuals who split from the original 1998 households in the intervening period are also tracked and interviewed together with their entire household. Of the 8,371 households interviewed in 2006, 3,701 were households that were interviewed in ELMS 1998, 2,167 were splits from the original households, and 2,498 were part of an entirely new refresher sample. Sample size is 17,364 individuals and 8,371 households. The surveys contain rich information about individuals' education, employment status, occupation, economic activity, firm size, wage, pension contribution, and so on.
Egypt, Arab Rep.	Household Income, Expenditures and Consumption Surveys (HIECS)	2005–2008	HIECSs have been conducted every five years since 1995 by CAPMAS, and they have been the main (and the only official) source for poverty and inequality data in Egypt. In late 2007, faced with multiple policy demands arising from social tensions, the authorities decided to make the data collection more frequent, and they decided to revisit in 2008 the households interviewed in the February during HIECS 2004–2005. The new survey was conducted during 2008–2009. As part of these efforts, CAPMAS revisited in 2008 the households from one month of 12-month HIECS 2004–2005, applying the same questionnaire. In February 2009 CAPMAS repeated the panel, revisiting again the full set of addresses of the 2004–2005 February sample. The data used in this report come from the last survey conducted in April 2008–March 2009. The sample provides information on informality, earnings, and poverty for 9,228 individuals of working age 16–64 and 3,456 households.

table continues next page

Annex Table 2A.1 Description of the Data Used for the Micro-Analysis *(continued)*

Country	Survey	Year	Description
Iraq	Household Socioeconomic Survey (IHSES)	2006–2007	In an effort to reduce poverty and promote social development, the Ministry of Planning and Development Corporation and the Central Organization for Statistics and Information Technology had undertaken IHSES with the support of the World Bank. Providing essential data for understanding the nature and causes of poverty among Iraqi households, IHSES is the largest household social and economic survey ever conducted in Iraq and reached a total of 18,144 households. IHSES provides information about education, labor, health, income, and expenditure in Iraq. IHEES has a sample size of 17,822 households and 127,189 individuals.
Jordan	Labor Market Survey (JLMPS)	2010	The Jordan Labor Market Panel Survey (JLMPS 2010) was carried out by the Economic Research Forum in cooperation with the National Center for Human Resource Development and the Jordanian Department of Statistics. For the first time in Jordan, detailed information about labor market experiences and behaviors is available in JLMPS. JLMPS has a sample size of 25,969 individuals, containing rich information about individuals' education, employment status, occupation, economic activity, firm size, wage, pension contribution, and decision making of labor force participation. JLMPS allows for a much richer linking of individual characteristics with labor market outcomes.
Lebanon	National Survey of Household Living Conditions (NHS)	2004	The NHS is the multipurpose survey conducted by the Ministry of Social Affairs, the Central Administration for Statistics, and the UNDP in 2004. The purpose of this survey is to assess the economic and social conditions of the households in Lebanon. It provides varied data and social indicators on Lebanese households' demographic status, educational conditions, employment and unemployment, health insurance, chronic diseases, disability, and leisure activities. The survey also provides data concerning the characteristics of residences and their available appliances. Out of the sample size of 14,948, 13,003 households—consisting of 56,513 individuals—completed the data in the questionnaire. The response rate reached 87% of the households sampled.

table continues next page

Annex Table 2A.1 Description of the Data Used for the Micro-Analysis *(continued)*

Country	Survey	Year	Description
Lebanon	Lebanon Employer-Employee Survey	2011	The Lebanon Employer-Employee Survey was conducted by the World Bank under the Lebanon MILES program. It is a nationally representative household-based survey covering a sample of 1,841 households. The survey collects basic information such as age, education, employment for the entire household, detailed information on employment (current and history), skills and training, wages, work benefits for each individual in the household who is over 15 years of age and is either unemployed, self-employed, or a salaried employee, and the level of cognitive and noncognitive skills of workers.
Morocco	Household Consumption and Expenditure Survey (HCES)	2000–2001	HCES was conducted in 2000–2001 by the Ministry of Economic Forecasts and Planning. The purpose of this survey was to provide information concerning the living condition of households and the structure of their consumption and expenditure. HCES provides demographic characteristics of the family members, education, employment, household consumption and expenditures, and income. HCES has 14,243 household and 85,509 individual observations.
Morocco	Morocco Household and Youth Survey (MHYS)	2009–2010	MHYS 2009–2010 was administered from December 2009 through March 2010 and collected information from a nationally representative sample of 2,000 households across the country (1,216 households were urban and 784 were rural) on their demographic and educational characteristics, economic activities, migration, and social program participation. Data on household asset ownership were used to construct a household wealth index and classify households into welfare deciles. In addition to the household module, which collected information on all members, a separate youth module focused on young people aged 15 to 29 in the 2,000 surveyed households. Consequently, information related to youth economic inclusion, community participation, and use of key public services was collected from 2,883 young people. The survey thus gathered information on understudied issues related to youth, such as labor force participation and intermediation, career choices and perceived employment opportunities, use of free time, and use of youth-oriented recreational and educational services that complement formal education.

table continues next page

Annex Table 2A.1 Description of the Data Used for the Micro-Analysis *(continued)*

Country	Survey	Year	Description
Syrian Arab Republic	Household Income and Expenditure Survey (HIES)	2003–2004	HIES 2003–2004 was conducted by the Central Bureau for Statistics, Syria's official statistical agency. HIES provides information on education, employment, household expenditure, and housing conditions. HIEA has a sample size of 29,790 households and 173,330 individuals.
Syrian Arab Republic	Syria Employer-Employee Survey (EES)	2010–2011	EES 2010–2011 was conducted by the World Bank in the context of the Syria MILES program. EES collects matched employer-employee data from firms and workers in registered firms in the manufacturing and services sector in Syria. A representative sample was drawn from firms interviewed in the 2009 World Bank Investment Climate Assessment. A random sample of workers in each firm was drawn systematically. EES has a sample of 116 firms and 961 individuals. The survey collects information on employment (current and history). skills and training, wages, and work benefits.
Yemen, Rep.	Household Budget Survey (HBS)	2005–2006	HBS 2005–2006 was conducted by the Central Statistical Organization of Yemen. The HBS data contain information on household roster, economic activities, dwelling conditions, health, education, anthropometrics, income, durable goods, and consumption. One of the main objectives of the HBS 2005–2006 is producing aggregates of the statistical indicators at the level of the urban and rural communities of each governorate to serve the purposes of economic and social development planning on the central and local levels. HBS 2005 consists of 13,136 household and 98,941 individual observations.

Annex Table 2A.2a Informality Profile (All Workers)

	Iraq		Egypt, Arab Rep.		Lebanon		Morocco		Syrian Arab Republic		Yemen, Rep.		Jordan	
	% Pop.	% Inf.	% Pop.	% Inf.	% Pop.	% Inf.	% Pop.	% Inf.	% Pop.	% Inf.	% Pop.	% Inf.	% Pop.	% Inf.
All workers														
National level	100.0	66.9	100.0	58.3	100.0	56.2	100.0	81.9	100.0	71.0	100.0	91.4	100.0	44.2
Urban	72.9	63.5	43.0	42.7	50.1	48.3	56.5	72.7	50.4	65.9	28.2	84.7	82.9	47.5
Rural	27.1	76.1	57.0	70.0	49.9	66.7	43.5	93.8	49.6	76.3	71.8	94.0	17.1	28.3
Gender														
Male	89.8	70.5	76.9	57.9	76.2	62.5	84.0	83.5	81.8	72.8	44.0	82.1	83.0	47.8
Female	10.2	35.3	23.1	59.3	23.9	36.1	16.0	73.2	18.2	63.0	56.0	98.7	17.0	26.7
Marital status														
Single	30.8	73.7	29.4	76.4	41.4	62.3	40.3	86.4	64.4	95.4	64.4	95.4	35.7	43.3
Married	69.2	63.85	70.7	50.7	58.6	53.4	59.7	78.8	57.9	63.3	35.6	89.2	64.4	44.7
Age group														
15–24	22.3	84.7	19.5	87.1	16.4	69.1	17.1	90.9	29.2	89.0	38.0	97.3	18.5	49.9
25–34	35.6	61.9	31.5	61.4	30.8	55.8	28.7	85.2	26.5	69.1	25.5	85.8	35.8	36.9
35–54	36.5	62.1	40.6	43.4	43.3	52.3	43.1	76.8	37.5	58.0	30.2	87.8	40.7	45.6
55–64	5.64	58.8	8.4	51.2	9.5	53.3	11.1	79.2	6.9	73.2	6.2	95.2	5.0	63.9
Education														
Primary or below	45.9	82.2	42.4	77.8	38.8	75.7	64.2	90.9	64.6	86.2	80.2	97.4	10.8	71.9
Preparatory/ secondary general	24.1	67.6	6.4	63.7	36.7	56.6	27.8	74.1	19.6	60.6	13.7	83.9	46.7	48.1
Secondary vocational	17.2	35.2	34.4	50.0	7.4	45.1	—	—	8.4	19.1	0.7	56.1	16.7	34.2

table continues next page

118

Annex Table 2A.2a Informality Profile (All Workers) *(continued)*

	Iraq		Egypt, Arab Rep.		Lebanon		Morocco		Syrian Arab Republic		Yemen, Rep.		Jordan	
	% Pop.	% Inf.	% Pop.	% Inf.	% Pop.	% Inf.	% Pop.	% Inf.	% Pop.	% Inf.	% Pop.	% Inf.	% Pop.	% Inf.
Tertiary education	12.8	25.4	16.8	23.7	17.2	28.4	8.0	36.5	7.4	24.3	5.4	40.7	25.8	22.0
Employment status														
Wage worker	68.9	51.7	64.3	42.6	65.4	43.1	51.4	67.1	55.6	52.2	23.9	63.7	81.7	32.4
Employer	—	—	13.2	78.4	4.8	84.0	3.9	98.4	6.7	89.4	—	—	7.2	94.6
Self-employed	20.5	100.0	9.9	82.1	27.2	80.1	29.6	98.1	24.0	93.4	20.3	100.0	9.9	98.5
Unpaid worker	10.6	100.0	12.6	98.3	2.6	86.0	15.2	99.0	13.8	99.2	55.9	100.0	1.1	100.0
Industry[a]														
Primary sector	4.6	52.2	25.5	94.1	6.6	94.4	28.4	94.1	31.6	92.4	18.4	95.6	4.4	82.3
Secondary sector	30.7	78.7	21.3	65.8	24.5	75.3	12.6	78.9	6.1	75.5	3.4	86.0	20.6	61.8
Tertiary sector	27.5	71.8	28.0	62.7	68.9	46.0	54.5	82.2	37.7	87.2	40.0	93.3	31.9	71.3
Public administration and social services	37.2	12.2	25.3	11.0	—	—	4.5	18.5	24.6	17.6	38.2	11.7	43.0	6.17
Ownership (only for wage workers)														
Public enterprises	36.9	11.8	30.0	5.3	13.5	9.5	19.2	24.4	26.8	10.8	38.6	7.8	35.6	1.1
Private enterprises	63.1	99.1	70.0	81.0	86.5	63.6	80.8	77.3	73.2	93.1	61.4	97.9	64.4	68.0

Note: Inf. = informality; Pop. = population; — = not available.

a. Industry = primary sector (agriculture); secondary sector (manufacturing and construction); tertiary sector (wholesale, transport, services); public administration; and social services (including education and health).

Annex Table 2A.2b Informality Profile (Private Sector Workers)

	Iraq		Egypt, Arab Rep.		Lebanon		Morocco		Syrian Arab Republic		Yemen, Rep.		Jordan	
	% Pop.	% Inf.	% Pop.	% Inf.	% Pop.	% Inf.	% Pop.	% Inf.	% Pop.	% Inf.	% Pop.	% Inf.	% Pop.	% Inf.
Private sector														
National level	100.0	99.1	100.0	81.0	100.0	63.5	100.0	88.7	100.0	93.1	100.0	99.7	100.0	68.0
Urban	68.7	99.0	37.4	67.3	58.1	53.8	53.5	83.0	47.7	90.4	26.0	99.0	89.7	67.7
Rural	31.3	99.4	62.6	89.2	41.9	76.9	46.5	95.2	52.3	95.6	74.0	99.9	10.4	70.8
Gender														
Men	94.6	99.2	79.7	78.2	76.4	70.7	84.5	89.8	84.0	92.7	39.4	99.2	85.1	71.9
Women	5.4	98.9	20.3	91.9	23.6	40.1	15.5	82.5	16.0	95.1	60.7	100.0	14.9	45.7
Marital status														
Single	34.1	99.3	35.2	88.2	43.0	67.6	42.0	90.2	37.1	99.8	37.1	99.8	37.1	63.6
Married	65.9	99.1	64.8	77.1	57.0	62.2	58.0	87.6	53.9	91.1	62.9	99.6	62.9	70.6
Age group														
15–24	28.3	99.5	25.7	92.4	17.8	72.6	18.4	92.2	33.9	96.9	40.5	99.9	20.3	69.6
25–34	32.7	98.9	33.6	78.9	31.2	61.9	29.8	89.3	26.5	92.1	23.9	99.6	32.3	62.8
35–54	33.9	99.2	33.0	74.9	42.2	60.6	41.1	87.1	32.3	90.1	29.1	99.4	41.0	69.8
55–64	5.1	98.5	7.8	78.0	8.9	64.7	10.7	87.4	7.4	91.9	6.5	99.9	6.4	77.5
Education														
Primary or below	60.0	99.4	52.9	88.3	41.8	80.4	67.7	93.5	77.3	95.5	84.9	99.9	14.1	88.2
Preparatory/ secondary general	25.8	99.1	7.2	80.1	36.0	66.0	26.4	84.8	17.0	89.8	12.4	99.3	48.0	74.3
Secondary vocational	9.2	98.4	30.4	77.8	7.3	51.5	—	—	2.3	82.8	0.4	97.1	16.3	55.6

table continues next page

Annex Table 2A.2b Informality Profile (Private Sector Workers) (continued)

	Iraq		Egypt, Arab Rep.		Lebanon		Morocco		Syrian Arab Republic		Yemen, Rep.		Jordan	
	% Pop.	% Inf.	% Pop.	% Inf.	% Pop.	% Inf.	% Pop.	% Inf.	% Pop.	% Inf.	% Pop.	% Inf.	% Pop.	% Inf.
Tertiary education	4.9	97.5	9.5	50.5	14.9	34.3	5.9	50.7	3.5	61.9	2.3	94.9	21.5	40.2
Employment status														
Wage worker	50.6	98.3	49.0	75.3	60.2	51.8	46.0	77.3	39.6	90.6	16.3	97.9	71.7	56.5
Employer	—	—	18.8	78.4	5.6	84.1	4.3	98.4	9.2	89.6	—	—	11.2	94.6
Self-employed	32.6	100.0	14.1	82.1	31.3	80.2	32.8	98.1	32.6	93.5	22.3	100.0	15.4	98.5
Unpaid worker	16.8	100.0	18.1	98.3	3.0	85.7	16.9	99.0	18.7	99.3	61.4	100.0	1.7	100.0
Industry[a]														
Primary sector	4.3	98.6	35.1	97.3	7.7	94.4	30.8	95.2	41.1	96.7	29.6	98.0	6.4	92.6
Secondary sector	50.8	98.7	25.7	76.5	27.6	76.7	13.3	81.6	7.4	83.9	5.1	94.1	32.7	63.1
Tertiary sector	41.2	98.6	35.3	70.4	64.7	54.5	55.3	87.4	47.5	93.9	61.6	98.7	49.0	75.1
Public administration and social services	3.7	88.9	4.0	61.5	—	—	0.6	29.3	4.0	63.8	3.7	87.9	12.0	30.7

Note: Inf. = informality; Pop. = population; — = not available.

a. Industry = primary sector (agriculture); secondary sector (manufacturing and construction); tertiary sector (wholesale, transport, services); public administration; and social services (including education and health).

Notes

1. Because of data restrictions, the analysis in the remainder of this chapter as well as in chapters 3 and 4 is restricted to non-GCC MENA countries. Tunisia is excluded from the analysis because of a different and not comparable definition of informality. An overview of informality trends in Tunisia is given in box 2.1.

2. Results including agricultural employment are very similar to those presented in the chapter and are available upon request.

3. The cognitive test used "Raven's Progressive Matrices," a nonverbal test in which individuals have to identify the missing piece of a particular pattern among multiple choices. Respondents are given five minutes to answer as many of the 12 matrices that are included in the test as possible. The matrices become progressively more difficult and require greater cognitive capacity. This test is independent of language, reading, or writing skills and focuses on measuring observation skills, analytical ability, and intellectual capacity. A score (out of 12) for each respondent is calculated based on the number of correct answers completed in the allocated time frame. See chapter 4 for a detailed description.

References

Angel-Urdinola, D., S. Brodmann, and A. Hilger. 2011. "Labor Markets in Tunisia: Recent Trends." Mimeo. Washington, DC: World Bank.

Angel-Urdinola, D., and A. Semlali. 2010. "Labor Markets and School-to-Work Transition in Egypt: Diagnostics, Constraints, and Policy Framework." MPRA Paper 27674, University Library of Munich, Germany.

Angel-Urdinola, D., and K. Tanabe. 2011. "Micro-Determinants of Informal Employment in the Middle East and North Africa Region." Mimeo. Washington, DC: World Bank.

Assaad, R. 2009. "Labor Supply, Employment and Unemployment in the Egyptian Economy, 1988–2006." In *The Egyptian Labor Market Revisited*, ed. R. Assaad, 1–52. Cairo: American University in Cairo Press.

Assaad, R., C. Binzel, and M. Gadallah. 2010. "Transitions to Employment and Marriage among Young Men in Egypt." *Middle East Development Journal* 2 (1): 39–88.

Elbadawi, I., and N. Loayza. 2008. "Informality, Employment and Economic Development in the Arab World." *Journal of Development and Economic Policies* 10 (2): 25–75.

Klasen, S. 1999. "Does Gender Inequality Reduce Growth and Development? Evidence from Cross-country Regressions." Policy Research Report Working Paper 7. Washington, DC: World Bank.

Perry, G., W. Maloney, O. Arias, P. Fajnzylber, A. Mason, and J. Saavedra-Chanduvi. 2007. *Informality: Exit and Exclusion*. Washington, DC: World Bank.

Radwan, S. 2007. "Good Jobs, Bad Jobs, and Economic Performance: A View from the Middle East and North Africa Region." In *Employment and Shared Growth*, ed. P. Pace and P. Semeels, 37–52. Washington, DC: World Bank.

World Bank. 1999. "Kingdom of Morocco: Private Sector Assessment Update." Report 19975-MOR. Washington, DC: World Bank.

———. 2003. "Unlocking the Employment Potential in the Middle East and North Africa toward a New Social Contract." MENA Development Report. Washington, DC: World Bank.

———. 2009. "Morocco: Skills Development and Social Protection within an Integrated Strategy for Employment Creation." Mimeo. Washington, DC: World Bank.

CHAPTER 3

Informality and the Firm

SUMMARY: Analyzing firms' incentives to be informal is an important complement to understanding informal employment. This chapter characterizes informality among firms and their workers using data from (1) Investment Climate Assessment (ICA) surveys on registered firms, (2) ICA survey data on micro- and informal firms, including matched employer-employee information, and (3) firm-level data on formal and informal small and medium enterprises. Important regularities emerge. First, informality is prevalent among firms in the Middle East and North Africa (MENA). Many firms never formalize, and even those that eventually register still operate informally for a significant amount of time. Micro- and small enterprises in the region, which account for the lion's share of enterprises and private sector jobs, are mostly unregistered and employ workers informally. Among currently formal firms, MENA has the world's highest share of firms that start out as informal (one-fourth) and the longest operating period before formalization (four years). Registered firms in the region do not report up to one-fifth of their sales and workers to the tax and social security agencies, respectively. Second, business regulations (taxes, entry regulation, and tax and labor regulation) are an important determinant of informality among firms. High taxation burden is the most significant constraint to formalization. Entry regulations seem to be strict, with longer and more cumbersome procedures than in comparator countries. Tax and labor regulations are relatively rigid and are accompanied by strong enforcement but also corruption. Third, among registered firms, worker underreporting for social security purposes is associated with some characteristics of firms, such as size, manager's education, and labor productivity. Fourth, among informal small and micro-firms in MENA countries, the quality and determinants of employment are diverse, offering satisfactory employment for entrepreneurs (often previously unemployed) but lower

quality jobs for informal salaried workers. The correlates of informal employ-
ment and labor market outcomes in micro-firms suggest that informal employ-
ment might in itself be a way to cope with vulnerability and the need for flexible
work arrangements.

Introduction

This chapter characterizes informality among firms and their workers.
Analyzing informality among firms is an important step toward understanding the institutional determinants and policy levers that might
affect formalization in MENA, including implications for job quality and
exclusion of workers from formal risk-sharing mechanisms. The evidence
shows that micro- or small firms that do not register officially with the
relevant government agency also typically do not register their workers
with the social security agency. In addition, even firms that register often
underreport a part of their workforce for social security purposes, which
indicates that there is a continuum of informality.

Different data sources are available to characterize informality from
the firm's perspective in MENA, including (1) Investment Climate
Assessment (ICA) survey data, which are based on a sample of registered
firms; (2) ICA survey data on samples of micro- and informal firms in
Egypt and Morocco; and (3) firm-level data collected by the Economic
Research Forum on formal and informal small and medium enterprises
in the Arab Republic of Egypt, Lebanon, and Morocco (MEAS). Data
from these various sources provide useful information on the extent of
incomplete reporting for tax purposes and social security contributions,
as well as on perceived constraints of complying with formalization
requirements. This chapter also focuses on the determinants of informal
salaried work, gaining insights from matched firm and worker data.

The first section of this chapter discusses the definition and extent of
informality among firms. The next section describes the costs and benefits of informality from a firm's perspective and discusses the main stylized facts on informality among firms. Finally, the last two sections
discuss informality among firms in more detail, outlining profiles of
informality for both registered firms and micro–informal firms.

Description of Informality among Firms

Informality among firms is best understood as a continuum along different
margins. As discussed earlier in the report, informality can be defined as an

activity that is unregulated by the formal institutions that govern economic activities, such as registration, labor laws, and taxation (ILO 1993, 2002; De Soto 1989). This definition covers two main dimensions: (1) the firm's perspective, which focuses on the legal documentation of a firm and the extent to which its activities are reported to public agencies (for example, the social security or tax authority), and (2) the workers' perspective, which focuses on employment conditions such as contractual ties and provision of social security and health insurance coverage. Typically, a firm that is not registered with the relevant government agency is considered to operate informally. Among small or micro-firms, the concept of a fully informal firm is broader, including firms that fail either to be registered or licensed or to keep financial accounts. This usually includes small-scale production units with no legal separation from their owners, such as family-based businesses in which one or more family members participate, and micro-enterprises with at most five employees.[1] Nevertheless, informality is not unique to fully informal firms. In fact, a significant share of the activities of registered firms is often unreported, including sales for tax purposes and the wage bill for social security contributions.

Among micro- and small firms, there is an overlap between the lack of firm registration or tax identifier and a firm's affiliation with a social security agency. Using a new set of data for micro- and small enterprises in Morocco (Oviedo 2008), Silva and others (2010) found that a firm's lack of registration or tax identifier and its affiliation with social security were not mutually exclusive. Although only 40 percent of firms were informal with respect to all three margins simultaneously, 90 percent were informal in at least one of them (figure 3.1). The most frequent margin of informality was the lack of affiliation with a social security agency (89 percent of firms), followed by a lack of registration (55 percent of firms). Using responses from the workers of each firm, Silva and others (2010) found that 55 percent of informal workers were employed by formal firms. Using the Micro- and Small Enterprises Survey (MEAS) of the Economic Research Forum (ERF) for Lebanon, a similar picture emerges: 41 percent of firms were unregistered in all three regulatory agencies simultaneously, and 78 percent of firms lacked affiliation with a social security agency, again the most common margin of informality.

Informality among firms is prevalent by all definitions in MENA. The region has the highest share of firms that start out as informal and has the longest operating period without formalizing in the developing world: On average, a quarter of firms with more than 20 workers start out as informal and operate for about four years without registration.[2] This is

Figure 3.1 Margins of Informality among Micro- and Small Firms in Morocco and Lebanon

a. Morocco

N = 219

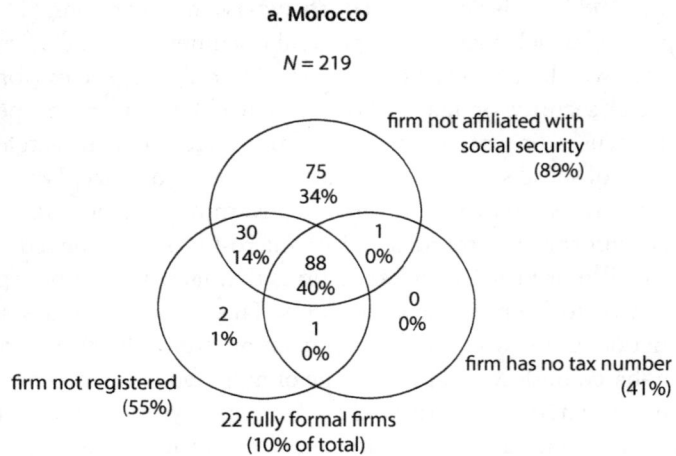

firm not affiliated with
social security
(89%)

75
34%

30
14%
88
40%
1
0%

2
1%
1
0%
0
0%

firm has no tax number
(41%)

firm not registered
(55%)

22 fully formal firms
(10% of total)

Source: Calculations using informal ICA survey (2008) for Morocco.

b. Lebanon

N = 1,341

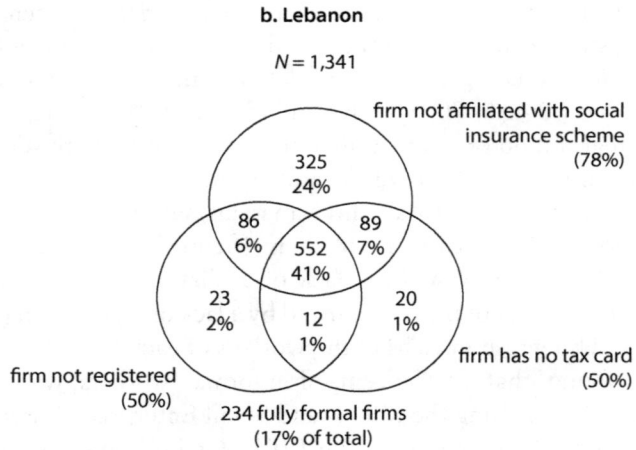

firm not affiliated with social
insurance scheme
(78%)

325
24%

86
6%
552
41%
89
7%

23
2%
12
1%
20
1%

firm has no tax card
(50%)

firm not registered
(50%)

234 fully formal firms
(17% of total)

Source: Calculations using ERF MEAS data (2004).

followed by the East Asia and Pacific region (16 percent of firms and 0.9 year on average) and the Latin America and Caribbean region (7 percent of firms and six months on average) (figure 3.2). In MENA, micro- and small enterprises represent the largest share of all firms and of total nonagricultural private jobs (Galal 2005). For example, according to Elbadawi and Loayza (2008), in Egypt, micro- and small enterprises

Figure 3.2   Unregistered Firms, by Region

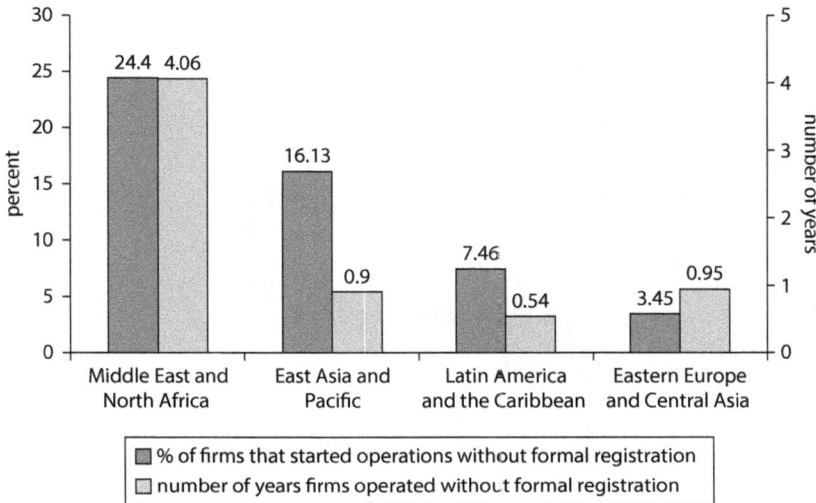

Source: World Development Indicators 2011.
Note: These data are collected from currently formal firms with more than 20 workers.

account for 97 percent of the enterprises, of which 81 percent are informal. Similarly, in Morocco and Lebanon, more than 50 percent of small and micro-firms are unregistered, employ workers informally (for example, the probability of being a formal worker if employed by a firm with fewer than five workers is about 20 percent in Lebanon and Egypt and below 5 percent in Morocco; table 3.1), and have lower labor productivity (evidence from Morocco is described in box 3.1). Among registered firms, an estimated one-fifth of both sales and workers are not reported for tax and social security purposes. This share is lower than in Sub-Saharan Africa, comparable to that in Latin America, and higher than in South Asia and Europe and Central Asia (figure 3.3).

In MENA firm informality is significantly associated with informal employment. Among small and micro-firms, the share of workers who do not have social security coverage is higher in informal than in formal firms: Although the share of informal employment relative to total micro- and small enterprise employment ranges from 47 percent for Egypt to between 66 and 70 percent in Morocco and Lebanon, most of these workers are hired by informal firms (figure 3.4). Similarly, in Egypt, when formal and informal firms were asked "What percentage of total employment would you estimate the typical establishment in your sector

Table 3.1   Firm Size and Worker Informality

	Lebanon (2011)		Morocco (2010)		Egypt, Arab Rep. (2006)		Jordan (2010)	
	% of all informal	Probability of being formal	% of all informal	Probability of being formal	% of all informal	Probability of being formal	% of all informal	Probability of being formal
<5 workers	42	16	56	4	73	20	60	9
5–9 workers	16	48	15	16	14	13	17	32
10–19 workers	15	65			8	32	16	65
20–49 workers	13	75	20	49				
50–99 workers	5	79						
100–149 workers	3	85	9	77	5	91	3	84
150 or more workers	6	82					5	90
Total	100	60	100	17	100	43	100	50

Source: Calculations using Morocco Household and Youth Survey (2010), Lebanon Employer-Employee Survey (2011), Egypt Labor Market Panel Surveys (1998–2006), and Jordan Labor Market Survey (2010).
Note: See annex table 2A.1 in chapter 2 for a detailed description.

Box 3.1   Job Creation and Productivity: Small versus Large Firms in Morocco

Data from the Longitudinal Census of Manufacturing Firms for Morocco (1995–2006) show the following:

- Labor productivity, measured as sales per worker, of the smallest firms (with up to 10 workers) is about 2.6 times lower than labor productivity of the largest firms (with 100+ workers).

Productivity and firm size, 2006

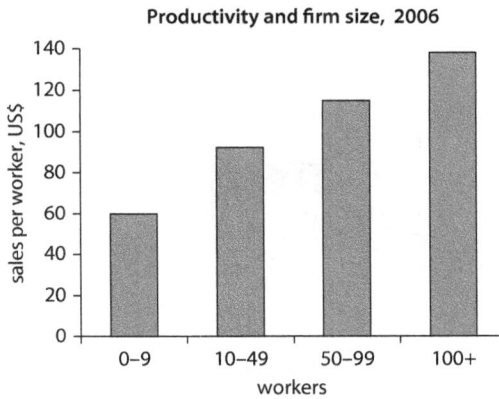

Source: Calculations using Morocco industrial longitudinal census.

Firm exit and birth annual rate by firm size, 1995–2006 (average)

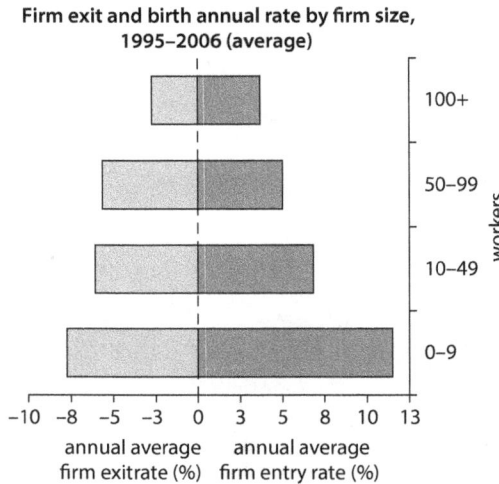

Source: Calculations using Morocco industrial longitudinal census.

box continues next page

Box 3.1   Job Creation and Productivity: Small versus Large Firms in Morocco *(continued)*

- Smaller firms have higher rates of entry and exit than larger firms.
- Small firms in Morocco appear to have employment growth rates lower than larger firms and have a smaller share of total job creation.

Annual employment growth by firm size, 1995–2006 (average)

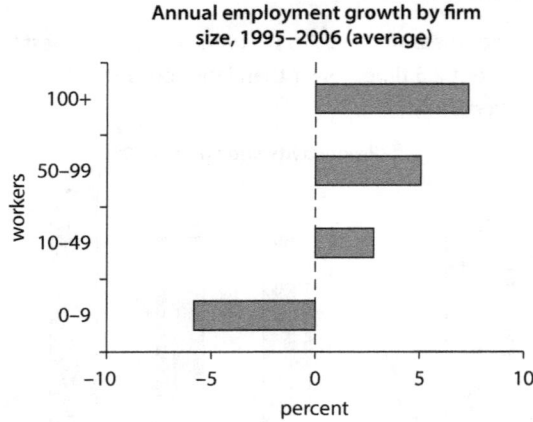

Source: Calculations using Morocco industrial longitudinal census.

Annual share of new jobs created by existing firms by firms size, 1995–2006 (average)

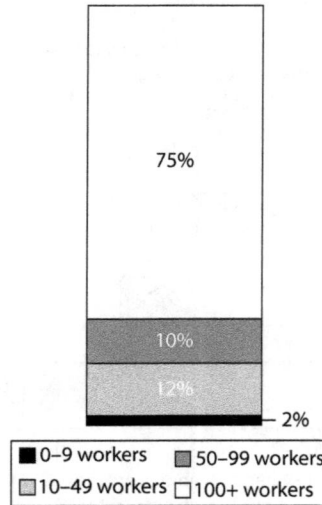

Source: Calculations using Morocco industrial longitudinal census.

Figure 3.3 Informality among Registered Firms, by Region

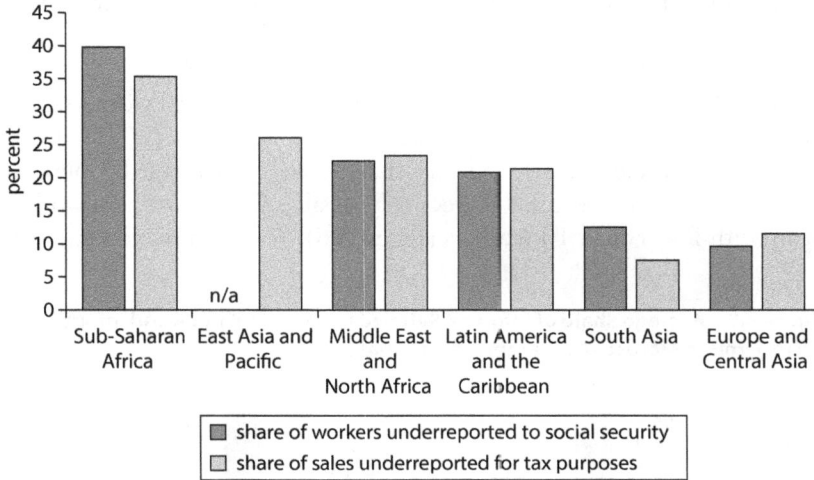

Source: Calculations using individual country ICA surveys for MENA and South Asia; 2005–10 consolidated data for Sub-Saharan Africa, Latin America and the Caribbean, Europe anc Central Asia; and 2002–05 standardized data for East Asia and Pacific.

Note: This figure was computed using firms' responses in the enterprise surveys to the questions: "What percentage of total sales would you estimate the typical establishment in your sector reports for tax purposes?" and "What percentage of the work force would you estimate the typical establishment in your sector reports to social security?" The MENA economies included are Syria (2009), the West Bank and Gaza economy (2006), Egypt (2008), Jordan (2006), Lebanon (2009), and the Republic of Yemen (2010). n/a = not available.

Figure 3.4 Informal Workers in Formal and Informal Micro- and Small Firms

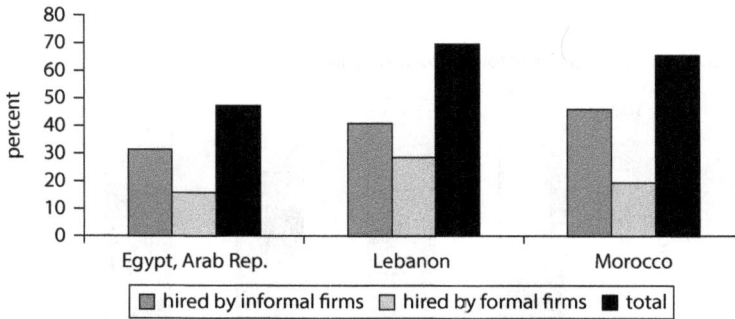

Source: Calculations using data from the MEAS survey of the ERF on 4,958 firms in Egypt (2003), 2,948 firms in Lebanon (2004), and 5,210 firms in Morocco (2002).

reports for social security purposes?" the estimated share of underreporting by informal firms was higher than that reported by formal firms (annex table 3A.1). Even among micro-firms, the share of informal workers is significantly higher among informal firms (figure 3.5).

Most informal workers work in firms with fewer than 10 workers. Data from household surveys for Morocco (2010), Lebanon (2011), Egypt (2006), and Jordan (2010) indicate that up to 71 percent, 87 percent, 58 percent, and 77 percent, respectively, of all informal workers work in firms with fewer than 10 workers (figure 3.6). Those employed in a firm

Figure 3.5   Average Share of Informal Salaried Workers in Formal and Informal Micro-Firms in Morocco by Margins of Informality

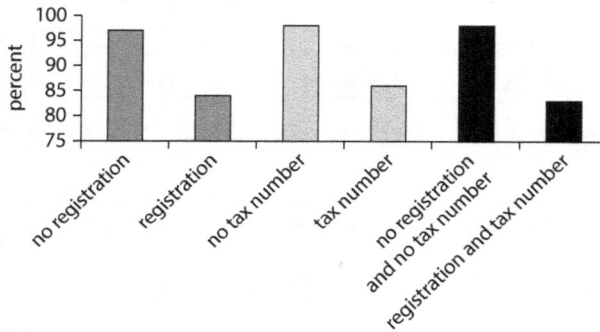

Source: Calculations using ICA survey sample of micro- and informal firms in Morocco, 2007.
Note: Shares of informal salaried workers in each firm's workforce were calculated. Bars represent the average of these shares in each firm category.

Figure 3.6   Where Do the Informal Workers Work?

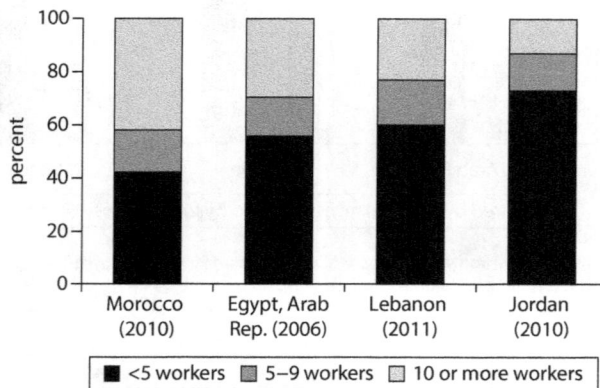

■ <5 workers   ■ 5–9 workers   □ 10 or more workers

with fewer than five workers in Lebanon, Morocco, Egypt, and Jordan have a 16 percent, 4 percent, 20 percent, and 9 percent probability, respectively, of having social security coverage through their job, five times smaller than the probability of having this benefit if employed in a large firm (table 3.1).

Main Costs and Benefits of Informality for Firms

Three main approaches in the literature explain the full or partial underreporting of the workforce (and sales) to authorities. The first line of thought follows De Soto (1989), who characterizes informality as a forced choice of firms to hide from a predatory state. In this case, bureaucratic burdens and rent seeking from public officials make underreporting the most rational choice for firms, especially those that are too small or unproductive to afford compliance.[3] Research by Johnson and others (2000) and Djankov and others (2006) supports this idea. Levenson and Maloney (1998) propose an alternative interpretation in the case of Latin America; they represent informality as the normal state of the nascent entrepreneurial sector. Their model presents informality as a continuum, where fully informal and fully formal behaviors are just two corner outcomes. Firms are modeled as choosing how much to comply with various institutions based on their desired degree of institutionalization, and on the costs and benefits associated with that degree. For instance, firms may register or become licensed but still not find it advantageous to report their entire workforce or all of their sales for taxation purposes. Finally, Friedman and others (2000) depart from the classical explanation of cost-benefit analysis at the firm level and focus on the quality of the institutional environment as a determinant of overall noncompliance.[4]

Numerous barriers might preclude firms from formalizing. In the literature[5] the costs and benefits of informality are categorized into three main groups: formalization costs (monetary, time, and information); compliance costs, which depend on the nature and degree of enforcement of the regulatory framework (the impact of stringency of regulation on firm costs, limits imposed on adjustment margins of employment and wages[6] and legal consequences of not registering);[7] and opportunity costs of operating informally[8] (table 3.2). As in the case of workers, informality can be the result of a profit-maximizing choice that weighs the costs and benefits of formality. People or firms locate in the informal sector because of their belief that informality's benefits outweigh its costs (for example, Ishengoma and Kappel 2006; Loayza and others 2004).

Striving for Better Jobs • http://dx.doi.org/10.1596/978-0-8213-9535-6

Table 3.2 Benefits and Costs of Formality

Benefits	Costs
• Avoidance of government penalties and expansion without fear of government intervention, which is particularly important if enforced	Initial registration
	• Monetary costs
	• Administrative costs and opportunity cost of time and effort
• Ability to issue formal receipts (needed to expand customer base to large firms and multinationals)	
• Ability to create legally enforceable agreements with suppliers and customers; more negotiating power, resulting in lower input prices	Ongoing compliance
	• Taxes and labor and other contributions (such as environmental or health taxes)
• Access to exporting and business with multinationals	
• Access to new and lower cost sources of financing (and government programs)	• Administrative costs and opportunity costs of time and effort
• Spillovers to personal life of entrepreneur (for example, access to personal loans often requires proof of income)	

Source: Based on Bruhn 2011.

According to a survey of micro- and small firms, high taxation burden is the most significant constraint to formalization. More than 50 percent of micro- and small firms in Morocco and 40 percent in Egypt indicate that the level of taxes is the major reason for not registering (figure 3.7). Similar results were found in Mexico, Brazil, and Bolivia (World Bank 2007). A high share of firms also report feeling constrained by both the minimum capital requirement and the level of administrative charges (about 30 percent for Morocco and 35 percent for Egypt). Although the share of Moroccan firms identifying taxes as an obstacle is significantly higher than those attributed to the other constraints, this difference is much less pronounced in Egypt, where corporate taxes were significantly reduced in 2005. Moreover, firms in Egypt did not identify the cost of registration and time necessary to register as major constraints to registration.

Objective measures of tax rates for Morocco corroborate firms' perceptions. Morocco's corporate tax rate is one of the highest among developing countries: In 2007, it was second only to Pakistan and remained significantly above the average for developing countries in 2008 (figure 3.8). Morocco's profit taxes are also high relative to countries with similar income levels (World Bank 2008).[9] In contrast, Egypt's corporate tax rate appears to be below average. As noted, Egypt reformed its corporate tax in 2005, reducing it from 42 percent then to 20 percent in 2007. Egypt also eliminated exemptions and tax holidays, clarified tax rules, replaced universal audits with self-assessment with sample audits,

Figure 3.7 Obstacles to Formalization

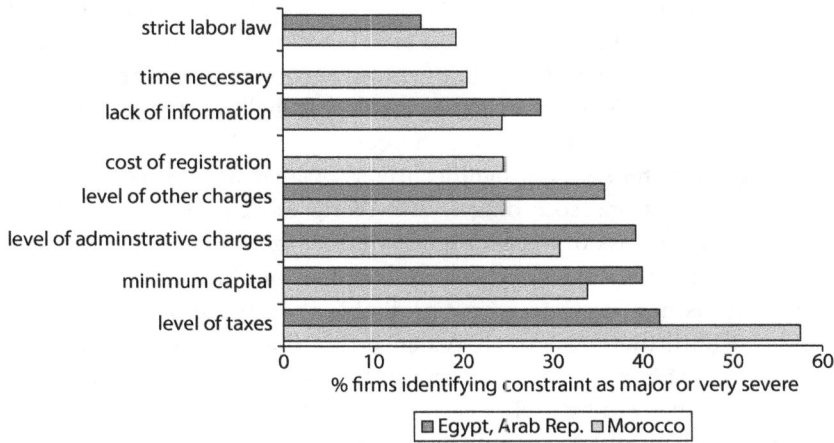

% firms identifying constraint as major or very severe

Egypt, Arab Rep. □Morocco

Source: Calculations using ICA surveys on samples of micro- and informal firms in Morocco 2007 and Egypt, Arab Rep., 2008.

Figure 3.8 Corporate Tax Rates in Developing Economies

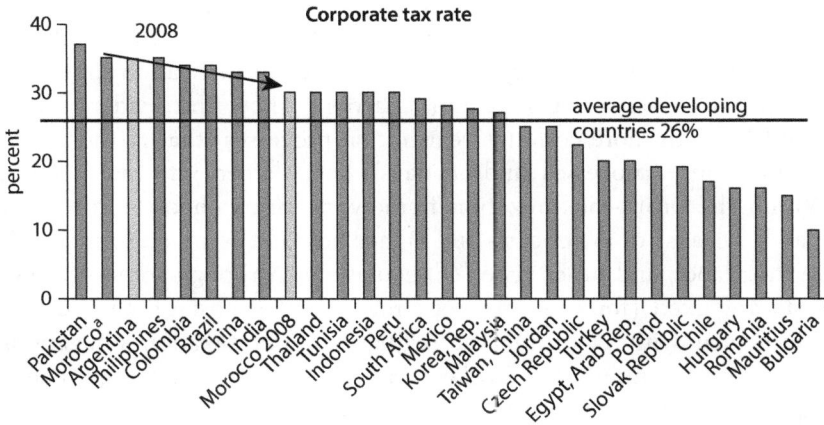

Source: World Bank 2008.
Note: a. Data from 2007.

and simplified forms. As a result, compliance became less onerous, and corporate tax revenues rose from LE 22 billion in fiscal year 2004 to LE 39 billion in fiscal year 2005.[10] A pioneering World Bank study in Brazil is now testing the hypothesis that firm owners in countries that reform tax laws do not register because they mistakenly believe that tax rates are higher than they actually are (see chapter 5, part 1).

Firms' characteristics are significantly associated with costs and benefits of formalization. According to the World Bank (2007), small firms may face a lower risk of being caught by inspectors and may find it more difficult to amortize the fixed costs of registration. In addition, recently created firms may not know how profitable their business will be; they may wait until there is enough evidence that they will stay in business, especially if the monetary and administrative costs of registration are high. As emphasized by McKenzie and Sakho (2010), owner characteristics and family wealth may influence the firm's ability to access credit to cover the minimum capital needed to register. These angles will be analyzed in detail for MENA using the ICA surveys, the largest comparable datasets available for MENA countries, providing information on the relationship between informality and firms' characteristics.

The regulatory context matters. International evidence shows that external obstacles that limit firms' and workers' access to the formal market are key constraints to formality. Djankov and others (2002) suggest that the main policy action to enhance formalization should be aimed toward lowering regulatory barriers. They find evidence that countries with more complex registration processes (that is, those that require more processes and/or days) have larger informal sectors. Within the profit-maximization framework, firms choose informality mainly because of lower costs and higher flexibility derived from avoiding tax, labor, and other types of regulations. Although some of these costs are fixed (for example, registration and licensing), the cost of compliance with labor market regulations and taxation obligations varies with the number of workers and revenues/sales. Noncompliance exposes firms to penalties and sanctions if detected by the corresponding regulatory entities. Firms must also outweigh other disadvantages of informality such as reduced access to financing and to legal enforcement options, and reduced business interaction with the government and other markets.

Labor regulations (particularly firing regulations) in some MENA countries are relatively rigid and labor taxes high compared with countries with similar levels of income. Hence, firms often identify labor laws as a major obstacle for business growth. Firing regulations in MENA are quite strict, and firing costs are high (figure 3.9). The cost of advance notice requirements and severance payments and penalties due when terminating redundant workers, expressed in weeks of salary, is rather low, accounting for 11 weeks of salary on average in MENA versus 15 weeks in Latin America and the Caribbean, but only 7 weeks in OECD countries. Labor taxes and mandatory contributions paid by businesses as a percentage of commercial profit are 25 percent in North Africa versus an average of 10 percent and 13 percent in a typical country in Latin America and East Asia, respectively. (See discussion in chapter 5, part 1, for more details.) Stringency of labor regulations is widely perceived as a major constraint by firms (figure 3.10), but this varies significantly across countries: In Syria and Lebanon, 50 percent and 36 percent of firms consider labor regulations as a major or severe obstacle for business, respectively, and in the West Bank and Gaza economy and the Republic of Yemen, it is 12 percent and 11 percent, respectively. In the following sections, it will be argued that these perceptions are strongly associated with informality. Evidence for Mexico shows that reforms that ease firms' registration are associated with an increased number of registered firms, but this is due more to creation

Figure 3.9   Difficulty of Redundancy Index

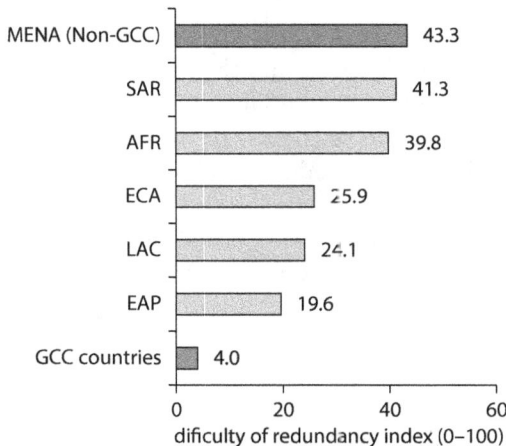

Region	Value
MENA (Non-GCC)	43.3
SAR	41.3
AFR	39.8
ECA	25.9
LAC	24.1
EAP	19.6
GCC countries	4.0

dificulty of redundancy index (0–100)

Source: *Doing Business* indicators 2011.
Note: The redundancy index ranges from 0 to 100. AFR = Sub-Saharan Africa; EAP = East Asia and Pacific; ECA = Europe and Central Asia; GCC = Gulf Cooperation Council; LAC = Latin America and the Caribbean; SAR = South Asia; LAC = Latin America and the Caribbean.

Figure 3.10 Percent of Firms Indicating Labor Regulations as a Major Obstacle to Business Development

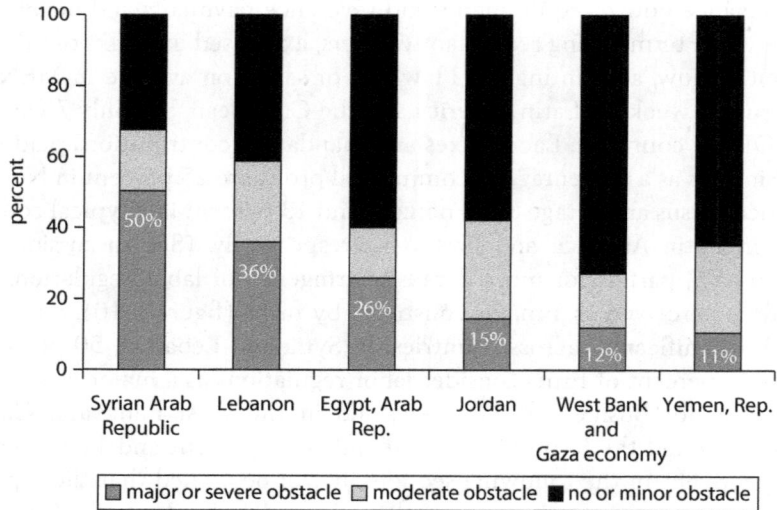

Source: Calculations using individual country ICA surveys.

of new businesses by former wage earners than to increased registration of existing informal businesses (Bruhn 2011).

Entry regulations in MENA countries seem strict (figure 3.11). In MENA the average number of procedures required to start a business is second only to Latin America and the Caribbean (LAC). Within the region, Algeria, Djibouti, and the West Bank and Gaza economy stand out as economies where this process is particularly cumbersome, requiring more than 10 procedures and an average of between 20 to 80 days to start a business. Besides the fact that the average time is long, the playing field might be unequal between different types of firms, with privileged firms likely benefiting from faster registration processes.

Tax regulations are accompanied by both strong enforcement and corruption (figure 3.12). Firms in MENA report an average of four tax inspections per year, the highest regional average in the world. Strict enforcement also appears to be accompanied by widespread corruption, as, according to firm-level surveys, informal payments were requested in 17 percent of inspections, which is significantly above the 7 percent reported in the LAC and ECA regions.

Figure 3.11   Entry Regulation across Regions and in Selected MENA Countries

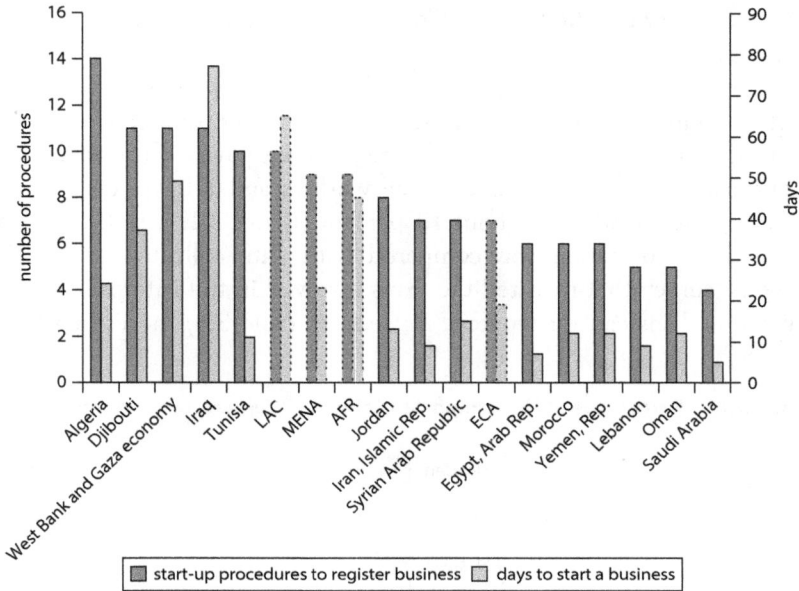

start-up procedures to register business   days to start a business

Source: World Development Indicators 2010.
Note: The dotted bars show values for regions. AFR = Sub-Saharan Africa; ECA = Europe and Central Asia; LAC = Latin America and the Caribbean; MENA = Middle East and North Africa.

Figure 3.12   Enforcement of Tax Regulations and Bribes during Tax Inspections

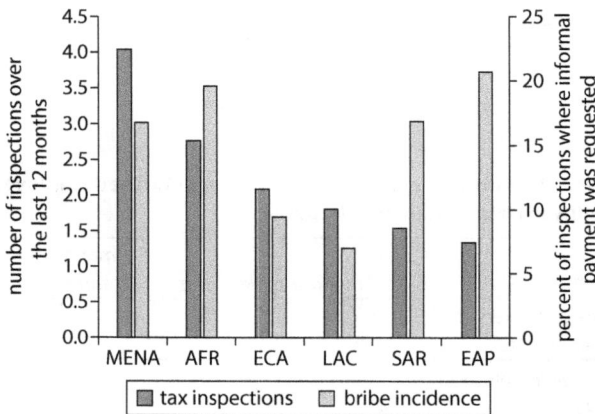

tax inspections   bribe incidence

Source: Latest available ICA survey data for individual MENA countries and standardized 2006–2010 ICA survey data for other regions.
Note: AFR = Sub-Saharan Africa; EAP = East Asia and Pacific; ECA = Europe and Central Asia; LAC = Latin America and the Caribbean; MENA = Middle East and North Africa; SAR = South Asia.

Stylized Facts on Informality among Firms in MENA

Informality among Registered Firms: Firm-Level Correlates

Underreporting employment (to social security) and sales (for tax purposes) is common among registered firms but is heterogeneous across MENA countries with relatively similar levels of income. For example, firms in Syria and the Republic of Yemen do not pay social security contributions for about 40 percent of their workers, and in Egypt the share of underreported workers is about 12 percent (figure 3.13). In the case of Syria, this information was compared with data collected in a 2011 workers' survey that revisited the firms involved in the enterprise survey but focused instead on workers. As seen in table 3.3, the estimates of

Figure 3.13   Percentage of Underreported Sales and Workers, by Economy

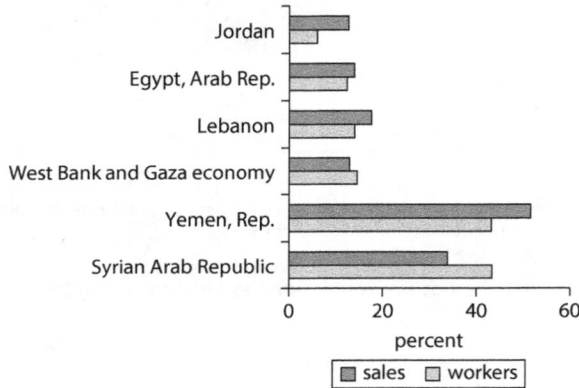

Source: Calculations using the World Bank Enterprise Survey database.

Table 3.3   Informality among Formal Firms: Matched Employer-Employee Data, Syrian Arab Republic, 2011

	Among sampled firms	Among workers at sampled firms
Share of workers underreported	43%	53%
Firm size (employees)		
10–49	49	52
50–99	46	30
100+	32	20

Source: Calculations using firm-data from ICA Syria 2009 and Syria matched-employer employee survey 2011.

informality based on firms' responses are a lower bound, but roughly in line with those based on workers' responses to enrollment in social security.

Regardless of the high cross-country variation, some firm characteristics are systematically associated with higher degrees of informality among registered firms. First, size matters: Smaller firms tend to underreport more than larger firms. The fraction of workers and sales that firms hide from the government is about twice as large in small firms than in large firms (with the exception of Lebanon; figure 3.14). In the Republic of Yemen and Jordan, for instance, about 50 percent and 13 percent, respectively, of workers go underreported among small firms, compared with about 20 percent and 3 percent, respectively, among firms with 100 workers or more. In Syria, small and medium firms are similar with regard to informality but differ considerably from larger firms where informality is less prevalent. In Egypt, size is also strongly correlated with worker underreporting, and the relationship is almost linear. In the West Bank and Gaza economy, the smallest and largest firms differ considerably with regard to the level of informality. In Jordan, worker underreporting seems to be prevalent mainly among the smallest firms. Sales underreporting exhibits different patterns: (1) although it tends to decrease with firm size in the Republic of Yemen, Syria, and Egypt, this is not the case in Lebanon, the West Bank and Gaza economy, and Jordan; and (2) sales underreporting is significantly higher than workers' underreporting among larger firms, with the exception of the West Bank and Gaza economy. The differences on underreporting between sales and workers might have important implications for productivity comparisons that use numbers on sales and employment from social security and tax administrative registries.

Doubling firm size is associated with a reduction in worker underreporting of more than 5 percentage points in Jordan and the Republic of Yemen and more than 2 percentage points in Syria and Egypt (figure 3.15). The negative relationship between underreporting and employment size in the case of Jordan, the Republic of Yemen, Syria, and Egypt is maintained even after controlling for the firm's length of time in business, location, and sector. This result is confirmed using a three-wave panel dataset for Egypt, suggesting that as a firm's employment grows, it is more likely to "hide" a smaller part of its production and workers (see columns 6–8 of annex table 3A.2).[11] The relationship between underreporting and size is found to be broadly linear across firms' sizes; that is, relative to small firms, both large and medium firms

Figure 3.14 Worker and Sales Underreporting by Firm Size

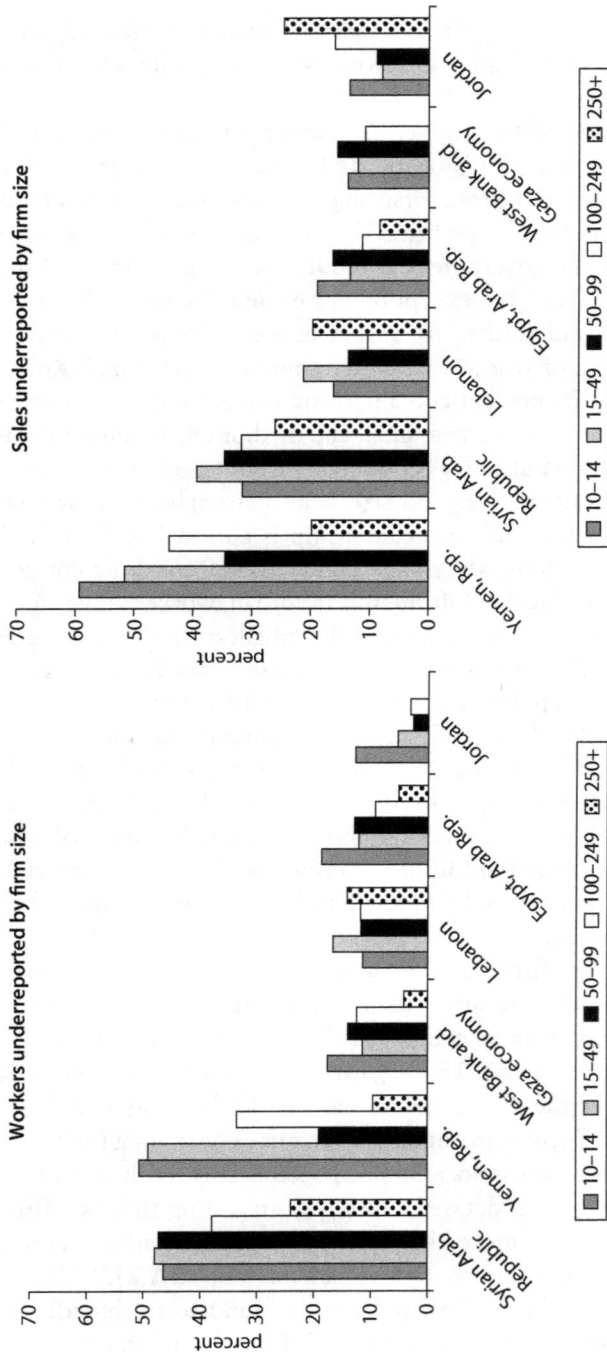

Workers underreported by firm size

Sales underreported by firm size

Legend: 10–14 | 15–49 | 50–99 | 100–249 | 250+

Source: Calculations using ICA survey data for MENA economies from the World Bank Enterprise Survey database.

Figure 3.15 Association between Doubling Employment Size and Worker Underreporting

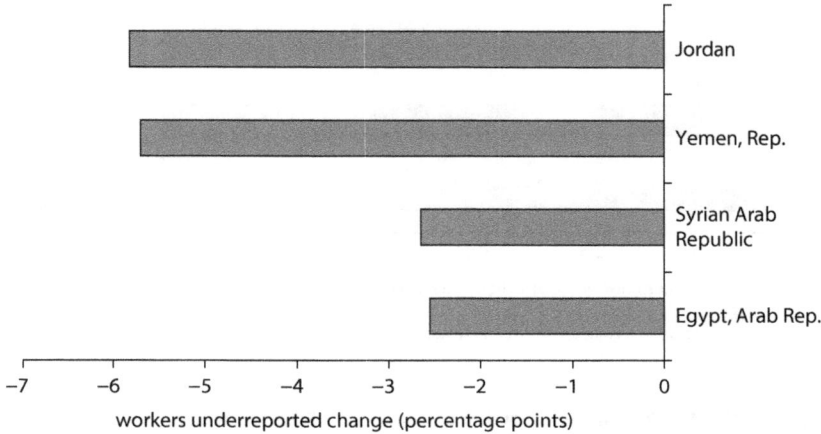

Source: Calculations using ICA survey data for MENA economies from the World Bank Enterprise Survey database.

underreport less, but the difference is greater for larger firms (see columns 1–2 of annex table 3A.2). Notably, underreporting of sales and underreporting of workers are highly correlated. In addition to reducing the revenue for taxation, sales underreporting may also have an effect on informal employment; that is, to pay its undeclared labor force, a firm may be forced to keep some of its sales off the books. For this reason, the incentive to sell informally may be correlated with an incentive to underreport workers. A simultaneous estimation of the determinants of sales and worker underreporting shows that similar determinants do affect underreporting of sales and workers (see columns 3–4 of annex table 3A.2).

More productive firms appear to report a larger share of their workers to social security. The association between sales per worker (a rough estimate of productivity) and informality appears to be negative and statistically significant, even after controlling for other firm-level correlates. This finding is robust to the different measures of productivity associated with both sales and worker underreporting and is also robust to using longitudinal data (annex table 3A.2). Though causality cannot be inferred in this setup, figure 3.16 depicts the change in worker underreporting that is associated with a doubling of productivity in selected countries in the region.

Figure 3.16   Association between Doubling Labor Productivity and Worker Underreporting

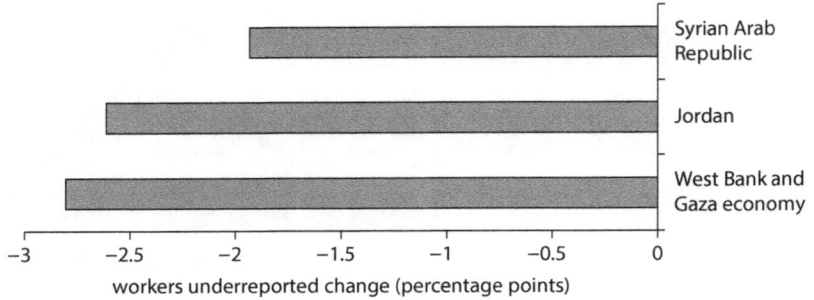

workers underreported change (percentage points)

Source: Calculations using ICA survey data for MENA economies from the World Bank Enterprise Survey database.

Figure 3.17   Worker Underreporting by Manager's Education Level

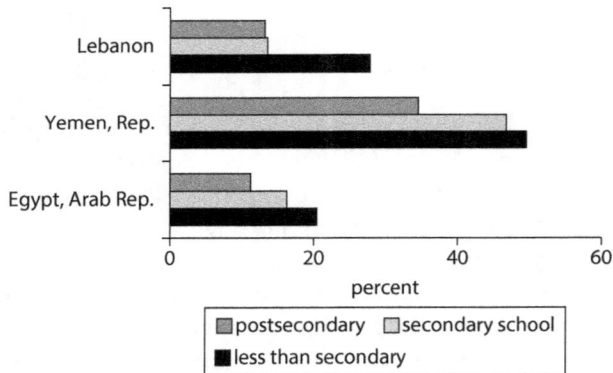

percent

□ postsecondary   □ secondary school
■ less than secondary

Source: Calculations using ICA survey data for MENA economies from the World Bank Enterprise Survey database.

Firms managed by highly educated individuals consistently report a higher share of the workforce to social security, controlling for other firm characteristics, including education of its workforce and the manager's prior experience. Firms whose top managers' highest level of education are below secondary school exhibit rates of worker underreporting of 50 percent in the Republic of Yemen and 20 percent in Egypt, and firms whose managers completed postsecondary education exhibit underreporting rates of 35 percent in the Republic of Yemen and 11 percent in Egypt (figure 3.17).[12] In Lebanon and Egypt,[13] a hypothetical increase in the education level of the top manager from less than

Figure 3.18 Changes in Worker Underreporting Associated with a Change in Manager's Education Level

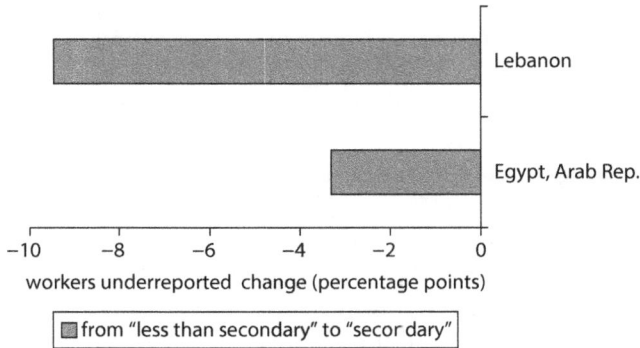

Source: Calculations using ICA survey data for MENA economies from the World Bank Enterprise Survey database.

secondary to secondary is associated with 9 percent and 3 percent decreases in worker underreporting, respectively (figure 3.18).[14] Cross-country regressions also suggest a strong association between the manager's education level and underreporting of workers as well as of sales. An analysis of panel data for Egypt (using both Tobit random effects and OLS fixed effects models) confirms this result (annex table 3A.3). Note that fixed effects regressions control for time-invariant firm characteristics and eliminate regression bias from omitted firm-specific variables. The results show that, all else equal, the arrival of a manager with a higher education level than the previous manager is associated with lower levels of underreporting. The relationship between a manager's education and informality is open to several interpretations. De Paula and Scheinkman's (2007) model shows that a manager's education is an imperfect measure of the person's ability, and that more able managers tend to be less likely to work in informal firms (that is, they are found more often in productive or larger firms). However, the results here suggest that the relationship between a manager's education and worker underreporting holds within the same firm (using firm fixed effects models and restricting the analysis to cases where the manager did not change), making this hypothesis less likely. A second hypothesis is that more educated managers may better understand the benefits of paying taxes or of hiring workers formally. Alternatively, more educated managers may have a lower tolerance for the risks associated with using informal hiring as a tool to avoid regulations.

Firms with a more educated workforce tend to exhibit lower levels of underreporting. In Syria and Lebanon, the level of compliance increases with workforce education (figure 3.19). For example, in Lebanon, in firms whose workforce consists mainly of workers with less than secondary education, underreporting is 27 percent; in firms where most of the workforce have a secondary or higher than secondary education, underreporting is 11 percent and 5 percent, respectively. Skill upgrading of the existing workforce could also be associated with increasing levels of formality. For a given firm size, age, location, and sector, a change in the most prevailing level of education of the firm's workforce from less than secondary to secondary is associated with a decrease in underreporting of almost 10 percentage points in Lebanon. Likewise, a change in the most prevailing level of education from secondary to postsecondary is associated with a decrease in underreporting of 7 percentage points in Lebanon and 8 percentage points in Syria (figure 3.20). Note that a more educated workforce is associated with higher productivity, and therefore, a higher opportunity cost of being informal. Hence the relationship between workforce education and informality might be open to several interpretations.

Informal firms are somewhat less connected and less likely to belong to a business network. As indicated by the World Bank (2010), the lack of network links might be an indication of "duality" in private

Figure 3.19 Worker Underreporting and the Workforce Education Level

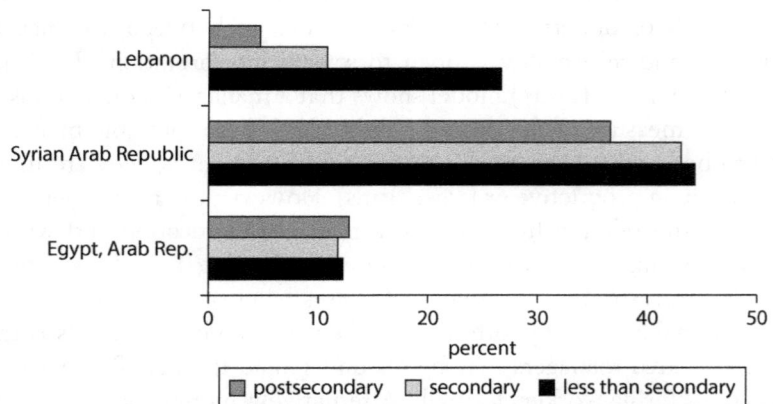

Source: Calculations using ICA survey data for MENA economies from the World Bank Enterprise Survey database.
Note: Workforce education level is reported according to the most representative education level within the firm.

149

Figure 3.20 Change in Worker Underreporting When Workforce Education Increases

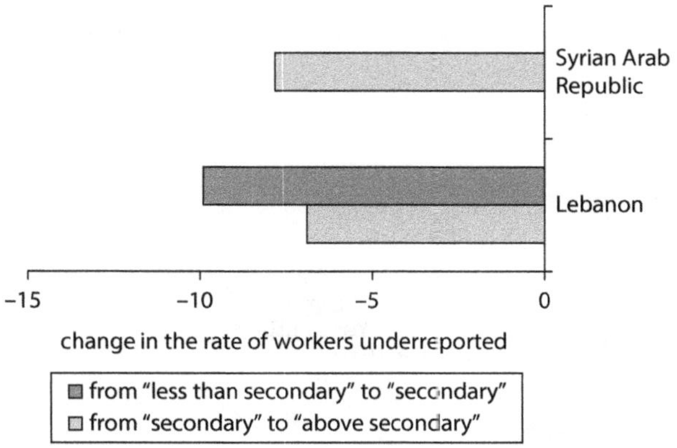

change in the rate of workers underreported

- from "less than secondary" to "secondary"
- from "secondary" to "above secondary"

Source: Calculations using ICA survey data for MENA economies from the World Bank Enterprise Survey database.
Note: Workforce education level is reported according to the most representative education level within the firm.

Table 3.4 Informality, Connectivity, and Networks among Firms in MENA Economies

Worker underreporting	E-mail	Web site	Association
Egypt, Arab Rep.	−0.0883*	−0.0918*	
Jordan	−0.1600*	−0.1335*	
Syrian Arab Republic	−0.0941*	−0.0984*	−0.029
Yemen, Rep.	−0.2542*	−0.3099*	−0.2335*
Lebanon	−0.1232*	−0.0666*	−0.0402*
West Bank and Gaza economy	−0.2221*	−0.2265*	

Source: Calculations using ICA survey data for MENA economies from the World Bank Enterprise Survey database.
Note: Correlation coefficients reported.
*Statistical significance at the 5% level.

sector dynamics. A relevant finding common to all countries is a significant negative association between the share of worker underreporting and the use of e-mail, existence of a Web site (as a proxy for connectivity), and belonging to a business association (as a proxy for networks) (table 3.4). The following chapter finds similar results for workers.

More informal firms are also less likely to provide training to their workers. Across countries and controlling for firm size, age, and sector, firms that are more informal are found to be less likely to provide training to their workers (figure 3.21).

Striving for Better Jobs • http://dx.doi.org/10.1596/978-0-8213-9535-6

Figure 3.21   Relative Provision of Worker Training in MENA Economies and Informality

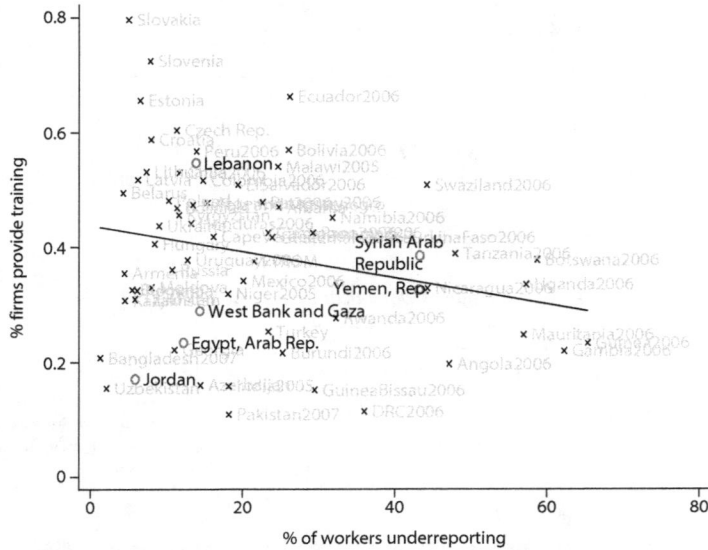

Source: Calculations using available enterprise surveys.

Firms and the Regulatory Environment

Firms with higher rates of underreporting are more likely to identify stringent labor and tax regulations as a major constraint. The literature suggests that more rigid de jure labor regulations can increase firms' incentives to hide part of their workforce (Botero and others 2004). A recent review of labor regulations in the region shows that MENA has fairly flexible hiring procedures but rigid dismissal rules that, according to employers, curb the employment potential (Angel-Urdinola and Kuddo 2010). Pierre and Scarpetta (2006) analyze an array of countries for which employment protection regulations have been evaluated in terms of stringency, and they show that employers' perceptions about labor regulations are closely related to the actual stringency of labor laws. In this analysis, the correlation between the perceived stringency of de jure labor regulations and a greater propensity to hire informally is analyzed (table 3.5). Following Pierre and Scarpetta (2006), employers' perceptions of labor and tax regulations are used as a proxy for regulatory stringency. In Egypt, the Republic of Yemen, and Lebanon, worker underreporting and perceptions of the stringency of labor regulations are

Table 3.5   Correlation between Worker Underreporting and Perceptions of Labor Regulations and Tax Rates

Economy	Labor regulation	Tax rate
Egypt, Arab Rep.	0.1295*	0.2270*
Jordan	0.0216	−0.0286
Lebanon	0.0682*	0.0471*
Syrian Arab Republic	−0.0109	0.0473*
West Bank and Gaza economy	−0.0504*	−0.0388*
Yemen, Rep.	0.1646*	−0.0203

Source: Calculations using ICA survey data.
Note: Correlation coefficients reported.
*Statistical significance at the 5% level.

positively and significantly associated. In contrast, in the West Bank and Gaza economy, this correlation is smaller and negative.

Firms that reported labor regulations to be a severe or very severe obstacle to their business are consistently more likely to underreport their workforce and their sales. This result is found in cross-country regressions and confirmed using panel data (annex table 3A.4). Consistent with this result is the fact that firms that reported taxes as being an important obstacle to their business also tended to hide more sales. The study finds that over time and for the same firm, the more labor obstacles are perceived as constraining, the lower the volume of sales reported.

Enforcement matters too. More frequent inspections are associated with less informality. The number of labor inspections that firms receive in a year is used to assess whether enforcement of regulations affect informality. In line with the results of Almeida and Carneiro (2009) for Brazil, more frequent labor inspections are found to be associated with less informal employment. Annex table 3A.4 reports the regression results for a pool of seven countries and for the panel of Egyptian firms. Tax inspections seem to be less effective than labor inspections in curbing sales evasion: Although labor inspections are significantly associated with less sales underreporting, the relationship between tax inspections and sales underreporting is not statistically significant.

When corruption is associated with inspections, underreporting is higher. The effectiveness of enforcement depends on the extent to which inspections are associated with corruption. To control for this effect, a binary variable is added for cases where firms reported that labor inspectors expected an informal payment with their visit. As expected, corruption in labor inspections is significantly associated with greater labor underreporting. Similarly, bribing of tax officials is also significantly associated with underreporting of sales, which may explain the previous result that tax inspections, unlike labor inspections, are not associated with lower informality. As was found for bribing, the share of informality among nonrespondents is higher for labor and taxes. Importantly, the more binding the regulations, the less inspections are associated with lower informality (annex tables 3A.4 and 3A.5).

In a survey of small firms, those that indicated they had transitioned from informality to formality reported that this was mainly driven by the fact that it became mandatory rather than beneficial. Data from the Micro- and Small Enterprises Survey (MEAS) of the Economic Research Forum (ERF) indicate that the reason for acquiring a business license or registering with the tax department after having started operations is primarily because it is mandatory rather than because it became advantageous or simpler to do. In Egypt, Lebanon, and Morocco, mandatory registration was identified by 69 to 86 percent of firms, and either advantageous or simpler registrations were identified by 4 to 21 percent and 3 to 13 percent of firms, respectively (figure 3.22). The only exception for registering to obey the law versus registering because it became advantageous was in Morocco, where 51 percent of the firms expressed perceived advantages to business registration as the main motivation. The requirement to register followed in second place (32 percent of firms). Consistent with this finding, a World Bank study on firm informality in Bolivia (World Bank 2007) shows that the main benefit as perceived by firms of having a tax number is compliance with the law (47 percent). Note, however, that not all small firms might be on the margin of formalizing. In particular, and in line with McKenzie and Sakho (2010), registration might lower profits for smaller firms because they might be too small to immediately benefit from formalization. Registering for taxes immediately involves more costs in the form of tax payments. If the firm is too small to benefit from an increased customer base or better access to credit, then immediate costs might outweigh benefits.

Informality among Micro- and Small Informal Firms

Some observers argue that the informal sector, and in particular informal small and micro-firms, is a vital employer of young and unskilled workers, a countercyclical employer for workers in transition, and an essential source of affordable goods and services for the poor. In this section, the informal ICA survey data on samples of micro- and informal firms in

Figure 3.22 Firms' Reported Reasons for Registering or Acquiring a License or Tax Card

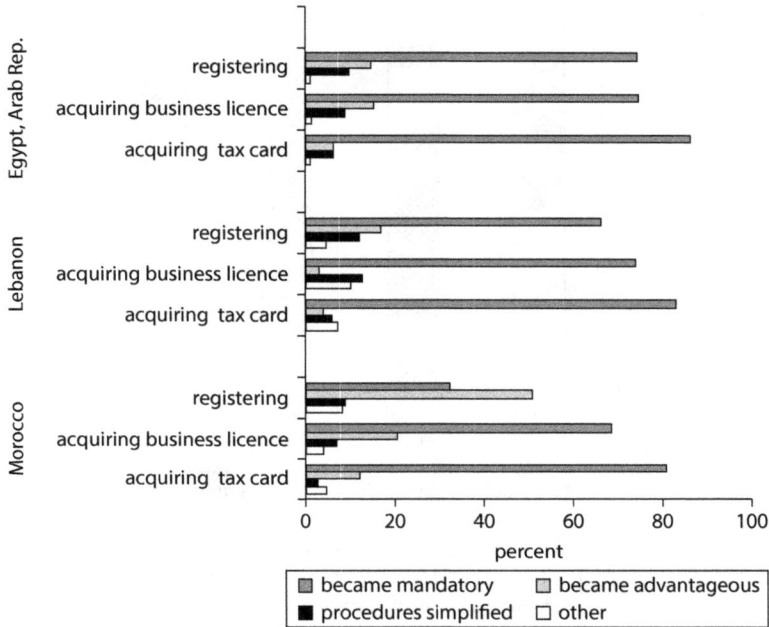

Source: Calculations using MEAS data (Egypt 2003, Lebanon 2004, and Morocco 2002).

Egypt and Morocco are used to analyze informality among micro- and small firms and understand the extent to which these hypotheses hold true in MENA.

Informality among micro- and small firms: A profile of employment. Among micro- and small firms in Egypt, entrepreneurs of informal firms are less qualified, on average, than entrepreneurs of formal firms. Using data from ICA survey (formal and informal firms) in Egypt, the World Bank (2010) indicates that managers of micro- and small informal firms have a lower level of education than those of formal firms. The share of managers with a primary education or less is 43 percent in informal firms and 7 percent in small formal firms. Similarly, the share of managers of informal firms with postsecondary education is significantly lower than that of formal firms (18 percent and 68 percent, respectively) (figure 3.23). In addition, 90 percent of informal firms indicated that the firm's manager did not have previous work experience in the formal sector.

Figure 3.23   Highest Education of Managers for Formal and Informal Manufacturing Firms in Egypt

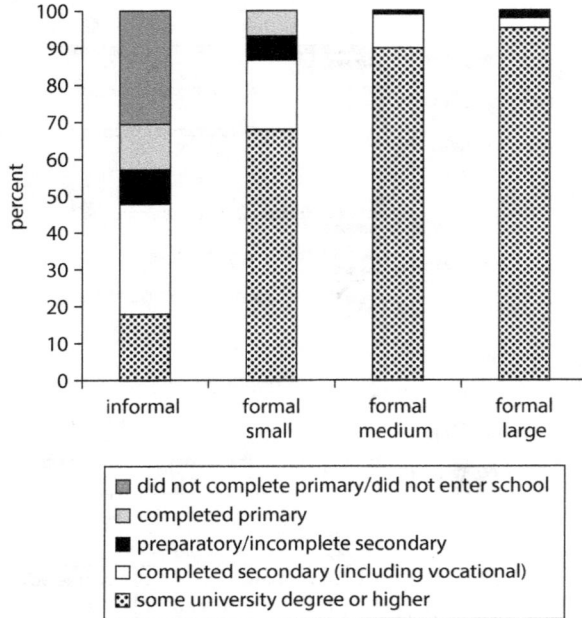

Source: World Bank 2010.

Similarly, workers in informal firms seem to be less qualified, have a higher job turnover, and have a greater likelihood of being relatives or members of the household of the firm owner. Among micro- and small firms in Egypt, the workforce of informal firms is less educated than that of formal firms. The largest difference is in the share of workers with no formal education (33 percent in informal firms versus 18 percent in formal firms) and the share that completed secondary education (29 percent in informal firms versus 39 percent in formal firms; figure 3.24). Notably, 27 percent of micro- and small firms identify skills and education of available workers as a major or very severe problem for their operations and growth. Nine percent of workers of these firms are part time, and 13 percent are relatives or members of the household of the firm owner.

Among micro-firms in Morocco, only 7 percent of all workers are covered by social security; the patterns and associations observed among formal, registered firms between underreporting of workers and

Figure 3.24 Highest Education of Male Workers in Formal and Informal Manufacturing Firms in Egypt

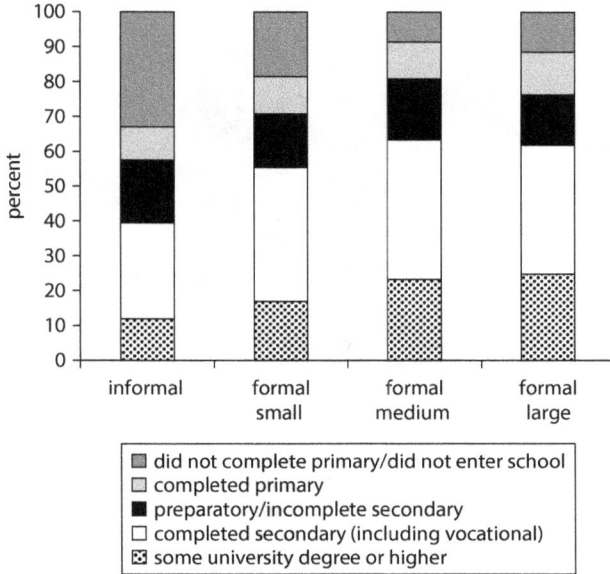

Source: World Bank 2010.

firms' characteristics also hold true among micro–informal firms. In the Morocco ICA survey on micro-firms, each worker was surveyed. Among other questions, each worker indicated whether he or she was contributing to social security. Results are depicted in figure 3.25. The largest part of the workforce of these firms consisted of informal salaried workers (58 percent), followed by informal entrepreneurs (34 percent). As in larger registered firms, informal employment among micro-firms spans beyond informal firms, with as many as 55 percent of all informal workers working in registered firms. This is not surprising considering that informal workers represent up to 84 percent of the labor force of firms with a business registration, and 68 percent of firms with tax registration (recall figure 3.5). Finally, among informal small and micro-firms in MENA countries, the strongest predictors of informality, measured as a firm's lack of registration, are the owner's level of education, having started the business following a period of unemployment, absence of business with larger firms, and concerns about tax increases and labor law enforcement.

Figure 3.25   Worker Categories in Micro-Firms in Morocco

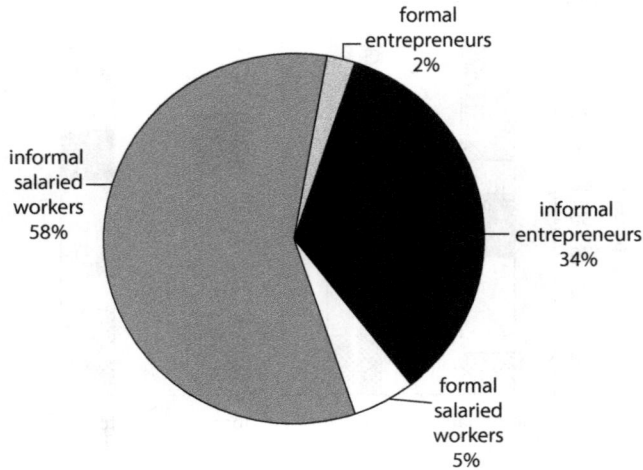

Source: Moroccan Enterprise Survey of micro-firms 2007. See description in the annex in chapter 2.
Note: Pie chart shows share of total work force in data set. Entrepreneurs are both self-employed and employers.

In Morocco, informal workers of micro-firms are a heterogeneous group, with informal salaried workers and entrepreneurs differing considerably with regard to age, gender, salary, and hours worked. The median informal salaried worker was 28 years old, male, had seven years of schooling, was not married and had no children, was paid weekly and received DH 6.9 ($0.83) per hour of work, worked 54 hours per week, and was most likely to be employed in manufacturing. The median informal entrepreneur was older (36 years old), male, had eight years of schooling, was married, was head of the household and had one child, received DH 7.9 ($1.00) per hour, worked 63 hours per week, and was most likely to work in the service sector. The median informal employer was 40 years old, male, had nine years of schooling, was married with two children, received DH 15.6 ($1.90) per hour, and worked 57 hours a week (table 3.6).

Looking beyond averages, variability in labor earnings among informal workers of micro-firms in Morocco is high, reflecting significant heterogeneity. Only 8 percent of all salaried workers are in the highest hourly wage quintile, and the rest are uniformly distributed among the other quintiles (figure 3.26). The self-employed category is likely to cover a variety of workers; most are in the two lowest and highest quintiles, and

Table 3.6   Informal Employment in Micro-Firms in Morocco

	Salaried worker		Self-employed		Employer	
	Mean	Median	Mean	Median	Mean	Median
Age	29.8	28	39.5	36	42.0	40
Female	23.9%		12.0%		16.9%	
Education (years)	7.3	7	8.6	8	8.2	9
Married	26.3%		64.0%		76.9%	
Number of children	0.6	0	1.6	1	2.5	2
Head of household	34.5%		68.0%		72.9%	
Paid daily	13.5%		50.0%		61.5%	
Paid weekly	54.6%		5.0%		13.5%	
Paid every two weeks	1.7%		0.0%		0.0%	
Paid every month	30.1%		45.0%		25.0%	
Hourly wage	8.1	6.9	9.1	7.9	19.3	15.6
Weekly hours worked	55.5	54	62.1	63	57.4	57
Manufacturing	40.9%		16.0%		35.6%	
Construction	12.0%		4.0%		13.6%	
Trade	14.9%		32.0%		16.1%	
Services	32.2%		48.0%		34.7%	

Source: Silva and others 2010.

Figure 3.26   Distribution of Workers by Hourly Wage Quintile in Micro-Firms in Morocco

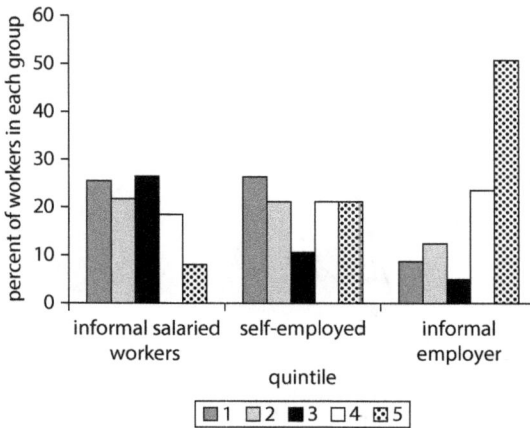

Source: Silva and others 2010.

about 10 percent are in the middle quintile. This may indicate an even distribution of successful (higher earning) and less successful self-employed workers. Employers are highly concentrated in the higher earnings quintiles; more than 50 percent of all employers earn an hourly wage in the top quintile of the hourly earnings distribution. The distribution of hourly earnings of formal salaried workers has two peaks, with a small group of formal salaried workers earning high wages. The distribution of earnings of informal entrepreneurs (self-employed and employers) is more dispersed and skewed to the right than that of both formal and informal salaried workers (figure 3.27).

Informal salaried workers differ considerably from formal salaried workers: They are significantly younger (mostly between 25 and 29 years old), less educated, have lower hourly wages, and are significantly more likely to be paid weekly. Figure 3.28 shows the distribution of workers' age by job status among informal workers in micro-firms. Salaried workers are highly concentrated between the ages of 25 and 29 years old. Although the distribution of employers is more dispersed than those of salaried workers, they tend to be older (concentrated around the age of 40). Similarly the largest age group of the self-employed is between 30 and 39 years old, with a second peak around age 60+, mainly following early retirement. Beyond differing in age, informal

Figure 3.27   Distribution of Hourly Earnings of Workers in Micro-Firms in Morocco

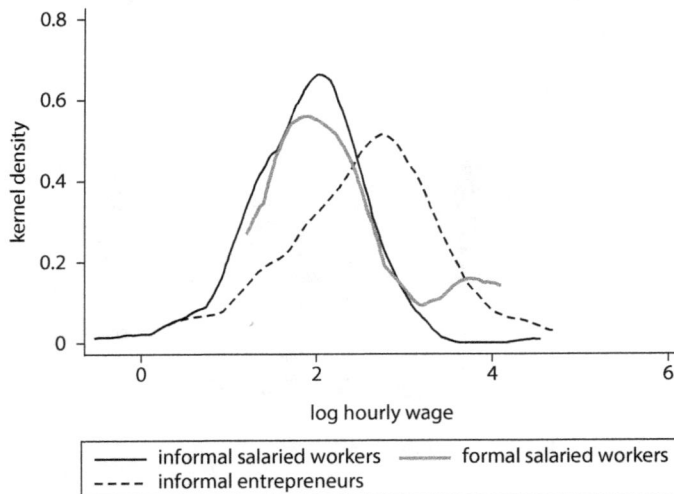

Source: Silva and others 2010.

Figure 3.28   Distribution of Workers' Age, by Type of Informal Employment

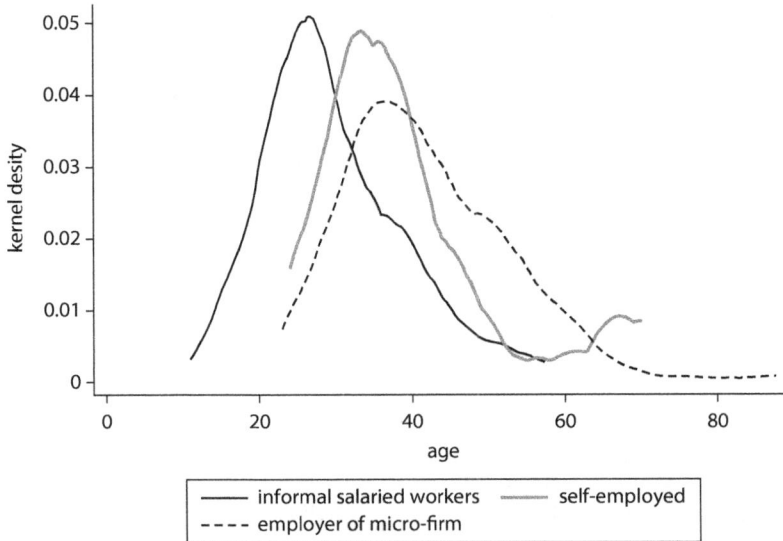

Source: Silva and others 2010.

salaried workers differ considerably from formal salaried workers in other dimensions: A significantly lower share have postsecondary education and lower hourly wages and are significantly more likely to be paid weekly (table 3.7).

The evidence from micro firms in Morocco suggests that labor informality might in itself be a way to cope with vulnerability and the need for flexible work arrangements. Silva and others (2010) show that in micro-firms in Morocco, the characteristics of workers that most strongly correlate with informal employment are household size and being a married woman. Gender is the sole systematic determinant of hours worked, with women working fewer hours than men. Besides being systematically related to age and education, wages of informal workers rise with the number of children and household size, and tend to be higher for the head of the household. Firms' characteristics play an important role in wage determination, particularly labor productivity and, to a lesser extent, size. Finally, in micro-firms, a significant wage (or hours worked) premium does not seem to exist between formal and informal salaried workers. Among informal workers, entrepreneurs command higher earnings.

Holding gender, owner's age, marital status, and education constant, owners of registered firms in Morocco are 8.3 to 20 percent more likely

Table 3.7 Differences between Informal and Formal Salaried Workers in Micro-Firms in Morocco

	Salaried worker	
	Informal	Formal
	Mean	Mean
Age	29.8***	34.5
Female	23.9%	31.8%
Married	26.3%	31.8%
Number of children	0.6	0.9
Head of household	34.5%	45.5%
Education (years)	7.3	8.8
Primary education or less	47.5%	36.4%
Secondary education	39.3%	31.8%
Postsecondary education	13.2%**	31.8%
Hourly wage	8.1***	14.7
Weekly hours worked	55.5	60.0
Paid daily	13.5%	9.1%
Weekly	54.6%***	4.5%
Every two weeks	1.7%	0.0%
Every month	30.1%***	86.4%

Source: Silva and others 2010.
Note: Asterisks indicate statistical significance of mean differences.
*$p<.10$, **$p<.05$, ***$p<.01$.

to indicate that they earn a good income from their activity than their peers who own unregistered firms of the same sector, region, age, and size (see figure 3.29 and Silva and others 2010).[15]

Informality as countercyclical employment for those out of work. Among micro-firms in Morocco, one-fourth of firm owners were unemployed before starting their business. This suggests that this type of entrepreneurship might often be a choice of last resort.

Micro-firms in Morocco operate with relatively low product margins. Among micro-firms there, the median sales margin on products is about 15 percent. Figure 3.30 shows the average cost share in micro-firms' expenditures. Human resources and production materials constitute the largest shares with 42.1 percent and 29.4 percent, respectively. The expenditure share on the rent of machines is much smaller (12.2 percent), but distinctively larger than the energy and communication expenditure shares. For labor and production materials, informal firms might have a cost advantage over formal firms, because informal labor and acquisitions without a receipt are usually not subject to taxes, leading to lower production costs.

Figure 3.29   Likelihood of Earning "Satisfactory Income" in Registered versus Unregistered Micro-Firms in Morocco

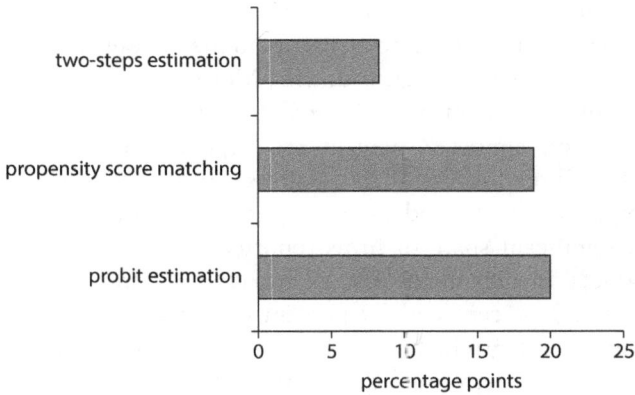

Sources: Silva and others 2010 and calculations using Morocco Enterprise Survey of micro-firms 2007.

Figure 3.30   Cost Categories among Micro-Firms in Morocco

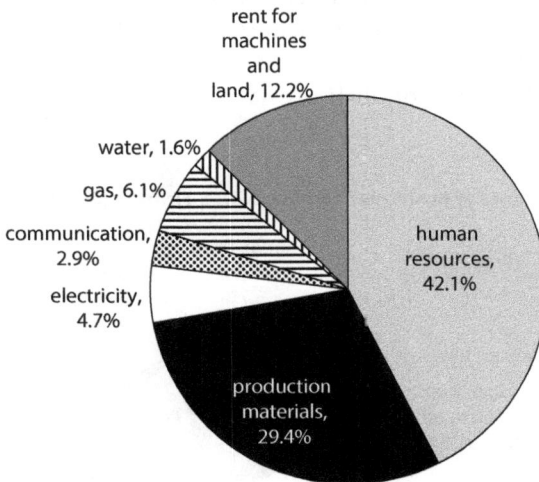

Source: ICA survey on sample of micro- and informal firms in Morocco 2007.
Note: Pie chart shows average cost shares of firms in data set.

On the revenue side, Moroccan micro-firms' sales mainly target local markets and are not subject to taxes. Over 80 percent of their sales are directed to the local market; of the remaining sales, 12.5 percent goes to the regional market, nearly 5 percent goes to the national market, and less than 1 percent goes to foreign countries. Moroccan consumers make up 87 percent of their client base; 9 percent of clients are other Moroccan micro-firms, and almost 2 percent are large Moroccan firms (annex table 3A.6.). Three-fourths of micro-firms report that they do not provide receipts to clients, and only 49 percent report that they accept checks. A significant share of firms reported innovating and improving their products' quality in the last 12 months in response to increasing competition: 30 percent and 19 percent of firms reported introducing new products and production processes, respectively, and 40 percent indicated they had performed quality upgrades. Notably, as many as 77 percent reported being recently forced to either reduce price or sales to respond to increasing competition (annex table 3A.6).

Among micro–informal firms in Morocco, financing is also mainly informal. Financing of micro-firms in Morocco depends heavily on internal financing (such as savings before starting the business) and amounts to an average of 84 percent of all investment (figure 3.31). On average, each firm mobilizes as little as 1.4 percent of its total resources from bank credit; fewer than 13 percent of all firms have ever demanded a bank credit.

Figure 3.31   Sources of Investment among Micro-Firms in Morocco

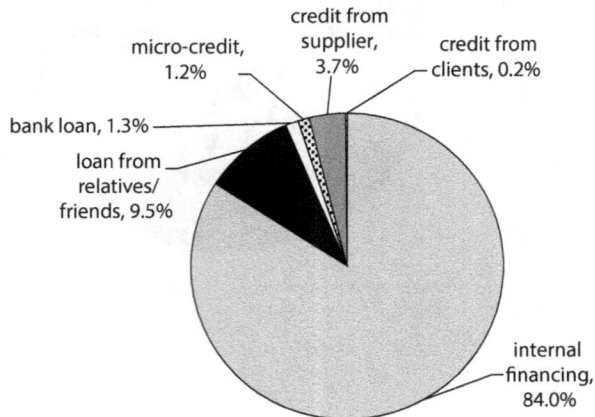

Source: Moroccan Enterprise Survey of micro-firms 2007.
Note: Pie chart illustrates average shares of firms' sources of investment.

Striving for Better Jobs • http://dx.doi.org/10.1596/978-0-8213-9535-6

Figure 3.32   Obstacles to Credit Requests among Micro-Firms in Morocco

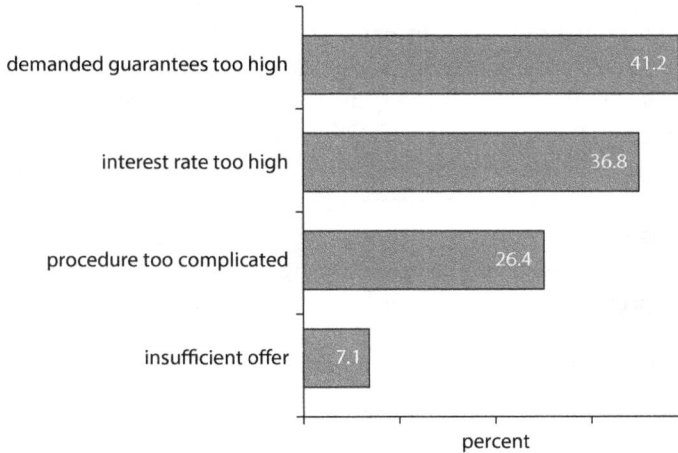

Source: Moroccan Enterprise Survey of micro-firms 2007.
Note: Limited to firms not requesting credit; bars show the share of firms identifying a constraint.

This is not surprising given that 79 percent of owners indicated they do not have a business bank account, and 62 percent do not have separate household and firm expenses. Firms indicated that high guarantees were the main obstacle for requesting credit (41 percent of firms), followed by the high level of interest rate (37 percent) and complicated procedures (26 percent) (figure 3.32).

Conclusions

Chapter 3 characterizes informality among firms and their workers. The main findings are fourfold. First, informality is prevalent among firms in MENA. Many firms never formalize, and even those that eventually register still operate informally for a significant amount of time. MENA's micro- and small firms are mostly not registered and typically do not pay social security contributions for their employees. Larger, registered firms, although operating within the broad regulatory framework, do not report up to one-fifth of their sales and workforce to the tax and social security agencies, respectively. The region has the world's highest share of firms that start out as informal (one-fourth) and has the longest operating period before formalization (four years) among firms with more than 20 workers.

Striving for Better Jobs • http://dx.doi.org/10.1596/978-0-8213-9535-6

Firms in MENA report that business regulations (taxes, entry regulation, and tax and labor regulation) are an important determinant of informality. Informal firms identify compliance costs and, in particular, the fiscal burden of taxes as the most significant constraint to formalization and, vice versa, the fact that registration became mandatory (as opposed to advantageous) as the main reason for formalizing. In the region and, in particular in economies such as Algeria, Djibouti, Iraq, and Tunisia and the West Bank and Gaza economy, a large opportunity exists for simplification of entry regulations. International evidence indicates that this may enhance employment creation through establishment of new formal firms by previously salaried workers. In contrast, a response based on increasing enforcement might have important limitations, because MENA already has the world's highest average number of inspections reported by registered firms over the last 12 months, and in more than 15 percent of cases these are reported to be accompanied by requests for informal payments. Firms that reported labor regulations to be a severe or very severe obstacle to their business are consistently more likely to underreport their workforce and their sales. Enforcement matters too: More frequent inspection is associated with less informality. However, corruption, also prevalent, reduces the effectiveness of inspections in curbing informality.

Among registered firms, worker underreporting is heterogeneous and appears to be a reflection of firm characteristics, in particular size, manager's education, and labor productivity. These variables are all strong correlates of worker underreporting. In particular, all else equal, an increase in firm size is associated with lower underreporting, even among similar firms (that is, with the same sector, location, or age). Specifically, among similar firms, doubling firm size is associated with a reduction in worker underreporting of more than 5 percentage points in Jordan and the Republic of Yemen, and roughly half of those effects in Syria and Egypt. In addition, at the firm level, the manager's and workers' education are strong predictors of a firm's level of registration, particularly in Lebanon, Egypt, and Syria. Furthermore, low firm productivity and high worker informality are strongly correlated among registered firms in MENA. For example, doubling labor productivity is associated with a 2 to 3 percentage point reduction in firms' underreporting in economies such as Jordan and Syria and the West Bank and Gaza economy.[16] Panel data confirm statistical significance of the effects of size, productivity, and manager's education. More informal firms are also somewhat less connected (for example, a lower share have e-mail and a Web site) and less likely to belong to a business network. Importantly, they are also less likely to offer training to workers than their formal counterparts.

Among informal small and micro-firms in MENA countries, the quality and determinants of employment are heterogeneous. Small informal firms appear to offer satisfactory opportunities for entrepreneurs but lower quality jobs to informal salaried workers, who are young, likely to work long hours, and earn a relatively low hourly wage. These workers are employed in jobs with high turnover rates and are often related to the entrepreneur. In Moroccan micro-firms, only 8 percent of all salaried workers are in the highest hourly wage quintile, and the rest are uniformly distributed among the other wage quintiles. Moreover, the two characteristics of workers that most strongly correlate with informal employment are household size and being a married woman. Gender is the sole systematic determinant of number of hours worked, with women working fewer hours. Wages of informal workers rise with the number of children and household size and tend to be higher for the head of the household. These results suggest that labor informality might in itself be a way to cope with vulnerability and the need for flexible work arrangements.

In summary, in MENA, although many firms stay informal, those that eventually register still operate informally for a significant amount of time. Compliance costs and entry regulations seem to be at the root of the problem, as is corruption. Worker underreporting is heterogeneous among registered firms and appears to be correlated with some characteristics of MENA firms, in particular size, manager's education, and labor productivity. Among informal small and micro-firms, only a minority of all workers are covered by social security. Micro- and small firms provide employment to young and unskilled workers, and opportunities to unemployed or informally employed salaried workers who might later decide to become entrepreneurs themselves.

Annex

Annex Table 3A.1 Informality Profile among Firms

Variable	All			Egypt, Arab Rep. (2008)			Jordan (2006)		
	% of sample	% workers under-reporting	% sales under-reporting	% of sample	% workers under-reporting	% sales under-reporting	% of sample	% workers under-reporting	% sales under-reporting
Workers underreporting	19			12			6		
Sales underreporting	20			14			13		
Firm size (employees)									
0–10					23				
11–14	32	24.8	24.4	25	18.8	18.9	26	12.8	13.5
15–49	33	18.6	19.0	33	12.3	13.4	34	5.3	7.9
50–99	12	19.0	20.2	11	13.0	16.3	15	2.6	8.9
100–249	12	15.3	17.2	13	9.4	11.3	14	3.2	16.0
250+	12	7.3	12.9	18	5.2	8.3	12	0.0	24.6
Firm's age									
0–5	15	19.9	20.1	10	14.7	13.8	31	7.3	15.8
6–10	19	20.5	20.0	17	14.0	14.3	21	10.3	10.9
11+	66	18.0	19.7	73	11.6	13.8	48	3.1	11.4
Sector									
Manufacturing	65	18.5	20.0	69	11.7	13.7	70	4.8	13.7
Service	24	15.9	16.0	28	12.0	12.4	23	7.5	9.0
Construction	5	21.0	23.6	3	31.0	34.6	7	11.0	13.2
Trade	7	33.9	33.0						
Sales per worker (log, PPP)									
1st tertile	33	20.7	20.9	38	13.4	13.4	10	12.5	22.7
2nd tertile	33	18.1	19.6	34	12.3	14.1	44	6.8	11.5
3rd tertile	33	17.5	19.1	28	10.7	14.2	46	4.0	12.1
Loan	19			11			30		
Manager's education									
Less than secondary	11	34.3	43.6	6	20.4	24.6			
Secondary	14	24.0	23.9	11	16.3	12.6			
Postsecondary	75	13.0	15.4	83	11.2	13.3			
Manager's experience									
0–3	16	11.6	13.1	28	11.2	11.3	9	9.8	28.6
4–10	28	17.8	20.6	33	14.4	17.3	30	5.0	12.5
11+	56	21.8	21.7	39	11.2	12.7	61	5.7	10.1
Workforce education									
Less than secondary	38	21.0	21.0	30	12.3	10.6			
Secondary	41	16.9	16.9	49	11.8	16.1			
Postsecondary	21	17.4	17.4	21	12.8	14.9			
Labor regulatory obstacle	25			26			15		
Labor inspections	3			5					
Bribing _ labor inspections	12			7					
Nonresp. _ labor inspections	36			6					
Nonresp. _ bribing labor inspections	38			12					
Tax obstacle	46			46			52		
Tax inspections	3			3			2		
Bribing _ tax inspections	14			5			40		
Nonresp. _ tax inspections	24			10			18		
Nonresp. _ bribing tax inspections	16			10			2		

Source: Calculations using individual country ICA survey data for MENA economies that included the questions: "What percentage of the workforce would you estimate the typical establishment in your sector reports to social security" and "What percentage of total sales would you estimate the typical establishment in your sector reports for tax purposes?

Syrian Arab Republic (2009)			Yemen, Rep. (2010)			Lebanon (2009)			West Bank and Gaza economy (2006)		
% of sample	% workers under-reporting	% sales under-reporting	% of sample	% workers under-reporting	% sales under-reporting	% of sample	% workers under-reporting	% sales under-reporting	% of sample	% workers under-reporting	% sales under-reporting
43			43			14			14		
34			52			18			13		
26	46.4	31.6	52	50.7	59.2	36	11.5	16.1	46	17.6	13.7
30	48.0	39.3	25	49.1	51.5	36	16.7	21.2	38	11.5	12.0
18	47.2	34.6	11	19.1	34.5	13	11.8	13.6	9	14.1	15.6
16	38.0	31.8	7	33.6	44.0	9	11.9	10.4	5	12.5	10.8
10	24.0	26.0	5	9.7	19.9	6	14.3	19.7	2	4.2	0.0
18	44.7	36.2	12	41.4	44.0	8	16.5	15.3	18	15.2	13.1
15	45.9	38.8	25	43.6	47.9	13	10.5	11.0	30	15.0	13.1
67	42.3	32.0	62	43.3	53.9	79	14.3	19.0	52	13.8	12.6
69	43.6	36.8	51	45.6	55.6	37	19.8	25.8	81	15.2	12.4
20	39.6	24.6	18	37.1	50.4	31	9.4	11.2	12	9.8	13.4
2	46.4	49.8	1	0.0	2.5	12	16.0	16.7	7	13.8	17.9
9	48.4	28.7	30	45.3	48.7	20	10.1	14.5	0		
22	43.0	35.1	48	44.3	54.0	48	14.2	14.5	26	27.1	24.0
24	48.5	36.4	35	44.3	52.0	9	22.8	29.7	48	10.3	10.3
54	41.1	32.1	17	38.4	46.0	43	11.5	18.1	26	9.7	6.5
15			12			53			18		
			36	49.5	61.5	2	27.8	46.1			
			28	46.7	50.9	12	13.5	22.7			
			36	34.5	41.8	86	13.2	15.9			
2	23.6	15.6	3	57.0	66.6	27	10.1	12.4	3	5.7	4.3
17	47.7	38.1	23	41.0	45.5	27	13.5	19.1	21	12.6	16.7
81	42.9	33.4	74	43.7	53.4	45	17.7	19.9	76	15.4	12.3
70	44.3	34.0				25	26.7	25.8			
12	43.1	30.4				49	10.8	15.9			
19	36.6	33.9				26	4.7	8.5			
49			10			36			12		
4			2			0					
53			18			4					
23			0			76					
24			1			74					
42			43			59			37		
3			6			1			2		
46			45			8			1		
24			21			58			63		
25			23			56			0		

Annex Table 3A.2   Underreporting, Firm Size, and Productivity

	All economies			
	Tobit (censored), marginal effects		Seemingly unrelated regression	
	(1)	(2)	(3)	(4)
Variable	Workers	Sales	Workers	Sales
Size: 15–49 (over 10–14)	−2.076	−1.107	−3.862	−2.971
	[0.000]***	[0.028]**	[0.001]***	[0.023]**
Size: 50–99	−3.178	−1.617	−6.549	−4.66
	[0.000]***	[0.018]**	[0.000]***	[0.008]***
Size: 100–249	−4.128	−2.385	−8.967	−6.218
	[0.000]***	[0.001]***	[0.000]***	[0.000]***
Size: 250+	−7.532	−3.684	−14.514	−7.946
	[0.000]***	[0.000]***	[0.000]***	[0.000]***
Log size				
Productivity	−7.166	−3.007	−7.557	−1.882
(log sales/worker, PPP)	[0.000]***	[0.000]***	[0.000]***	[0.274]
Country dummies	Y	Y	Y	Y
Year dummies	N	N	N	N
Firm effects	N	N	N	N
Cluster firm-level	N	N	N	N
Governorate dummies	N	N	N	N
Sector dummies	Y	Y	Y	Y
Observations (N)	3,547	3,525	3,453	3,453
No. of firms	1,623	1,617	1,617	1,617
R^2 or pseudo-R^2	0.046	0.028	0.2133	0.1265

Source: Calculations using ICA survey data for MENA economies.

Note: Columns 1 and 2 were estimated using Tobit (censored). Although in column 1 the dependent variable was the share of workers underreported to social security, in column 2 the dependent variable is the share of sales underreported for tax purposes. Marginal effects are reported throughout. Columns 3 and 4 were jointly estimated, using seemingly unrelated regressions. Column 5 uses pooled data for Egypt covering the three waves of data (2004, 2007, and 2008) and including year dummies. Columns 6, 7, and 8 use panel data for Egypt for 2004, 2007, and 2008. Columns 6 and 7 have the share of workers underreporting as a dependent variable. Results in column 6 were estimated using firm-fixed effects in a linear probability model, and results in column 7 were estimated using firm-random effects in a censored Tobit model. The dependent variable in column 8 was the share of sales underreported. Results were estimated using a censored Tobit model. Columns 1 to 4 include control for firm age.

p values in brackets. *significant at 10 percent; **significant at 5 percent; ***significant at 1 percent.

Egypt panel			
Pooled	Panel		
(5)	(6)	(7)	(8)
Workers	Workers		Sales

−2.781	−2.085	−1.895	−1.472
[0.000]***	[0.001]***	[0.000]***	[0.000]***
−0.775	−1.324	−0.524	−0.451
[0.002]***	[0.008]***	[0.002]***	[0.006]***
N	N	N	N
Y	Y	Y	Y
N	FIXED	RANDOM	RANDOM
N	Y	N	N
Y	N	Y	Y
Y	N	Y	Y
3,022	3,028	3,028	3,022
1,623	1,623	1,623	1,617
0.018	0.028		

Annex Table 3A.3   Underreporting and Manager's Education

	All economies			
	Tobit (censored), Marginal effects		Seemingly unrelated regression	
	(1)	(2)	(3)	(4)
Variable	Workers	Sales	Workers	Sales
Size: 15–49 (over 10–14)	−1.949	−1.247	−4.133	−3.156
	[0.012]**	[0.089]*	[0.004]***	[0.074]*
Size: 50–99	−1.961	−0.983	−3.656	−2.311
	[0.070]*	[0.334]	[0.069]*	[0.345]
Size: 100–249	−3.38	−3.03	−6.928	−7.194
	[0.001]***	[0.003]***	[0.000]***	[0.002]***
Size: 250+	−5.878	−4.412	−10.41	−8.271
	[0.000]***	[0.000]***	[0.000]***	[0.000]***
Log size				
Productivity	−0.0512	0.133	−0.218	0.185
(log sales/worker, PPP)	[0.595]	[0.141]	[0.205]	[0.376]
Secondary education	−2.63	−3.765	−4.772	−13.29
(base: less than secondary)	[0.065]*	[0.005]***	[0.092]*	[0.000]***
Postsecondary education	−2.695	−3.392	−4.925	−9.992
	[0.045]**	[0.007]***	[0.052]*	[0.001]***
Manager's years	0.0236	0.0611	0.0523	0.117
of managerial experience	[0.451]	[0.037]**	[0.350]	[0.085]*
Worker education: secondary	−2.202	1.142	−5.138	5.044
(base: less than secondary)	[0.115]	[0.378]	[0.045]**	[0.106]
Worker education: postsecondary	−6.216	−3.848	−9.545	−4.889
	[0.000]***	[0.014]**	[0.001]***	[0.167]
Country dummies	Y	Y	Y	Y
Year dummies	N	N	N	N
Firm effects	N	N	N	N
Cluster firm-level	N	N	N	N
Governorate dummies	N	N	N	N
Sector dummies	Y	Y	Y	Y
Observations (N)	1,801	1,790	1,782	1,782
No. of firms	1,801	1,790	1,782	1,782
R^2 or pseudo-R^2	0.012	0.010	0.046	0.036

Source: Calculations using ICA survey data for MENA economies.
Note: Columns 1 and 2 were estimated using Tobit (censored). In column 1 the dependent variable was the share of workers underreported to social security, but in column 2 the dependent variable is the share of sales underreported for tax purposes. Marginal effects are reported throughout. Columns 3 and 4 were jointly estimated, using seemingly unrelated regressions. Columns 5, 6, 7, and 8 use panel data for Egypt for 2004, 2007, and 2008. The dependent variable (columns 5 and 7) is the share of workers underreported, whereas in columns 6 and 8 it is the share of sales underreported. Results in columns 5 and 6 were estimated using firm-fixed effects in a linear probability model, and results in column 7 and 8 were estimated using firm-random effects in a censored Tobit model. Columns 1 to 4 include control for firm age.
p values in brackets; *significant at 10 percent; **significant at 5 percent; ***significant at 1 percent.

Egypt panel			
Linear probability model		Censored Tobit	
(5)	(6)	(7)	(8)
Workers	Sales	Workers	Sales
−1.535	−1.349	−1.628	−1.325
[0.021]**	[0.099]*	[0.000]***	[0.000]***
−1.172	−0.281	−0.444	−0.364
[0.022]**	[0.606]	[0.012]**	[0.031]**
−7.364	−11.005	−1.551	−1.713
[0.042]**	[0.003]***	[0.100]*	[0.062]*
−9.591	−11.024	−2.834	−1.905
[0.003]***	[0.001]***	[0.002]***	[0.026]**
−0.163	−0.092	−0.065	−0.029
[0.014]**	[0.198]	[0.004]***	[0.182]
4.424	10.989	0.551	2.38
[0.183]	[0.002]***	[0.614]	[0.024]**
5.84	1.382	−1.767	−4.009
[0.290]	[0.823]	[0.340]	[0.026]**
N	N	N	N
Y	Y	Y	Y
FIXED	FIXED	RANDOM	RANDOM
Y	Y	N	N
N	N	Y	Y
N	N	Y	Y
2,999	2,993	2,999	2,993
1,613	1,607	1,613	1,607
0.039	0.020		

Annex Table 3A.4 Underreporting, Regulations, Enforcement, and Corruption

| | All economies: pooled | | | |
| | Workers | | | |
Variable	(1)	(2)	(3)	(4)
Size: 15–49 (over 10–14)	−2.031	−2.031	−1.993	−1.995
	[0.000]***	[0.000]***	[0.000]***	[0.000]***
Size: 50–99	−3.216	−3.198	−3.179	−3.221
	[0.000]***	[0.000]***	[0.000]***	[0.000]***
Size: 100–249	−4.229	−4.25	−4.203	−4.212
	[0.000]***	[0.000]***	[0.000]***	[0.000]***
Size: 250+	−7.21	−7.205	−7.203	−7.172
	[0.000]***	[0.000]***	[0.000]***	[0.000]***
log size				
Productivity (log sales/worker, PPP)	−0.105	−0.106	−0.104	−0.102
	[0.074]*	[0.072]*	[0.077]*	[0.083]*
Regulation obstacle	2.253	2.56	2.212	0.566
	[0.000]***	[0.000]***	[0.000]***	[0.462]
Inspections (log)	−0.833	−0.829	−1.222	−1.416
	[0.027]**	[0.028]**	[0.005]***	[0.001]***
Bribe inspectors	2.632	3.269	0.451	2.458
	[0.000]***	[0.000]***	[0.743]	[0.001]***
Nonresponse bribe inspectors	5.514	5.541	5.023	5.257
	[0.000]***	[0.000]***	[0.000]***	[0.000]***
Regulation obst_bribe		−1.437		
		[0.231]		
Inspections*bribe			1.488	
			[0.065]*	
Regulation obst*insp.				1.565
				[0.003]***
Country dummies	Y	Y	Y	Y
Sector dummies	Y	Y	Y	Y
Location dummies	Y	Y	Y	Y
Firm random effects	N	N	N	N
Observations (N)	3,537	3,537	3,537	3,537
Pseudo-R^2	0.0508	0.0509	0.0510	0.0513

Source: Calculations using ICA survey data for Egypt 2004, 2007, and 2008.
Note: Columns 1 to 8 were estimated using Tobit (censored) using pooled data for Egypt with year dummies. Columns 6 to 8 use the panel dimension of the data with firm-random effects. In columns 1 to 4 and 9 to 10, the dependent variable was the share of workers underreported to social security, but in columns 5 to 8 and 11 the dependent variable is the share of sales underreported for tax purposes. Marginal effects are reported throughout. Columns 1 to 4 include control for firm age.
p values in brackets; *significant at 10 percent; **significant at 5 percent; ***significant at 1 percent.

	All economies: pooled				Panel		
	Sales				Workers		Sales
	(5)	(6)	(7)	(8)	(9)	(10)	(11)
	−0.992 [0.052]*	−0.966 [0.060]*	−1.003 [0.050]*	−0.966 [0.060]*			
	−1.620 [0.020]**	−1.574 [0.024]**	−1.636 [0.019]**	−1.574 [0.024]**			
	−2.17 [0.003]***	−2.156 [0.003]***	−2.204 [0.002]***	−2.156 [0.003]***			
	−3.826 [0.000]***	−3.75 [0.000]***	−3.87 [0.000]***	−3.75 [0.000]***			
					−1.651 [0.000]***	−1.626 [0.000]***	−1.542 [0.000]***
	−0.0721 [0.196]	−0.0726 [0.193]	−0.0697 [0.212]	−0.0726 [0.193]	−0.551 [0.003]***	−0.554 [0.003]***	−0.396 [0.025]**
	1.152 [0.007]***	1.76 [0.000]***	1.124 [0.008]***	1.76 [0.000]***	3.141 [0.000]***	3.128 [0.000]***	2.113 [0.037]**
	0.546 [0.115]	0.537 [0.122]	0.913 [0.029]**	0.537 [0.122]	−1.232 [0.001]***	−0.779 [0.069]*	0.018 [0.972]
	2.716 [0.000]***	4.554 [0.000]***	4.282 [0.000]***	4.554 [0.000]***	1.714 [0.018]**	5.612 [0.002]***	−0.151 [0.830]
	0.145 [0.854]	0.116 [0.884]	0.386 [0.633]	0.116 [0.884]	−2.742 [0.389]	−2.787 [0.380]	1.023 [0.746]
		−3.256 [0.002]***					
			−1.104 [0.116]				
				−3.256 [0.002]***		−2.226 [0.016]**	−0.609 [0.321]
	Y	Y	Y	Y	N	N	N
	Y	Y	Y	Y	Y	Y	Y
	Y	Y	Y	Y	Y	Y	Y
	N	N	N	N	Y	Y	Y
	3,483	3,483	3,483	3,483	2,696	2,696	2,713
	0.0321	0.0327	0.0323	0.0327			

Annex Table 3A.5 The Effect of Firm Size and Productivity on the Association between Regulations and Underreporting

	X = Regulation			X = Inpections		
	MENA countries: pooled	Egypt panel		MENA countries: pooled	Egypt panel	
		Linear probility model	Censored Tobit		Linear probility model	Censored Tobit
Variable	(1)	(2)	(3)	(4)	(5)	(6)
Regulatory obstacle	−0.745	15.428	7.332	2.276	8.317	2.972
	[0.568]	[0.016]**	[0.001]***	[0.000]***	[0.000]***	[0.000]***
Inspections (log)	−0.833	−3.606	−1.335	−1.93	−3.778	−2.925
	[0.028]**	[0.002]***	[0.000]***	[0.007]***	[0.334]	[0.018]**
Bribes	2.549	3.88	2.444	2.441	3.933	2.492
	[0.001]***	[0.100]	[0.001]***	[0.001]***	[0.097]*	[0.001]***
Nonresponse bribes	5.481	5.37	−0.875	5.212	5.513	−0.718
	[0.000]***	[0.556]	[0.749]	[0.000]***	[0.548]	[0.795]
X_size15_49	0.224			−1.237		
	[0.852]			[0.047]**		
X_size50_99	3.049			−0.474		
	[0.065]*			[0.564]		
X_size100_249	1.521			−1.256		
	[0.363]			[0.137]		
X_size250+	0.492			0.367		
	[0.802]			[0.681]		
X_size		−1.624	−1.008		0.103	0.095
		[0.128]	[0.008]***		[0.875]	[0.692]
X_productivity	0.282	−0.268	−0.043	0.212	−0.054	0.33
	[0.016]**	[0.813]	[0.905]	[0.000]***	[0.947]	[0.185]
Country dummies	Y	N	N	Y	N	N
Sector dummies	Y	N	N	Y	N	N
Firm effects	N	Y-F	Y-R	N	Y-F	Y-R
Observations (N)	3,537	2,696	2,696	3,537	2,696	2,696
Pseudo-R^2	0.0514	0.052		0.052	0.051	

Note: Columns 1, 4, 7, and 10 include control for firm size, age, sector, location dummies and year dummies; and columns 2–3, 5–6, 8–9, and 11–12 include control for firm size and age, and year dummies.

p values in brackets; *significant at 10 percent; **significant at 5 percent; ***significant at 1 percent.

Y-F stands for firm fixed effects and Y-R stands for firm random effects.

	X = Bribes			X = Nonresponse labor bribe		
	MENA countries: pooled	*Egypt panel*		*MENA countries: pooled*	*Egypt panel*	
		Linear probability model	*Censored Tobit*		*Linear probability model*	*Censored Tobit*
	(7)	*(8)*	*(9)*	*(10)*	*(11)*	*(12)*
	2.233	8.229	2.92	2.269	8.352	2.982
	[0.000]***	[0.000]***	[0.000]***	[0.000]***	[0.000]***	[0.000]***
	−0.823	−3.592	−1.326	−0.762	−3.588	−1.329
	[0.03]**	[0.003]***	[0.000]***	[0.046]**	[0.003]***	[0.000]***
	−0.2	12.864	9.352	2.468	3.994	2.511
	[0.907]	[0.130]	[0.002]***	[0.001]***	[0.092]*	[0.001]***
	5.529	5.233	−0.776	7.044	4.358	−4.59
	[0.000]***	[0.568]	[0.778]	[0.000]***	[0.902]	[0.605]
	0.57			1.574		
	[0.716]			[0.169]		
	3.28			1.699		
	[0.09]*			[0.289]		
	2.817			1.896		
	[0.161]			[0.258]		
	2.78			1.893		
	[0.245]			[0.348]		
		−0.867	−0.564		4.878	1.699
		[0.628]	[0.289]		[0.175]	[0.311]
	0.17	−1.613	−1.055	−0.376	−5.713	−0.861
	[0.244]	[0.236]	[0.018]**	[0.001]***	[0.362]	[0.655]
	Y	N	N	Y	N	N
	Y	N	N	Y	N	Y
	N	Y-F	Y-R	N	Y-F	Y-R
	3,537	2,696	2,696	3,537	2,696	2,696
	0.0512	0.052		0.0516	0.052	

Annex Table 3A.6 Description of Data Sources

Economy	Survey	Description
Egypt, Arab Rep.; Jordan; Syrian Arab Republic; Yemen, Rep.; Lebanon; West Bank and Gaza economy	Investment Climate Assessment (ICA) Surveys	Data from the World Bank Enterprise Survey repository, which assembles data from the ICA survey,[17] are used. The countries included were those where the ICA surveys asked questions about the percentage of sales and the percentage of workers that a typical firm of a specific sector would report for tax or social security purposes.[18] Information provided through this type of question has been widely used in the literature with consistent results. Informality is measured using the percentage of workers that firms do not report for social security purposes. Although the percentage of sales reported for tax purposes are also considered, the main focus in this report is on worker underreporting.
Morocco (2007)	Investment Climate Assessment Surveys of micro- and small firms	Survey of micro-firms with up to five workers in Morocco in 2007. These data include matched employer-employee information for 219 firms, 264 salaried workers, 127 employers, and 26 self-employed workers. All workers in each firm were interviewed in the context of this survey. Data cover the cities of Casablanca, Rabat, Salé, Témara, and Fès, which are located in urban and rural areas. Four sectors were chosen for the survey: manufacturing, construction, trade, and services. The survey covers all the key sectors of informal employment identified by the 2004 Morocco national survey on the nonagricultural informal sector (ENSINA): trade, services, construction, textile, clothes, and shoes. ENSINA indicates that these sectors employ 37 percent, 20 percent, 7 percent, and 50 percent of their workforce informally, respectively (Direction de la Statistique 2004; Alami 2008). It also indicates that entrepreneurship[19] forms an important part of the national informal sector by representing 69 percent of the total informal employment. These data consist of 219 firms and 417 individuals (264 salaried workers, 26 self-employed,[20] and 127 employers[21]). Summary statistics on firms, firm owners, and employees in the sample are presented below.
Egypt, Arab Rep. (2008)	Investment Climate Assessment Surveys of micro- and small firms	Survey of micro- and small firms in Egypt 2008. The survey covers 500 firms selected from a sample frame of 25,000 firms of the Center for Social Research at the American University of Cairo. Firms have up to 50 workers. This sample frame includes firms that are either unregistered or unlicensed or do not keep formal accounts. It covers eight governorates: Cairo, Alexandria, Damittra, Gharbia, Giza, Fayoum, Assuit, and Souhag. About 89 percent of firms in the sample have fewer than five employees; 115 of the sample have between 6 and 50 employees; 134 are manufacturing firms; and 366 are in services, including retail. Summary statistics on the sample are presented below.
Lebanon (2004); Egypt, Arab Rep. (2003); Morocco (2002)	Firm-level data collected by the Economic Research Forum (ERF) (MEAS)	Data from the ERF on surveys in Lebanon, Egypt and Morocco of small and medium enterprises with up to 50 workers. The sample for Egypt includes 4,958 firms, for Lebanon 2,948 firms, and for Morocco 5,210 firms. For a more detailed description of the data see Elbadawi and Loayza (2008).

Annex Table 3A.7 Descriptive Statistics on Moroccan Micro-Firms, Their Workers, and Their Owners

		Firms				Mean	Median
		Mean	Median				
General	Manufacturing	31%		Infrastructure and innovation	Owns computer	20%	
	Construction	7%			Has telephone service	31%	
	Trade	21%			Connected to public electricty	86%	
	Services	41%			Uses Internet	21%	
	Urban	66%			Improved quality within last year	40%	
	Suburban	33%			Introduced new product within last year	29%	
	Rural	2%			Introduced new materials within last year	16%	
					Location rented by firm	43%	
Firm characteristics	Age of firm (years)	10.19	7		Location owned by firm	50%	
	Permanent workers	1.92	2		Location is mobile	7%	
	Profit (DH)	5,756	1,850				
	Productivity	5,453	3,625	Market orientation	Local market (% of sales)	81%	
	Sales margin (%)	17.77	15		Regional market (% of sales)	13%	
					National market (% of sales)	5%	
	Invoices clients	25%			Export market (% of sales)	1%	
	Accepts checks	49%			Moroccan consumers (% of client base)	87%	
Finance	Has business bank account	21%			Moroccan micro-firms (% of client base)	9%	
	Requested bank credit in the past	13%			Large Moroccan firms (% client base)	2%	
					Quality problems with clients	7%	
	% of firm resources from bank credit	136%					

table continues next page

Annex Table 3A.7 Descriptive Statistics on Moroccan Micro-Firms, Their Workers, and Their Owners *(continued)*

Firms		
Competition	Mean	Median
Intense competition: informal producers	33%	
Intense competition: small and medium producers	36%	
Intense competition: large producers	31%	
Intense competition: imports	19%	
Impact of competition: forced to reduce price	25%	
Impact of competition: forced to reduce sales	18%	
Impact of competition: forced to reduce both	24%	
Impact of competiton: none	33%	

Firms		
Government	Mean	Median
Bribe as % of market to receive public market	32%	41%
Application of law is foreseeable and consistent	48%	
Bribe often expect by inspectors	43%	
Firm knows level of bribe expected in advance	31%	
% of sales devoted to bribes	11%	19%
Firm subject to inspections	46%	

Firms' Owners

	Mean	Median
Female owner	17%	
Education of owner (years)	8.63	9
Age of owner (years)	42.03	39
Owner is married	74%	
Number of children	2.45	2
Owner was previously unemployed	26%	
Household income for owner (DH)	4,109.62	3,500

Workers

	Mean	Median
Age (years)	30.17	28
Education (years)	7.46	7
Paid daily	13%	
Paid weekly	50%	
Paid every two weeks	2%	
Paid every month	35%	
Male	75%	
Hourly wage (DH)	8.71	7
Weekly hours of work	55.89	54
Married	27%	
Number of children	0.64	0
Employer himself	4%	
No relationship to employer	73%	
Married to employer	1%	
Child of employer	8%	
Sibling of employer	4%	
Parent of employer	2%	
Other blood relation to employer	8%	
Household income (DH)	3,141.26	3,000
Age of head of household	48.89	48
Size of household	8.00	5

Annex Table 3A.8 Descriptive Statistics on Egyptian Micro-Firms, Their Workers, and Their Owners

Small and micro-firms	Mean	Median
Micro- ≤ 5	89%	
Small >5	11%	
No. of employees	4	3
Industry sector	26.60%	
Trade sector	48.60%	

table continues next page

Annex Table 3A.8   Descriptive Statistics on Egyptian Micro-Firms, Their Workers, and Their Owners *(continued)*

Small and micro-firms	Mean	Median
Service sector	24.80%	
Urban Egypt, Arab Rep.	76.60%	
Lower Egypt, Arab Rep.	12.40%	
Upper Egypt, Arab Rep.	11.00%	
Age of firm	17	12
Sales (LE)	27,384	8,000
Productivity	7,835	2,498
Sales growth	−15.26%	−15.00%
Percent of sales not paid in 2004	4.85%	
Has checking account (0/1)	5.92%	
Number of visits by tax inspector	1.60	
Informal payment was expected by tax inspector (0/1)	4.38%	
Are skills and education of workers a constraint to growth?	27%	
In establishment, business activity varies by season	67%	
Percent of bank loan to total financing	2.95%	

Workers (%)	Mean
Share of workers with postsecondary education	16.89
Share of workers with secondary education	39.16
Share of workers with incomplete secondary education	11.49
Share of workers with complete primary education	6.88
Share of workers with incomplete primary education	25.58
Share of female employees	5.56
Share of relatives among employees	13.63
Lost production days due to strikes or absenteeism	8.40
Share of workers who left firm in the last 12 months	10.44

Firm owners (%)	Mean
Female owner	15
Education of owner/top manager	
Postsecondary education	29.40
Completed secondary education	35.20
Incomplete secondary education	5.20
Complete primary education	7.00
Incomplete primary education; no education	23.20
Age of the owner (years)	
Less than 21	0.40
21–30	11.42
31–40	29.46
41–50	28.66
51+	30.06
Manager had previous experience in formal firm (0/1)	9.60

Notes

1. See Oviedo (2008).

2. See La Porta and Shleifer (2008) for a recent review of this strand of the literature.

3. See Perry and others (2007) for a detailed description of these three viewpoints.

4. *Source:* World Development Indicators 2011 and calculation using ICSs.

5. See, for example, Asiedu and Freeman (2008), Chong and Gradstein (2006), Elbadawi and Loayza (2008), McKenzie and Sakho (2010), and World Bank (2009).

6. Informality may be chosen to avoid burdensome government regulations such as hiring and firing costs, government standards for products and production processes, and strict working hours and wages.

7. For example, impossibility of providing receipts to clients and risk of being caught.

8. For example, limited access to markets, formal financing, courts, or other forms of contract enforcement and government services.

9. For a more detailed analysis of the tax wedge see chapter 5. Note that for firms at the cusp of formalizing, factors such as how progressive the taxation system is (including income tax for individuals), and whether there are exemptions from taxes below a certain threshold, should be considered.

10. For more details, see Ramalho (2008).

11. Methodologically, in the regression analysis of worker underreporting, the dependent variable measures the share of the workforce that is not reported to social security; for sales underreporting, the dependent variable measures the share of sales that are not reported to the tax office. Following Johnson and others (2000), the presented results were estimated using censored estimation models (Tobit) to take into account the fact that sales and worker underreporting in MENA are left censored. Each estimation provides Tobit marginal effects at the censoring point, representing the marginal effect of each explanatory variable on the percent of sales or workers underreported, conditional on the probability that a firm is in the uncensored group (that is, an informal firm). The figures in the main text present the results of the country by country analysis. This analysis was complemented with cross-country and panel data analysis. The latter overcomes the issue of firm unobserved characteristics that might drive both shares of tax/social security reporting and other outcomes (for example, productivity). Sales and worker underreporting for tax purposes and social security have been widely used as proxy for informality (see, for example, Gatti and Honorati 2008; Johnson and others 2000; and Ingram and others

2007; Perry and others 2007). They are computed using the information from two questions: (1) "What percentage of total sales would you estimate the typical establishment in your sector reports for tax purposes?" and (2) "What do you think is the percentage of total workforce that is reported for purposes of labor regulation and social insurance in a typical establishment in your sector?"

12. Note that in MENA, the only countries where manager education and worker underreporting variables were collected in ICS surveys covering underreporting were Egypt, the Republic of Yemen, and Lebanon.

13. In contrast, in the Republic of Yemen, after controlling for firm size, changes in the manager's level of education are not significant correlated with worker underreporting. In fact, in the Republic of Yemen, firm size predicts almost perfectly the manager's level of education. For example, in small firms, 81 percent of managers have less than postsecondary education, whereas in large firms, fewer than 13 percent of managers are in this situation.

14. Lebanon's controls do not include location because of the unavailability of corresponding information in the survey data.

15. The two estimates are obtained from 2SLS and probit estimation techniques, respectively.

16. Note that this chapter is not arguing that being informal is causing firms to be less productive or to offer workers less protection. Formal firms might be more productive as a result of formalization, or just because they have more capital, use more technology, and have better skilled owners. Although some of these factors are controlled for and the findings tested for robustness using panel data, the results should not be interpreted as causal.

17. In this instance, a word of caution is necessary given that the collected information can indeed describe the incidence of informality on firms, but does not allow aggregates of informality over the entire population due to the lack of weighted data. Although the results might not be descriptive at the general level, they still remain indicative for the policy standpoint.

18. These questions are: "What percentage of total sales would you estimate the typical establishment in your sector reports for tax purposes?" and "What do you think is the percentage of total workforce that is reported for purposes of labor regulation and social insurance in a typical establishment in your sector?"

19. Defined as the job status of either self-employed or employer.

20. Firm owners who do not employ other workers are defined as self-employed.

21. Firm owners who employ other workers are defined as employers.

References

Alami, R. M. 2008. "Comment définir l'informel?" *La revue economia* 2 (Feb.): 80.

Almeida, R., and P. Carneiro. 2009. "Enforcement of Regulation, Informal Employment, Firm Size and Firm Performance." *Journal of Comparative Economics* 37 (1): 28–46.

Angel-Urdinola, D., and A. Kuddo. 2010. "Key Characteristics of Employment Regulation in the Middle East and North Africa." SP Discussion Paper 1006. Washington, DC: World Bank.

Asiedu, E., and J. Freeman. 2008. "The Effect of Corruption on Investment Growth: Evidence from Firms in Latin America, Sub-Saharan Africa and Transition Countries." Working Papers in Theoretical and Applied Economics 2008/02. Lawrence: University of Kansas, Department of Economics.

Botero, J. C., S. Djankov, R. La Porta, F. Lopez-de-Silanes, and A. Shleifer. 2004. "The Regulation of Labor." *Quarterly Journal of Economics* 119 (4): 1339–1382.

Bruhn, M. 2011. "License to Sell: The Effect of Business Registration Reform on Entrepreneurial Activity in Mexico." *Review of Economics and Statistics* 93 (1): 382–386.

Chong, A., and M. Gradstein. 2006. "Inequality and Informality." Discussion Paper 5545. London: CEPR.

De Paula, A., and J. A. Scheinkman. 2007. "The Informal Sector." Working paper 13486. Cambridge, MA: NBER.

De Soto, H. 1989. *The Other Path: The Invisible Revolution in the Third World*. New York: HarperCollins.

Direction de la Statistique. 2004. "L'enquête nationale sur le secteur informel non agricole." Rabat, Morocco: Direction de la Statistique.

Djankov, S., R. F. Lopez-de-Silanes, and A. Shleifer. 2002. "The Regulation of Entry." *Quarterly Journal of Economics* 117 (1): 1–37.

Djankov, S., C. McLiesh, and R. Ramalho. 2006. "Regulation and Growth." *Economics Letters* 92 (3): 395–401.

Elbadawi, I., and N. Loayza. 2008. "Informality, Employment and Economic Development in the Arab World." *Journal of Development and Economic Policies* 10 (2): 25–75.

Friedman, E., S. Johnson, D. Kaufmann, and P. Zoido-Lobaton. 2000. "Dodging the Grabbing Hand: The Determinants of Unofficial Activity in 69 Countries." *Journal of Public Economics* 76 (3): 459–493.

Galal, A. 2005. "The Economics of Formalization: Potential Winners and Losers from Formalization in Egypt." In *Investment Climate, Growth, and Poverty*, ed. G. Kochendorfer-Lucius and B. Pleskovic. Washington DC: World Bank.

Gatti, R., and M. Honorati. 2008. "Informality among Formal Firms: Firm-Level, Cross-Country Evidence on Tax Compliance and Access to Credit." Policy Research Working Paper 4476. Washington, DC: World Bank.

ILO (International Labour Organization). 1993. "Resolutions Concerning International Classification of Status in Employment." Adopted by the 15th International Conference of Labour Statisticians. Geneva: ILO.

———. 2002. "Decent Work and the Informal Economy: Sixth Item on the Agenda." International Labour Conference 90th: 2002. Report VII (2A) Geneva: ILO. http://www.ilo.org/public/english/standards/relm/ilc/ilc90/pdf/rep-vi.pdf.

Ingram, M., V. Ramachandran, and V. Desai. 2007. "Why Do Firms Choose to be Informal? Evidence from the Africa Investment Climate Surveys." Washington, DC: World Bank.

Ishengoma, E., and R. Kappel. 2006. "Economic Growth and Poverty: Does Formalization of Informal Enterprises Matter?" Working Paper Series 20. Hamburg: GIGA (German Institute of Global and Area Studies).

Johnson, S, D. Kaufmann, J. McMillan, and C. Woodruff. 2000. "Why Do Firms Hide? Bribes and Unofficial Activity after Communism." *Journal of Public Economics* 76 (3): 495–520.

La Porta, R., and A. Shleifer. 2008. "The Unofficial Economy and Economic Development." *Brookings Papers on Economic Activity* 2: 275–364.

Levenson, A., and W. Maloney. 1998. "The Informal Sector, Firm Dynamics, and Institutional Participation." Policy Research Working Paper WPS1988. Washington, DC: World Bank.

Loayza, N., A. M. Oviedo, and L. Serven. 2004. "Regulation and Macroeconomic Performance." Washington, DC: World Bank.

McKenzie, D., and Y. S. Sakho. 2010. "Does It Pay Firms to Register for Taxes? The Impact of Formality on Firm Profitability." *Journal of Development Economics* 91 (1): 15–24.

Oviedo, A. 2008. "Economic Informality: Causes, Costs, and Policies: A Critical Survey of the International Literature." Washington, DC: World Bank.

Perry, G., W. Maloney, O. Arias, P. Fajnzylber, A. Mason, and J. Saavedra-Chanduvi. 2007. *Informality: Exit and Exclusion*. Washington, DC: World Bank.

Pierre, G., and S. Scarpetta. 2006. "How Labor Markets Can Combine Workers' Protection with Job Creation: A Partial Review of Some Key Issues and Policy Options." Social Protection Discussion Paper 0716. Washington, DC: World Bank.

Ramalho, R. 2007. "Adding a Million Taxpayers." *Doing Business 2008*. Washington, DC: World Bank.

Silva, J., M. Benyagoub, and G. Wallner. 2010. "Informality, Firm Performance and Labor Market Outcomes: Evidence from Matched Employer-Employee Data for Morocco." Mimeo. Washington, DC: World Bank.

World Bank. 2007. "Republic of Bolivia: Policies for Increasing Firms' Formality and Productivity." Report 40057-BO. Washington, DC: World Bank.

———. 2008. "Climat de l'Investissement au Maroc: Créer les conditions du changement structurel." Washington, DC: World Bank.

———. 2009. "From Privilege to Competition: Unlocking Private-Led Growth in Middle East and North Africa." Washington, DC: World Bank.

———. 2010. "Egypt Investment Climate Assessment 2009: Accelerating Private Enterprise-Led Growth." Washington, DC: World Bank.

CHAPTER 4

Informality: Choice or Exclusion?

SUMMARY: Building on the analysis of earning differentials, job mobility patterns, self-reported attitudes toward moving jobs, and self-rated satisfaction, this chapter provides a characterization of the quality of informal jobs. The existing evidence corroborates the view that segmentations exist across formal and informal jobs and that much of the observed informality is likely due to exclusion factors. Returns to human capital differ sharply, with estimated formality premiums ranging up to 50 percent for salaried workers. Informal salaried workers also report lower access to nonpension benefits, including annual, maternity, and official leave, and to training and skills upgrading. Moreover, informal jobs in MENA countries have longer durations than in comparator countries, thus dispelling the notion that informal jobs are mainly an entry point to the labor market to help employers and new entrants (youth) overcome asymmetric information constraints. In some countries, notably Egypt, a prominent margin of segmentation is along the public/private employment margin, as indicated, for example, by the extremely long duration of public jobs. The lack of information on earnings for the self-employed for most countries limits a full analysis of self-employed work. However, where these data are available, as in Lebanon, the evidence suggests that the self-employed have higher earnings than informal salaried workers, but overall lower earnings than formal salaried workers, while a small percentage of them earns more than both. The large majority of self-employed workers, who tend to be older and have lower education than both informal and formal salaried workers, do not have access to social security.

Introduction

The previous chapters, in particular chapter 2, discussed the profile and characteristics of informal workers, pointing at common trends but also important heterogeneities. Overall, a large informal sector and the resulting coverage gap represent a suboptimal equilibrium that calls for policy action: Welfare can be improved by extending instruments to better manage risk. However, the ultimate drivers of informality are critical for identifying the appropriate policies. This chapter investigates the attributes of formal and informal jobs, including earnings, job mobility, access to leave and other benefits, and investment in training, as well as workers' subjective perceptions. In addition to providing a full characterization of informal work, this evidence can help document empirically the extent to which informality is the result of workers' voluntary choice or exclusion. This chapter first uses a variety of techniques, from simple comparisons of wage distributions to multivariate regression analysis, including the use of interesting and innovative controls for measured ability, to estimate whether a formality premium exists. Although persistent formality premiums are prima facie evidence that returns to skills are not equalized across formal and informal jobs for individuals of observed similar skills, wage differences cannot be taken alone as evidence that segmentations prevent arbitrage between the two sectors. Many factors can confound comparisons between earnings from different jobs but are unmeasured (for example, flexibility and independence). To gain a better understanding, this chapter complements the information on wage differentials with evidence on job mobility. High mobility is an indicator of integrated labor markets, where workers and enterprises, following market signals, search for matches between skills and vacancies. In countries with integrated labor markets, informal jobs help reduce asymmetric information for new labor market entrants, who, once they have proven their skills, would move rapidly to formal employment or self-employment. Thus workers that are observed working informally might indeed choose to do so, because in labor markets with easy transitions they could move out of informality if they so wished. In line with evidence from around the world, formal jobs have a longer duration than informal jobs. However, high persistence in informal, lower-paying jobs (for workers of skills comparable to those in the formal sector) is likely to indicate that many barriers, including labor regulations, prevent informal workers from moving to better jobs. In addition to analyzing data on actual job transitions and associated wage differentials, this chapter discusses newly collected data on self-reported attitudes toward job search, as well as the role of networks. Finally, the chapter discusses access to benefits (beyond old-age pensions) and training, and overall working conditions.

Informality and Wages

On average, wages in the formal sector are higher than in the informal sector. Wage data from surveys in Egypt (2006, and youth, 2009), Lebanon (2010), Morocco (available for youth only, 2010), Syria (2010), and the Republic of Yemen (2006) are used to quantify whether a premium to formal work exists beyond the returns to specific measured skills and experience. To address the high degree of heterogeneity among informal workers, the analysis is restricted to those individuals living in urban areas who are wage earners and working full time (between 30 and 60 hours a week). Data from Egypt, Morocco, and the Republic of Yemen include public and private sector workers, but data for Lebanon and Syria include only the private sector.[1] Whenever possible, a distinction is made between private and public sector formal wages. Table 4.1 provides information about average wages by gender of formal and informal workers across different education levels and sectors. Informal sector wages are uniformly lower than formal sector wages, especially if compared with the formal private sector. Women systematically command lower wages than men. In Egypt, public sector wages are higher than private formal sector wages for low-to-medium-skill workers, thus providing incentives for a large share of the population to queue for public sector jobs. Kernel density plots provide a useful representation of differences in wages among formal and informal workers because they plot (smoothed) densities at all wage levels. The heavy solid line in figure 4.1 shows informal salaried workers' wages. In Egypt and Lebanon (to a larger extent), the distribution of wages for workers in the informal sector is such that wages in the informal sector are always "'within'" the distribution of public and formal sector wages; that is, they are stochastically dominated by them, confirming the existence of a formality wage premium throughout the wage distribution and lending prima facie support to the view that informality is an exclusion phenomenon. In other words, workers would prefer to move from the low-paid informal sector to the high-paid formal sector if possible. In the Republic of Yemen, however, this is not the case. Although in that country the average formal worker earns slightly more than the average informal worker, a small pool of workers at the high end of the wage distribution is

Table 4.1 Average Hourly Wages in Local Currency

	Yemen, Rep., 2006			Egypt, Arab Rep., 2006			Lebanon, 2010		Syrian Arab Republic, 2010	
	Public	Private formal	Private informal	Public	Private formal	Private informal	Private formal	Private informal	Private formal	Private informal
Educational attainment										
Primary and below	104.48	111.12	148.35	3.31	2.95	2.32	5.09	3.13	78.08	60.88
Preparatory/secondary	140.25	229.12	149.51	3.33	2.87	2.26	5.38	3.60	93.58	75.65
General										
Secondary vocational	129.22	142.14	114.34	3.52	3.20	2.19	5.74	4.07	113.76	110.34
University and above	198.46	296.52	222.62	5.22	8.27	3.13	8.21	6.45	168.55	132.10
Gender										
Female	124.01	207.55	69.93	2.83	2.68	1.37	6.85	4.00	91.76	72.61
Male	158.42	219.80	164.45	3.03	3.25	2.08	6.85	4.87	110.75	92.45
Age group										
15–24	87.70	74.32	124.06	2.76	2.68	1.78	5.89	4.05	76.21	72.51
25–34	136.04	182.49	161.16	3.54	5.27	2.66	6.80	4.88	97.34	83.43
35–54	184.26	248.48	196.94	4.32	5.55	2.85	7.57	3.82	114.62	94.58
55–64	163.63	367.91	181.51	5.65	8.37	2.69	5.47	—	156.91	149.94
Sector of employment										
Primary	138.33	185.93	157.53	3.67	5.13	2.09	6.50	3.38	—	—
Secondary	182.95	174.68	105.85	4.60	5.15	2.42	6.17	3.79	—	—
Tertiary	161.47	237.40	170.24	5.08	5.88	2.41	6.98	4.73	—	—
Total average	154.48	218.87	158.03	4.21	5.29	2.39	6.85	4.55	107.43	87.31

Sources: Angel-Urdinola and Tanabe, 2011; Alloush and others, 2011.

Note: — = not available.

Figure 4.1   Kernel Density Plots of Hourly Wages by Employment Sector

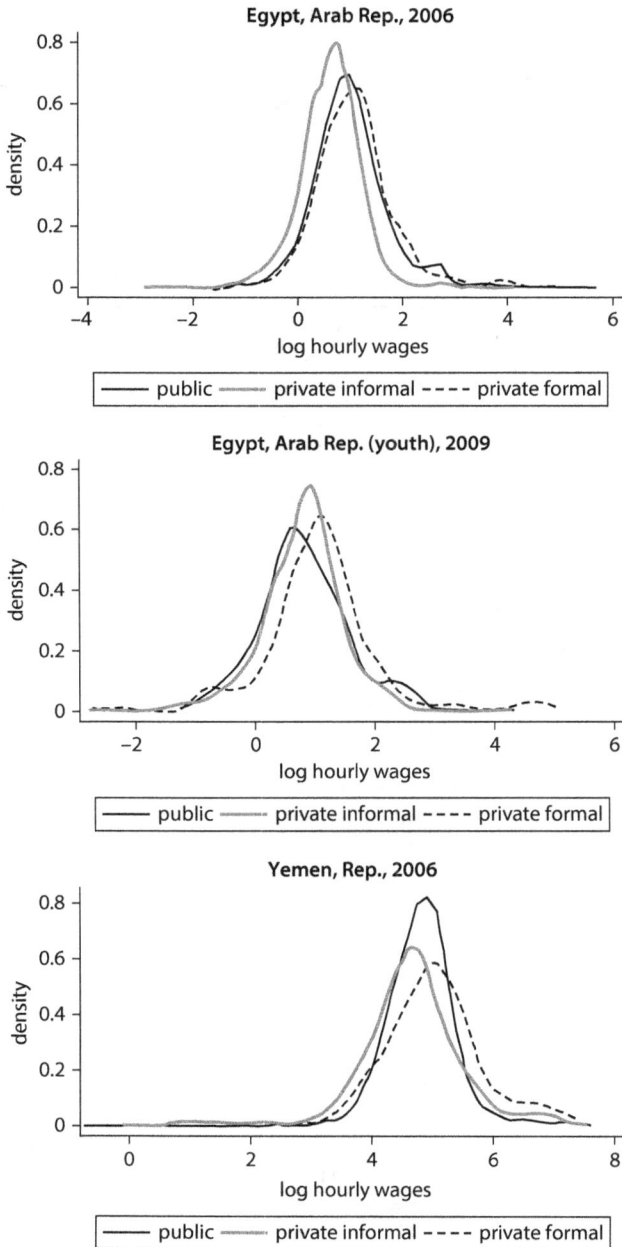

figure continues next page

Striving for Better Jobs • http://dx.doi.org/10.1596/978-0-8213-9535-6

Figure 4.1   Kernel Density Plots of Hourly Wages by Employment Sector *(continued)*

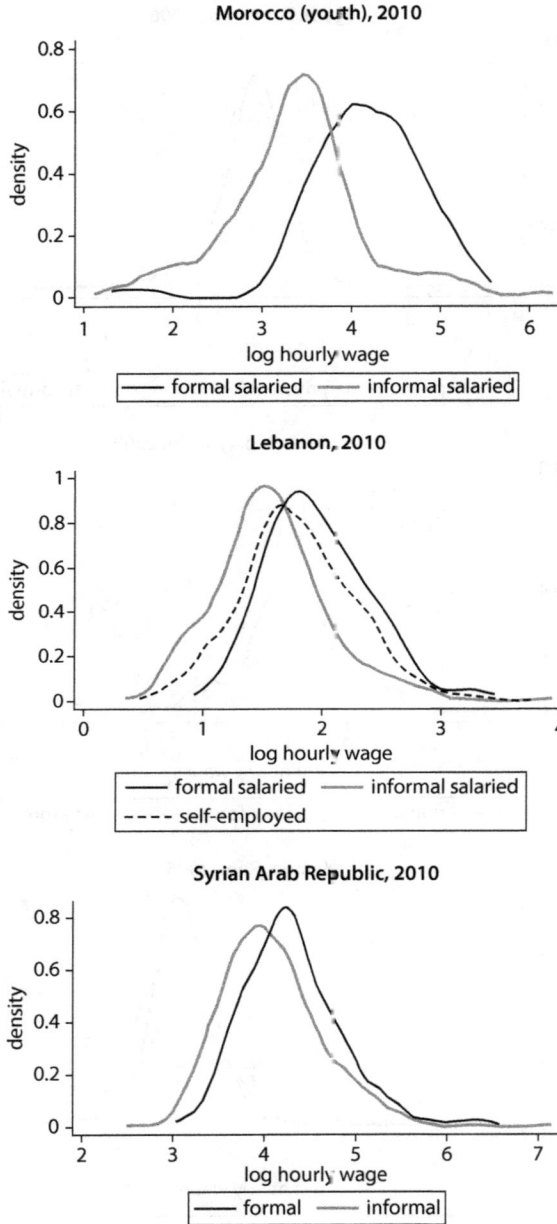

Morocco (youth), 2010

Lebanon, 2010

Syrian Arab Republic, 2010

Sources: Angel-Urdinola and Tanabe 2011; Alloush and others 2011.

able to earn higher wages in the private informal sector than would be earned in the public sector (seen at the right tail of the wage distribution). For this small pool of workers, working in the informal sector is probably a profitable choice.[2]

A wage gap in the earnings of formal and informal workers persists, especially for women, even after controlling for a number of observable factors. Although kernel density plots are informative, they represent unconditional distributions; that is, they compare wages in the formal and informal sectors without controlling for observed characteristics that might affect the distribution (such as lower education and/or age). To overcome this limitation, standard Mincerian regressions were used. In their basic form, Mincerian regressions estimate wages as a function of a number of key observable characteristics, such as gender, age (nonlinear), and years of education. A binary variable for working in the formal sector is then added to this standard specification. The coefficient on this variable captures an estimate of the formality premium.[3] This estimate varies significantly from country to country, highlighting the heterogeneity of the informality phenomenon in the region (figure 4.2). In Lebanon, the

Figure 4.2   Estimated Formality Premiums by Gender in Different Countries

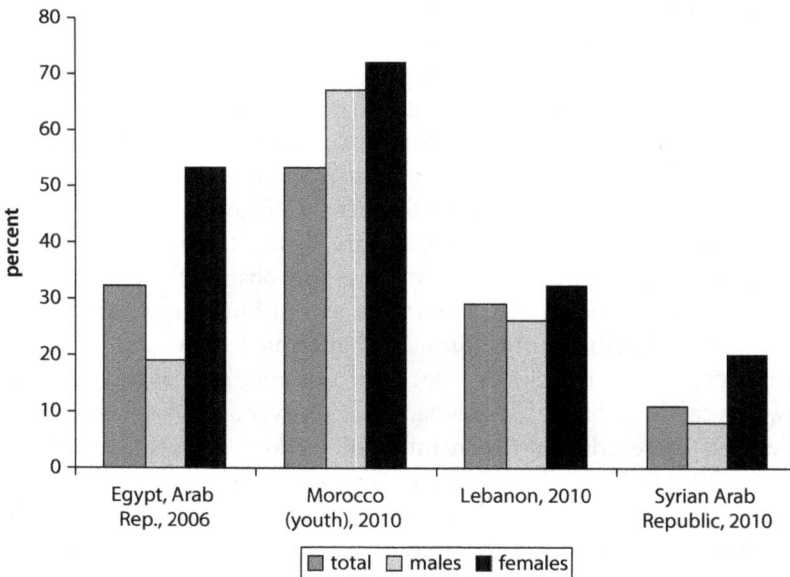

Sources: Angel-Urdinola and Tanabe, 2011; Alloush and others, 2011.

Striving for Better Jobs • http://dx.doi.org/10.1596/978-0-8213-9535-6

average estimated formality premium is 29 percent, in Egypt, 32 percent, and among Moroccan youth, as high as 53 percent.[4] The formality premium is higher among female workers in all cases. In Egypt this phenomenon is particularly notable, where, on average, a female worker in the formal sector earns 1.5 times as much than an otherwise similar woman in the informal sector. Very low wages paid to female workers in the informal sector often explains why many women decide not to participate in the labor market at all, especially if the opportunities to find formal jobs are limited. This finding is quite relevant in a country such as Egypt, where female participation rates remain low by international standards.[5] In both Lebanon and Syria, the formality premium is higher for workers with a low level of education, which suggests that unskilled informal workers might have lower bargaining power in wage setting (Alloush and others 2011).

The differences in wages between the formal and the informal sector are explained by differences in the characteristics of formal and informal workers, as well as by differences in how the labor market rewards those characteristics. It is interesting to assess whether the observed differences in wages of formal and informal workers are mainly due to differences in the characteristics (endowments) of workers in the two groups, or to differences in the extent to which formal and informal jobs reward those endowments. Returns to observed skills can differ for many reasons between formal and informal jobs, depending on firm scale, complementarities with physical capital investment, and incentives to acquire experience and upgrade skills. Although many observed and unobserved variables affect workers' distribution into formal and informal occupations, a simple Oaxaca decomposition provides an alternative insight into the likely drivers of observed wage differences.[6] Figure 4.3 plots the result of this decomposition: The dark gray bars illustrate the share of the difference in wages explained by differences in observable characteristics between formal and informal workers, as attributed to characteristics (endowments), returns (how formal and informal jobs reward these characteristics), and an interaction effect. For example, part of the difference in wages can be explained by the fact that, on average, formal workers are older and more educated than informal workers (Angel-Urdinola and Tanabe 2011). These differences in "endowments" explain about one-third of the wage differential in Lebanon and about half in Egypt. One could argue that this component of the wage differential is "fair," because the market should positively reward higher education attainment and experience.

Figure 4.3   Oaxaca Decomposition of the Differences in Wages

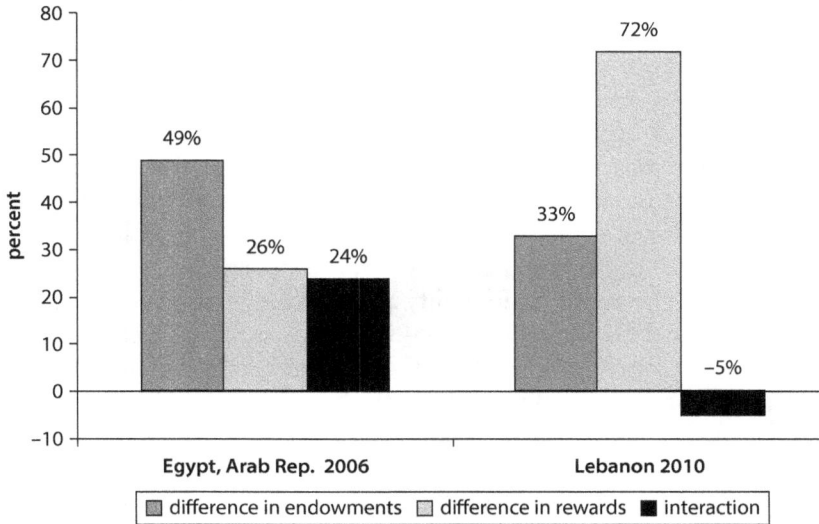

Source: Based on Angel-Urdinola and Tanabe 2011.
Note: For Egypt these are wages for urban workers in private and public sectors. For Lebanon, the wages are for private sector employees with no distinction between rural and urban areas.

The light gray bars in figure 4.3 illustrate the gap in returns to endowment due to being an informal rather than a formal worker, or the extent to which equal endowment/work is not rewarded by equal pay across the two sectors (for example, having a university education is rewarded less if the degree holder works as a taxi driver than if he works in the financial sector). These differences in rewards explain a large share of wage differences in Lebanon but a smaller share in Egypt. The higher the share of the wage differential that is explained by differences in "rewards," the higher the chance that informality is an exclusion phenomenon (because workers would prefer to be rewarded more for a given observable characteristic, such as educational attainment, if they could). Last, the black bars represent the share of the difference in wages that arises because of the interaction between how the market rewards characteristics of formal versus informal workers and their differences in endowments.

Looking beyond individual characteristics, where workers are employed (small firms or large firms) affects the formality premium. However, the formality premium still persists after controlling for size.

Where people work can potentially make an important difference in the earnings that they command. In particular, it is expected that informal wage workers in micro-enterprises (two to five employees) will earn significantly less than workers in larger firms, because smaller firms usually have lower productivity. In turn, firm productivity could account for much, if not all, of the formality premium across workers. Omitting this variable from an analysis of wage differentials could lead one to erroneously attribute the formality premium to informal employment when it might instead reflect firm characteristics. Once firm size in included in the regressions, the earnings gap between formal and informal workers still persists. The resulting formality premium is now estimated to be between 10 and 50 percent (figure 4.2). However, ample heterogeneity is observed in how firm size affects the estimated formality premium. In Syria, working in micro-firms does not change the formality premium significantly. This could be because of the nature of the survey sample, since survey participants all work in registered firms. Small micro- "formal" firms might share some of the key productivity attributes of larger firms so that controlling for firm size might not make a significant difference. In Egypt the formality premium continues to be significant but increases. In Lebanon, up to one-third of the informality premium is attributable to firm characteristics, with workers in micro-firms earning 23 percent less than workers in medium size firms (10 to 49 employees). Unlike in Egypt, informal workers in Lebanon are not primarily concentrated in micro-enterprises, because a large share of them work in larger firms. In this sense, returns to informal workers' skills might differ in important respects because of the widely different productivity levels of the firms where they work (ranging from micro-informal to large formal). If uncaptured, this difference would be spuriously attributed to workers' status (formal versus informal) rather than to firms' characteristics and productivity.

Note that, when direct measures of individual ability are explicitly accounted for, the formality premium is virtually unchanged. Quality of education and skills often differ starkly across social strata and are correlated with the likelihood of working in the informal sector. Assignment to the informal sector is not random, and so it is important to control in some way for individual ability/skills to ensure that the attribution of the formality premium does not instead reflect other factors. In particular, unmeasured individual ability, which is likely negatively correlated with selection into the informal sector, could be spuriously driving these results, because years of education are unlikely to capture well actual quality of education and skills. To overcome this limitation in the interpretation of the estimation, the results of direct cognitive and noncognitive tests are included in the regression. These tests were administered in conjunction with the Lebanon labor force survey and the Syria matched employer-employee survey. Both surveys fielded a battery of ability tests to all participants as well as a questionnaire to self-assess personality and relational skills (box 4.1 describes the methodology and main features of these tests). The results of these tests are translated into scores and added as additional controls in the wage regressions. Although concerns have been expressed related to possible

---

Box 4.1   Cognitive and Noncognitive Tests

Traditionally, studies have focused on measuring skills through educational attainment and experience, without measuring ability directly. Cognitive and noncognitive tests can be good proxies for individual ability. In fact, an individual's skill set can be defined as a combination of his or her cognitive, noncognitive, and technical skills (see table below). In turn, given that human capital is multidimensional, both cognitive and noncognitive skills can serve as good predictors of economic outcomes such as income and wealth (Bowles and others 2001; Cawley and others 2001; Hansen and others 2004; Heckman and others 2006).Two innovative labor market surveys conducted in the MENA region (in Syria and Lebanon) have measured cognitive and noncognitive skills of labor force participants and have produced interesting results.

Relationship between technical, cognitive, and noncognitive skills

Type of skill	What it measures	Measurable concepts
Cognitive	Ability	Verbal, math, logic reasoning
Noncognitive	Ability, interaction	Personality, communication
Technical	Knowledge, experience	Breadth, depth of field of knowledge

The cognitive test used "Raven's Progressive Matrices," a nonverbal test in which individuals have to identify the missing piece of a particular pattern among multiple choices. Respondents are given five minutes to answer as many as they can of the 12 matrices included in the test, which become progressively more difficult and require greater cognitive capacity. This test is independent of language, reading, or writing skills and focuses on measuring observation skills, analytical ability, and intellectual capacity. A score (out of 12) is calculated for each respondent based on the number of correct answers completed in the allocated time.

box continues next page

Box 4.1   Cognitive and Noncognitive Tests *(continued)*

The noncognitive test consists of a list of statements describing personal behaviors and characteristics corresponding to the five core dimensions of personality used in psychology literature to classify human personality (referred to as the "Big Five"):

- Conscientiousness: tendency to be organized, responsible, and hardworking
- Emotional stability: tendency to be predictable and consistent in emotional reactions
- Agreeableness: tendency to act in a cooperative and unselfish manner
- Extraversion: tendency to orient one's energies toward the outer world of people and things
- Openness to experience: tendency to be open to new cultural or intellectual experiences.

These traits are considered to be relatively stable throughout one's lifetime. The noncognitive test used in the Syria and Lebanon surveys, an adaption of the Goldberg test, asks respondents to rank the applicability of a total of 15 traits/behaviors to themselves (three of each corresponding to one of the "Big Five") from a scale of 1 to 7. Accordingly, a score for each of the "Big Five" traits is calculated.

Main observed patterns: Cognitive skills are positively correlated with educational attainment, but more strongly so in Syria than in Lebanon. A positive difference in the average cognitive score between formal and informal workers is observed, which is significant in Lebanon but not in Syria.

	Cognitive Score Means and Correlations			
	Syria Arab Republic		Lebanon	
	Mean	Unconditional correlation between years of education and cognitive score	Mean	Unconditional correlation between years of education and cognitive score
Total	4.56	0.41	4.93	0.29
Salaried formal	4.44	0.37	5.54	0.26
Salaried informal	4.86	0.51	4.85	0.23
Self-employed	—	—	4.53	0.26

Note: In Lebanon, 9.4 percent of the total population surveyed did not take the test. The highest nonresponse rate was for the illiterate (50 percent). Note, however, that only 10 workers in Lebanon reported themselves as illiterate. The results in Lebanon are in line with the "Flynn effect," which describes an intergenerational increase in scores.

box continues next page

Box 4.1   Cognitive and Noncognitive Tests *(continued)*

Noncognitive Score Means in the Syrian Arab Republic and Lebanon

	Syrian Arab Republic		
	Total	Informal	Formal
Conscientiousness	0.89	0.88	0.89
Emotional stability	0.16	0.17	0.16
Agreeableness	0.75	0.80	0.74
Extraversion	0.31	0.29	0.31
Openness to experience	0.52	0.52	0.52

	Lebanon		
	Total	Informal	Formal
Conscientiousness	0.89	0.9	0.89
Emotional stability	0.22	0.17	0.23
Agreeableness	0.5	0.55	0.51
Extraversion	0.39	0.35	0.39
Openness to experience	0.49	0.54	0.46

Source: Alloush and others 2011.

endogeneity of cognitive and noncognitive score measures, the inclusion of these scores is likely a good proxy for individual ability. Note that when cognitive and noncognitive scores are included in the estimation, they do not affect the estimate of the informality coefficient. Even after taking ability and personal characteristics into account, formality still has a 20 percent premium in Lebanon, and a 12 percent premium in Syria (tables 4.2 and 4.3).[7]

Unobserved firm characteristics can also affect earnings differentials between formal and informal occupations. In most household surveys, information on the types of establishments where individuals work is not available, with the exception of information on firm size. For example, characteristics such as whether an individual firm is registered with tax authorities or the average level of education of its workforce are not known. These characteristics might matter and drive the ability of firms to reward skills. If unmeasured, they can also confound the size and attribution of estimated wage gaps between formal and informal workers. The Syrian data, which allow for these controls, are collected as part of a matched employees-employer survey, so that workers can unequivocally

Table 4.2   Formality Premium, Lebanon: Ordinary Least-Squares (OLS) Estimates for Private Sector Formal and Informal Workers

	OLS	OLS	OLS	OLS
	(1)	(2)	(3)	(4)
Dependent variable	Log hourly wage	Log hourly wage	Log hourly wage	Log hourly wage
Informal (dummy)	−0.2920***	−0.1915***	−0.2024***	−0.1953***
Controls	Gender, age, age squared, Years of education	Gender, age, age squared, Years of education, firm size dummies	Gender, age, age squared, Years of education, firm size dummies, sector cognitive score	Gender, age, age squared, Years of education, firm size dummies, sector cognitive score, noncognitive score

Source: Annex tables 4.1 and 4.2 from Alloush and others 2011.
***Significant at 1 percent.

be mapped to their firms and firm-specific effects controlled for. Even after controlling for individual cognitive and noncognitive ability and for firm fixed effects, the formality premium is unaffected; workers who are hired as informal command a lower wage.

The wage analysis developed in this section suggests that informal workers command uniformly lower pay than formal workers with similar characteristics. One could argue that, given the overall worse terms of informal jobs (that is, lower duration and limited or no access to leave and pension benefits), informal jobs would have to pay higher wages to attract workers. However, in economies such as those in the MENA region where job creation is rationed, lower pay and worse conditions in the informal sector might be seen by workers as a preferable alternative to unemployment, especially for workers with low skills and education.

Job (Im)Mobility

Although wage comparisons can be informative, differences in earnings alone cannot unequivocally prove segmentations in labor markets. Earnings differences between the formal and informal sector might reflect a range of unobservable job characteristics, including flexible hours, value of training, and value (or lack) of social security benefits, all of which can affect the salary wedge between observationally similar jobs (Maloney 1999, 2004). Moreover, selection into formal or informal jobs

Table 4.3 **Formality Premium, Syrian Arab Republic: Ordinary Least-Squares (OLS) Estimates for Private Sector Formal and Informal Workers**

	OLS	OLS	OLS	OLS	Firm fixed effects
	(1)	(2)	(3)	(4)	
Dependent variable	Log hourly wage	Log hourly wage	Log hourly wage	Log hourly wage	Log hourly wage
Informal (dummy)	−0.109**	−0.123***	−0.123***	−0.119***	−0.127***
Controls	Gender, age, age squared,	Gender, age, age squared,	Gender, age, age squared,	Gender, age, age squared,	Gender, age, age squared,
	Years of education	Years of education, firm size dummies	Years of education, firm size dummies, cognitive score	Years of education, firm size dummies, cognitive score, noncognitive score	Years of education, cognitive score, noncognitive score

Source: Annex tables 4.1 and 4.2 from Alloush and others 2011.

**Significant at 5 percent; ***significant at 1 percent.

might be driven by unobservable workers' skills and ability, which might in turn affect earnings. The concern that this might lead to estimation bias is mitigated in wage regressions for Lebanon and Syria, due to inclusion of direct test score measures of cognitive and noncognitive ability. These controls did not affect the size of the formality premium, hence suggesting that "informality" status did not, to a large extent, spuriously reflect ability. However, other unobservables might still persist. To complete and complement this analysis, patterns of labor mobility in and out of informality and wage differentials for individuals moving from informal to formal jobs and vice versa were examined using actual transitions from the Egypt panels as well as data on self-reported jobs search.

Workers' mobility patterns in MENA provide evidence that segmentations exist in the region's labor markets. Mobility patterns can provide important insights on the extent to which labor markets are segmented or integrated. A good level of mobility and integration in labor markets indicates that workers and employers have the chance to find productive matches between labor demand and supply of skills. In this section, longitudinal data from two separate sources for Egypt are used to study mobility patterns between the formal and informal sectors: the ELMPS, which surveyed individuals in 1998 and 2006, and the HIECS panel, which surveyed individuals in 2008 and 2009. Over the eight-year span of the two ELMPS surveys, persistence in formal or informal status was high (figure 4.4): 46 percent of informal salaried workers in 1998 continued to be informal salaried in 2006. By 2006, only 19 percent had transitioned to formal employment, either in the private or in the public sector. In the second panel survey, 65 percent of informal salaried workers in 2008 remained so in 2009. Upward mobility was minimal, with only 9 percent of informal salaried workers transitioning toward jobs with social security coverage (public or private).

Only a minority of all informal workers in 2008 became unemployed in 2009 despite the financial crisis. It is interesting to note that when the financial crisis struck Egypt in 2008, formal private sector employment shrank substantively (35 percent) with a large share of workers transitioning to informal salaried jobs in the private sector (about 28 percent). In a crisis year, many of these transitions are likely involuntary and might have been the result of termination of temporary contracts (initially with benefits) and their subsequent conversion into informal jobs, as well as of firm closures after which workers rapidly found informal subsistence employment. It is notable that transitions into unemployment from formal jobs are almost nonexistent.

Lacking effective unemployment insurance, informal work (which commands average lower wages) represents a safety net type of employment.[8] Table 4.4 depicts the 1998–2006 transition matrix, and table 4.5 depicts the 2008–2009 transition matrix. The yearly transition probabilities in 2008 translate into an estimated job duration of about three years for informal salaried workers,[9] above that observed in comparator countries in other regions, such as Mexico (where movement in and out of salaried informal jobs is high and average job duration is estimated at about two years).[10] Bosch and Maloney (2010) offer a sophisticated approach to reading transition matrices, which adjusts for the extent to which vacancies open up and workers leave in different sectors (for example, formal private, public, or private informal).[11] Applying their

Figure 4.4   Distribution of Labor Market Transitions in Egypt

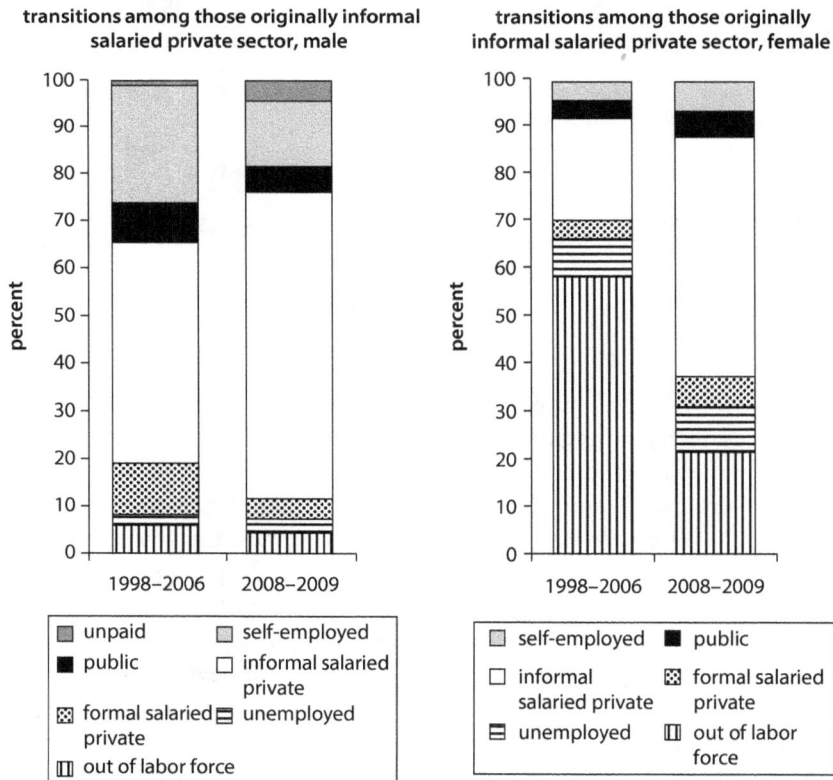

transitions among those originally informal
salaried private sector, male

transitions among those originally
informal salaried private sector, female

unpaid   self-employed
public   informal salaried private
formal salaried unemployed
private
out of labor force

self-employed   public
informal   formal salaried
salaried private   private
unemployed   out of labor force

box continues next page

Figure 4.4   Distribution of Labor Market Transitions in Egypt *(continued)*

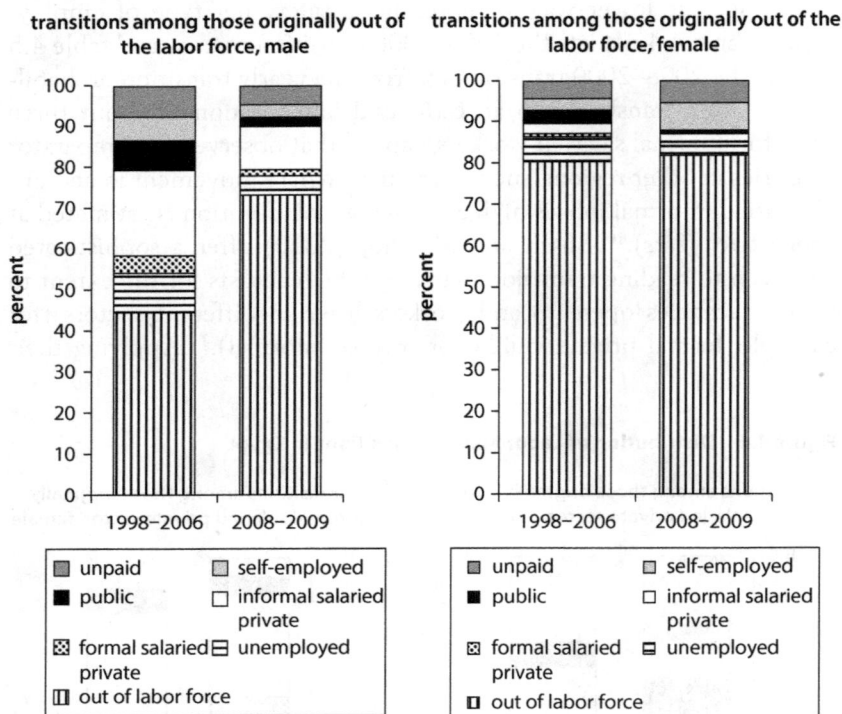

transitions among those originally out of the labor force, male

transitions among those originally out of the labor force, female

Legend (male):
- unpaid
- public
- formal salaried private
- out of labor force
- self-employed
- informal salaried private
- unemployed

Legend (female):
- unpaid
- public
- formal salaried private
- out of labor force
- self-employed
- informal salaried private
- unemployed

Source: Silva and others 2010.

methodology to the Egypt context confirms that the public sector continued to be an engine of employment growth in the crisis, second only to informal salaried work, absorbing 28 percent of formal private sector workers. Overall, persistence in informal status (including, in addition to informal wage workers, the self-employed, many employers, and unpaid workers) is extremely high, at about 90 percent.

Panel data also allow for observing earning changes along transitions. On average, when a worker moves from an informal to a formal job, his or her net earnings increase by about 24 percent and even more if benefits are accounted for (table 4.6). Note that by tracking earnings changes for the same individual across the informal-formal transition, the concern that higher earnings in formal jobs might reflect unobserved workers' characteristics is eliminated.

Table 4.4 Labor Market Transitions in Egypt (1998–2006)

	Out of labor force 2006	Unemployed 2006	Formal salaried private 2006	Informal salaried private 2006	Public 2006	Self-employed 2006	Unpaid work 2006	Total
Out of labor force 1998	**45%**	**10%**	**4%**	**21%**	**7%**	**6%**	**8%**	**100%**
No. of observations	1,283	279	121	602	207	168	216	2,876
Unemployed 1998	**8**	**9**	**9**	**37**	**11**	**23**	**3**	**100**
No. of observations	26	30	31	122	37	77	10	333
Formal salaried private 1998	**5**	**1**	**55**	**14**	**10**	**15**	**0**	**100**
No. of observations	13	4	149	37	28	41	1	273
Informal salaried private 1998	**6**	**2**	**11**	**46**	**8**	**25**	**1**	**100**
No. of observations	53	20	98	414	76	225	9	895
Public 1998	**11**	**0**	**2**	**2**	**81**	**3**	**0**	**100**
No. of observations	150	6	29	77	1057	40	1	1310
Self-employed 1998	**5**	**2**	**3**	**7**	**6**	**78**	**1**	**100**
No. of observations	30	10	18	44	39	511	6	658
Unpaid work 1998	**7**	**1**	**5**	**19**	**10**	**32**	**27**	**100**
No. of observations	16	2	11	45	23	78	66	241
Total	**24**	**5**	**7**	**20**	**22**	**17**	**5**	**100**
No. of observations	1,571	351	457	1,291	1,467	1,140	309	6,586

Source: Silva and others 2011.

Note: Percentages are reported in bold. The shaded area highlights transition among employed workers. Sample: Male workers, 15–64 years old in 2006.

Table 4.5 Labor Market Transitions in Egypt (2008–2009)

	Out of labor force 2009	Unemployed 2009	Formal salaried private 2009	Informal salaried private 2009	Public 2009	Self-employed 2009	Unpaid work 2009	Total
Out of labor force 2008	**73%**	**5%**	**2%**	**10%**	**2%**	**3%**	**5%**	**100%**
No. of observations	760	48	16	109	24	32	47	1,036
Unemployed 2008	**16**	**31**	**3**	**29**	**13**	**3**	**5**	**100**
No. of observations	26	49	5	45	20	4	9	158
Formal salaried private 2008	**2**	**2**	**32**	**28**	**28**	**7**	**0**	**100**
No. of observations	8	7	105	92	94	25	0	332
Informal salaried private 2008	**4**	**3**	**4**	**65**	**5**	**14**	**4**	**100**
No. of observations	41	28	40	607	51	132	40	940
Public 2008	**2**	**0**	**2**	**3**	**90**	**2**	**0**	**100**
No. of observations	21	2	25	25	886	22	1	982
Self-employed 2008	**3**	**0**	**2**	**14**	**3**	**76**	**2**	**100**
No. of observations	29	3	20	129	30	713	17	941
Unpaid work 2008	**14**	**1**	**1**	**23**	**6**	**7**	**49**	**100**
No. of observations	39	3	2	62	16	19	135	276
Total	**20**	**3**	**5**	**23**	**24**	**20**	**5**	**100**
No. of observations	924	140	214	1,071	1,121	948	249	4,666

Source: Silva and others 2011.

Note: Percentages are reported in bold. The shaded area highlights transition among employed workers. Sample: male workers, 15–64 years old.

Table 4.6 Average Level of Earnings Increase When Moving from Formality to Informality

percent

	Mover I-F	Stayer I-I	Mover F-I	Stayer FF	Mover formal salaried private to public	Stayer formal salaried private
Earnings (mean % change) (1)	24	2	−9	2	7	2

Source: Silva and others 2010 using Egypt HIECS 2008/09.
Note: Line (1) presents the mean percentage change in real earnings between 2008 and 2009. For this calculation, nonadjusted earnings (take-home pay), which exclude social security benefits, were used. Sample: Male, 15–64 years old, employed in 2008 and 2009.

Patterns of social security contribution densities from administrative data confirm the limited mobility between formal and informal jobs. Social security contributions offer an alternative data source to understand job duration patterns. Contribution density is defined as the share of time an individual contributes to the pension system during his or her active life period. Individual contribution densities are the longitudinal companion of the coverage rate, which measures the share of employed who are contributing to social security at a certain moment in time. Figure 4.5 illustrates the age-specific contribution density patterns toward the mandatory social insurance scheme administered by the Social Security Corporation (SSC) in Jordan. The SSC dataset used for the analysis includes everyone who contributed to or received benefits from the SSC between 1980 and 2010. The pattern indicates that in Jordan, individuals tend to complete either long contributory spells or long noncontributory spells (that is, they stay in or out of the system for long periods of time). As illustrated by the figure, adult individuals between ages 25 and 55 are expected to stay in the system for about 30 years (which is generally the time needed for full retirement). Across all individuals and cohorts, contribution densities are low for youth, but they increase rapidly as individuals reach adulthood, leave school, and establish themselves in formal employment. As expected, contribution rates drop significantly when individuals are in their late fifties, because early and statutory retirement rules drive down contributions (a pattern that is observed in most countries).[12]

Contribution density patterns show the coexistence of two different groups of workers: some with an established contributory status, and

Figure 4.5   Contribution Density and the Distribution of Contributory and Noncontributory Spells in Jordan

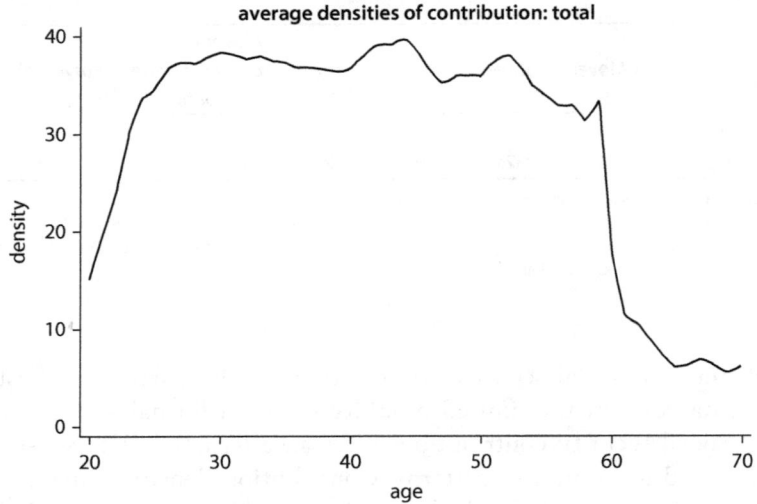

Source: Calculations using administrative datasets from the SSC of Jordan.

some who hardly ever contribute. The average length of a continuous contributory spell in Jordan is longer than four years, with little difference between women and men (49 and 53 months, respectively), and with 40 percent of all contributors contributing for at least three years (figure 4.6). Only 16 percent of all contributors (mainly new entrants to the labor market) have a contributory period shorter than six months. The distribution of the length of noncontributory spells signals the existence of a group consistently out of coverage. For example, once workers who are enrolled in a contributory job (that is, registered with SSC) at some point in their career start a noncontributory spell, 69 percent of them stay out of coverage for a minimum of three years and an average of approximately six years (94 months).

Changes in contributory status in Jordan are significantly less frequent than in a comparator country such as Chile. The third and fourth panels of figure 4.6 illustrate the transition patterns in and out of contributory status based on monthly administrative data on social insurance contributions from Chile. In the case of Chile, the most frequent length category for both being in or out of social insurance contributory status is less than six months: 42 percent of those contributing to the social insurance system in Chile are likely to discontinue contributions within six months, and 37 percent of those registered with social security will restart contributions within six months. In contrast, the Jordanian contributory pattern is extremely skewed: 40 percent of contributors are likely to complete a spell longer than three years, and

Figure 4.6   Distribution of the Length of Social Insurance Contributory and Noncontributory Spells in Jordan and Chile

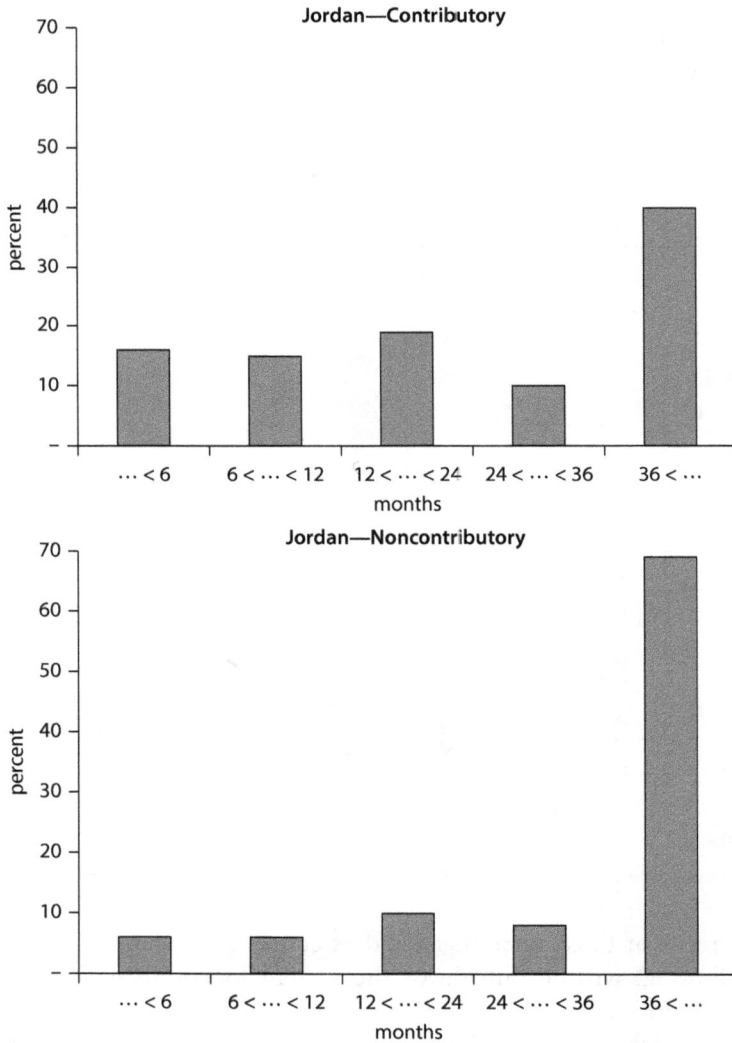

Jordan—Contributory

Jordan—Noncontributory

box continues next page

Figure 4.6   Distribution of the Length of Social Insurance Contributory and Noncontributory Spells in Jordan and Chile *(continued)*

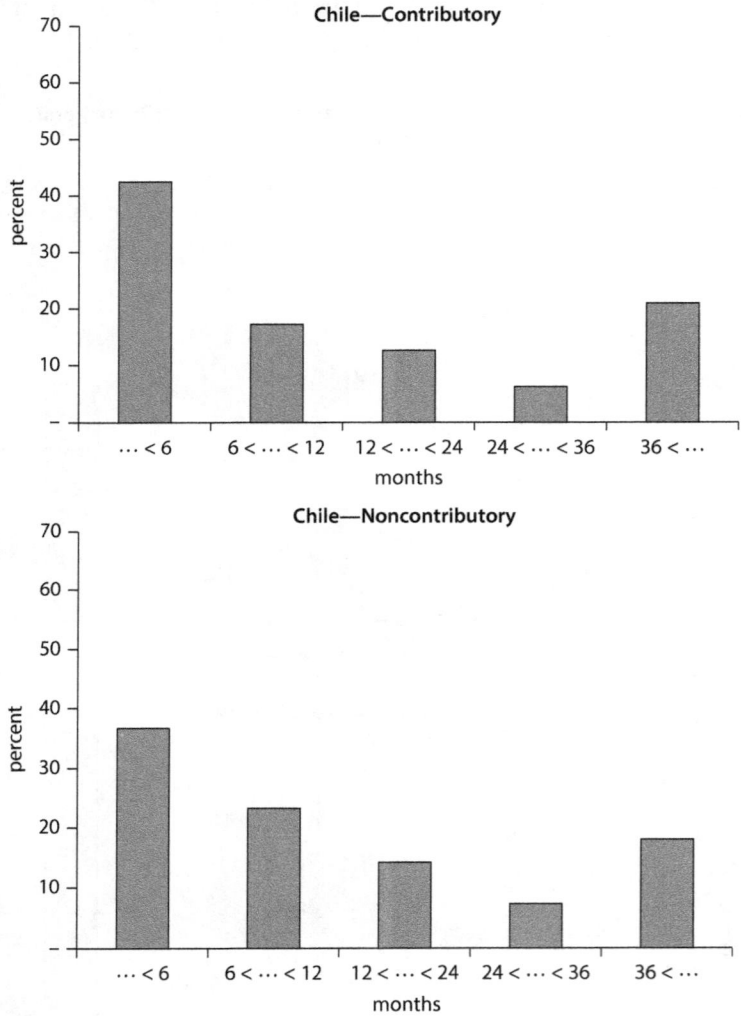

Chile—Contributory

Chile—Noncontributory

Source: Administrative datasets from the SSC of Jordan and the Chilean Pension Supervisory Agency.

69 percent of those once registered as contributors, but currently not contributing, will be outside of the system longer than three years. These results confirm the existence of an insider/outsider structure in MENA labor markets that is notably different from other parts of the world.[13]

What Are Informal Jobs Like?

This section aims to provide as assessment about the quality of informal employment. To begin with, available evidence indicates higher levels of job dissatisfaction among informal workers.[14] Table 4.7 reports responses to the question "Would you like to change your job?" for Lebanon, Egypt, and Syria. In Lebanon and Egypt, informal workers were significantly more likely to want to change jobs or were searching for a job. A higher level of job dissatisfaction persists in Egypt and Lebanon even after many individual characteristics are accounted for, including age, education, and pay (with the expectation that workers with higher pay are less likely to want to change jobs). In Syria, where differences between formal and informal workers are less pronounced in the surveyed sample, formal workers actually appear to be marginally more willing to change jobs than informal workers, but this difference is insignificant when individual characteristics are accounted for (Alloush and others 2011).

In general, informal jobs entail worse working conditions. Table 4.8 presents descriptive statistics related to self-perception of employment quality for formal and informal workers in Lebanon and Syria. Results indicate that, in many dimensions, formal workers experience better job quality, as measured by higher earnings, having a written contract, longer employment tenure, and higher chances of choosing when to work overtime (and be paid for such work). A noticeable feature is that informal jobs have a significantly shorter tenure than formal private sector jobs, which suggest that informal jobs provide firms with the needed flexibility in hiring and firing (especially relevant in countries where labor regulations are particularly restrictive).[15] Little difference is seen in the amount of work time (hours per day and days per week) between formal and informal workers in Lebanon and Syria. However, access to annual or other leave is much lower for informal workers (as discussed below), so

Table 4.7   Individuals Who Want to Change Jobs
percent

	Egypt, Arab Rep., youth	Lebanon	Syrian Republic Arab
Formal workers	11.6	21.8	37.1
Informal workers	36.9	45.5	34.4
N	3,180	757	961

Sources: Egypt youth survey 2010, Lebanon Labor Force Survey 2011, Syria Employee-Employer matched module 2011.

Table 4.8   Differences in Job Quality between Formal and Informal Jobs

	Lebanon		Syrian Arab Republic	
	Informal	Formal	Informal	Formal
Are you currently looking for another job? (% yes)	20.6%	8.1%	22.7%	20.2%
Hours (weekly)	48.42	46.96	50.80	48.73
Days of work per week	5.78	5.66	5.96	5.83
Earnings per hour (pounds)	4.55	6.85	72.36	89.48
Earnings per hour (bonuses taken into account)	4.57	6.9	89.92	110.77
Length at job (years)	5.12	7.81	4.35	8.03
Implicit annual growth rate of earnings per hour	9.8%	8.4%	9.3%	10.8%
Can request overtime	27.2%	38.4%	—	—
Can refuse overtime	33.4%	47.4%	—	—
Paid overtime	36.9%	49.3%	—	—
Written contract	18.4%	64.1%	21.7%	68.2%
Would like to be formal (registered in NSSF)	67.9%	—	68.6%	—
Prefer to be self-employed	63.6%	57.1%	63.5%	65.2%
Confidence in stability of job	83.4%	65.8%	77.6%	84.0%
% full time	84.2%	95.2%	—	—
Secondary job	5.6%	5.9%	7.7%	5.6%
Secondary source of income	4.7%	4.2%	16.9%	16.5%
Financial need to work	76.0%	73.5%	—	—
Personal satisfaction	24.0%	26.5%	—	—

Source: Alloush and others 2011. — = Not available.

that they may end up working a significantly greater number of days per year than formal workers.

As expected, informal workers enjoy fewer benefits than formal workers. In Lebanon, 56 percent of informal workers do not have any annual leave versus 13 percent of formal workers. Similarly, informal workers have significantly less access to benefits of family, sick, or maternity leave (figure 4.7). Although no significant difference is seen between formal and informal workers in terms of their access to benefits, such as provision of a firm nursery or a lunch allowance, large differences emerge for benefits that are fairly common in the formal sector. The evidence from Egypt suggests that informal jobs require, on average, shorter commutes, indicating that they are more likely to be "local." Still, transport expenses (which are not factored in the reported wage) can be substantial. For example, in Lebanon, daily transportation costs are anecdotally reported to be somewhat higher (at about 0.8–1.2 times the average hourly wage).

Figure 4.7 Lack of Access to Job Benefits between Informal and Formal Sectors (% of Workers without Access)

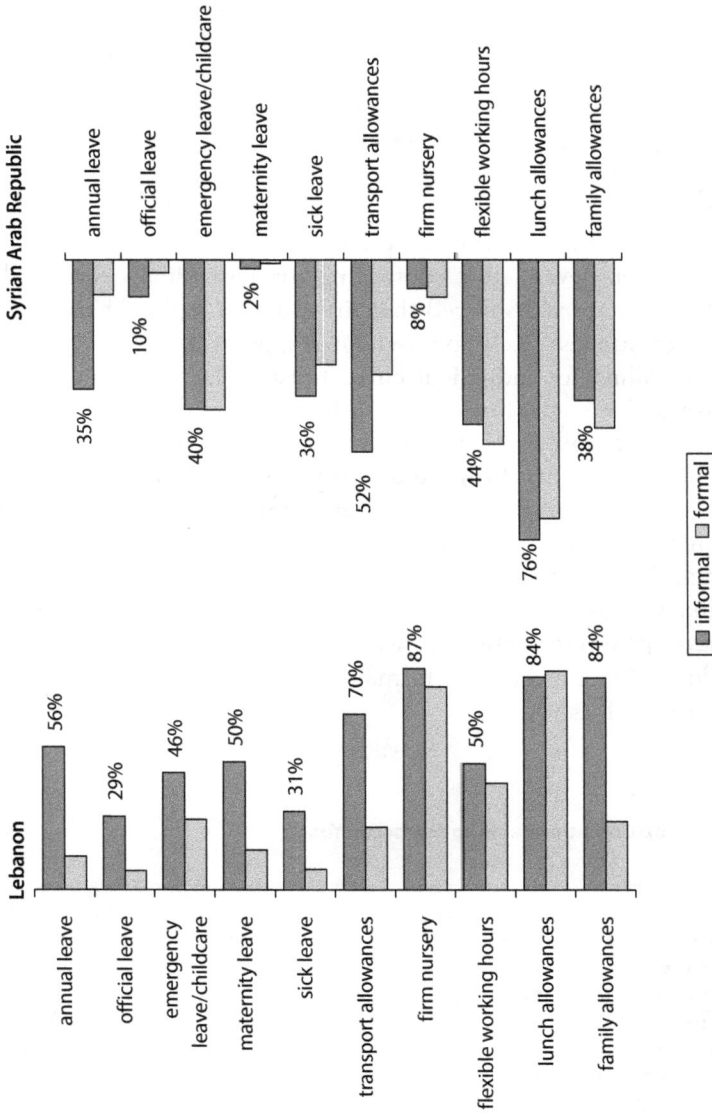

Lebanon

- annual leave: 56%
- official leave: 29%
- emergency leave/childcare: 46%
- maternity leave: 50%
- sick leave: 31%
- transport allowances: 70%
- firm nursery: 87%
- flexible working hours: 50%
- lunch allowances: 84%
- family allowances: 84%

Syrian Arab Republic

- annual leave: 35%
- official leave: 10%
- emergency leave/childcare: 40%
- maternity leave: 2%
- sick leave: 36%
- transport allowances: 52%
- firm nursery: 8%
- flexible working hours: 44%
- lunch allowances: 76%
- family allowances: 38%

■ informal □ formal

Source: Alloush and others 2011.

213

Furthermore, informal workers are more likely to be working in unsafe conditions. Data from the Morocco youth survey provide additional information on job safety and dignity at the job place for formal and informal workers (table 4.9). Results indicate that informal workers are systematically worse off: more likely to be physically or verbally abused, more likely work longer period of time for less pay, more likely to be harassed at the workplace, and more likely to feel they are exposed to exhausting workloads. Finally, informal workers are much more likely to feel that their job is not challenging and/or not interesting, which supports the view that informal jobs might entail waste of talents.

Informal workers appear to be less likely to receive training than formal workers, even after controlling for individual characteristics. Evidence in chapter 3 showed that firms with a higher share of informal workers are less likely to provide training. In the Syria sample, and after controlling for individual characteristics such as education and cognitive and noncognitive scores, informal workers are found to be significantly less likely to receive training. However, this association loses significance once firm fixed effects are included, indicating that the correlation identified cross-sectionally might all be due to differences in firms' types. Among Moroccan workers who did not report benefiting from technical training, informal workers were significantly more likely to report that no training is accessible to them, and that they have little information on what training to take. Moreover, they were almost twice as likely as formal workers to report that they could not afford the fees.

Table 4.9   Job Conditions among Moroccan Youth
percent

	Total	Formal	Informal
Verbal abuse from clients or colleagues	18	14.3	18.9
Physical abuse	2	0.0	2.5
Long hours many days in a row	35	25.6	36.5
Too little pay	51	33.6	54.1
Exhausting work load	39	21.5	42.7
Harassment from clients or colleagues	3	2.7	3.5
Hazardous workplace	14	8.7	14.5
Harassment during commute	4	3.9	4.1
Unchallenging/very boring	29	12.0	32.2
Working without definite information about pay	8	5.9	8.8

Source: Morocco Household and Youth Survey 2010.

Striving for Better Jobs • http://dx.doi.org/10.1596/978-0-8213-9535-6

Self-Employment: A Choice?

For some self-employed, informality may be a matter of choice. As mentioned in chapter 2, self-employed workers are somewhat different from other informal workers (mainly wage earners). Results from Egypt and Lebanon indicate that self-employed workers are mainly male (72 percent in Egypt and 85 percent in Lebanon), belong predominantly to the age group 35–54 (about 50 percent in both countries), and have attained at most a secondary education (93 percent in Egypt and 87 percent in Lebanon). On average, self-employed workers are older and less educated than informal wage earners (see chapter 2). Nevertheless, as illustrated in figure 4.8, self-employed workers in Lebanon generally earn, on average, 32 percent higher wages than informal wage earners (although they still earn lower wages than formal wage earners in net terms). This holds true all along the wage distribution. Indeed, a small

Figure 4.8 Net Wages by Employment Status (Lebanon, 2010)

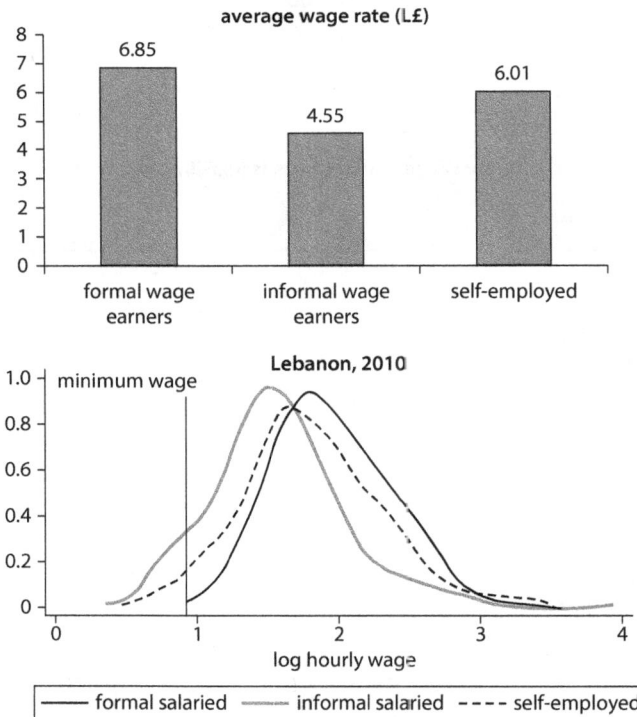

pool of self-employed is seen at the top end of the wage distribution (see figure 4.8) earning even higher wages than formal wage earners. These results would be consistent with self-employed workers preferring their employment status versus that of informal wage earners and even versus formal wage earners (that is, those at the very high end of the wage distribution).

Self-employed workers enjoy being independent, although they would like to be covered by a social security scheme. Table 4.10 provides information on self-stated preferences and perceptions of being self-employed versus being a wage earner. Results indicate that 70 to 75 percent of all workers would like to be wage earners mainly for job security reasons (that is, having social security and greater employment security). Note that only 7 to 15 percent of all workers interviewed claimed that better opportunities and/or greater job satisfaction would be a reason for wanting to be a wage earner. At the same time, the majority of workers interviewed claimed that greater independence and higher earnings are the main two reasons for wanting to be self-employed. Although enjoying the benefits of independence and higher earnings, the majority of self-employed workers (53 percent) would like to be registered in a social security scheme.

Table 4.10   Preferences for Wage Earning versus Self-Employment (Lebanon, 2010)

percent

	Informal wage earners	Formal wage earners	Self-employed
Reasons for wanting to be a wage earner			
Greater job security	64.5	57.7	52.3
Access to social security	10.3	13.8	24.4
Better prospects	4.7	9.0	4.7
Greater professional satisfaction	4.7	5.8	2.3
Reasons for wanting to be self-employed			
Greater independence	57.1	53.6	63.2
Higher income level	19.9	21.7	20.4
More flexible hours	5.8	4.9	6.5
Better prospects	6.3	8.0	4.2
Greater professional satisfaction	6.8	8.4	2.3
Would like to be formal (registered in NSSF) (% yes)	67.9		53.5

How Much Are Workers Willing to Contribute to Social Security?

By and large, informal workers would like to have access to social security benefits and are willing to pay for them. In Lebanon and Syria, 70 percent of informal workers indicate they would like to have social security benefits and are willing to give up on average 5.8 percent of their salary. This compares to a contribution rate of 2 percent for NSSF, which provides health insurance coverage with an additional 9 percent paid by the employer. Of the 30 percent of informal salaried workers who are not interested in being registered in NSSF, 37 percent say that having private health insurance from a different source is the main reason for their lack of interest (table 4.11). Although only limited inferences can be made because of the small sample size (these questions were asked only of informal workers who did not want to contribute to social security), it should be noted that both the poor perceived quality of the public service and lack of information are reported as leading reasons for opting out of the system. Similarly in Morocco, lack of information and how the system works are the top reasons for not wanting social security (table 4.11). Although no strong correlations emerge, generally males and the better educated are more likely to know how social security works. It is interesting that a high share of noncontributing workers in Syria report that they are not concerned about retirement.

Table 4.11   Reasons Why Informal Workers Do Not Want to Contribute to Social Security

percent

	Lebanon	Syrian Arab Republic	Morocco (youth)
Informal workers who do not want to contribute	28	30	
Reasons for not wanting to contribute			
Private health insurance	37	—	0.9
Reduction of earnings too much	22	39	15.3
Low quality of service	39	42	6.7
Do not know how it works	19	55	50.9
Not concerned about retirement	—	56	—
Employer does not want to pay	—	—	26.9
Does not think current job gives right to social security	—	—	66.7

Source: Salaried workers (Lebanon Labor Force Survey 2011, Syria 2010, Morocco Household and Youth Survey 2010).

It is not clear whether this is attributable to myopia or to the existence of strong informal social safety nets that would substitute for retirement savings. Also in Syria, half of the noncontributing respondents report that "not knowing how it works" is an important reason for not contributing. This suggests that improving financial literacy and communication about pension systems' roles and rules might be an important component of effective risk protection.

Networks and Intergenerational Persistence

Networks constitute an important mechanism for workers to find formal and informal employment. The large majority of workers in the MENA region report having found jobs through personal connections. This is particularly the case for informal workers. For example, 85 percent and 74 percent of informal workers in Lebanon and Syria, respectively, report finding jobs through personal contacts (table 4.12). Overall, this evidence points at a very limited role for private and public institutional mechanisms to support broad matching of skills. Employers seem to fulfill their labor demand through mechanisms that bypass market signals of skills or quality of education, either because these signals might not be informative or because other factors, such as trust, are dominant and unlikely to be picked up by market matching mechanisms. To the extent that personal contacts and networks develop within, rather than across, specific social

Table 4.12   How People Find Jobs

percent

Lebanon	Formal	Informal
Personal contacts	77.3	84.5
Other	10.4	6.3
Advertisement	7.3	6.6
Online job search	4.2	1.7
Recruitment agency	0.66	0.99
National employment agency	0.22	0.0
Syrian Arab Republic		
Personal connections	62.3	74.1
Direct contact with company	21.5	16.3
Advertisement (newspaper)	6.1	6.6
Other	4.6	2.2
National employment agency	3.8	0.2
Private employment agency	1	0.5
Online advertisement	0.6	0.16

Source: Lebanon Labor Force Survey 2010 and Syria 2010.

and economic strata, these job search methods are likely to perpetuate segmentations within labor markets, particularly across formal and informal jobs, thus preventing the best matches and highest returns to skills from being realized.

Evidence from Lebanon and Syria stresses the importance of family relationships for finding informal employment. Table 4.13 presents the self-reported relationship to the firm owner for employed individuals in Lebanon and Syria. Results indicate that informal workers tend to be related to the firm owner (that is, be family or friend) more often than are formal workers. Among informal workers, this phenomenon is particularly present among family-owned companies and almost absent in large enterprises. The opposite is observed among formal workers, for whom the importance of networks does not change substantially across firm size. Consistent with these findings, in Lebanon and Egypt, informal jobs are less likely to require significant commutes because networks are generally built within the community of residence (for example, in Egypt, youth are less likely to have a lengthy commute if working informally).

Networks seem to be an important determinant for finding "formal" employment. Regression analysis indicates that in Morocco, having a father with a formal job significantly increases one's chances of having a formal job, even after controlling for own and parental education, as well as for whether one's father speaks French (used here as a proxy for social status; table 4.14). Moreover, the probability of being informal decreases significantly if another member of the household holds a formal job. In Morocco, the formality definition captures both pension and health insurance coverage, because the benefits are bundled. The literature on informality often makes the assumption that informality is higher because, with bundled and family coverage, incentives to participate in

Table 4.13   Relationship to Owner
percent

Relationship to firm owner	Lebanon		Syrian Arab Republic	
	Formal	Informal	Formal	Informal
Member of household	3.6	7.3	1.4	2.8
Relative outside household	1.8	5.9	2.1	6.3
Friend/neighbor	7.8	16.3	8.9	13.4
From the same town	4.4	10.6	0.8	0.3
Unrelated	82.4	59.8	86.7	77.3

Source: Lebanon Labor force survey 2010 and Syria 2010.

Table 4.14 Determinants of Informality: Networks in Morocco

	OLS (1)	OLS (2)	OLS (3)	OLS (4)
Dependent variable	Informal	Informal	Informal	Informal
Father has formal job	−0.124***	−0.118***	−0.109***	−0.108***
Controls	Gender, age, age squared, Education, province, urban	Gender, age, age squared, Education, province, urban, father education, father French speaking	Gender, age, age squared, Education, province, urban, father education, father French speaking, wealth	Gender, age, age squared, Education, province, urban, father education, father French speaking, wealth, cell phone ownership

Source: Gatti and others 2011.
***Significant at 1 percent.

220

the system for family members of a formal worker are very limited. However, the evidence for Morocco points at the opposite: Formal jobs appear as a privilege of the few, and family connections are successfully leveraged to access them.

Conclusions

Results indicate that the average worker in the formal sector earns higher wages compared to the average worker in the informal sector. Controlling for other factors such as education, experience, and gender, workers in the formal sector earn higher wages than otherwise similar workers in the informal sector. This "formality premium" is generally high, ranging from 10 percent in Syria to up to 53 percent among youth in Morocco. The formality premium is higher among female workers in all cases. On average, a female worker in the formal sector earns 1.5 times as much as an otherwise similar worker in the informal sector. Very low wages paid to female workers in the informal sector often explain why many women decide not to participate in the labor market at all, especially if the opportunities to find formal jobs are limited.

The observed differences in wages between the informal and formal can be attributed to differences in the characteristics of formal and informal workers (endowments), as well as to differences in how the labor market rewards those characteristics (returns). About one-third of the wage differential in countries such as Egypt and Lebanon can be explained by the fact that, on average, formal workers are older and more educated than informal workers. In Lebanon, the wage differential is explained mostly by the labor market treating similar skills of formal and informal workers differently.

Where workers are employed (small versus large firms) and their skills and ability can both potentially affect the observed formality premium, but the formality premium is found to persist even when these additional factors are accounted for. A priori there might be important differences in workers' wages across small and large firms because of differences in firms' productivity. Omitting this factor could be problematic in estimating the formality premium, especially when informal workers for the most part find employment in micro-firms. When firm size is controlled for, workers in micro-firms in Lebanon earn 23 percent less than workers in medium size firms (10 to 49 employees) and about one-third of the formality premium is attributable to firm characteristics. However, a formality premium of about

20 percent still persists. In Egypt and Syria, the formality premium is virtually unaffected by inclusion of controls for where workers are employed. Although firm size might be an imperfect measure of firm productivity, even using firm fixed-effects estimation (Syria) confirms that informal workers earn less than formal workers, independent of where they work.

Individual ability does not seem to be an additional important determinant of the formality premium. Quality of education and skills often differ starkly across social strata and are correlated with the likelihood of working in the informal sector. Assignment to the informal sector is not random, and so it may be important to control for individual ability and skills to ensure that the attribution of the formality premium does not instead reflect other factors. Data from Lebanon and Syria allow proxying for individual ability through results of direct cognitive and noncognitive tests. When cognitive and noncognitive scores are included in the estimation (and controlling for other factors), the observed informality premium remains largely unchanged. These results suggest that informal workers are generally worse-off, because individual ability is better rewarded by formal jobs than by informal jobs.

Limited mobility between formal and informal employment points at the existence of segmentations in the region's labor markets. The fact that measured rewards (wages) to skills are consistently different across formal and informal workers cannot be taken alone as an indicator of labor market segmentation, because many other features of jobs are usually unmeasured. Mobility patterns provide important insights into the extent to which labor markets are segmented or integrated. In this chapter longitudinal data from two separate sources for Egypt are used to study mobility patterns between the formal and informal sectors. Results indicate that between 1998 and 2006, persistence in formal or informal employment status was very high and upward mobility was minimal, with only 9 percent of informal salaried workers transitioning into formal jobs. Transition from informal to formal jobs was associated with an average increase in earnings of 24 percent, confirming the hypothesis that formal workers are generally better off.

Beyond earnings, workers in the informal sector are generally disadvantaged in many other dimensions. Informal workers are more likely to be unsatisfied with their job relative to formal workers. This is explained by the fact that informal jobs entail worse working conditions. Results in this chapter indicate that, in many dimensions, formal workers display better job quality indicators, such as higher earnings, having a written contract, longer employment tenure, and higher chances to choose when to work overtime (and be paid for such work). Furthermore, informal workers enjoy fewer benefits than formal workers, such as paid leave and maternity leave. On the positive side, evidence from Egypt suggests that informal jobs require, on average, shorter commutes, which indicates that they are more likely to be "local."

Finally, results in this chapter indicate that individual networks are important to explain the likelihood that individuals find formal and informal employment. The large majority of workers in the MENA region report having found jobs through personal connections. This is particularly the case for informal workers. For example, 85 percent and 74 percent of informal workers in Lebanon and Syria, respectively, report finding jobs through personal contacts. Informal workers tend to be somewhat more related to the firm owner (that is, a family or friend) than formal workers. Networks are also important for individuals to find formal employment. Evidence from Morocco indicates that, controlling for other factors, having a father with a formal job significantly increases one's chances of having a formal job. In Morocco, the evidence also suggests that, everything else equal, workers are more likely to find a formal jobs if someone else in the family already has a formal job. In countries where pension and health insurance are bundled and where spouses and dependents can rely on the worker's coverage, this evidence suggests that formality is likely driven by the use of network to secure the "good jobs."

Annex

Annex table 4A.1 Estimating the Formality Premium in Lebanon

Variables	(1)	(2)	(3)	(4)	(5)
	ln(earnings/hr)	ln(earnings/hr)	ln(earnings/hr)	ln(earnings/hr)	ln(earnings/hr)
Informal	-0.2920***		-0.1915***	-0.2024***	-0.1953***
Years of education	0.0325***		0.0264***	0.0247***	0.0260***
Male	0.0982***		0.0926**	0.0859**	0.0645
Age	0.0133		0.0117	0.0147	0.0161
Age²	-0.0001		-0.0001	-0.0001	-0.0001
Firm size <5 (base 10–49)			-0.2312***	-0.2195***	-0.2157***
Firm size 5–9			-0.0374	-0.0629	-0.0668
Firm size >50			0.0165	-0.0065	-0.0117
Cognitive score quintile 2				0.0523	0.0549
Cognitive score quintile 3				0.1325**	0.1268**
Cognitive score quintile 4				0.1446**	0.1615***
Cognitive score quintile 5				0.1347**	0.1514**
Open to experience					-0.0451
Conscientious					-0.0072
Extravert					0.0044
Agreeable					-0.1303***
Emotionally stable					-0.0607
Constant	1.1544***		0.9748***	0.8845***	0.9322***
Observations	582		582	533	519
R^2	0.2526		0.3379	0.3430	0.3769

Source: Alloush and others 2011.

Note: Estimation with OLS, robust standard errors.

***$p<.01$, **$p<.05$, *$p<.1$.

Annex table 4A.2   Estimating the Formality Premium in Syria

Variables	(1) Log hourly wage	(2) Log hourly wage	(3) Log hourly wage	(4) Log hourly wage	Firm fixed effects Log hourly wage
Informal	−0.109**	−0.123***	−0.123***	−0.119***	−0.127***
Years of education	0.0436***	0.0420***	0.0349***	0.0334***	0.0302***
Male	0.133***	0.136***	0.132***	0.122***	0.156***
Age	0.0459***	0.0458***	0.0472***	0.0465***	0.0415***
Age^2	−0.000477***	−0.000465***	−0.000468***	−0.000470***	−0.000384**
Firm size 1–5		0.0470	0.0314	0.000480	
Firm size 6–10		−0.0740	−0.0555	−0.0460	
Firm size >50		−0.0738	−0.0722	−0.0683	
Cognitive score quintile 2			0.00837	−0.00731	−0.00632
Cognitive score quintile 3			0.0668	0.0397	0.0197
Cognitive score quintile 4			0.112*	0.0903	0.0522
Cognitive score quintile 5			0.258***	0.229***	0.126
Open to experience				0.0882***	0.0991***
Conscientious				−0.00841	0.0113
Extravert				−0.0324	−0.00719
Agreeable				−0.168***	−0.135***
Emotionally stable				−0.0361	0.0152

Source: Alloush and others 2011.

Note: Estimation with OLS, robust standard errors.

***p<.01, **p<.05, *p<.1.

Annex table 4A.3 Estimating the Formality Premium in Egypt

Dependent variable = log hourly wage	Informality defined by not having access to social security			Informality defined by not having access to social security and not having a work contract		
	Total	Male	Female	Total	Male	Female
Informal dummy	-0.262*** [0.031]	-0.192*** [0.033]	-0.583*** [0.065]	-0.145*** [0.032]	-0.116*** [0.033]	-0.515*** [0.083]
Middle school	0.196*** [0.042]	0.163*** [0.045]	0.413*** [0.127]	0.208*** [0.042]	0.170*** [0.045]	0.402*** [0.123]
High school	0.324*** [0.026]	0.311*** [0.027]	0.478*** [0.084]	0.342*** [0.026]	0.322*** [0.027]	0.490*** [0.087]
Tertiary	0.714*** [0.033]	0.743*** [0.037]	0.826*** [0.088]	0.740*** [0.033]	0.759*** [0.037]	0.843*** [0.093]
Experience	0.037*** [0.003]	0.031*** [0.003]	0.040*** [0.005]	0.039*** [0.003]	0.031*** [0.003]	0.046*** [0.005]
exp^2	-0.000*** [0.000]	-0.000*** [0.000]	-0.000*** [0.000]	-0.000*** [0.000]	-0.000*** [0.000]	-0.000*** [0.000]
Alexandria	-0.068** [0.034]	-0.018 [0.041]	-0.189*** [0.059]	-0.060* [0.034]	-0.015 [0.041]	-0.147** [0.059]
Urban upper	-0.107*** [0.030]	-0.124*** [0.037]	-0.157*** [0.051]	-0.113*** [0.031]	-0.131*** [0.037]	-0.142*** [0.052]
Urban lower	-0.140*** [0.032]	-0.122*** [0.039]	-0.260*** [0.054]	-0.143*** [0.032]	-0.125*** [0.039]	-0.245*** [0.054]
Rural upper	-0.112*** [0.033]	-0.151*** [0.037]	-0.163* [0.097]	-0.126*** [0.033]	-0.163*** [0.037]	-0.172* [0.104]
Rural lower	-0.191*** [0.030]	-0.192*** [0.035]	-0.300*** [0.063]	-0.196*** [0.030]	-0.196*** [0.035]	-0.300*** [0.064]
Secondary sector	0.267*** [0.025]	0.222*** [0.026]	0.167** [0.073]	0.267*** [0.025]	0.221*** [0.026]	0.174** [0.072]
Tertiary sector	0.244*** [0.027]	0.222*** [0.030]	0.211*** [0.062]	0.253*** [0.028]	0.228*** [0.030]	0.239*** [0.064]

table continues next page

Annex table 4A.3 Estimating the Formality Premium in Egypt *(continued)*

Dependent variable = log hourly wage	Informality defined by not having access to social security			Informality defined by not having access to social security and not having a work contract		
	Total	*Male*	*Female*	*Total*	*Male*	*Female*
Public sector dummy	−0.113*** [0.032]	−0.088** [0.035]	−0.007 [0.066]	−0.047 [0.032]	−0.045 [0.035]	0.056 [0.069]
Married dummy	0.090*** [0.025]	0.079*** [0.030]	0.084* [0.044]	0.103*** [0.025]	0.091*** [0.030]	0.100** [0.045]
Constant	0.151*** [0.055]	0.263*** [0.062]	−0.139 [0.123]	0.024 [0.054]	0.188*** [0.061]	−0.331*** [0.123]
Observations	5,144	3,960	1,184	5,144	3,960	1,184
R^2	0.249	0.234	0.423	0.24	0.228	0.404
Formality premium	23.0	17.5	44.2	13.5	11.0	40.2

Source: Angel-Urdinola and Tanabe 2011, using the 2006 Egypt ELMPs.

Note: Omitted variables: Education: Primary; Region: Cairo; Sector of employment: Primary sector (agriculture); Secondary sector (manufacturing and construction); Tertiary sector (wholesale, transport, services); Public administration and social services (including education and health).

Notes

1. To appropriately control for hours worked, the analysis is based on hourly wages in current local currency (that is, wage rates).

2. Formal workers are required to pay taxes, and so some high-earning workers have an incentive to evade taxes and earn higher net wages, especially if they have access to health insurance through a family member and/or to a pension.

3. Because of the likely presence of omitted variables, the estimate of this coefficient is likely biased. In particular, if (unobservable) ability is positively correlated with formality, this coefficient is likely biased upward. However, when direct measures of individuals' cognitive and noncognitive ability are introduced for Lebanon and Syria, the size of the coefficient remains unchanged.

4. Herrera and Badr (2011) estimate a formality premium for Egypt of 13.2 percent using a different definition of informality (workers not having a contract and not contributing to social security). Using the same definition, very similar results are found in this analysis and are available upon request.

5. Controls are year of education, age, age squared, and a gender dummy.

6. See, for example, Arias and Khamis (2007) and Pianto and others (2009) for approaches that correct for selectivity bias.

7. Two main sources of concern are found when it comes to endogeneity. First, ability influences education outcomes, which in turn affect measured ability. This would tend to overestimate the coefficients on skills and underestimate that of schooling. Second, reverse causality may exist between labor outcomes and socioemotional skills. Personal characteristics can influence labor market outcomes, but labor market outcomes can also influence the way one feels about oneself. For example, having a low paying job can lower one's self-esteem and emotional stability (Heckman and others 2006).

8. Note that the two rounds of surveys are likely to capture the early crisis impact because they were fielded in April 2008 and March 2009. Unfortunately, because of the lack of information on type of contracts (temporary vs. permanent), it is not possible to further disentangle mobility across formal/informal states.

9. Following Maloney (1999), job duration can be calculated as $1/(1-P_{ii})$ where P_{ii} is the individual probability of not leaving sector/state i. See Silva and others (2011) for a detailed discussion.

10. See Maloney (1999).

11. Bosch and Maloney (2010) compute an adjusted propensity to transit from sector i to sector j (C-stats). This statistic weighs the raw transition probabilities by the rates of leaving the origin sector and the relative opening in the receiving sector compared to the economy as a whole.

12. Note that contribution density here, in contrast to the coverage rate, is not defined in relation to the labor force, but rather to the population registered with the social insurance administration. This population includes (at least temporarily) inactive people who exited the labor force after a period of past contributions; therefore the contribution density defined in this manner is naturally smaller than the coverage rate for the identical population.

13. The Chile and Jordan datasets differ somewhat, which may confound the interpretation of these results. For example, the underlying Jordanian administrative data cover a period of 363 months, whereas the Chilean data cover only 288 months; that is, it might be more likely to observe long (in excess of 36 months) contributory and noncontributory spells in Jordan than in Chile because of data differences. However, it is unlikely that the radical difference in the shape of the distributions can be explained solely by this sample difference.

14. In this chapter "job quality" is referred to in a way that is akin to the "decent work" definition. Decent work involves opportunities for work that is productive and delivers a fair income, security in the workplace and social protection for families, better prospects for personal development and social integration, freedom for people to express their concerns, organize and participate in the decisions that affect their lives, and equality of opportunity and treatment for all women and men. The private sector and innovation literature usually refers to job quality as "high value-added jobs." The discussion of which policy interventions can promote the development of high value-added production (for example, moving from textiles to electronics) is complementary to the treatment of informality herein. However, it is beyond the scope of this report.

15. An interesting exception is in Lebanon, where informal workers report having higher confidence in the stability of their jobs than do formal workers.

References

Alloush, M., C. Chartouni, R. Gatti, and J. Silva. 2011. "Informality and Exclusion: Evidence from Lebanon and Syria." Mimeo. Washington, DC: World Bank.

Angel-Urdinola, D., and K. Tanabe. 2011. "Micro-determinants of Informal Employment in the Middle East and North Africa Region." Mimeo. Washington, DC: World Bank.

Arias, O., and M. Khamis. 2007. "Comparative Advantage and Informal Employment." Mimeo. Washington, DC: World Bank.

Bosch, M., and W. Maloney. 2010. "Comparative Analysis of Labor Market Dynamics Using Markov Processes: An Application to Informality." *Labour Economics* 17: 621–631.

Bowles, S., H. Gintis, and M. Osborne. 2001. "The Determinants of Earnings: A Behavioral Approach." *Journal of Economic Literature* 39 (4): 1137–1176.

Cawley, J., J .J. Heckman, and E. J. Vytlacil. 2001. "Three Observations on Wages and Measured Cognitive Ability. *Labour Economics* 8 (4): 419–442.

Gatti, R., M. Ivanic, and J. Silva. 2011. "It's Who You Know: Networks and the Chance of Getting a Formal Job." Mimeo. Washington, DC: World Bank.

Hansen, K. T., J. J. Heckman, and K. J. Mullen. 2004. "The Effect of Schooling and Ability on Achievement Test Scores." *Journal of Econometrics* 121 (1–2): 39–98.

Heckman, J. J., J. Stixrud, and S. Urzua. 2006. "The Effects of Cognitive and Non-cognitive Abilities on Labor Market Outcomes and Social Behavior." Working Paper 12006. Cambridge, MA: National Bureau of Economic Research.

Herrera, S., and K. Badr. 2011. "Why Does the Productivity of Education Vary across Individuals in Egypt? Firm Size, Gender and Access to Technology as Sources of Heterogeneity in Returns to Education." Mimeo. Washington, DC: Word Bank.

Maloney, W. F. 1999. "Does Informality Imply Segmentation in Urban Labor Markets? Evidence from Sectoral Transitions in Mexico." *World Bank Economic Review* 13 (2): 275–302.

———. 2004. "Informality Revisited." *World Development* 32 (7): 1159–1178.

Pianto, D. M., M. Tannuri-Pianto, and O. Arias. 2009. "Informal Employment in Bolivia: A Lost Proposition?" Mimeo. Washington, DC: World Bank.

Silva, J., M. Benyagoub, and G. Wallner. 2010. "Informality, Firm Performance and Labor Market Outcomes: Evidence from Matched Employer-Employee Data for Morocco." Mimeo. Washington, DC: World Bank.

Silva, J., Y. Dukhan, and D. Marotta. 2011. "Determinants and Earnings Consequences of Mobility In and Out of Informality in Egypt." Mimeo. Washington, DC: World Bank.

CHAPTER 5

Barriers to Coverage and Policy Options

SUMMARY: Widespread informality implies that large portions of the workforce are not protected against old age, disability, and, often, health risks. Although the need to address these vulnerabilities provides a clear rationale for government intervention, the actual drivers of informality should inform policy levers and choices. Many institutional constraints determine the labor market segmentation that underpins informality in MENA, such as the design of pension systems, business and labor regulation, incentives and pay in the public sector, and the design of interventions to improve skills upgrading. This chapter analyzes these institutional constraints and presents a related set of policy interventions to effectively expand coverage and promote the creation of better quality jobs. First, the chapter discusses the importance of a healthy business environment that fosters competition and facilitates firm entry. Easing certain provisions of the labor legislation and keeping the cost of labor at a realistic level can help employment creation and reduce informality, especially if coupled with reforms geared toward protection of workers' transitions. Realigning the pay and benefit package that is offered by public sector employment can reduce important distortions. Moreover, the low productivity dimension of informality, a phenomenon that is particularly relevant among the poorest countries in the region, calls for productivity-enhancing interventions, including those that aim to improve access and realign training and skill-upgrading programs to the needs of the informal sector. Second, the chapter discusses how reforms in the design of the social insurance system in MENA are critical for addressing informality. Limited legal coverage, the short minimum vesting requirements, generous early retirement provisions, and the use of an average wage measure from the final years before retirement for pension benefit calculation all contribute to limited coverage. Addressing the coverage gap will require governments to look beyond reforming the existing social insurance system to seek special coverage extension schemes targeted to the informal sector and to those with limited savings capacity.

This chapter is organized in two parts and addresses five distinct and complementary policy angles, each linked to the drivers of informality in the MENA region. Part 1 discusses institutional barriers to formality in MENA, including (1) the business environment, (2) labor market regulations, and (3) public sector employment bias, and provides relevant policy options. Part 1 also discusses the need for (4) addressing the productivity trap faced by informal workers, particularly through training and skills-upgrading interventions. Part 2 of this chapter focuses on (5) the social insurance system and presents barriers to coverage linked to the incentive design of pension systems in MENA. It presents policy options and recommendations for coverage extension through both improving the design of existing social insurance systems and introducing new special schemes targeting informal workers.

Part 1. Addressing Institutional Barriers and the Low Productivity Trap

Introduction to Part 1

Although growth materialized in the last decade in MENA, not enough good jobs were created. Instead, informal employment grew, characterized by lower pay, lack of access to training, worse working conditions, and lower job tenure than formal employment. These conditions affect the vast majority of workers, whereas relatively few "insiders," including those employed in the public sector, benefit from privileged circumstances. Reforms aimed at decreasing informality can potentially affect two aspects of this process: (1) by generating direct productivity gains and increasing job creation (increasing the "size of the pie") and (2) by improving how equitably rents and benefits from the development process are redistributed. In this sense, many of the policy options discussed here can have an impact both on employment creation as well as on formalization and moving toward fulfilling work for all. Because of the multidimensionality of informality, it is important to acknowledge that a complex set of policy interventions might be needed to effectively overcome barriers to formality in a sustainable manner and help the growth process to become progressively more inclusive. Here, too, the mechanism through which formalization is achieved matters greatly for its effects on employment, efficiency, and growth. If formalization is based purely on enforcement, it will likely lead to unemployment and low growth. If, on the other hand, it is based on improvements in both the regulatory framework and the quality and availability of public services, it is likely to bring about more efficient use of resources and higher growth.

Certain features of the regulatory framework in MENA, encompassing the business environment, set of labor regulations, and nature of employment in the public sector, pose barriers to formality. Informality appears to be strictly intertwined with the development process and can be largely explained as a suboptimal private sector response to restrictive regulation. The first part of this chapter describes institutional barriers to formality and provides relevant policy options that extend beyond mere enforcement. In particular, this section addresses the need for a conducive business environment, the importance of less restrictive labor regulations, and, at the same time, more effective protection of workers' income during employment transitions. Moreover, the first part of this chapter argues that the preference for public sector jobs in many MENA countries affects informality outcomes, requiring a realignment of incentives to limit queuing for these jobs. Finally, recognizing that many informal workers face a low-productivity trap because of their limited access to relevant skill acquisition, numerous skills-upgrading interventions are explored for specific MENA context.

Improving the Business Climate
Having to obey more stringent regulations may imply lower flexibility in firms' employment and production decisions, and therefore, lower profits and productivity (Almeida and Carneiro 2005).

Excessive entry regulations and high taxes matter for informality and growth. Across countries, a significant correlation is found between the size of the informal sector and the ease of doing business (figure 5.1). Barriers to firm entry give discretion to public officials to exclude or advantage specific investors (World Bank 2009) and thus continue to perpetuate a dual model of development in which a few "protected" firms thrive and share rents while many small firms strive to survive. These barriers work as an impediment to growth, especially for the most productive among these outsiders, who might be excluded from

Figure 5.1   Correlation across Countries between the Size of the Informal Sector and the Ease of Doing Business

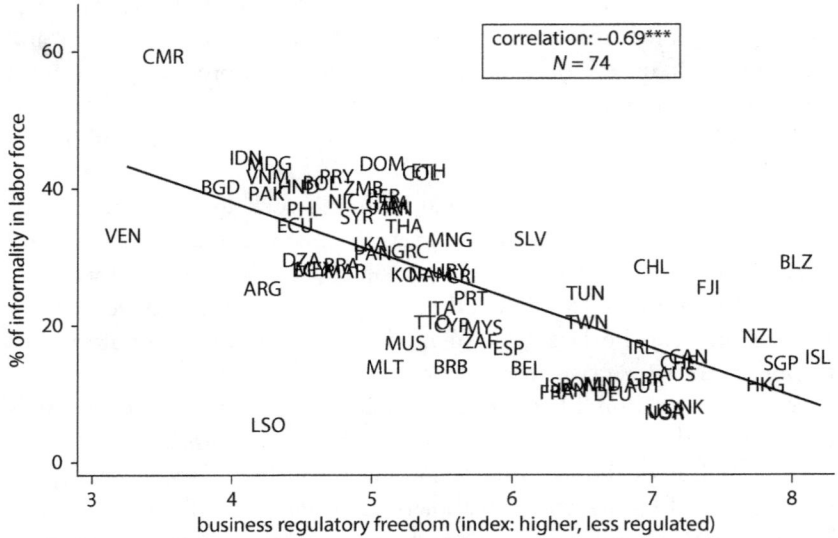

Source: Loayza and others 2005.
Note: *** = 1% significance level.

important opportunities (or alternatively, who might have to divert resources from productive activities to rent-seeking activities). In parallel, corporate taxes are also systematically identified as a constraint to business and formalization. These constraints are particularly powerful in MENA. As highlighted in chapter 3, many firms in MENA never formalize, and even those that eventually register still operate informally for a significant amount of time. The region has the developing world's highest share of firms that start out as informal (one-fourth) and the longest operating period before formalization (four years) among registered forms. The following discussion focuses on two main margins along which business environment reform can promote a more inclusive and dynamic private sector: (1) regulation of entry and (2) corporate tax reform.

Could reforms in the regulation of entry improve firms' incentives to formalize? Regulation is understood to be an important determinant of formalization. First, monetary and administrative registration costs (for example, a high number of procedures requiring extensive time and effort) increase formalization costs. After LAC, MENA is the region with the highest average number of procedures to start a business. Economies such as Algeria and Djibouti and the West Bank and Gaza economy stand out as places where the registration process is particularly cumbersome, requiring more than 10 procedures and an average of between 20 to 80 days to start a business (see chapter 3). Second, discretion in the application of these procedures (for example, with connected firms potentially benefiting from less strict enforcement) increases barriers to formalization for those firms that, quality-wise, would have the potential to compete on a larger scale and fully within the regulatory framework. Thus, uneven enforcement sustains an equilibrium where few connected firms thrive, a large number of firms operate informally, and new entrants face the choice of either investing in rent seeking to secure the benevolent eye of the bureaucracy or being virtuous and thus bearing the disproportionate brunt of taxation and regulation.

Reforms to the regulation of entry have been shown to have had positive, albeit moderate, effects on formalization. Interventions include (1) reducing the costs of registration, number of procedures, and minimum capital; (2) providing information and training to entrepreneurs (such as filling out forms); and (3) facilitating registration by establishing one-stop shops for registration. No experimental evidence exists in MENA on the likely impact of these reforms. In Mexico experiments were conducted and the impact evaluated (Bruhn 2011; Kaplan and others 2011). Broadly, these studies found that simplifying the process of business registration had a moderate impact on formalization of existing firms. In contrast, they indicate that the intervention increased formalization because of more creation of new businesses by former wage earners (Bruhn 2008). Another potential reason for the limited impacts on formalization of existing firms is that results might take time because of uncertainty about reform reversal, which is not captured by these analyses. Finally, the effect of these policies tends to depend on how many firms are at the margin of formalizing. Given the differences between MENA and LAC in this domain, the effects of this type of intervention could be significantly larger in the MENA region.

High taxation burden was the constraint to formalization most widely identified by micro- and small firms in Egypt and Morocco (figure 5.2). High taxes imply high costs of regulatory compliance if a formal business. Morocco's corporate tax rate is one of the highest among developing

Figure 5.2   Obstacles to Formalization in Egypt and Morocco

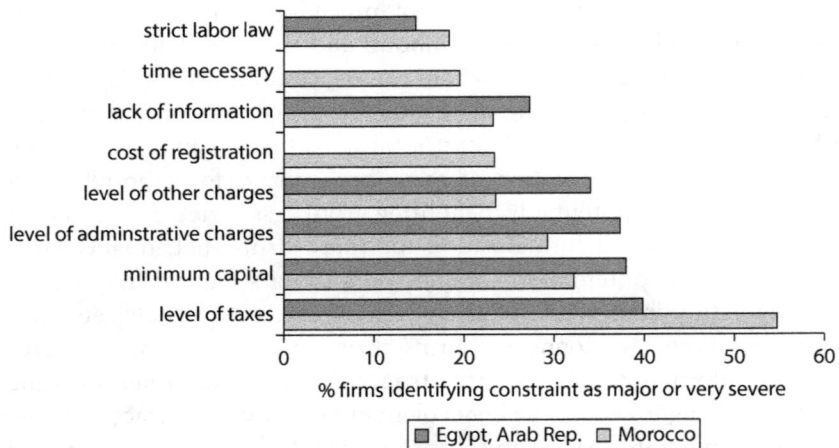

Source: Calculations using informal ICA surveys from Morocco 2008 and Egypt 2010.

countries: In 2007, it was second only to Pakistan and remained significantly above the average for developing countries in 2008. It is interesting that in Egypt (where corporate tax rates are below the developing countries average), a significantly smaller share of firms than in Morocco identified tax rates as being a major obstacle to formalization. The country's profit taxes are also high relative to countries with similar income levels.[1] Similar results were also found in countries such as Mexico, Brazil, and Bolivia. Lowering the corporate tax rate can affect tax revenue through three main channels: (1) existing formal firms may invest more and earn more income on which they pay taxes, (2) existing informal firms may be induced to formalize and start paying some taxes, and (3) new firms might be induced to operate formally. Evidence from other regions suggests that the net effect is likely to depend on whether a reduction in the tax rate is accompanied by additional enforcement and a reduction in exceptions. The short-run impact may also be negative; for example, Turkey lowered its corporate tax rate from 30 to 20 percent in 2007 and experienced a drop in overall tax revenues (Otonglo and Trumbic 2008).[2] However, the converse happened in Egypt: When its corporate tax rate was lowered from 42 to 20 percent, it was accompanied by a significant increase in overall tax revenues. An experimental study in Brazil evaluated the impact of a reform that combines business tax

reduction (of up to 8 percent among eligible firms) and regulation simplification and found interesting results. The emerging evidence indicates
that the reform led to a significant increase in formality along several
dimensions (Fajnzylber and Reyes 2010). In particular, the reform consisted of implementing a new simplified tax system for micro- and small
firms, referred to as "SIMPLES." The new national system consolidated
several federal taxes and social security contributions into one single
monthly payment, varying from 3 to 5 percent of gross revenues for
micro-enterprises, and from 5.4 to 7 percent of revenues for small firms.
Program eligibility excluded some sectors. This intervention suggests that
this type of program can increase levels of registration and government
revenues. Enforcement matters too. Overall, and not surprisingly, more
frequent inspections are associated with lower underreporting of workers
and sales (Almeida and Carneiro 2009). In MENA, firms report an
average of four tax inspections per year (the highest regional average in
the world). Such strict enforcement appears to be accompanied by widespread corruption, because informal payments were requested in
17 percent of inspections, significantly above the 7 percent reported in the
LAC and ECA regions.

In the MENA region, investment climate reforms have accelerated
in many countries in recent years. The evidence suggests that the implementation of reform matters greatly to private sector development. The
recent MENA Development Report *From Privilege to Competition*
(World Bank 2009) estimates that in response to previous reforms,
private investment in the MENA region increased by only 2 percent of
GDP, compared with between 5 and 10 percent in Asia, Eastern
Europe, and Latin America. The same report estimates that the number
of registered businesses per 1,000 people in MENA is less than one-
third that in Eastern Europe and Central Asia, and with less entry and
exits of firms, the average business is 10 years older than in East Asia or
Eastern Europe. Close to 60 percent of business managers surveyed did
not think that the rules and regulations were applied consistently and
predictably, whereas policy uncertainty, unfair competition, and corruption were identified as major concerns for investors. Discretionary
enforcement of regulation is a strong deterrent to small entrepreneurs
who start their businesses informally but are then forced to stay small
to escape controls. Staying small may, in turn, make it prohibitively
costly to formalize over time.[3] Overall, the paucity of existing data on
firms' dynamics has not yet allowed identification of which margins
matter most to promote formalization in the context of MENA. This is

an important area where experimental evidence can effectively inform policy making.

Addressing Constraints in Labor Market Regulation

Labor policies can affect informality through three main channels. First, excessive labor costs, whether due to labor regulation (such as high minimum wages, severance costs, or labor taxes) or strong worker bargaining power, can depress labor demand in the formal sector. Second, legislation can create incentives for workers to voluntarily work informally if perceived contributions exceed the benefits. Third, labor market institutions can impact productivity growth. Productivity gains arising from adoption of new technologies and production processes account for half of the differences in levels of economic development (the most important determinants of informality), not to mention long-run worker productivity and welfare more generally (World Bank 2007). Yet excessive restrictions on job reallocation or layoffs for economic reasons, or state- or union-induced inflexibilities, may reduce the adoption of such innovations.

Across countries, there is debate whether overly rigid employment protection legislation (EPL) is an important determinant of the labor market segmentations underlying informality. EPL is the set of rules governing the hiring and firing process that is provided through both labor legislation and collective bargaining agreements (box 5.1). Strong evidence suggests that overly rigid EPL tends to not only discourage hiring and firing but also may slow down adjustment to shocks, impede the reallocation of labor, and promote informality (OECD 2010). Recently, Fialová and Schneider (2010) established a statistically significant effect of EPL on the size of the informal sector in European Union (EU) countries. In the countries that have the most rigid EPL, the share of the informal sector is estimated to be about 3.5 percentage points higher than in countries that have the most flexible EPL. This result supports the view that unduly strict EPL leads some employers to hire workers informally to avoid costs imposed by the EPL. Specifically, strict EPL typically makes it harder for certain groups, including youth, women, and displaced older workers, to enter or reenter the labor market, at least on an open-ended contract.

Perceptions of employers. The extent to which labor regulations are perceived by employers as a constraint to expanding their formal employment varies among MENA countries but in general is higher

Box 5.1 Employment Protection Legislation (EPL)

EPL, a key state intervention in the labor market, aims to protect workers from arbitrary, unfair, or discriminatory actions by their employers, while addressing potential market failures stemming from insufficient information and inadequate insurance against risk. As such, EPL governs the individual employment contract, including flexibility of hiring through part-time and fixed-term contracts, and conditions of employment, including maximum number of hours in a work week, premiums for overtime work, paid annual leave, and minimum wage. It also governs flexibility of firing, including grounds for dismissal, notification rules for dismissal, priority rules for dismissal, and severance pay.

The literature on EPL describes positive and negative effects on labor market performance. Among the former, it highlights the benefits of long-term employee-employer contracts, including greater willingness to invest in on-the-job training. Among the latter is the concern that workers hired on regular contracts may enjoy a high degree of employment security to the detriment of other workers hired on temporary contracts or without formal contract and coverage. In addition, employment protection may diminish firms' ability to cope with a rapidly changing environment driven by globalization, technological change, and the derived organizational innovation (OECD 2004).

Source: Angel-Urdinola and Kuddo 2010.

Table 5.1 Employment Regulations and Skills and Education of Labor as a Major or Severe Obstacle for Expanding Employment

percent of firms

Region	Employment regulations	Skills and education of labor
Eastern Europe and Central Asia	18.7	43.2
Africa	17.3	32.6
East Asia and Pacific	14.5	33.8
Latin America and the Caribbean	29.5	42.5
South Asia	19.0	24.8
Middle East North Africa	36.2	54.4

Source: BEEPS 2008 and Enterprise Surveys.

than in other regions. According to ICA surveys, labor regulations and mandatory contributions are considered by firms as a factor that constrain many enterprises from expanding formal employment. Table 5.1 shows the percent of firms indicating employment regulations and skills and education of labor are a major or severe obstacle. The MENA

region has the highest share of employers dissatisfied with the existing
labor regulations, although it should be noted that the skills and education of the labor force are a more significant problem for all regions
than employment regulations. In Egypt, Lebanon, and Syria, labor
regulations are perceived by firms as a major constraint to expanding
formal employment, although this is true to a lesser extent in Algeria,
Jordan, Morocco, and the West Bank and Gaza economy (figure 5.3).
Manufacturing firms, service firms, and hotels in Egypt report that they
would hire a net of 21 percent, 9 percent, and 15 percent more workers, respectively, if there were fewer restrictions on hiring and firing
workers (Angel-Urdinola and Kuddo 2010). Similarly, according to
enterprise surveys, firms in Lebanon would be willing to hire more
workers (by an average of more than one-third of the workforce) in the
absence of existing restrictions on labor regulation. The results of the
enterprise survey analysis support those of previous studies (Pierre and
Scarpetta 2006), showing that firms in countries with more stringent
employment regulations are more likely to report labor regulations as
a major or very severe obstacle, even after controlling for other factors
such as GDP and unemployment. Overall, EPL as an obstacle to business growth tends to be more pronounced in countries that are more

**Figure 5.3   Share of Firms Identifying Labor Regulations as a Major Constraint in
Doing Business in MENA (%)**

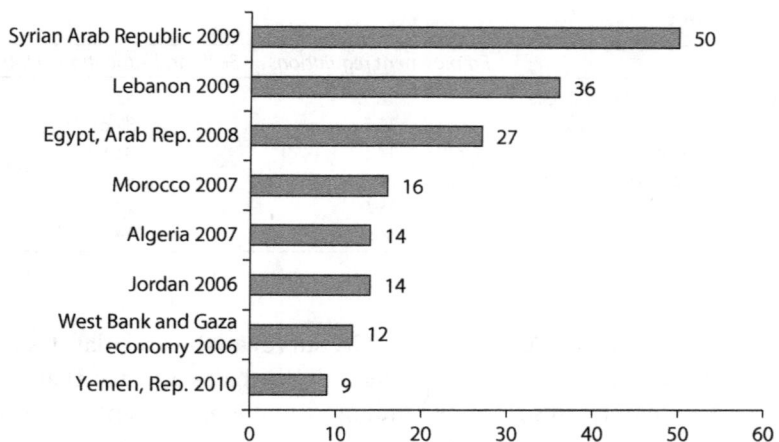

Source: World Bank: www.enterprisesurveys.org.

Striving for Better Jobs • http://dx.doi.org/10.1596/978-0-8213-9535-6

likely to enforce it (including through court challenges) and less of a problem in countries where the capacity of labor market institutions is weaker.

In most MENA countries, labor regulation is a key mechanism for protecting workers' rights, because collective bargaining is not widespread. Trade unions in MENA rarely represent many workers effectively (although exceptions are found, as in Tunisia, where unions are influential social partners). Moreover, workers have limited ways of challenging private employers; for instance, in many countries in the region, strikes remain illegal. Thus, labor regulations have an important role to play in protecting workers (Angel-Urdinola and Kuddo 2010). Below, key aspects of EPL that can affect informality are explored, including (1) hiring regulations and contract types, (2) minimum wage, (3) firing regulations, and (4) tax wedges.

Hiring regulations and contract types. Hiring regulations in MENA are generally aligned with international standards, and MENA countries are joining the international trend in increasing the prevalence of fixed-term work contracts. In general, MENA countries do not have strict hiring regulations compared with international standards. In reforming labor legislation in the region, most attention is paid to relevant arrangements associated with fixed-term employment, which in the past was deemed to be an exceptional form of employment, conditioned by the nature of work or other objective conditions. In recent years, fixed-term work has been increasing not only in EU15 countries[4] but also in MENA (table 5.2).[5] Fixed-term contracts are heavily concentrated among young people and other new labor market entrants, such as the formerly unemployed and those with lower education levels, that is, among people who have weaker bargaining power. For these workers, fixed-term work can provide a bridge to formal employment and an opportunity to gain experience and skills. Among MENA countries, Morocco has the most restrictive laws: Fixed-term contracts are prohibited for permanent tasks, the duration is limited to 12 months, and renewal is prohibited. At the other end of the spectrum, no restrictions or limits are placed on the use of fixed-term contracts in Bahrain, Egypt, Jordan, Kuwait, Oman, and the Republic of Yemen.

Fixed-term employment contributes to more flexible labor markets. It provides a buffer for cyclical fluctuations in demand, allowing companies to adjust employment levels without incurring high firing costs. Fixed-term work also allows companies to reap market opportunities by

Table 5.2   Arrangements for Fixed-Term Contracts around the World in 2010
number of countries

Region	Total	Fixed-term contracts are prohibited for permanent tasks	Maximum cumulative duration of a fixed-term employment relationship including all renewals (months)					
			No limit	12	24	36	48	60+
East Asia and Pacific	24	5	20	1	1	1	0	1
Europe and Central Asia	25	15	10	1	2	4	0	8
Latin America and the Caribbean	32	16	22	2	6	0	0	2
Middle East and North Africa	18	4	12	1	3	0	1	1
High income: OECD	30	9	13	1	10	1	1	4
South Asia	8	3	6	1	1	0	0	0
Sub-Saharan Africa	46	20	23	3	8	2	7	3
Total	183	72	106	10	31	8	9	19

Source: Doing Business 2011 database.

engaging in projects of short duration without bearing disproportionate personnel costs. This is especially important in labor markets where permanent employment is protected by strict regulations and high firing costs. To counterbalance the latter, some countries have established a minimum service length of one to three years with the same employer for a worker to be eligible to claim severance pay, making short fixed-term contracts less attractive.

Although temporary jobs can be useful for promoting employment opportunities, they can also lead to undesirable labor market outcomes and informality. From the firm's perspective, temporary jobs can provide a "screening" device, allowing the firm to evaluate workers' ability or adequacy for the job. They can also act as a buffer, facilitating a firm's adjustment to temporary demand shocks, thereby avoiding costly adjustments to its "core" labor force (European Commission 2010). Conversely, temporary contracts can simply be a convenient way for firms to reduce labor costs. From the workers' perspective, fixed-term jobs are subject to higher turnover and pay lower wages on average. Estimates show that in the EU, temporary workers earn on average 14 percent less than workers on open-ended contracts after controlling for a number of personal characteristics. Temporary workers also tend to have reduced access to training provided or subsidized by firms. Labor market reforms are met with resistance by the segments of the society benefiting from the status quo, and so it is likely that fixed-term contracts will become more and more common. From the perspective of improving coverage, more temporary work contracts are desirable if they provide access to basic social risk management tools to workers.

Minimum wage and wage rigidities. Minimum wages affect informality through at least two channels. First, if the minimum wage is set higher than what employers are willing to pay for an unskilled worker, the latter's employment is likely to be undeclared. Second, minimum wage policy can reduce tax evasion where underreporting is a problem (World Bank 2008) (see box 5.2 for a brief overview of minimum wages).

Although the evidence of the impact of statutory minimum wages on informality is limited, a large body of empirical literature, albeit inconclusive, exists on the impact of statutory minimum wages on worker flows, particularly in the United States. In the United States, although early studies tended to find a negative impact of minimum wages on job retention for individuals at, or close to, the minimum wage, more recent studies have generally found no significant impact (Abowd and others 2005; Zavodny 2000). Draca and others (2008) found that the introduction of a minimum wage in the United Kingdom in 1999 led to insignificant changes in firm entry and exit patterns (OECD 2010). Evidence from other countries is limited. Abowd and others (2005) found no impact of real minimum wages on entry into employment in France, but a strong positive impact on exit from employment. By contrast, Portugal and Cardoso (2006), exploring a specific Portuguese reform that in 1987 dramatically lifted minimum wages for very young workers, found that raising minimum wages had a significant negative effect on both separations and hirings. The effect of introducing a higher minimum wage appears to be large and negative in Colombia and small or negligible in Costa Rica and Mexico. In Brazil, evidence was found of a positive effect of an increase of minimum wage on employment; however, this was mainly the result of changes in the composition between hours worked and number of jobs (Maloney and Medez 2003).

Less is known about the impact of minimum wages on informal employment, but some findings show that a rise in the minimum wage has a positive impact on wages in the informal sector, through what is known as the "lighthouse" effect—as workers in the informal sector use the

---

Box 5.2   Minimum Wages

Setting minimum wages is a common practice in many countries: Both OECD and developing countries set minimum wages with the intended objectives to promote a *fair wage structure,* to provide *minimum acceptable standards of living* for low-paid workers, and to eventually *alleviate poverty.* Minimum wage legislation exists in more than 90 percent of countries, with "universal" minimum wage for both public and private sectors the most dominant, although not the only, practice.[a]

Minimum wage regulations have many dimensions: (1) the level set, (2) coverage, (3) differentiation in the level (such as by age, sector, or region), (4) methods of adjusting levels to reflect inflation, (5) how the level is set (for example, by the government or by the social partners), (6) whether the level applies to the private and/or public sector, and (7) sanctions for noncompliance.

International evidence demonstrates that if the minimum wage is set at a moderate level, then it is not likely to entail substantial employment losses. At the same time, minimum wages tend to have only a limited and often transitory impact on earnings of low-wage workers. Overall, this suggests that statutory minimum wages have at best second-order impacts on labor reallocation (OECD 2010). If minimum wages (in relation to the average wage) are set too high, they can be counterproductive. Higher minimum wages can have a non-negligible adverse impact on employment in low-wage sectors.

Minimum wage as a policy tool to improve the living standards of low-paid workers has clear advantages. First, depending on its level, the minimum wage could be a less distortionary policy tool compared with alternative mechanisms that include changes in tax policy (reduction in income taxes for low-skilled workers, non-distortive negative income tax, or implicit subsidies). Second, a minimum wage may be easier to implement and enforce than a change in taxes (Smits 2008). Nevertheless, minimum wage should be viewed as only one option in a menu of policy instruments available to governments to affect income distribution, poverty, and employment levels of low-income earners.

Source: Angel-Urdinola and Kuddo 2010.
a. An overview of the minimum wages in about 100 countries can be found in the ILO online database: http://www.ilo.org/travaildatabase/servlet/minimumwages.

---

minimum wage as a reference for their own wages. Although minimum wages are not legally binding in the informal sector, they still seem to influence informal sector wage distribution. From the labor supply side, the minimum may be a benchmark for "fair" wages. On the demand side, employers may pay a wage comparable to the formal sector market wage for a particular occupation so that employees will not leave for a similar job in the formal sector, or employers may not be willing to provide all legislated labor benefits but at least will pay the minimum wage. In particular, Lemos (2004) found adverse effects of higher minimum wages on employment in both the formal and informal sectors in Brazil. Based on data from Costa Rica, a country with a complex minimum wage policy, Terrel and Gindling (2002) found that employers responded to a minimum wage increase by increasing the hours of full-time workers and decreasing them for part-time workers, who, in turn, switched to self-employed work in the informal sector. The subsequent increase in supply of workers in the informal sector then placed downward pressure on wages in the informal sector.

About half of all MENA countries do not have a legal minimum wage; those that do set them with considerable variation. Djibouti and the West Bank and Gaza economy are examples of MENA members that have no minimum wage in practice (Angel-Urdinola and Kuddo 2010). In countries with minimum wages, settings vary, complicating cross-country comparisons. For example, minimum wages are set at a monthly rate in Egypt, Jordan, Lebanon, and Tunisia, whereas Morocco has a minimum hourly wage. Figure 5.4 presents the ratio of minimum wages to average value added per worker in selected countries. In countries that have minimum wages in some form, the ratio of minimum wage to average value added per worker varies from 1.80 in Zimbabwe and 1.17 in Mozambique to 0.05 in Burundi and Gabon. In the reviewed MENA countries, the ratio varies from 0.11 in Egypt to 0.72 in Morocco. A high minimum wage can be damaging in some low-paid sectors and regions with below-average wages; it is also typically more damaging for small and medium enterprises (SMEs) because these enterprises tend to be more labor intensive and financially weaker. This likely contributes to keeping many SMEs smaller than they might otherwise be and gives them an incentive to remain informal. In Egypt, despite the relatively low minimum wage, a significant number of workers earn below the minimum wage, which suggests low levels of enforcement. However, the wage distribution for both formal and informal workers in Egypt seems quite centered (and compressed) close to the minimum wage; this suggests that the minimum wage may serve as a benchmark wage for new entrants in the labor market (figure 5.5).

Overall, minimum wages do not appear to be binding in most MENA countries. In most MENA countries, minimum wages are rather low, and sanctions for noncompliance with minimum wage rules are weakly enforced. Independent of how high or low the minimum wage is relative

Figure 5.4   Ratio of Minimum Wages to the Average Value Added per Worker in Selected Countries in 2010

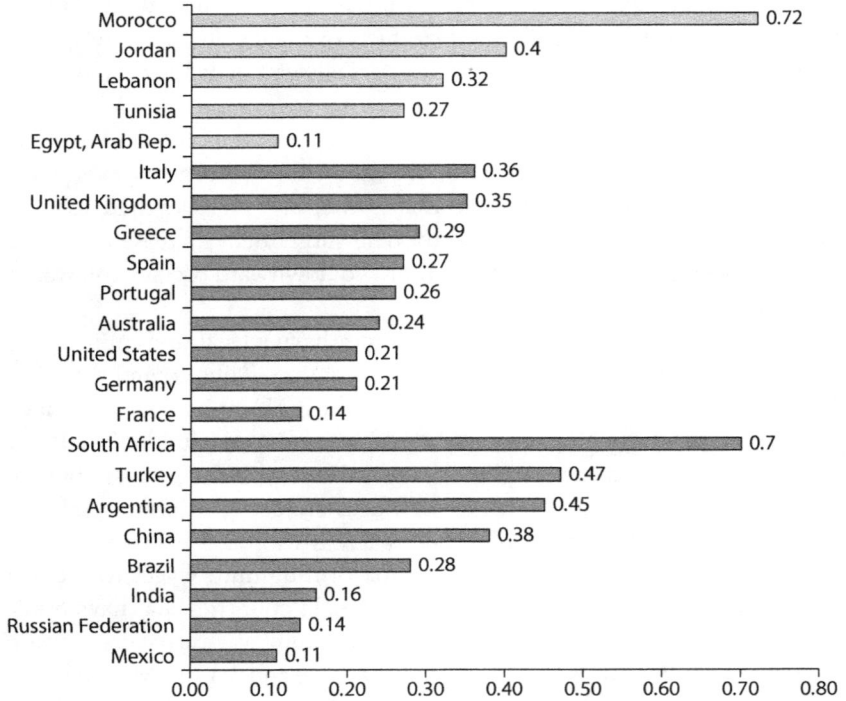

Morocco	0.72
Jordan	0.4
Lebanon	0.32
Tunisia	0.27
Egypt, Arab Rep.	0.11
Italy	0.36
United Kingdom	0.35
Greece	0.29
Spain	0.27
Portugal	0.26
Australia	0.24
United States	0.21
Germany	0.21
France	0.14
South Africa	0.7
Turkey	0.47
Argentina	0.45
China	0.38
Brazil	0.28
India	0.16
Russian Federation	0.14
Mexico	0.11

Source: Doing Business 2011 database.
Note: Because of a lack of consistent cross-country data on average earnings, the average gross national income per capita is used as a proxy for average earnings. This ratio is adjusted to represent the percentage of population of working age as a share of the total population.

to average wages, the extent to which minimum wage policy affects employment outcomes and the wage distribution depends on its enforcement. Although most MENA countries with defined legal minimum wage have regulations on enforcement, enforcement is rather weak, inspections are rare due to a lack of resources, and fines are rarely imposed. A fairly significant mass of workers (those to the left of the vertical bar in figure 5.5) report wages below the minimum wage, which indicates that the minimum wage is unlikely to be a significant constraint to formal employment in most MENA countries. Centralized wage setting can, however, be an important determinant of informality. In Tunisia, in parallel to the general minimum wage, employer and employee representatives negotiate a pay scale based on professional levels in each

Figure 5.5 Hourly Wage Distribution and Minimum Wages in Egypt, the Republic of Yemen, and Morocco

(kernel density plots of monthly wages)

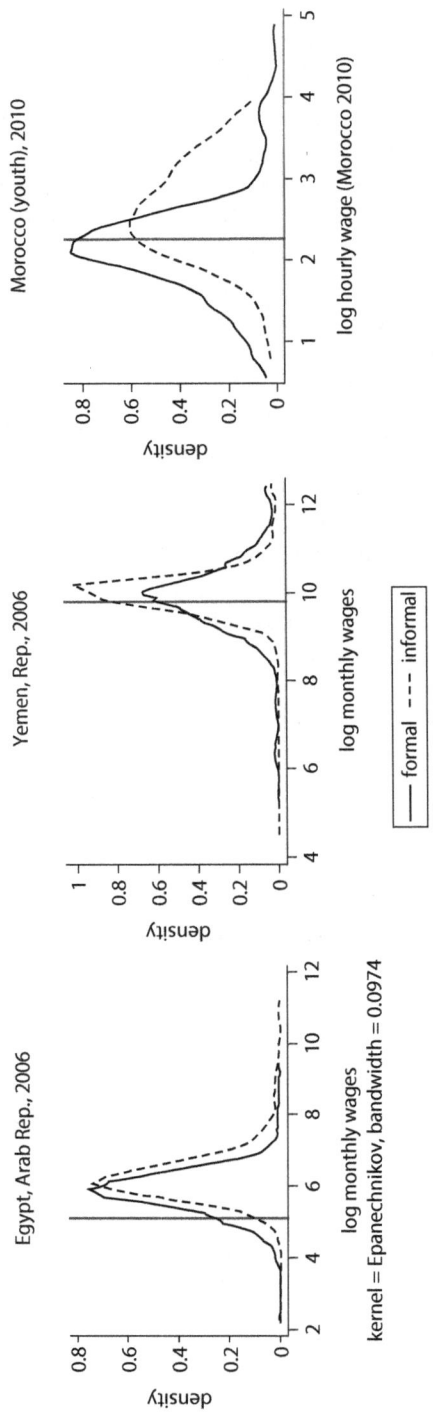

Egypt, Arab Rep., 2006

kernel = Epanechnikov, bandwidth = 0.0974

Yemen, Rep., 2006

Morocco (youth), 2010

— formal - - - informal

Source: Calculations using Egypt's 2006 Labor Market Panel Survey.

Note: The vertical line illustrates the level at which the minimum wage is set; only wages in urban areas are considered.

sector; the differences are significant in some sectors. In reality, a relatively high minimum wage for university graduates is institutionalized, which likely contributes to the high graduate unemployment. The bargaining process is such that on the employee side, wages are monopolistically negotiated by unions whose members are all employed, thus possibly resulting in artificially high wages. This especially affects first-time job seekers. Those who cannot afford to wait for a formal job at or above the minimum wage will tend to accept lower wages in informal jobs.[6]

Firing arrangements. The strictness of firing regulations and the associated cost can affect the incentives of firms to keep workers informal. In general, the procedures for dismissal often require notification or even approval by unions, workers' councils, the public employment service, a labor inspector, or a judge (table 5.3). Some countries also mandate retraining and reassignment to another job and establish priority rules for dismissal or reemployment of redundant workers. In Tunisia, companies must notify the labor inspector of planned dismissals in writing one month ahead, indicating the reasons and the workers affected. The inspector may propose alternatives to layoffs. If these proposals are not accepted by the employer, the case goes to the regional tripartite committee comprising the labor inspector, the employers' organization, and the labor union. The committee decides by a majority vote: If the inspector

Table 5.3 Firing Regulations around the World, 2010

number of countries

| | | Where employers must | | | |
| | | Before dismissal of one redundant worker | | Before collective dismissal | |
Region	Total	Notify or consult third party	Obtain prior approval of third party	Notify or consult third party	Obtain prior approval of third party
East Asia and Pacific	22	10	3	13	4
Europe and Central Asia	29	6	0	9	0
Latin America and the Caribbean	29	10	6	12	6
Middle East and North Africa	19	10	5	12	6
High income: OECD	24	9	1	13	2
South Asia	8	6	3	6	4
Sub-Saharan Africa	46	36	14	44	18
Total	177	87	32	109	40

Source: Doing Business 2011 database.

and union reject the proposal, no dismissal is possible. The committee may also suggest retraining, reduced hours, or early retirement. Only 14 percent of dismissals end up being accepted. As a result, annual layoffs occur in less than 1 percent of the workforce, compared with more than 10 percent in the average OECD country. In Egypt, the employer has the right to close down or downsize the establishment, but it is a cumbersome process. Currently the employer may pay terminated workers one month of salary for each of the first five years of service, and one and a half month's salary for each year after that, one of the most generous severance payments in the world. Eliminating or limiting some or all of the associated firing restrictions would give employers greater flexibility in responding to market fluctuations. Employers must have reasonable freedom to dismiss employees or they will be reluctant to hire and more inclined to operate in the informal sector.

Most countries mandate severance pay with layoffs but differ in important details including extent of coverage, eligibility conditions, cause of dismissals, generosity of benefits, and level of benefits associated with seniority. Some countries require a minimum number of years worked before a worker is entitled to severance pay. In MENA severance pay for redundancy dismissal (for workers with 10 years of job tenure) is the highest in Egypt with 27 weeks of salary paid, followed by the Islamic Republic of Iran, the West Bank and Gaza economy, and the Republic of Yemen, at 23 weeks each (figure 5.6). In general, firing costs in poor countries are 50 percent higher than in rich countries. Some argue that this is justified because governments in poor countries do not have enough resources to provide unemployment insurance, so the cost should be borne by businesses. However, heavy regulation of dismissal is also associated with more unemployment, so those who want to work in poor countries frequently get neither a job nor unemployment insurance (World Bank 2004).

In labor markets with less rigid and less costly firing regulations, appropriately designed unemployment insurance (UI) schemes can provide adequate protection to workers. This allows firms to discontinue unproductive employee–employer relationships, while maintaining adequate income protection through UI, a powerful support for creating higher productivity, good quality (formal) jobs. According to many (including Auer 2007; Auer and others 2004; Grazier 2007), legislative focus should be shifted from protection of jobs to protection of transitions, so that the individual risk of unemployment and income loss is reduced, while the potentially negative effects of job protection are avoided.

Workers themselves feel better protected by a support system for unemployment than by EPL (European Commission 2006). This is particularly important in a world characterized by the gradual disappearance of lifelong jobs and an increasing need for job mobility. Only a few countries in the region have UI systems, namely, Algeria, Bahrain, Egypt, the Islamic Republic of Iran, and Kuwait (table 5.4). Even in countries with UI systems in place, such as Egypt, systems are underutilized because of a lack of public awareness about UI benefits among plan members, restrictive eligibility conditions, the difficulty of and the stigma attached to documenting a "just-cause" firing decision, and low overall layoff risks among covered open-ended contract employees (Angel-Urdinola and Kuddo 2010). The shift from rigid firing rules to less restrictive regulation

Figure 5.6   Severance Pay for Redundancy Dismissal (Average for Workers with 1, 5, and 10 Years of Tenure, in Salary Weeks)

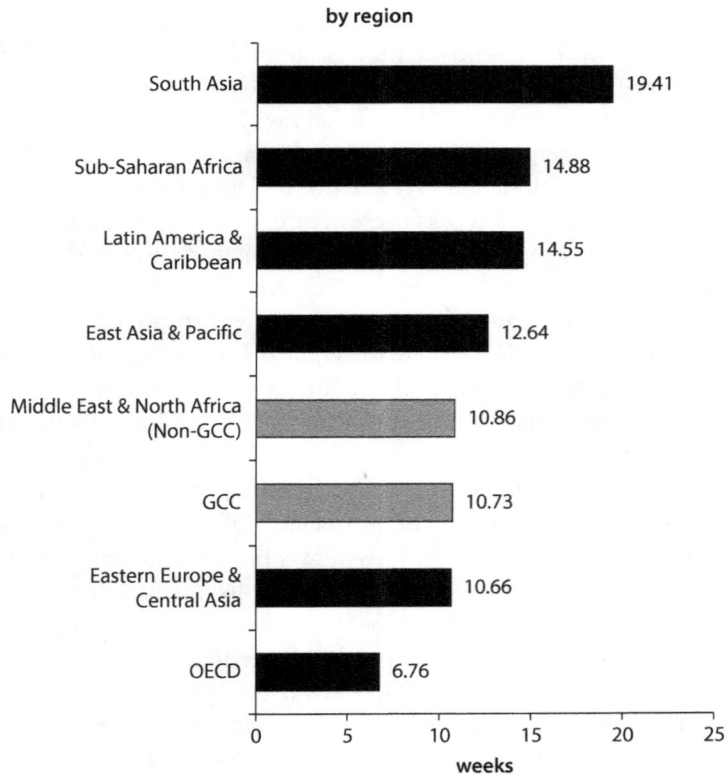

by region

Region	Weeks
South Asia	19.41
Sub-Saharan Africa	14.88
Latin America & Caribbean	14.55
East Asia & Pacific	12.64
Middle East & North Africa (Non-GCC)	10.86
GCC	10.73
Eastern Europe & Central Asia	10.66
OECD	6.76

weeks

figure continues next page

Figure 5.6   Severance Pay for Redundancy Dismissal (Average for Workers with 1, 5 and 10 Years of Tenure, in Salary Weeks) (continued)

by MENA country

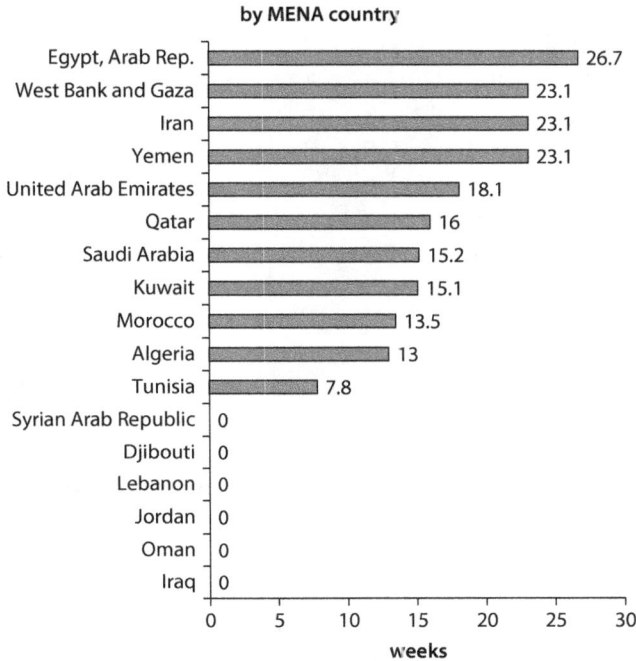

Table 5.4   Existence of Unemployment Protection Legislation around the World

	Number of economies with unemployment scheme/total number of economies in region	Economies and territories with unemployment scheme
East Asia and Pacific	9/24	China; Hong Kong SAR, China; Lao PDR; Mongolia; Papua New Guinea; Solomon Islands; Taiwan, China; Thailand; Vietnam
Europe and Central Asia	23/25	All countries except Georgia and Kosovo
Latin America and the Caribbean	8/32	Argentina, Brazil, Chile, Ecuador, Puerto Rico, St. Kitts and Nevis, Uruguay, R.B. Venezuela
Middle East and North Africa	5/18	Algeria; Bahrain; Egypt, Arab Rep.; Iran, Islamic Rep.; Kuwait
High income: OECD	30/30	All countries
South Asia	1/8	India
Sub-Saharan Africa	4/46	Mauritius, Seychelles, South Africa, Tanzania
Total	80/183	

Source: Doing Business 2011 database.

Striving for Better Jobs • http://dx.doi.org/10.1596/978-0-8213-9535-6

accompanied by unemployment insurance creates the precondition for a more efficient allocation of resources. In simple terms, the easier it is for firms to discontinue a formal employment contract tomorrow, the more likely the firm will create that job today. This is especially true in sectors exposed to a volatile product market. Of course, the argument for economic efficiency should not justify reducing worker protection to inadequate levels, but rather shifting the form of protection from protecting jobs to protecting income for workers in transition through UI. By contributing to UI, employees and employers share the social costs of unemployment, but not in a manner that forces firms to maintain unproductive employment in downturns or to limit their incentives to open up vacancies when demand is stronger (World Bank 2008).

Tax wedge. Labor taxes create a wedge between the labor cost to the employer and the worker's take-home pay. Studies suggest that a higher tax wedge reduces both employment and economic growth (World Bank 2007). For example, a 10 percent reduction in the tax wedge (the difference between the cost of labor and take-home pay) could increase employment between 1 and 5 percent (Kugler and Kugler 2003; Rutkowski 2003). The literature for developing countries and emerging markets economies is limited, but a World Bank study on Turkey concluded that labor tax cuts would not have a major impact on formal employment (Betcherman and Pages 2007). An across-the-board reduction of 5 percent in pension contributions paid by employers would bring about a 0.8 percent increase in employment overall and would reduce the unemployment rate by about 0.2 to 0.3 percent. The effect could be stronger (an increase in employment of almost 1.5 percent) if the reduction in pension contributions was targeted at workers younger than 30 years old, who have less bargaining power to capture most of the tax reduction in higher wages.

Labor taxes in countries such as Morocco (where they account for about 39 percent of total labor cost) and Egypt (37 percent) are as high as the average for OECD countries. In Egypt, Jordan, and Lebanon, social security contributions are the dominant component of labor taxes (table 5.5). Social security contributions in these countries (paid by both the employer and the employee) account for the bulk of the tax wedge. In all reviewed MENA countries, social security contributions are paid largely by the employer; employees pay only a minor part. Table 5.5 shows the calculation of the tax wedge in some MENA countries, and figure 5.7 shows the tax wedge in various countries.

Table 5.5   Contribution Rates for Social Security Programs, 2009/2010, and Tax Wedge on Average Wages in Private Sector

Country	Year	All social security programs			Personal income tax (%)[a]	Tax wedge (%)[b]
		Insured person	Employer	Total		
Egypt, Arab Rep.	2009	14	26	40	10	37.3
Jordan	2010	6	12.75	18.75	7	22.2
Lebanon	2010	2	21.5	23.5	7	24.9
Morocco	2009	6.29	18	24.29	24	39.4
Yemen, Rep.	2010	6	13	19	25	30.4

Source: Calculations based on SSA and ISSA (2008, 2009, and 2011).
a. Data refer to effective rates on average wage.
b. The tax wedge is calculated as a sum of social security contributions paid by the employer and the employee, and the personal income tax is expressed as a percentage of total labor cost. Total labor cost is gross wage plus employers' social security contributions. Gross wage is net wage plus employees' social security contributions and the personal income tax.

Figure 5.7   Percent Tax Wedge in Various Countries

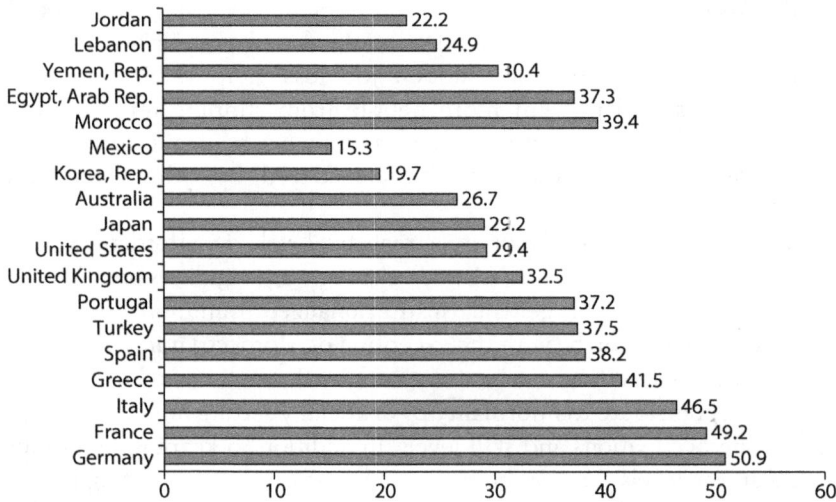

Sources: OECD 2010.

Policy implications for MENA. MENA countries could ease certain provisions of labor legislation to achieve more compliance and improved employment outcomes, while shifting from protection of particular jobs to protection of transitions. Overall, even though certain provisions in labor legislation in some MENA countries might be rigid de jure, de facto they are widely evaded. It is unlikely that merely improving enforcement would result in reducing informality.

As discussed in this section, the rigidity of certain labor regulations in some countries contributes to the prevalence of informality (for example, hiring arrangements in Morocco, and firing arrangements in Tunisia and Egypt). A shift toward a richer and more flexible set of labor contracts (including more fixed-term contracts and fewer open-ended contracts), despite their drawbacks, would provide opportunities for young workers and new entrants to join the formal sector through flexible working arrangements with social insurance coverage. Such policy reforms that ease regulations and make them more realistic to comply with should be supported by a reform of social protection systems to better protect the income position of workers and their employment transitions.[7] For example, recent experience shows that moderately strict EPL, when combined with a well-designed system of unemployment benefits and a strong emphasis on active labor market programs, can help create a dynamic labor market while also providing adequate employment security to workers (OECD 2008). Adequate safety nets could also play an important role in protecting workers from sudden job loss, help them transition between jobs, and prevent more people from slipping into poverty. The newly legislated unemployment insurance schemes in Jordan and Egypt provide an example to be considered by other countries in MENA.

Keeping the cost of labor at a realistic level via affordable social security contributions in MENA and relaxing wage rigidities are likely to reduce informality. In general, institutionalized minimum wages in MENA are neither high (with the exception of Morocco) nor binding. Yet centralized wage setting mechanisms, such as those discussed in the case of Tunisia, contribute to informality by artificially setting high wage floors for certain occupations and skill levels. In addition to keeping minimum wages at low levels that can be realistically enforced, wage-setting mechanisms in MENA should benefit from some kind of quantitative anchor to provide an objective baseline measure on changes in productivity. In countries where minimum wages are high (whether economy wide or sector specific), and where it is not politically feasible to reduce them, governments could consider reducing the minimum wage for youth to at least improve transitions of new entrants into formal employment, while maintaining the higher-level minimum wages that protect well-established workers. This section has also shown that the cost of labor attributable to labor taxes is not very binding in MENA, with the exception of Morocco and Egypt. In general, tax wedges could be reduced through social insurance reforms that reduce the social security contribution rates (as already legislated in Egypt) or by shifting a portion of the labor taxes toward other general revenue taxes such as consumption taxes.

Engaging in a more inclusive social dialogue is key to sustaining these types of reforms. Important political economy aspects to labor market reform are found. In particular, the traditional tripartite structure that convenes government actors, trade unions, and employer representatives is likely to show a bias for the status quo of protective regulation for employed, unionized workers. Including representation from the outsiders, informal workers, youth, and the unemployed would likely rebalance the dialogue toward facilitating entry in labor markets, improving mobility, and promoting a more equitable redistribution of returns across different strata of the population.

Addressing the Preference for Public Sector Employment

The widespread preference for public sector jobs in many MENA countries has important implications for informality. The presence of large public sectors has been explained as the consequence of an implicit social contract in the Arab region that promised well-compensated public sector jobs to those reaching higher levels of educational attainment (Yousef 2004). Recently hiring has slowed, and in practice, public sector jobs are offered only to those who are sufficiently patient to queue for them. Yet the preference for public employment is very widespread. For example, according to the 2010 youth survey in Egypt, 70 percent of youth say it is best to work for the public sector. This preference for public sector jobs is grounded in a rational evaluation of costs and benefits. On average, public sector jobs (1) are better compensated than similar private sector jobs; (2) offer full job security, good fringe benefits, and solid social status; and (3) tend not to require as much effort as private sector jobs. Jordan, Syria, and Egypt have the highest proportion of the workforce in the public sector in the region (30 percent in each of Jordan and Syria and 39 percent in Egypt). In Syria, the average public sector wage is 32 percent higher than the average private sector wage (representing both formal and informal workers). Even in Egypt, where public sector pay is considered low, the average wage in the public sector is 6 percent higher than the average wage in the formal private sector.[8] The public employment bias and the queuing phenomena also exist in Jordan, where public sector wages are on average 20 percent higher than private sector wages.[9] Bodor and others (2008) show that in Morocco public sector employees, regardless of the level of education, have better career paths, in terms of wages and pension benefits, than those working in the private, formal nonagricultural sector and the informal agricultural sector.

The existence in some countries of a distinct single registry for those seeking public sector jobs indirectly contributes to the prevalence of informality. In Jordan and Syria, those who wish to work in the public sector must register with an agency. This registry is the institution of the "queue"; once registered, an individual does not need to exert any effort to procure a public sector job, he or she just needs to wait for his or her turn in the queue. In Syria, the total number of registered jobseekers was over 1.7 million persons in 2009. When the Syrian government attempted to use this registry to offer training, with the opportunity for private sector placement upon conclusion, it found that those in the registry were typically unwilling to accept the prospect of formal private sector employment. They believed that presence in the social insurance agency's administrative records would lead to deletion from the public sector job queue. Therefore, only a quarter of those offered formal jobs took them.[10] In contrast, informal employment was acceptable to the same individuals; many of them were already engaged in informal employment.[11]

In the short run, MENA governments should consider eliminating institutionalized public sector employment queues. In the medium and long run, a reform of civil service by realigning incentives is needed. Modernized public employment and placement services should require active job search effort from applicants. Placement services should place workers based on their interests, training, and skills, instead of an expressed preference for public or private employment. Workers currently in formal private sector jobs should not be disqualified from moving into public sector jobs later in their careers. In the long run, civil service reforms should establish stronger performance evaluation measures, linking worker compensation to performance. Further, public sector wage scales should be rationalized so they no longer constrain flow of talent into the private sector.

Enhancing the Productivity of Informal Workers through Training and Skills Upgrading

The productivity dimension of informality is especially predominant in the poorer countries, in rural areas where low-skilled workers are engaged in micro-entrepreneurship and low-yield agricultural work. Programs aiming at increasing productivity in the informal sector are potentially important interventions to promote inclusive growth and avert a productivity trap. However, effectively tackling productivity improvements in the informal sector, particular in rural areas, is a complex agenda, which involves not only effectively upgrading skills, but also creating opportunities that would allow for returns to training to materialize. As such, complementary investments in infrastructure and access to markets are needed. An exhaustive analysis of policies to increase productivity is outside the scope of this report; this section focuses on policy and program options that improve access to training opportunities and realign training programs to the needs of informal workers.

Improving access to training. Informal workers have limited opportunities to benefit from training provided by governments, employers, and private training providers. Active labor market programs (ALMPs), which include training and skills-upgrading programs, are interventions provided by the government or by nongovernmental organizations that aim at increasing workers' employability. In MENA, government provision of such programs is mainly directed to the unemployed. This may be because of the belief that the unemployed are more vulnerable and worse off than the employed, regardless of job quality. However, the working poor could actually be worse off than certain groups of the unemployed in some countries. Workers from higher income households might be able to afford to be unemployed and queue for better quality jobs, whereas those from poor households are forced to take available low-quality and low-wage informal sector jobs. Figure 5.8 shows that unemployment is lowest among those with the lowest skill levels. This would suggest that those who can afford to stay in the education system could also be those who can afford to stay unemployed and wait for better jobs. In addition to government provision, the private sector plays a large role in providing fee-based training programs in MENA. However, an evaluation of privately provided ALMPs targeting young people in MENA revealed that the informal sector rarely has access to such programs: 80 percent of beneficiaries are educated males from middle- or high-income groups in urban areas (Angel-Urdinola, Semlali, and Brodmann 2010). It is also worth mentioning that only 5 percent of all surveyed training programs target rural areas, where a large share of informal workers reside. Finally, as shown in chapter 3, informal salaried workers working in informal firms or small firms are less likely to receive on-the-job training where they work.

Figure 5.8   The Relationship between Educational Attainment and the Unemployment Rate in Urban Egypt and the Republic of Yemen

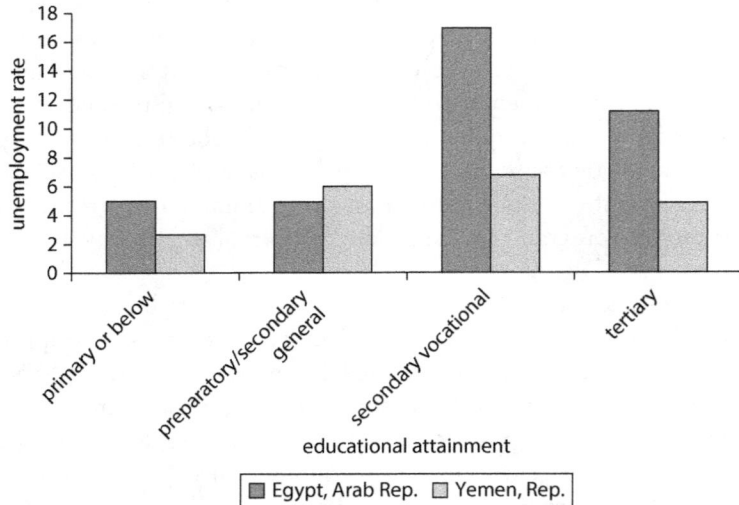

Sources: Egypt 2006 Labor Market Panel Survey, the Republic of Yemen 2006 Household Budget Survey.

To address low access to training, as well as to provide incentives for firms and workers themselves to pursue training, governments may extend their provision of ALMPs to informal sector workers through direct targeting (for example, through training cooperatives or vouchers). Training vouchers can be used to empower recipients to buy training in the open market and thereby promote competition between public and private providers of training and the efficient delivery of training services. The Jua Kali program in Kenya, which offered training vouchers to those working in the informal sector in the mid-1990s, provides an interesting perspective on the response of public training institutions to the demand for skills created by the vouchers. The Jua Kali vouchers produced a positive supply response to the demand created for skills, but mainly from master craftspersons in the informal sector and nongovernmental organizations (NGOs). Programs were tailored to the needs of voucher recipients and offered in off-hours to fit work schedules. The Jua Kali voucher program was successful in its pilot stage in expanding the supply of training to workers in the informal sector. Evidence was also noted of its positive impact on the earnings of participants as well as strengthened capacity of local Jua Kali associations responsible for distribution of the vouchers (Steel and Snodgrass 2008). A commonly used policy intervention to address the underprovision of training by firms is the establishment of training funds, financed through general revenue or some payroll taxes. However, financing training through general revenues is regarded as less distorting to employment outcomes than through payroll taxes (and thus preferable). Training funds can be used to target firms with low levels of training, such as SMEs. For example, in the Republic of Korea, all firms pay a training levy, but the government provides reimbursement to employers who offer training. When the government found that mostly larger firms were actually providing training and benefiting from the reimbursement, they provided additional incentives to SMEs to establish a training consortium through which they could collectively mobilize resources for training while benefiting from a higher reimbursement rate and a subsidy to hire financial managers (Lee 2009).

Tailoring training to informal workers' needs. Traditional training programs generally require a minimum level of literacy and proficiency and do not adequately address the need for a general and flexible set of skills that is typical of informal employment, especially in rural areas. General literacy skills are a barrier to productivity as well as a barrier for informal workers to access and benefit from training programs, especially in rural areas. Although the expansion of the basic education system in MENA has been remarkably successful in initially enrolling almost all children in rural and urban areas, the dropout rates are still high, and education quality often lags behind in rural areas, leaving rural agricultural workers with low levels of literacy.[12] This is especially important given the evidence that literacy is associated with increased productivity. An often cited example is that literacy improves the use of fertilizers when workers can adequately read and comply with directions written on the labels. General education reforms addressing the low literacy and quality of education, particularly among rural workers, are necessary conditions for improved productivity in the medium term. However, in the shorter run, rural workers could benefit from training programs that are made accessible to them, and for which literacy is not a necessary precondition. Such training should also be associated with support for micro-entrepreneurship and accessing markets, so as to broaden the set of available opportunities.

How training is delivered matters too. Training programs for the informal poor need to offer clear, concrete, and immediate reasons to

motivate enrollment and ensure that individuals participate and benefit
from the program. Many informal workers are too poor to take time off
from work to participate in daytime training. Thus, programs should
provide opportunities to combine earning and learning as well as flexible
schedules. If alternative schedules are offered, such as evenings and week-
ends, beneficiaries can then continue to contribute to household income
and/or take care of their children during regular hours, thereby increasing
beneficiary retention (Singh 2005). Moreover, experience shows that
nonformal training programs should be adapted to the work context sur-
rounding the beneficiaries, that the teaching methods should be partici-
patory, and that some of the program instructors should ideally come
from the neighborhood itself, because they bring with them insights on
community needs. Unless the training is provided in the rural villages or
is hands-on at the homes of the informal workers, it can be difficult to
attend for several reasons: lack of transportation, insufficient infrastructure,
and lack of lights along roads. Women face additional challenges because
they may not be allowed to travel without male company.

Although school dropouts constitute a majority of informal workers in
many MENA countries, very few "second-chance" programs are aimed at
providing learning in a nonformal manner. Second-chance programs can
provide enhancement of an individual's literacy, work skills, equivalency
education, and life skills training, crucial characteristics that facilitate
integration into society. Education equivalency programs are designed for
those who have missed opportunities for early and traditional education
and are unlikely to return to a formal learning environment. People who
have dropped out of school at an early age are generally poor and very
vulnerable. Second-chance programs are usually provided in a nonformal
manner (often via accelerated learning) because this increases the likelihood of reaching informal and vulnerable workers. Life skills include
social and coping skills, and improving relations with family, community
members, and authority figures, while increasing the beneficiary's own
self-confidence. They can also include counseling and mentoring and
components related to risky behaviors. Participants are more likely to
benefit from work skills training once life skills and coping mechanisms
are included in the general training (Angel-Urdinola and Semlali 2010).

The traditional approach to training programs in the MENA region is
not well suited for the informal sector. Training appears to be associated
with a positive impact on labor market outcomes when offered as part of
a comprehensive package. According to the survey of privately provided
ALMPs in MENA, about 70 percent focus solely on hard skills and are

provided in classrooms, less than 20 percent provide some type of practical experience and/or apprenticeships, less than 35 percent focus on soft skills, and only 14 percent provide some type of employment services and/or labor market intermediation (Angel-Urdinola, Semlali, and Brodmann 2010). Country-specific evidence confirms that similar approaches also prevail among publicly provided ALMPs. Many countries, particularly in the OECD and Latin America, have moved toward a comprehensive training model that includes provision of classroom and workplace training, monitoring, job search and placement assistance, and soft skills training. Evaluations of "comprehensive" youth programs from Latin America indicate that programs can have a significant positive impact on employment and earnings of program participants, especially for women, if they are organized with flexible schedules, based on public-private partnerships (that is, demand driven), combined with internships and practical experience (in addition to in-class training), provide a combination of soft and hard skills, and are monitored and assessed for impacts. In many Latin American economies, youth unemployment rates soared during the late 1990s. To address this, the Chilean government designed what is known as the "Chile Joven" program, which offered comprehensive "demand-driven" training programs to unemployed youth. The program was so successful that similar models were customized in Argentina, Colombia, the Dominican Republic, Panama, Paraguay, Peru, and República Bolivariana de Venezuela. Depending on the specific needs identified, these programs can be targeted to either the general unemployed youth population or to specific marginalized groups.

If improved and combined with theoretical knowledge taught by Technical and Vocational Education and Training (TVET), traditional apprenticeships[13] could contribute to more productive employment within the informal sector in MENA. Traditional apprenticeships are distinct from formal apprenticeships, which are registered with a government agency and administered by employers. The flexibility of traditional apprenticeships in combining hands-on training, work and learning, their affordability and self-financing, their connection with future employment, and their generally low entry standards make them attractive to disadvantaged informal workers. However, master craftspersons rarely provide theoretical knowledge alongside practical experience and often teach outdated technologies, and there are few market standards available for judging the quality of the training provided. Traditional apprenticeships suffer from the low education of those being trained, and the choice of trades tends to follow gender biases (Johanson and Adams 2004). If public

financing for TVET institutions shifted to focus on outcomes (such as success in serving target populations of master craftspersons and apprentices)
rather than financing inputs (such as classrooms, courses offered, or
instructors hired), both apprenticeships and TVET could be made more
relevant. Performance-based budgeting for public institutions could provide incentives to upgrade technical skills for master craftspersons and
improve their pedagogy (Ziderman 2003). More attention and account-
ability could be given to these institutions in partnership with apprenticeships for addressing the low levels of basic education that handicap
training of apprentices and master craftspersons and for providing the
complementary theoretical training needed to accompany the practical
training of apprenticeships (Van Adams 2008).

Training programs targeted toward the low-skilled, self-employed, and
micro-entrepreneurs among informal workers, or those individuals with the
inclination to become self-employed, could help informal workers transition into higher productivity and higher value-added self-employment. The
great majority of participants in informal self- or household-based enterprises have had little formal education or training when entering self-
employment. Some, especially woman entrepreneurs, may have had none
at all. The knowledge and skills used in their businesses have likely been
acquired from parents and other relatives in family enterprises. The self-
employed can benefit from both technical training specific to their industry, such as on the use of modern production techniques in agriculture, as
well as general entrepreneurship and business skills training. The latter
could include bookkeeping, financial literacy, marketing, communication,
life skills, and simple risk management. International experience has shown
that a comprehensive package offering a set of services that both includes
training and facilitates access to credit can be successful in improving entrepreneurial ventures. Moreover, micro-franchising programs are an emerging
approach that entails helping individuals replicate an existing business
rather than starting an original one. Box 5.3 presents two case studies of
productivity-enhancing programs from Egypt and Jordan.

Finally, moving toward more integrated and innovative social safety
net systems that link income support to the poor with strategies to
foster productivity should be considered in the context of MENA. The
"Chile Solidario" Conditional Cash Transfer Project provided the poor
with the means to attend training while linking them to employment
opportunities. This well-targeted social protection project assisted
extremely poor families, mostly in Chile's rural areas. A social worker
worked with anyone in the family in need. Each individual's needs

Box 5.3   MENA Case Studies of Productivity-Enhancing Programs in Urban Areas

The Cairo Earnings and Learning Project of the Children and Youth Garbage Collectors provides an example of an urban community-based nonformal project. By working directly with the garbage-collecting community itself, this project, headed by a grass-roots NGO, has managed to reach several hundred children. The beneficiaries asked for training that would not alienate the children from their trade and families and for an education that would respect and build on the children's existing skills of sorting and recycling waste. A curriculum was developed within the context of recycling: Participants were taught basic math and literacy, marketable skills within the weaving industry, waste recycling, health skills, family planning, personal hygiene, and sanitation. Children were removed from their hazardous environment and given opportunities to earn money in a clean and safe environment while also learning. The children would most likely not have been able to participate to the same extent had they not been able to work. The woven products they produced were sold through a cooperative system for young artisans and became popular among Egyptians and tourists alike, leading to a source of pride for the young weavers. Sales earnings were divided between the weavers. Results show that after six years, some 500 young women have graduated and achieved functional literacy. Moreover, 64 percent reported that they were practicing family planning, 56 percent said they would not circumcise their daughters, and 70 percent of single girls said they would not circumcise their daughters when they got married (Madhu 2005).

Jordan's "Questscope Program" provides urban street children, school dropouts, and young workers in the informal sector with a nonformal equivalency education, jobs, and life skills. In 2007 the Ministry of Education made the program an official alternative to tenth grade certification. The program was a response to the Department of Labor's initiative to ensure that working children under the age of 16 (the legal age for work) are withdrawn from the labor force and reinserted into nonformal education (accelerated learning) or formal education. In addition to equivalency education, job training, and life skills, the program provides income support to the beneficiaries as they attend evening classes in public schools. Certified teachers help beneficiaries earn a proficiency certificate (equivalent to tenth grade level). Vocational graduates also receive business-management training, thereby enhancing future employability and livelihood options. Other program elements include coaching in life and social/coping skills aimed at facilitating the integration of youth into society. The program is provided by a grassroots NGO with strong linkages to the community. The classes are flexible to ensure that attendance and learning are centered on the realities of the participants. The cost per beneficiary is around $350 per year (Semlali 2008).

Source: Semlali 2008.

were evaluated and the social worker then linked the person to the appropriate services, including literacy classes, soft skills training, help with job searches, links to internship opportunities/subsidized employment opportunities, or self-employment assistance programs. The connection to the social worker was important for understanding the needs of the client and for accurately informing the client of available opportunities, because many poor are not aware of the services available to them. Conditional Cash Transfers in the form of a stipend were provided conditional upon training participation. Without this stipend, the poorest would not have been able to participate (Angel-Urdinola and Semlali 2010).

Conclusions to Part 1

Numerous barriers to formality exist in MENA, requiring a complex set of policy interventions. Restrictive business and labor market regulation, the prominent role of the public sector as employer in a number of countries, and the productivity gap facing informal workers are all important barriers to inclusive growth and formalization. Although different and complementary policy interventions that relax these barriers can be effective toward this goal, the process of formalization matters, and policy interventions to address informality should extend beyond mere enforcement and should aim to reduce informality in a sustainable manner while helping the growth process become progressively more inclusive.

A healthy business environment and labor regulations that foster more mobility in labor markets, while protecting workers during job transitions, are important. The evidence suggests a negative correlation between the ease of doing business and the size of the informal sector. In MENA, barriers to entry, high taxes, and discretionary enforcement of regulation all collude to promote informality. Simplifying entry regulation, reducing compliance costs, and moving toward a fairer implementation of regulation are all necessary, and emerging evidence from other countries suggests that these interventions can be effective to move beyond informality. A large portion of employers in MENA perceive labor regulations as a major obstacle to business development and more employment growth. In some MENA countries, certain labor regulation provisions are rigid, including hiring arrangements in Morocco and firing arrangements in Tunisia and Egypt. Rigid EPL promotes informality, because firms can respond to rigid labor regulations by reducing overall employment or shifting employment into conditions of informality. Easing certain provisions of labor legislation to achieve more compliance, supported by a reform of social protection systems to better protect the income position of workers and their employment transitions (for instance, through the introduction of unemployment benefits and a strong emphasis on active labor market programs), can decrease informality and promote employment creation. In parallel, it is also important to keep the cost of labor at a realistic level, including through affordable social security contributions. The generosity of public sector employment conditions (including pay, benefits, and job security) in some countries also contributes to higher informality and important segmentations, making the need for a reform of civil service even more pressing.

Many informal workers face a productivity trap. Especially in the poorer countries and in rural areas, the low productivity of jobs is the predominant aspect of informal employment. Low productivity is a result of different factors, including poor skills and limited opportunities, particularly in rural areas. The evidence shows that informal workers consistently have limited access to training and skills-upgrading opportunities. Although complementary investments in infrastructure and access to capital and markets will be necessary to increase the returns associated with skills upgrading, targeting such programs to informal workers can be one effective way to address the productivity trap. Providing incentives to firms (such as through training cooperatives for small firms) and workers (such as with vouchers) to engage in training will address some of the determinants of underprovision of these programs. To make these interventions more effective, reorienting and tailoring the delivery and design of training toward the particular needs of informal workers is necessary. Second-chance programs, traditional apprenticeship, and training specifically designed for the self-employed and micro-entrepreneurs are examples of interventions that are likely to be effective in the context of MENA.

Part 2. Extending Social Insurance Coverage

Introduction to Part 2

Lack of social insurance coverage exposes workers and their families to important risks and vulnerabilities. In MENA, these vulnerabilities loom large, with about 67 percent of the labor force not protected against a plethora of social risks, of which loss of income in old age may be the most pressing. Government interventions that effectively expand access to risk management instruments can be beneficial both from the perspective of individual/household welfare and for society as a whole, because evidence exists that private markets are likely to underinsure social risks, such as loss of income-generating capacity due to old age, disability, health conditions, or layoffs. This is particularly true for the poor, who might engage in suboptimal strategies, such as selling productive assets or withdrawing children from school, to respond to shocks. From a societal point of view, important negative externalities can be found from having too much uninsured risk, including an adverse impact on productivity. If the rationale for government intervention is clear, assessing what drives lack of coverage is key to informing which policies are most likely to succeed in expanding it. For example, if most workers are observed to voluntarily opt out of social security systems because of a rational cost-benefit analysis, then improving the perceived quality of public service, including outreach and communication about benefits, would be needed. Specific design features of pension systems, including vesting periods, early retirement, and legal coverage provisions, might also provide different incentives for workers to contribute to social insurance. Furthermore, a significant portion of the population might not possess sufficient saving and contributory capacity to pay for the true cost of the socially optimal degree of protection against these risks, which would justify government intervention to improve coverage with some level of subsidy beyond traditional contributory mandatory social insurance schemes. A complex set of reforms is likely to be needed, which includes moving beyond a sole focus on enforcement of mandatory social insurance rules (especially under existing designs and lack of financial sustainability) toward a coverage extension strategy that acknowledges the realities of the informal economy in MENA.

Part 2 of this chapter introduces a conceptual framework for social insurance coverage extension policies. In this context, it discusses design features of pensions systems in MENA, with special attention to the need for improving the design and incentive structure of existing formal sector pension schemes as a precondition for feasible and successful coverage extension efforts. Following that, a structured description of alternative coverage extension strategies is presented, including a set of guiding principles to select such strategies for specific vulnerable population groups. Finally, it concludes with a section on how the often disregarded evidence from the emerging field of behavioral economics could support better designed social insurance coverage extension policies.

A Framework for Social Insurance Coverage Extension Policies: Why Does It Matter?

Although the costs and benefits to informality have been discussed, the vulnerability associated with informal employment is a social concern requiring government action. The main objectives of this section are to describe (1) how the design of social insurance systems affects incentives to be informal and (2) the policies governments should consider to alleviate the social problems caused by informality. In line with the emphasis of this report on informal employment, policies aimed at extending social insurance coverage are the focus of the following discussion, because they provide a means for individuals to reduce vulnerability and excessive exposure to social and economic shocks, and to ultimately improve social welfare.

The ultimate objective of coverage extension policies is to improve social welfare by providing individuals with access to the risk management tools of social insurance systems. A framework for social insurance/coverage extension policies is illustrated in figure 5.9. Social insurance systems provide protection against certain social and economic risks, such as the loss or sudden reduction in income (generating capability) due to old age, disability, work-related injury, death of an income-generating family member, sickness, loss of income due to maternity, or loss of a job.[14] The realization

Figure 5.9 A Framework for Social Insurance/Coverage Extension Policies: Objectives, Social and Economic Risks, Policies, Instruments, and Behavioral Impacts

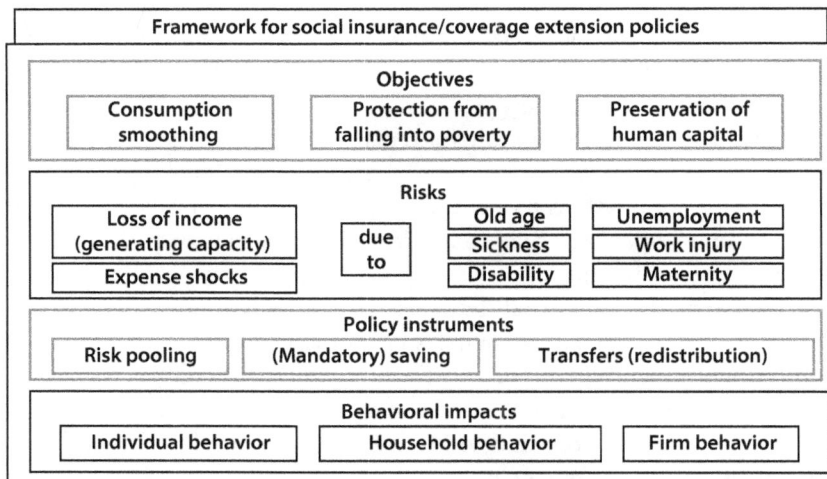

Source: Adaptation of the broader framework presented in Robalino and others 2010.

of any of these risks, at least temporarily, undermines an individual's employment income-generating capacity, and in some cases a medical care-related expense shock is incurred as well (for example, with sickness, disability, and work injury). The social insurance system is designed to intervene in such cases to at least temporarily provide income support and cover a significant portion of the shock's expenses. These interventions are in line with the underlying objectives of (1) consumption smoothing (limiting the extreme fluctuation of individual and household consumption and welfare), (2) poverty alleviation (preventing social and economic shocks from forcing individuals or households into poverty), and (3) preserving investment in human capital (in the cases of health insurance, disability, and work injury benefits, there is a direct objective to prevent the—further—deterioration of health). In a broader social insurance context, temporary income support measures are justified as an attempt to prevent households from reducing their investment in human capital (such as spending on education) when social and economic shocks occur.

Social insurance programs typically entail a combination of risk pooling, (mandatory) saving, and explicit redistributionary transfer mechanisms (Holzmann and Koettl 2010). The optimal choice of a policy instrument depends on the nature of the risk. In general, low-probability shocks with potentially devastating impact are best protected against through risk pooling. In contrast, the loss of income-generating capacity in old age is a high-probability (thus predictable) event; therefore (mandatory) saving-type pension schemes are more appropriate. Saving and risk pooling are, in theory, contributory mechanisms ensuring the financial sustainability of the social insurance systems and ensuring that any redistribution among plan members happens based only on the ex ante unknown realization of risks (that is, in a random manner). The discussion to follow defines a necessary role for redistributionary transfers, especially for ensuring protection to low saving capacity individuals (and households) who cannot afford to pay the true cost of a universally guaranteed social insurance package. Such transfers play an especially critical role in coverage extension policies.

Understanding behavioral impacts is especially important for the design of coverage extension policies given the need to induce voluntary compliance and enrollment. Given the nature of informality, relying only on enforcement of mandates is not sufficient and can be counterproductive. Economic actors respond to incentives. For example, self-employed individuals decide to register and enroll in social insurance schemes based on whether they find their participation beneficial given the information they have and the level of effort required. Firms make employment offers with or without associated enrollment in the mandatory pension system dependent on factors such as the related additional cost of labor. Employees and employers may negotiate over a worker's enrollment as part of a total compensation package. Households may optimize social insurance participation of one household member based on the degree of protection offered to the entire household. A focus on expected behaviors is necessary for understanding the true effect of policy interventions. Later in this chapter it will be shown that the lessons learned from behavioral economics about bounded rationality can significantly inform the design of coverage extension policies.

Improving the Design of the Existing Social Insurance System
The link between pension design and coverage: A review of key options.
This section describes an array of pension system designs and their features as related to coverage. The designs of old-age pensions vary greatly in achieving wide coverage, and few systems manage to provide access specifically to informal sector workers. In their simplest form, old-age pension systems are mandatory saving schemes that prevent myopic undersavings for old age and curb intentional undersavings and abuse of often generous social safety nets that redistribute income to those in need.

Earnings-related pension schemes (see panel 1 of figure 5.10) provide old-age pension benefits dependent on individual contributions; they work, in effect, as saving mechanisms from the perspective of the individual and can be designed as defined benefit (DB) or defined contribution (DC).[15] In MENA, pension benefits are determined through a set of parameters taking into account the individual's contribution performance over the active life cycle (such as number of contributory periods, and some average wage measure reflecting earnings before retirement or over the entire contributory life span). These are known as DB schemes. The expected value of pensions may be quite different than the value of lifelong contributions. If the pension benefits are systematically higher than the value of contributions, contingent government liabilities emerge, giving rise to implicit pension debt. Mandatory pension schemes in MENA tend to be pay-as-you-go (PAYG), as opposed to "funded," in their underlying financing mechanism, with pension benefits financed by the contributions of active age plan members.[16] Pure earnings-related mandatory pension schemes are rare and lack the minimum old-age income feature that most modern pension schemes possess in one way or another.

Figure 5.10   Old-Age Pension Design and Coverage: Options Ranging from Pure Earnings-Related Pensions to Pure Noncontributory Flat Pensions

(1) Earnings-related pension   (2) Minimum pension guarantee   (3) Universal basic pension

(4) Universal basic pension

(5) Means targeted matching defined contribution

■ income level–dependent subsidies   ☐ income level–dependent contributions

By definition, mandatory earnings-related pension schemes in general, regardless of their design or financing mechanism, do not offer protection to informal sector workers; these schemes typically require that employers register their employees with the social insurance authority, report their earnings. and pay wage-proportional employee and employer contributions, while earnings of informal sector workers are rarely observed. Later in this section, the specific design features of PAYG pensions systems in MENA that pose challenges to participation are explored.

In contrast to earnings-related pension schemes, noncontributory basic (flat) pension schemes do not take into account an individual's income position before retirement to determine his or her benefit amount. Such schemes assume a social responsibility for providing everyone with a minimum standard of living at old age regardless of their saving capacity before retirement (see panel 4 of figure 5.10). As such, they have limited scope for controlling myopic behaviors, a disadvantage over earnings-related pension schemes. Although earnings-related pension schemes attempt to smooth consumption patterns between an individual's active and retired life, flat noncontributory pensions do not necessarily prevent a radical drop in consumption in retirement but offer wider coverage. By design, noncontributory pensions rely on general revenue financing and cover formal and informal sector workers as well as those outside the labor force. Noncontributory pension schemes can provide 100 percent coverage in exchange for government spending as low as 1 to 2 percent of GDP.[17] The most commonly cited universal flat pension scheme is in New Zealand, where no other pension program is offered by the government.[18]

Establishing a minimum pension floor in an earnings-related pension scheme improves income protection compared with a pure earnings-related design but does not improve the potential for coverage. Additionally, it can undermine contribution incentives. The minimum pension is a redistributory feature of earnings-related pension schemes, which ensures an income floor in old age to anyone with an acceptable lifetime contribution effort (for example. with a sufficiently large number of contributory years), regardless of what the earnings-related pension benefit determination would yield (see panel 2 of figure 5.10). The cost of a minimum pension (that is, the "top-up" over the earnings-related pension) is financed from general revenues or redistribution from other plan members. Its potential to increase coverage is limited because it does not extend benefits beyond the Bismarkian (earnings-related) scheme for the formal sector. Moreover, it may create incentives for individuals to hide income, move certain employment activities into informality, or save outside the system, so that lower levels of observed income and contributions will create eligibility for the top-up.

A recent innovation that addresses the flaws of the minimum pension combines an earnings-related pension scheme with a universal (flat) basic pension. One policy option is to combine a pure earnings-related scheme with a universal basic (flat) pension without any connection between the two components. This solution provides smooth income patterns across active and retired life for formal sector workers and establishes an income floor in old age for everybody. The criticism of this solution is its overall high cost, involving uniform general revenue-financed universal pension benefits to those with already high earnings-related pensions. An innovation over this simple unlinked combination is the so-called "universal basic pension with claw-back," which attempts to combine the high coverage of the universal basic pension with the incentive design of a pure earnings-related pension, by gradually phasing out the universal basic pension component as old-age income from the earnings-related pension increases (see panel 3 of figure 5.10).[19] This mechanism provides complete old-age income protection coverage while avoiding the contribution incentive trap of the minimum pension. Under the latter, for a class of low-income workers, any contribution that will not eventually elevate earnings-related pensions above the minimum pension is a sunk cost. In contrast, the claw-back feature reduces the marginal benefit from contributions among low-income contributors but does not eliminate it. Universal basic pensions with a claw-back are always cheaper than an otherwise identical flat universal benefit scheme because of the built-in targeting mechanism and benefit reduction. However, a universal pension with a claw-back is more expensive than an otherwise identical earnings-related pension scheme with a minimum pension because it covers more individuals using general revenue funding and the top-up is larger, as apparent in figure 5.10. This innovation was recently enacted (but has yet to be implemented) in Egypt and already exists in Chile and South Africa.

The most recent innovation for incentive-compatible pension coverage extension is the matching defined contribution (MDC) design. MDCs are voluntary defined contribution saving mechanisms, offering old-age or other social insurance benefits, where the government or employer provides incentives to enroll by matching individual contributions at a given rate and threshold. MDCs increase the incentive to save through matching contributions, effectively increasing the return on savings. Many employer-sponsored pension programs, such as the 401(k) scheme with employer matching in the United States, already have this feature. In panel 5 of figure 5.10, the dark gray columns show the income level–dependent subsidies, and the light gray columns show the income level–dependent contributions under a general MDC design. The figure reflects a further extension to MDCs, combining the matching mechanism with a targeting mechanism (such as means testing or proxy means testing) to induce participation by those with limited saving capacity, without regressively offering higher matches to individuals with higher income or savings capacity. This feature makes MDCs suitable for coverage extension. It is conceivable that a significant number of households desire social insurance services, but their income position does not allow them to pay for the true cost of their social insurance coverage in the form of contributions (see box 5.4 for an example of a targeted MDC in the case of health insurance in Lebanon). The MDC innovation demonstrates that targeting mechanisms often used to reach the poorest and most disadvantaged households can also be used to target those above the extreme poverty level, but below the income level that would allow them to enroll in the contributory social risk management mechanisms.

In fact, the relative income status of households can be used to determine the amount of matching subsidies for which households are eligible if they are willing to enroll in the related social insurance mechanism. The MDC scheme is likely more affordable than universal basic pensions due to the targeting mechanism and the consequently reduced inclusion error. However, MDCs do not ensure complete coverage as well as universal schemes do; their potential to increase coverage can only be met if (1) the matching design adequately motivates contributions at all income levels, (2) the transaction cost of enrollment is small, and (3) lessons learned from behavioral economics on irrational behavior are used in the program design (discussed later in this chapter.)[20]

The key issues with increasing coverage through noncontributory (or heavily subsidized) special schemes are the potential unintended

---

Box 5.4   Proposal for Expansion of Health Insurance in Lebanon through a Targeted MDC

The government of Lebanon has embarked on reforms to expand health insurance coverage to individuals who are not covered by the National Social Security Fund (NSSF) and other contributory schemes. The NSSF, which covers about 40 percent of the population, provides health insurance to formal sector workers in the private sector and to civil servants through earnings-related contributory schemes. For those not covered by the NSSF, the Ministry of Public Health acts as the insurer of last resort. These are mostly poor or near poor, low-income self-employed, and informal wage earners. The recent reforms (Health Card Initiative) launched by the government entail subsidizing the low-income population who cannot afford the premium to be covered. Figure B5.4.1 is an illustration of how the consolidation of the health plans can be achieved if the government chooses to use a targeting strategy offering three plans (a basic plan, an intermediate plan, and the more comprehensive NSSF plan) and allocates subsidies based on the level of earnings. As shown in the figure, a universal subsidy is provided to all individuals regardless of income that covers externalities and public goods. Additional subsidies are allocated based on the income quintile to which beneficiaries belong. The proxy means testing system currently being developed under the National Poverty Targeting Program could be used to indicate beneficiaries' income brackets. As income increases, subsidies decline, and the required individual contributions rise. Thus, individuals with some savings capacity would contribute to the cost of the plan to receive the subsidy. Individuals who can afford to pay additional contributions can finance more "generous" health packages.

box continues next page

Striving for Better Jobs • http://dx.doi.org/10.1596/978-0-8213-9535-6

**Box 5.4   Proposal for Expansion of Health Insurance in
Lebanon through a Targeted MDC** *(continued)*

Figure B5.4.1   Subsidized and Individual Contributions by Income Quintile

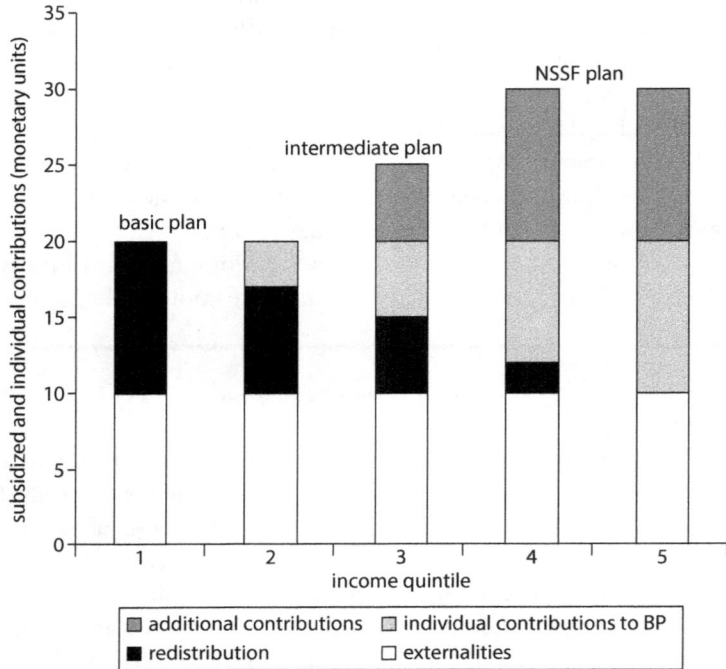

Source: World Bank 2010.
Note: BP = Basic Plan ; NSSF = National Social Security Fund.

consequences in the form of behavioral responses; such schemes may reduce willingness to participate in the contributory mechanism among those who are able to and could ease the path for firms to offer jobs without social insurance coverage. Clearly, the easiest way to extend coverage is through universal general revenue–funded noncontributory transfers such as the universal basic (flat) pension. In addition to the higher costs of a universal program, the availability of noncontributory benefits may create incentives for current contributors (and some uncovered who otherwise would exert effort to contribute) to transition to the noncontributory scheme. Even if the services of the noncontributory system are of lower quality, this argument still holds as long as the services are valuable and include a higher subsidy component than the contributory benefit alternative. Levy (2006) provides evidence in this regard, indicating that the availability of subsidized social insurance programs for uncovered workers may unintentionally allow firms to shift employment into contractual relationships not covered under the formal social insurance scheme or into self-employment. The macroeconomic result of such a shift may be that aggregate labor is overemployed in the informal sector and underemployed in the formal sector. This increases labor costs in the formal sector, and thus these programs can have an economy-wide negative effect on productivity competitiveness, and potentially on growth. Alterido and others (2009) have shown that expansion of a noncontributory health insurance program in Mexico (Seguro Popular)[21] has a moderate downward influence on participation in the formal contributory social insurance scheme covering health insurance as well as pension and unemployment benefits. The authors show that 55 percent of Seguro Popular beneficiaries are nonpoor. Overall, the availability of noncontributory special schemes is likely to decrease incentives to participate in contributory social insurance mechanisms. In addition, access to noncontributory schemes allows employees and firms to collude by not incurring the cost of enrolling the employee in the contributory social insurance system to share the emerging surplus. In cases of weak bargaining power on the side of employees, the availability of noncontributory schemes can give rise to firm behaviors that shift the creation of new jobs to informality, justifying this by the access of workers to the noncontributory benefits. Theoretically, the MDC design would not suffer from this problem if the matching subsidy were truly aligned with the income position of the contributor. In particular, the better the targeting in assessing saving capacity, the less likely that undesirable behavioral responses would emerge.

Design of pension systems in MENA and determinants of coverage.
Universal social insurance coverage is a relatively modern policy goal; current coverage patterns in MENA reflect a history of social security provision initially limited to the civil service, without the ambition of universality. Most social insurance systems in MENA were born in the late 1960s or early 1970s through the establishment of schemes specific to civil service employees. In fact, worldwide, public sector employees were usually the first to be covered by pensions and other social insurance schemes sponsored by governments in their role as employers.[22] Gradual expansion to formal private sector employees and other groups took place at later stages. In MENA, though expansion of pension schemes beyond the civil service has been achieved in all countries, it has happened

in a fragmented manner. As shown in figure 5.11, the share of MENA countries that have already integrated civil service schemes within larger schemes that cover workers in other sectors (such as the private sector) is lower than in the ECA and LAC regions, comparable to EAP, and greater than in SSA and SAR.[23] Currently, 11 of the 19 MENA countries still operate a separate or only partially integrated scheme covering civil servants and private sector workers. Concerns regularly surface regarding the legacy costs of integrated civil service schemes in countries where the integration has already been implemented (such as in Jordan and Syria). None of the countries operate one single national scheme that covers all types of workers. The fragmentation of the system poses various problems, especially as MENA economies seek efficient and productive resource allocation across sectors. First, if benefits are not portable across schemes, labor mobility across sectors with different schemes is constrained (box 5.5). Moreover, generous sector specific schemes (such as civil service schemes) may crowd out labor supply in other sectors (such as the private sector) and create inequities (Robalino 2005). The following sections discuss three features that are common to many MENA pension systems and that are problematic for informality: legal coverage, early retirement, and calculation of benefits.

Outside the public sector, pension system coverage in MENA is still limited, and legal provisions for covering the self-employed and agricultural workers are sporadic. MENA social insurance schemes reflect the traditional view that coverage is associated with a formal employment relationship, and they rarely accommodate special employment status categories. In several MENA countries, certain types of workers are legally excluded from coverage. Thus, in some cases, coverage extension may need to start with expansion of "legal coverage," as was done recently for workers of agricultural cooperatives in Morocco. Traditional social insurance coverage implies that the self-employed are excluded from coverage by default. Only half of the MENA countries offer mandatory or voluntary coverage for the self-employed (table 5.6; see Robalino 2005; SSA 2009, 2010). However, integrating the coverage of the self-employed under the current DB pension schemes in MENA is challenging because it would put a significant burden on the often low-productivity self-employed. Moreover, the existing pension schemes in the majority of MENA countries exclude a large portion of rural workers; at best, workers in large agricultural organizations such as cooperatives can enroll. As for unpaid family workers, coverage relies exclusively on household members accessing social insurance benefits (such as survival pensions or

Figure 5.11   Path Dependency in the Evolution of Pension Systems: Degree of Integration of Civil Service Pension Schemes in MENA and Other Regions

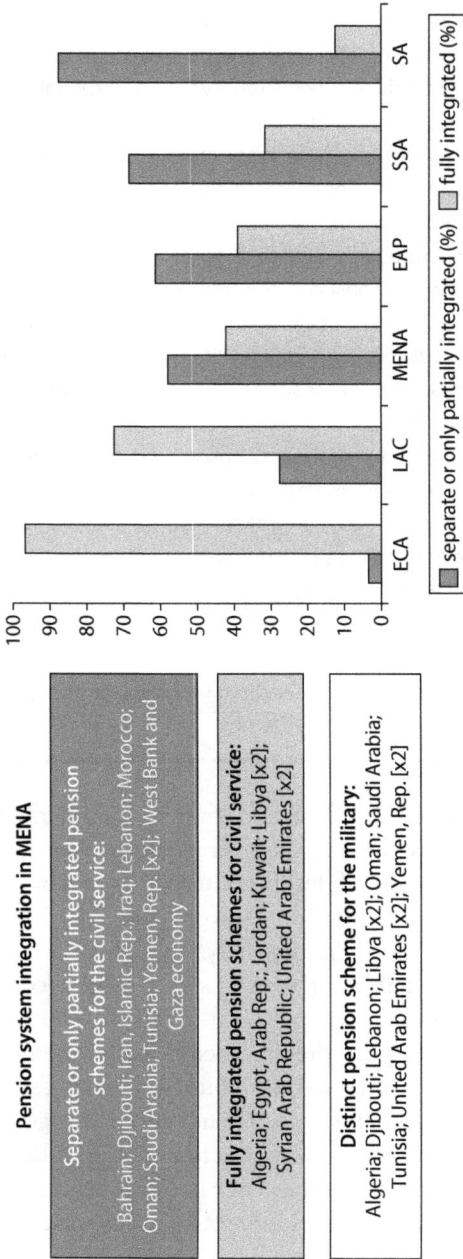

Pension system integration in MENA

Separate or only partially integrated pension schemes for the civil service:
Bahrain; Djibouti; Iran, Islamic Rep; Iraq; Lebanon; Morocco; Oman; Saudi Arabia; Tunisia; Yemen, Rep. [x2]; West Bank and Gaza economy

Fully integrated pension schemes for civil service:
Algeria; Egypt, Arab Rep.; Jordan; Kuwait; Libya [x2]; Syrian Arab Republic; United Arab Emirates [x2]

Distinct pension scheme for the military:
Algeria; Djibouti; Lebanon; Libya [x2]; Oman; Saudi Arabia; Tunisia; United Arab Emirates [x2]; Yemen, Rep. [x2]

■ separate or only partially integrated (%)   ▨ fully integrated (%)

Source: World Bank pension systems database.
Note: Integration refers to integration of civil service pension schemes within schemes covering workers in other sectors, including the formal private sector. ECA = Europe and Central Asia; EAP = East Asia and Pacific; LAC = Latin America and the Caribbean; SA = South Asia; SSA = Sub-Saharan Africa.

Box 5.5   Integration and Portability of Social Insurance Schemes

The integration of distinct public and private sector social insurance schemes is driven by the need for reduced distortionary forces in the labor market. Programs covering distinct groups in the labor force without explicit portability arrangements of vested social insurance rights limit labor mobility and therefore cause economic and labor market distortions. For example, public sector workers who are vested in the public sector pension scheme for many years, but not long enough to draw pension benefits, may be reluctant to accept otherwise desirable job offers from the private sector, because their past contributions may become a sunk cost, and future private sector vestment may not be long or secure enough to yield pension benefits either. To diminish this distortion, and to facilitate labor mobility, governments either integrate public and private sector social insurance programs or establish arrangements for their portability.

With integration, the same set of rules applies for all enrolled plan members regardless of their employment sector. Portability arrangements are often thought of as "second best solutions" for labor mobility; distinct social insurance contribution requirements and benefits still apply to different groups in the labor force, and the difference in generosity (often favoring those working in the MENA public sector) may induce reluctance to switch jobs. Segmentation of social insurance systems also limits international labor mobility, further motivating the current trend toward integration of sector specific schemes domestically, and establishing cross-border portability among integrated national social insurance schemes.

health insurance) through covered family members. Temporary and casual workers are excluded from coverage in the Republic of Yemen and Syria. Another example of legal exclusion from coverage is in Syria, where employees in firms with fewer than five employees receive coverage limited to work injury only. In Lebanon, all private sector employees are not eligible for pensions, but rather receive a lump-sum end-of-service indemnity.

Further contributing to the fragmentation of pension systems and labor markets in MENA, various countries have established specific occupational schemes that are usually not subject to government regulation. Occupational schemes exist in the Islamic Republic of Iran, Morocco, Egypt, and Tunisia. Tunisia's experience in expanding coverage to the self-employed is based on the development of an income estimation system for different occupational groups. Based on the estimated lowest income bracket assigned to each occupational group, the required personal

Table 5.6 Legal Coverage for Self-Employed Workers and Agricultural Workers in Non-GCC MENA Economies

Economy	Coverage for self-employed mandatory (M) or voluntary (V)	Coverage for agricultural workers	Remark
Egypt, Arab Rep.	Mandatory coverage	Covered	In agriculture, casual workers covered
Morocco	No coverage	Covered	Agricultural workers in cooperatives covered
Tunisia	Mandatory coverage	Covered	Agricultural workers in cooperatives and agricultural wage earners covered
Syrian Arab Republic	No coverage	Covered	Agricultural workers with formal jobs (a marginal segment) covered under general social insurance scheme
Algeria	Voluntary coverage	No coverage	Special scheme for self-employed
Jordan	Voluntary coverage		
Lebanon	No coverage	No coverage	
Iran, Islamic Rep.	Mandatory coverage	No coverage	Coverage of self-employed within scheme for private sector employees
Yemen, Rep.	Mandatory coverage	No coverage	Coverage of self-employed within scheme for private sector employees
Djibouti	No coverage	Covered	Agricultural workers in cooperatives covered under general social insurance system
West Bank and Gaza economy	No coverage	No coverage	Excludes self-employed
Libya	Mandatory coverage	No coverage	Coverage of self-employed within general social insurance scheme
Iraq	No coverage	No coverage	Excludes self-employed

Sources: Robalino 2005; SSA 2009, 2010.

contributions are identified. Workers can choose to contribute more, or they can contribute less if they prove that their real income is lower than the bracket assigned to them. This kind of approach suffers from challenges of financial sustainability and inaccuracy of estimated income. Although specific mandatory occupational schemes have been used as a gradual approach to expanding coverage, and have been sought in countries such as South Africa, Korea, and Costa Rica (Von Ginneken 2009), their potential as an approach to increase coverage (especially compared with more wide-scale extension of coverage strategy) is very much affected by whether the groups are large and sufficiently homogenous (Olivier 2009; Robalino and Palacios 2009). Arguably, such a coverage extension approach increases the segmentation of the social insurance system and could ultimately undermine integrated coverage extension efforts that attempt to attract voluntary participation regardless of the nature of workers' employment status.

In terms of design, mandatory earnings-related pension schemes in MENA all follow the DB pension system design. Figure 5.12 illustrates the relative share of each of four mandatory pension design types (DB, DC, notional defined contribution [NDC], and provident fund [PF]) that exist around the world. In MENA, DB systems dominate. The widespread design weaknesses of these schemes in MENA contribute to the observed high degree of informality. Modern versions of DB pension design are capable of creating favorable participation incentives similar to those of DC schemes. In fact, it has been proven that DB and DC design can be identical if the DB design (1) adjusts the benefit level in an actuarially fair manner for early or delayed retirement before or after the statutory retirement age, (2) has an automatic mechanism to change the statutory

Figure 5.12   Mandatory Pension Design Types across Regions of the World

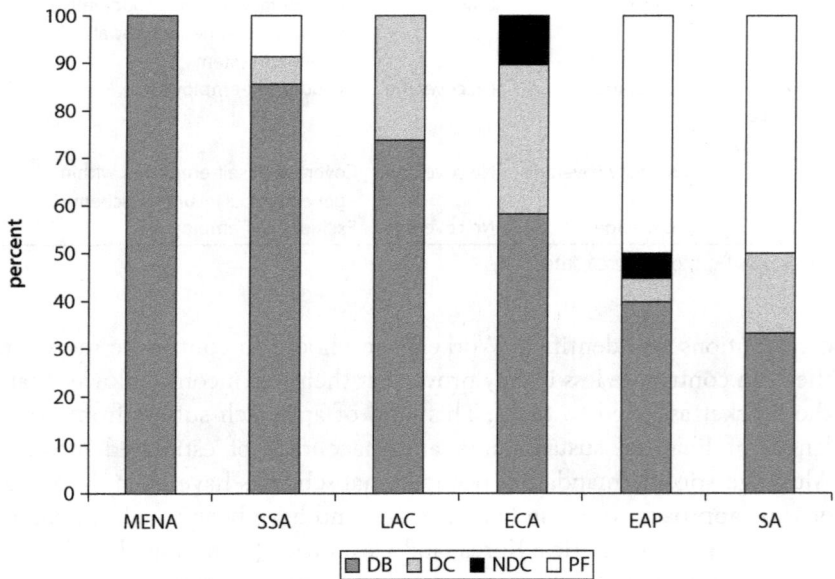

Source: Pallares-Miralles and others forthcoming.
Note: ECA = Europe and Central Asia; EAP = East Asia and Pacific; LAC = Latin America and the Caribbean;
SA = South Asia; SSA = Sub-Saharan Africa; DB = defined benefit; DC = defined contribution; NDC = notional
defined contribution; PF = provident fund.

retirement age in line with changing life expectancy, and (3) uses an average wage measure in the benefit formula, which incorporates the wage level of all contributory periods in a revalorized manner.[24] However, the mandatory DB schemes in MENA do not meet these criteria. In addition to the problem of financial sustainability, MENA's DB schemes have flaws in many of the critical design features, such as the minimum vesting period, early retirement provision, and average wage measure in the benefit formula, that provide disincentives to participate in the system.

Minimum vesting period: Minimum vesting periods can promote informality. Table 5.7 summarizes some of the design parameters of mandatory pension schemes in MENA. With the exception of the recently modernized Iraqi pension system, none of the featured MENA countries require individuals to contribute for longer than half of a potentially 35- to 45-year active life cycle (that is, between a labor market entry age of 15 to 25 years and retirement at the age of 60) to qualify for full pensions. Primarily, a short vesting period causes either unsustainability or inadequate income protection. In many cases, the length of the minimum vesting period is close to or less than the length of time for receiving pension benefits, even without taking advantage of early retirement provisions. Theoretically, this can be sustainable only at prohibitively high contribution requirements or very low benefits. Low benefits would not protect against poverty in old age, so that the protection offered is not adequate. Another consequence of a short vesting period is that individuals provide only what is required from them in terms of system participation and exert a significant portion of their income-generating effort in some form of informality hidden from the social insurance system. The best strategy for workers is to limit the length of contributions to the minimum necessary to draw full benefits (see further below). Gaming the pension system with strategically shortened life-cycle contributions not only undermines sustainability but also increases informality. Conversely, a long minimum vesting requirement would exclude from pension eligibility those who cannot contribute sufficiently long in the formal sector.

Under DC schemes, no need for a required minimum vesting period is required, and thus such schemes can be considered more "coverage friendly" than DB schemes. With funded DC or NDC[25] pension designs, the saving effort during the active life cycle is measured only by the actual amount of the saving. Furthermore, the earnings-related DC mechanism could be augmented with a minimum old-age income guarantee feature (see the summary in the previous section), and the eligibility of the

Table 5.7 Pension Design Parameters of Mandatory Formal Sector Schemes in MENA Retirement Age, Minimum Vesting Period, and Early Retirement Provisions

	Life expectancy at birth	Statutory retirement age		Minimum vesting period		Early retirement age		Vesting for early retirement age	
		Female	Male	Female	Male	Female	Male	Female	Male
Algeria	73.5	55	60	10	15	any age/45	any age/50	32/14	32/20
Djibouti	58.5	55	55	—	—	any age	any age	25	25
Egypt, Arab Rep.	73.5	60	60	10	10	any age	any age	20	20
Iran, Islamic Rep.	73.3	55	60	19	19	any age/45	any age/50	35/30	35/30
Iraq	70.2	60	60	25	25	55/50	55/50	25/30	25/30
Jordan	73.6	55	60	15	15	50	50	22	25
Libya	75.1	60	65	20	20	—	—	—	—
Morocco	72.5	60	60	14	14	55	55	if employer pays	if employer pays
Syrian Arab Republic	76.1	55	60	15	15	any age/50	any age/55	25/20	25/20
Tunisia	74.4	60	60	10	10	50	50	30	30

Sources: Pallares-Miralles and others forthcoming; SSA 2009, 2010.

Note: — = not available.

pensioner for a subsidy could be determined based on the annuity level
he or she receives given his or her saving effort and age. Such a scheme
would avoid gaming behaviors that are prevalent under the vesting period
requirement of DB design. The minimum vesting period requirement also
puts upward pressure on informality through another channel. Jobseekers
with access to temporary formal employment who are uncertain whether
they can maintain formal employment status for the minimum required
DB vesting period may decide to stay informal since any contributions
could eventually become a sunk cost to them.[26] Conversely, under DC
schemes, no sunk cost risk is found for engaging in formal sector employment for those who are uncertain about the stability of their formal
employment status. Overall, DC design can be considered as the desirable
"coverage friendly" system benchmark (as long as it is augmented with
some minimum old-age income guarantee) under which there is no need
to use proxies for contribution performance that are prone to be abused.
The path dependency reality suggests that DB will continue to be the
dominant design in MENA in the foreseeable future. However, it is possible to incorporate features into a DB design pension to approximate the
advantages of a DC scheme, although doing so is more difficult than taking advantage of the DC design's simplicity. For example, under a still
uncommon but theoretically interesting DB design solution, the flaws
associated with a minimum vesting period could be overcome. The
requirements for drawing full pensions or accessing the minimum pension
top-up could be conditioned on age and the true value of past contributory effort (see box 5.6 on recent Jordanian pension reform).

Early retirement provisions: Generous early retirement provisions
cause problems similar to those of the short minimum vesting period
by radically undermining financial sustainability and encouraging
people to reduce the length of their formal sector employment.
Providing a degree of flexibility in determining the actual individual age
of retirement is a logical feature of pension systems. In good practices
of pension design, such flexibility is achieved through an actuarially fair
adjustment of benefits. In particular, those who decide to retire before
the statutory retirement age should compensate the pension system, in
the form of reduced pension benefits, for their shorter contributory
period and their longer term of benefit receipt. An upward adjustment
should also be allowed for those who delay retirement beyond the statutory age and therefore contribute longer and receive benefits for a shorter
period. MENA pension schemes are lax in defining the age at which
individuals can start drawing benefits, and it is the exception rather than

Box 5.6 Social Insurance Reform in Jordan

In 2010 the Jordanian parliament passed a complex social insurance reform law. First, the reform implements a parametric readjustment of the mandatory DB pension program of the Social Security Corporation (SSC) to improve sustainability and incentives in line with the recommendations of this report, including the reduction of benefits in cases of early retirement. This is, in effect, a degree of approximation toward a DC design. Second, it extends the scope of social risk management by introducing maternity benefits and an unemployment insurance saving account mechanism, while also declaring health insurance as the next phase of the scope extension. Third, the reform extends full social insurance coverage to workers of small firms, in particular, firms with fewer than five employees; previously these workers were not covered due to the coverage assignment in accordance with firm size. This coverage extension effort is being supported by public communication activities and implementation efforts that make it easy for small firms to register and do business with the SSC, which has so far been used to collaborate with firms possessing their own human resource departments to serve as counterparts in administering social insurance contributions.

Source: Razzaz 2011.

the rule that the actual benefit amount is less than that defined by the benefit formula.[27] In many MENA countries, the actual age of retirement is not constrained at all. For example, in Algeria, males must complete 32 contributory years; in Djibouti, 25; in Egypt, 20;[28] in the Islamic Republic of Iran, 35; and in Syria, 25. An individual who starts a formal sector job at the age of 20 could retire with a full pension at the age of 40 in Egypt or 45 in Syria, in other words, at ages still suitable for economic activity. Many of these individuals do decide to start drawing pension at this age, stop contributing to the pension system, and seek other informal employment income while officially retired. These "noncontributing active age pensioners" are then counted as uncovered in widely used coverage definitions. Even when the pension system actually imposes an age floor, the set ages are still considered suitable for economic activity; for example, in Iraq, Jordan, and Tunisia, the floor is age 50 for men. The flip side of this practice is that no incentive is given for delayed retirement. To the contrary, mandatory retirement-age rules are set at or close to the statutory retirement age, especially in the public sector. It is likely that this practice is related to the bias toward public sector employment. Without mandatory retirement, many would "overstay" in their relatively well-compensated and low-effort public sector jobs. Allowing early retirement for the public sector–dominated formal employees may be viewed as making room for the many young graduates who queue for public sector jobs, a situation exacerbated by the ever lengthening queue associated with the youth bulge and expansion of the higher education system. High informality rates among those 55 and older have been observed in the data used herein. If these are early retirees, they are already covered by pensions, and the vulnerability argument does not apply to them.

Average wage measure in the DB pension formula: Another design flaw of MENA pension schemes is that the wage measure used in the DB formula does not represent full career wages; this feature provides incentives to report only high income in the years before retirement. If the average wage measure used in the DB pension formula represents all contributions throughout the active life cycle where past wages are revalorized to the changes in the average wage levels over time, then DB systems could have desirable incentive effects similar to those of DC systems. Table 5.8 summarizes the average wage measures applied in the national DB schemes of MENA; they tend to use an unrevalorized average wage measure of the last few years before retirement. As a result, individuals tend to avoid reporting low earnings in these critical years and artificially inflate wages during the same period through side agreements with the employer. The average wage measure effects of the DB MENA pension schemes are stronger from a sustainability or a general equity perspective but can also contribute to gaming of earnings for reporting contribution purposes.

What are optimal life-cycle pension system participation strategies? Pension systems in MENA are extremely generous and have a high internal rate of return for contributors. Given the existing design, individuals often have the incentive to contribute for the minimum period required and still draw generous pensions once retired. MENA pension schemes are excessively generous and, not surprisingly, financially unsustainable. For anyone able to find formal employment and registered with the pension administration, it is worthwhile to enroll in the pension system, although the optimal strategy is not necessarily to contribute all the time. Figure 5.13 shows that in Egypt and Jordan (before the recent reforms) and in Syria, contributing to the pension system yields real returns in the ranges of 6 to 10.5 percent, 7 to 17 percent, and 7 to 14 percent, respectively, much higher than the riskless 2 to 4 percent real return one could achieve through saving outside

**Table 5.8   Average Wage Measures in the Pension Benefit
Formula in Selected MENA Countries**

Country	Average wage measure
Algeria	Maximum of the average of the wages of five last years and the average of five best years without revalorization
Djibouti	average of the wages of the last 10 years/last month's wage
Egypt, Arab Rep.	convoluted combination of unrevalorized average basic wage of the last two years and unrevalorized full career average variable wages
Iran, Islamic Rep.	average of unrevalorized wages in the last two years
Iraq	gradually expanding to revalorized full career average wages in public sector/unrevalorized average of last three years of wages in private sector
Libya	average of unrevalorized wages in the last three years
Syrian Arab Republic	average of last year's unrevalorized wages with wage increase not to exceed 15 and 30 percent in the last two and five year periods, respectively
Tunisia	average revalorized wages in the last 10 years in main scheme; different rules in four other national schemes
Yemen, Rep.	last month's salary

Sources: Pallares-Miralles and others forthcoming; SSA 2009, 2010.

the pension system.[29] Figure 5.13 also illustrates that returns and contribution length are inversely related under the flawed design of MENA DB pension schemes. The highest return is associated with just completing the minimum vesting period necessary to draw full pensions, with contributions completed either early in the career (for example, a "frontloading strategy," taking advantage of the generous early retirement provisions) or very late in the career, to raise the average wage measure with the highest wages reached during a career (for example, a "backloading strategy"). Note that limiting the number of contributory years, if they are nearly evenly distributed between the years of labor market entry and the statutory retirement age, does not increase the return on contributions; the constant contribution density strategy (that is, a "homogeneous life-cycle strategy") is suboptimal from the perspective of the individual. If individuals are in a position to move income between the formal and informal sectors, or if they strategically plan their life-cycle formal employment participation behavior, they further undermine the sustainability of the pension schemes and increase observed informality. The patterns of the derived optimal contribution strategies can explain some of the coverage patterns observed at the aggregate level.

Reforms toward DC pension design (regardless of the financing mechanism) or improvements in DB scheme design would address the

Figure 5.13 **Internal Rate of Return under Various Pension System Participation Strategies in Egypt, Jordan, and Syria**

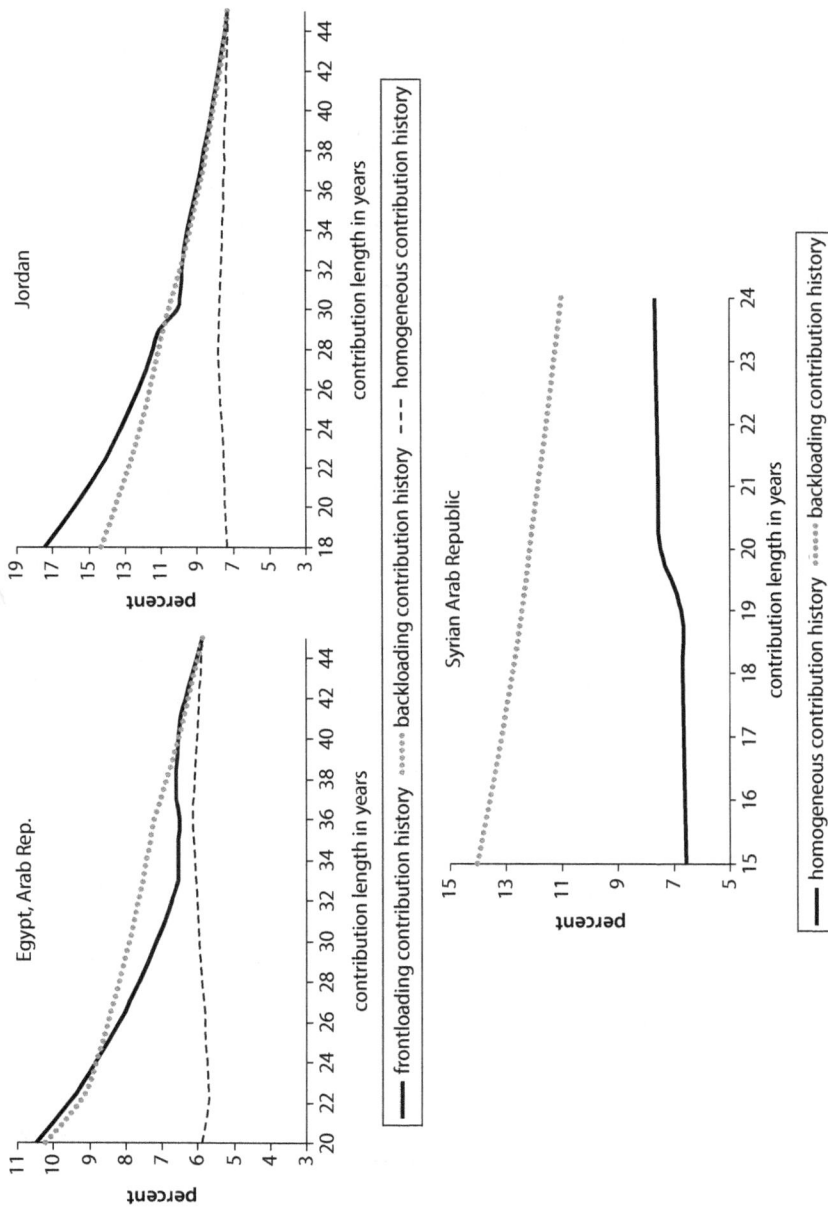

Source: di Filippo and Bodor forthcoming.

adverse incentives of the current MENA pension schemes. Figure 5.14 illustrates the changing internal of rate of return profile under the recently legislated NDC of a funded DC pension reform in Egypt and a hypothetical DB reform in Syria. The Egyptian legislature passed a complex pension reform in 2010, which changed the PAYG pension scheme from DB to NDC design, and introduced a smaller funded DC mandatory pension component, as well as a universal basic pension for all, while reducing the tax wedge imposed by the pension system. One of the goals of this reform was to reinstate the pension system's financial sustainability, so it is not a surprise that the current system's extreme generosity is reduced (as evidenced by the lower internal rate of return). It is also notable that the rate of return differential across various contribution lengths and strategies of "frontloading," "backloading," or keeping contribution density nearly constant is diminished; the pension system no longer provides incentives to work informally during the work career. Similar results can be achieved under a well-designed DB architecture as well. The second panel of figure 5.14 shows that the payoff for short career contribution (and system participation) strategies disappears if an actuarially fair benefit reduction for early retirement is introduced and is combined with an average wage measure that represents all career contributions in a revalorized manner. (These reform features are combined with reduced accrual rate,[30] increased retirement age to improve sustainability, and a reduced contribution rate/tax wedge to reduce the system's burden on the economy.)

By design, pure DC pension schemes promote desirable incentives and are financially sustainable, yet on their own they cannot provide adequate income protection in old age for those who could not save enough during their active life period. As the name "defined contribution" suggests, benefits are solely dependent on the contributions/savings. The implications of this design are especially problematic among those who save too little, not because of a lack of effort, but rather because of labor market conditions and the marketability of their skills. That is why DC pension schemes are almost always augmented with some feature guaranteeing a minimum income level in old age. In this case, the minimum guarantee could be conditional on contributory effort rather than the value of contributions. Moreover, the income guarantee could be a top-up subsidy to augment the saving in the DC scheme, a broader noncontributory social pension, or a combination in the form of a social pension claw-back based on the DC saving.

Figure 5.14 Internal Rate of Return Patterns of the Egyptian Pension System before and after Recently Legislated Pension Reform and of Hypothetical DB Reform in Syria

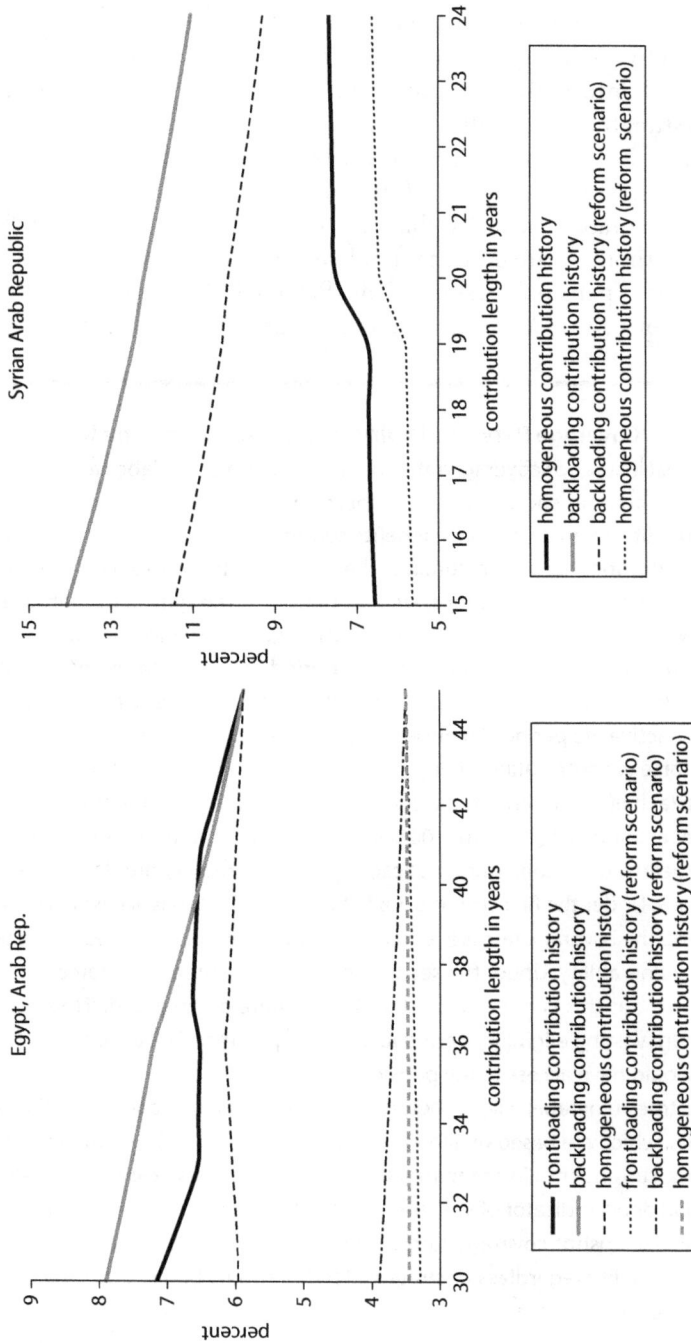

Egypt, Arab Rep.

— frontloading contribution history
— backloading contribution history
– – homogeneous contribution history
······ frontloading contribution history (reform scenario)
–·–·– backloading contribution history (reform scenario)
– – – homogeneous contribution history (reform scenario)

Syrian Arab Republic

— homogeneous contribution history
— backloading contribution history
– – – backloading contribution history (reform scenario)
······ homogeneous contribution history (reform scenario)

Source: di Filippo and Bodor forthcoming.

The discussion in the previous subsections on the various distortions created by the design features of MENA DB pensions implies that the observed informality in the form of the coverage rate is likely to overestimate vulnerability, at least when it comes to access to old-age benefits. Box 5.7 discusses how the coverage rate overestimates the informality-related vulnerability problem when it comes to accessing social insurance benefits that are based on life-cycle contributions, even without strategic behavioral responses to the rules of the social insurance (pension) systems. The flawed DB design of many of the mandatory MENA pension schemes further contributes to reducing

---

Box 5.7   Coverage Rates and Vulnerability Due to Informality

The social insurance coverage rate (that is, the share of the labor force contributing to the mandatory social insurance scheme at a point of time) adequately signals vulnerability when it comes to benefits conditional on current enrollment (such as health insurance) but overestimates the vulnerability for social insurance benefits based on lifetime contributions, such as pensions. The typical DB pension scheme in MENA sets minimum contributory length requirements for eligibility to draw full pensions (called the minimum vesting period). Consider a hypothetical case in which the minimum vesting period is 20 years, equivalent to roughly half of a 40-year active life period. An observed 50 percent coverage rate (that is, half of the labor force is contributing at any point in time) could represent two extreme scenarios: (a) half of the labor force contributes 100 percent of the time and the other half never contributes and (b) 100 percent of the labor force contributes half of the time. Clearly, the underlying implications for vulnerability are different in the two scenarios. Under the first scenario, half of the labor force has access to pension benefits, and the coverage rate is accurate and informative about access to benefits and about vulnerability. Under the second scenario, the entire labor force has access to pensions, but this is not reflected in the estimate of coverage. (Note that with a minimum vesting eligibility period just a bit longer than 20 years, none of the labor force would have access to full pensions.)

The true vulnerability lies in between these extreme scenarios for social insurance benefits, which are based on life-cycle contribution (saving) performance. For other benefits, current enrollment matters for eligibility; in these cases, the coverage rate is a good direct indicator of vulnerability. Note that this illustration explains how the observed snapshot coverage rate overestimates the true vulnerability associated with informality regardless of strategic (endogenous) behavioral responses to the rules of social insurance provision.

---

the observed coverage rate and increasing the gap between the informality measure provided by the coverage indicator and the actual access to old-age income benefits. It should also be stressed that this usually comes at the cost of financial sustainability and, as such, has implications for intergenerational equity.

Beyond pensions. In the previous section, the primary focus was on how pension system rules affect informality outcomes in detail, but a variety of other social insurance risk management mechanisms may have similar effects. With the notable exception of Lebanon, mandatory national pension schemes in MENA offer old-age pension benefits in the form of pension payments until death. The old-age pension benefits are almost always augmented with survivor and disability pension benefits. Eligibility for survivor benefits in MENA tends to be generous; significant anecdotal evidence suggests household-level strategic planning around fully utilizing survivor pensions. Work injury coverage, almost always bundled with old-age pensions, can be more extensive than that of old age. For example, in Syria, registered workers of firms with fewer than five employees are covered only for this risk. Work injury coverage for private sector workers in Morocco is mandatory (a unique case), but employers need to purchase coverage for their employees from competing private insurance providers. A survey from Syria[31] suggests that employees value this social insurance component more than others, such as family or survivorship benefits, but less than old-age benefits and perceived job security due to coverage. In any case, it is unlikely to significantly drive informality. Workers' behaviors are more likely to be affected by health insurance coverage, but in MENA, broad access to health insurance is ensured through public provision of heavily subsidized but often low-quality health services, and privately or publicly provided health insurance benefits typically augment this or offer access to higher quality care (for example, as in Iraq for private sector scheme members). Last, UI schemes in MENA rarely meet the international standards of UI provision, are hardly effective in ensuring the unemployment risk, and are unlikely to drive social insurance system participation decisions. However, recent UI reforms in Jordan and Egypt, which not only offer services to those laid off but also return the savings not used during periods of unemployment to the individual upon retirement, have the potential to make this a valued social insurance component.

Bundling or debundling coverage for the various social insurance components may influence informality outcomes. The bundling of benefits under a single social insurance package may exert downward pressure on coverage through mandating contributions for components widely viewed as less valuable. The Syria employer-employee survey showed that old-age coverage is significantly more valued than any bundled components, although health insurance is not provided through social insurance. On the other hand, in Lebanon, where old-age coverage in the traditional sense of pensions does not exist (only a lump-sum end-of-service indemnity), the health coverage component is viewed as the most valuable. The "price elasticity" of coverage is dependent on what services are provided under the coverage umbrella. If employees and employers are forced to pay for social insurance components that are less valued because of the bundled access to social insurance services, participation may be reduced under the formal sector social insurance scheme. At the same time, bundling of important social insurance components that are not valued by some workers because of myopia and the lack of immediate benefits (such as old-age income security compared with health insurance whose benefits could be immediately experienced) may improve coverage of such insurance types. Often benefits that are not associated with social risks are also financed through the social insurance mechanism, which increases the cost of participation without underlying theoretical justification. For example, in Syria, heating subsidies and family allowances are financed through the social insurance contributions of employees and employers. Such social benefits may be legitimate social benefits categories in a particular country context, but no reason exists to mix their financing with the financing mechanisms of protection against the realization of social risks such as old age, disability, or death of income-generating family members. Social support toward families is not an insurance service per se; this would be better matched with general revenue financing.

In summary, the set of risks covered by the social insurance mechanism should be linked to the underlying exposure to social risks and productivity of formal sector employment, so that a bundle of protection against the truly relevant risk is provided at an appropriate cost. Such bundling decisions should be revisited as MENA governments are now considering introducing unemployment insurance to protect against layoff risk in formal sector employment. This was less of a relevant risk in the past, but one that is getting increasingly more relevant given the private sector–driven growth path. It should be noted, however, that the limited existing evidence does not support the hypothesis that bundling significantly affects the participation decision in Morocco. There the chance of having a formal job was found to increase if another member of the family had a formal job. With health insurance extended to spouse and dependents, the "bundling" hypothesis would generate a negative correlation of formal jobs within the household. Instead, an explanation relying on networks and privileged access to formal jobs seems more plausible.

The coverage of social insurance (pension) systems in MENA is historically low. Coverage extension is required to provide tools to individuals and households to protect against various critical social risks including, but not limited to, health and unemployment risks and diminishing income-generating capacity in old age. Well-designed social risk management mechanisms increase welfare, but it is crucial that their design ensures adequate, affordable, and sustainable benefits in a manner that offers coverage to a large and increasing share of the population, without causing massive economic and labor market distortions. The first step in coverage extension is bridging the legal coverage gaps: coverage is rarely offered, for example, to the self-employed or agricultural workers. Beyond that, rethinking the design of existing MENA pension schemes should be a precondition for further coverage extension efforts. Vesting requirements, early retirement provisions, and average wage measures used for pension benefit calculation all contribute to reduced observed coverage. In general, the MENA pension systems provide high returns to those who have the chance to enroll, but paradoxically, this return can be made even greater by reducing the contribution length to a minimum and by taking advantage of the generous early retirement or by gaming representation of career wage by wages immediately before retirement. In addition to improving sustainability of the pension system and protecting against a wider array of social risks, social insurance reform is critical for addressing informality in MENA. Important political economy aspects to coverage extension can be identified. Given the generosity of existing systems and their financial unsustainability, current contributors have the incentive to extend coverage now to stave off reform. Without reestablishing financial sustainability first, extending coverage under the same conditions of existing pension systems is likely to magnify considerably the financial sustainability problem (box 5.8). Nevertheless, even if the existing formal sector pension schemes were reformed to match best practices, full, or even near full, coverage would still be an issue in MENA. Because many of informal workers have limited ability to save, it is unlikely that coverage extension can be achieved effectively without special subsidized social insurance features.

Box 5.8   Political Economy Considerations for Coverage Extension

The political economy of coverage extension and its interaction with pension reform matters significantly. For example, the true intent behind certain coverage extension efforts may be motivated by the need to temporarily improve the financial sustainability of otherwise unsustainable PAYG pension schemes. Particularly, DB pension schemes with PAYG financing are often financially unsustainable due to the political economy of pensions: The future generations who inherit the burden of the "pension Ponzi scheme" do not participate in the political system. When the demographic transition in developing countries accelerates the aging process of the society and the benefits of those already in or close to retirement become harder to finance even on a PAYG basis, then the search for alternative funding sources is intensified in the political arena, at least in the short term. Paradoxically, the mass enrollment of young workers who used to be excluded from participating in the formal sector pension scheme offers such a temporary financing solution. New young contributors pay contributions to the PAYG scheme to cover pension expenditures in the near future. Of course, improving the current financial position of a pension scheme through coverage extension without reinstating the overall sustainability of the design is hardly even a temporary correction measure; in fact, such a move accelerates the accumulation of unfunded government liabilities. In the future, when coverage extension is no longer available as a temporary measure, the government will be forced to default on the pension promises; that is, it will reduce the value of benefits promised in exchange for enrolling in the system. Ultimately, chances are that coverage extension without realigned sustainability will treat those formerly informal in an unfair manner, as it shifts forward the burden of the financial sustainability of the system. Because of this, covered (formal) workers are likely to support coverage extension, because it ensures system sustainability in the short run and eases the pressure for pension reform (which would likely reduce the generosity of their benefits). In this sense, reestablishing the sustainability of pension (and broader social insurance) schemes is a precondition to functionally adequate coverage extension efforts.

Extending Social Insurance Beyond the Existing Mandatory System: Guiding Tree with Application to MENA

This section addresses how governments can develop coverage extension program strategies for their country-specific needs, assuming that the incentive design issues in existing earnings-related schemes are addressed in line with the discussion above. The following discussion acknowledges that informality is a persistent reality, and that access to innovative social risk management tools needs to be developed and provided to the informal sector, as well as to those outside of the labor force.

Governments that opt to extend social insurance coverage beyond the existing mandatory social insurance system by targeting groups of informal workers are faced with a set of decisions related to strategy, design, and implementation of new schemes. Although modernization of social insurance systems is expected to contribute to improved coverage, certain groups are likely to remain vulnerable/excluded. For example, consider the case of workers with nontraditional jobs that have no easily identifiable employment relationship defined by a single employer, duration, frequency, and wage, and who experience high mobility between jobs and recurrent unemployment spells. It is difficult, if not impossible, to mandate such workers to enroll under the formal earnings-related social security system. Moreover, some groups of informal workers are likely not to be able to afford any contributions required by the social insurance system and the transaction costs associated with enrolling. Extending coverage to such groups of workers requires the introduction of one or more types of special coverage extension schemes. This section discusses the various decisions facing governments when introducing such schemes (figure 5.15). For example, schemes could be based on either a universal strategy, where all individuals in the broad population group are eligible to benefit from a certain scheme, or on a targeted strategy, where only a portion of individuals within the broad population group is eligible, based on some kind of means test or categorical differentiation. Additionally, the scheme might or might not require contributions on the part of the beneficiaries. Examples of contributory schemes include MDC schemes in which the matching for the employee's contribution may be financed by the government or by employers. Noncontributory schemes include social pensions and free health insurance (figure 5.10 illustrates these types of schemes in the context of pensions). Governments may even consider introducing different schemes serving distinct homogenous social groups and/or different objectives. This section also presents guiding indicators that can be used to assess the relevance of different strategies in light of existing country conditions. The indicators are chosen based on evidence from international literature and experience on different social insurance schemes. Based on the decision framework presented, this section also provides policy implications specific to MENA countries regarding the relevance of different types of coverage extension strategies.

Figure 5.15 Guiding Tree for Introducing Coverage Extension Strategies

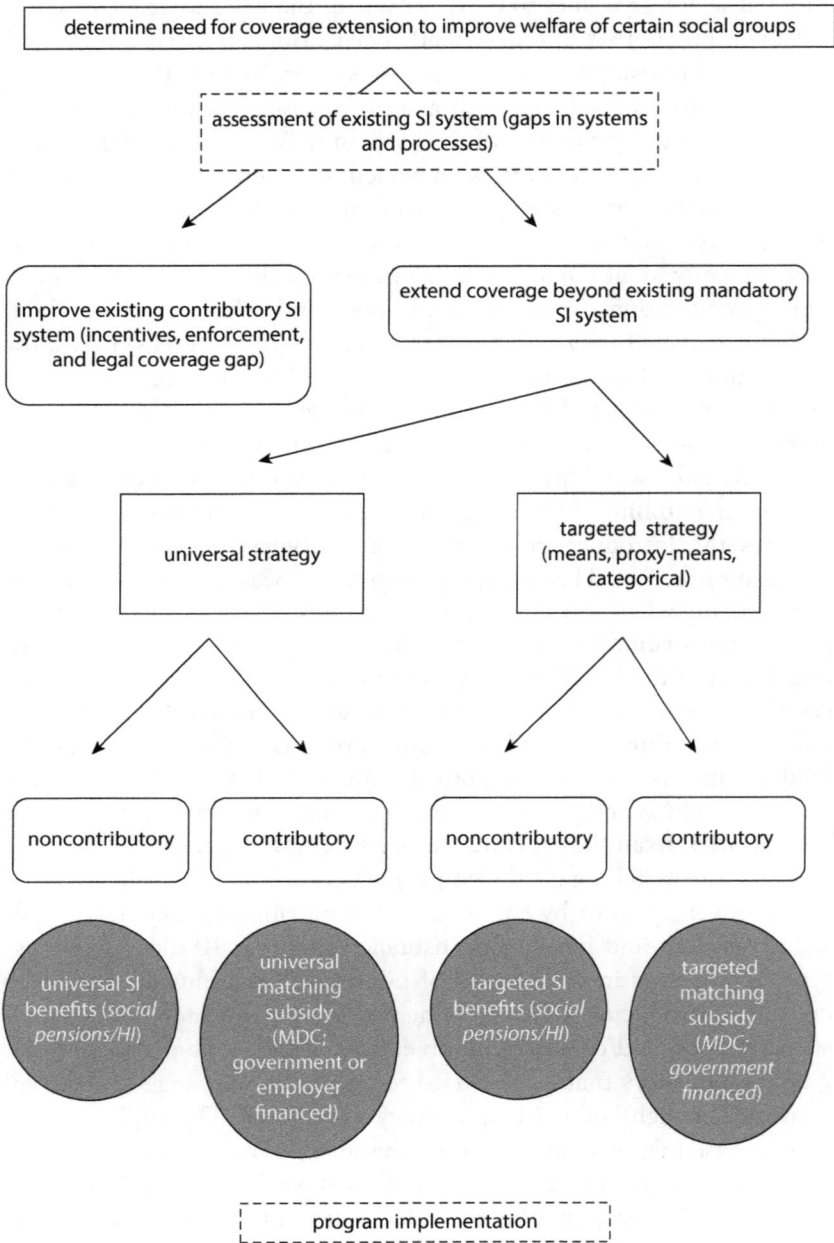

determine need for coverage extension to improve welfare of certain social groups

```
                    assessment of existing SI system (gaps in systems
                                  and processes)
```

improve existing contributory SI system (incentives, enforcement, and legal coverage gap)		extend coverage beyond existing mandatory SI system

universal strategy	targeted strategy (means, proxy-means, categorical)

noncontributory	contributory	noncontributory	contributory
universal SI benefits (*social pensions/HI*)	universal matching subsidy (MDC; government or employer financed)	targeted SI benefits (*social pensions/HI*)	targeted matching subsidy (*MDC; government financed*)

```
                        program implementation
```

Note: SI = social insurance.

A Framework to Assess the Existing Social Insurance System in Light of Coverage Extension

Most countries are not starting with an empty slate when it comes to social insurance. The first step of decision making requires an assessment of the existing system with the objective of identifying possible reasons for low coverage outcomes resulting from implementation shortcomings. Palacios (forthcoming) presents a framework that can be used to identify gaps in social protection programs based on five main implementation "tasks," presented as different layers of the pyramid in figure 5.16: (1) identification, (2) targeting, (3) enrollment, (4) benefit definition, and (5) management information systems. This framework suggests that a rough estimation can be made of the share of the eligible population that did not receive a certain social protection benefit due to shortcomings in each of the five main tasks. This then provides guidance on improving the implementation of existing programs as well as on the design and implementation of new programs. Figure 5.16 also presents examples of indicators associated with each of the five tasks in the framework.

A robust and integrated national identification system is an important prerequisite. In MENA, although a national identification (ID) system exists in all countries and national IDs are mandatory for adults, the robustness and integration of these systems across various public agencies and service providers vary among countries but remain under-developed in most. Moreover, exclusion from the ID system is heavily dependent on income level. Morocco, the Republic of Yemen, and Djibouti have recently taken steps to develop a multiuse biometric national ID system. The national ID in Egypt is used for receiving various public services as well as for employment and some private transactions. In other countries, the use of national IDs is limited to election purposes. Overall, modernization of national ID systems is underway in the region, although completion may take time, and program-specific IDs can be used, with an outlook toward future development of an integrated unique ID. With respect to the second layer of the pyramid, targeting/eligibility, the key question for governments is whether some people are being excluded because they cannot prove their eligibility or because of the quality of the targeting system. It is also important to determine if ineligible people are erroneously included as well. The upper levels of the pyramid consider the need to assess the procedures through which potential beneficiaries enroll in the system and evaluate the effectiveness of the benefit delivery processes and the accuracy and maturity of the management information systems.

Striving for Better Jobs • http://dx.doi.org/10.1596/978-0-8213-9535-6

Figure 5.16 A Framework for Implementing Social Protection Programs

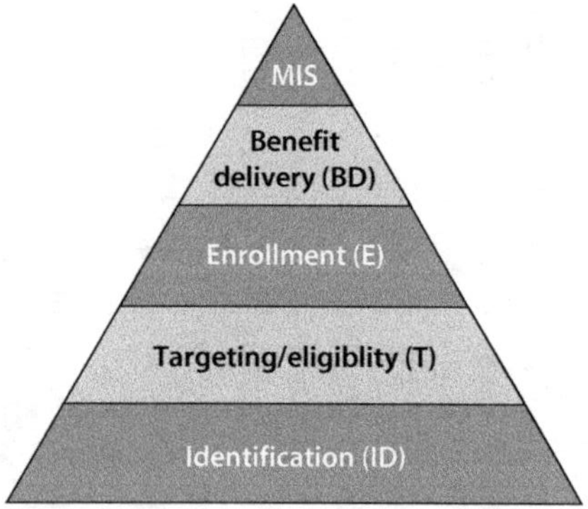

	Example of indicator
ID	• National Identification System Robustness • National Identification System Integration
T	• existence and quality of (proxy) means testing • National Identification System Integration
E	• bureaucratic transaction costs • legal constraints to enrollment • strength of enforcement • Internet/mobile penetration
BD	• access/availability of providers (such as hospitals, local offices, banks) • Internet/mobile penetration

Source: Based on Palacios forthcoming.

Extending Coverage beyond an Existing Mandatory Social Insurance System

Existing country conditions can serve as a good guide for governments to assist in making design decisions when introducing coverage extension strategies. Current country-specific conditions (such as the level of income of the target group, existing coverage patterns, government effectiveness, and effectiveness of existing programs and their supporting infrastructure) can be used to assess the relevance of each type of scheme in a specific country context. Various guiding indicators are collected in the score card presented in table 5.9. It summarizes considerations and examples of relevant indicators that can be used to evaluate existing country-specific conditions for guiding decisions on coverage extension strategies. The conditions are described in turn below. It is worth mentioning that although current country conditions will ultimately guide the decisions to be made when introducing new

Table 5.9 Existing Country Conditions Guiding Indicators (Score Card)

Universal vs. Targeted strategy		
	Universal	Targeting
1. Level of income and poverty in the country		
A. GDP per capita		+
B. Share of rural population	+	
C. Share of "no" and "low" savings capacity population	+	
D. Incidence of poverty among elderly	+	
2. Effectiveness of existing social assistance programs and systems		
E. Existence and effectiveness of social assistance programs		+
F. Existence and quality of means or proxy means testing		+
3. Government's ability to reach different population groups		
G. Mobile/Internet penetration		+
H. Local government presence/strength		+
Noncontributory vs. Contributory Scheme		
	Noncontributory	Contributory
4. Level of income and poverty in the country/target population		
A. GDP per capita		+
B. Coverage rate		+
C. Share of "no" to "low" savings capacity population	+	
5. Transaction costs (bureaucratic transaction costs)	+	
6. Trust in government (government accountability)		+
7. Financial literacy		+

Note: GDP = gross domestic product.

Striving for Better Jobs • http://dx.doi.org/10.1596/973-0-8213-9535-6

schemes, governments' future objectives and the projected enabling
environment of a country, as envisioned by various reforms, should be
taken into account. For example, although current country conditions
may motivate the introduction of temporary programs or temporary
design features, a different form of the system may be anticipated
under more developed conditions. The key is that design features
applied under current conditions should not serve as constraints toward
future modernization.

Deciding between a universal or a targeted strategy:

(1) Level of income and poverty: The richer the country, the more likely
    that a universal strategy will result in higher inclusion errors; that is,
    more middle- and high-income individuals with no need for govern-
    ment support are likely to benefit from the scheme. This group would
    otherwise be excluded from a means-tested targeted scheme. Thus, a
    universal scheme would be both more regressive in nature and more
    costly in richer countries. In addition, because income is more likely
    to be observable in richer countries, both inclusion and exclusion
    errors will be less significant under a targeted scheme. Indicators to
    consider under this category include GDP per capita, the share of
    rural population, and the savings capacity of the population. Finally,
    with respect to old-age benefits in particular, a higher share of elderly
    among the poor strengthens the argument for universal schemes.[32]
(2) Effectiveness of existing social assistance programs and systems: In
    countries with well-established, effective, and high-coverage social as-
    sistance programs, a universal scheme implies that individuals are
    likely to receive multiple benefits. Moreover, effective social safety net
    programs often rely on well-developed targeting systems, on which
    governments can depend when introducing a targeted coverage exten-
    sion strategy. Relevant indicators to be considered under this category
    include scope, coverage, and impact of social assistance programs and
    the existence/quality of means or proxy means testing systems in the
    country (see box 5.9 for a discussion of targeting methods).
(3) Government's ability to reach different population groups: In less
    urbanized countries with little government representation in rural
    and remote areas, a targeting strategy may be very costly. Examples
    of indicators that can be considered when assessing the government's
    ability to reach different population groups include local government
    presence/strength and mobile or Internet penetration rates.

Box 5.9   Targeting Methods

The ideal mechanism to target programs to low-income households is determining eligibility to a given program based on the household's level of income and available assets.[a] *Means testing* implies that benefits could go directly to those most financially in need. It requires the collection and verification of household income information, a costly exercise whose credibility could be threatened by the underestimation or misreporting of income by households, especially by the self-employed. Another mechanism of targeting based on means that is increasingly being used in the developing world is *proxy means testing (PMT)*. Under proxy means testing, individuals and/or households are assigned a score based on a number of household indicators that serve as a proxy for income and assets. The method requires the development of a regression formula that relates easily observed household characteristics to income (or expenditures). Common variables include number of household members and children, location, quality of housing, ownership of assets, and utility bills. Once individuals apply to a certain program, such information is usually collected through household visits, although in more developed targeting environments, a detailed national database such as the census could be used to create a proxy means score independently of applications to a specific program. This method can be less expensive than means testing and subject to less underreporting. However, the effectiveness of the overall mechanism depends on a strong correlation between income and easily observed household and individual characteristics.

In addition to targeting based on means or proxy means, some programs determine eligibility on the basis of specified geographic, socioeconomic, and demographic characteristics that are correlated with poverty (for example, age, number of children, disabled status, single parenthood, unemployed status, and geographic location). Such methods are called categorical and geographic targeting and are associated with relatively low administrative and economic costs, although they are more likely to include the nonpoor. Moreover, the success of geographic targeting depends heavily on an accurate and detailed poverty map of the country.

Source: Silva, Levin, and Morgandi 2012.
a. For a discussion of concepts, methods, results, and implementation of targeting strategies, refer to chapter 4 in Grosh and others (2008).

Although a higher share of rural population may make it more expensive and difficult to use a targeting strategy, the cost may be offset in varying degrees if the majority of people can be reached through mobile phones or the Internet and if the government has a strong local presence.

Besides country conditions, the fiscal implications of each scheme are also important. The average cost of a noncontributory pension scheme is estimated at about 1 percent of GDP, varying between universal and targeted schemes. For example, a means-tested scheme in Bangladesh costs 0.03 percent of GDP, whereas a universal scheme in Mauritius costs 2 percent of GDP. For the MENA region, Palacios and Sluchynsky (2006) estimate that the cost of a universal social pension that provides a benefit equal to 15 percent of GDP per capita at a retirement age of 65 would reach 1 percent in 2025 and 1.5 percent in 2040, depending on demographic evolutions. The cost of a universal scheme may be considered unaffordable for countries with a low tax base and revenues and an aging population. Moreover, capping the number of eligible beneficiaries, restricting benefits to one individual per household (as in Bangladesh), and disqualifying persons who receive other forms of assistance could also contain costs. Countries with means tested social pensions include Bangladesh, rural Brazil, Chile, Costa Rica, India, Moldova, Nepal, South Africa, and Thailand.

Deciding between a contributory and a noncontributory scheme: The choice between a contributory and a noncontributory scheme is, to a large extent, dependent on the ability and willingness of target social groups to contribute to a particular scheme and the extent to which their incentives to do so can be influenced. It is in this context that the following factors are evaluated (recall table 5.9).

(1) Level of income and poverty in country/target population: Indicators including GDP per capita, coverage rate of existing contributory schemes, and the ratio of "no" to "low" savings capacity population can be considered. If a large portion of the target population has no savings capacity, the take-up rate of a contributory scheme is likely to remain very moderate even when the government or employers offer to subsidize a portion of contributions. Moreover, if coverage of existing mandatory schemes is low (for example, below 20 to 25 percent), incentives are likely to play a less significant role compared with situations where coverage is higher (for example, above 50 percent). GDP per capita and coverage rates are correlated, and so this is in line with the argument presented earlier.

(2) Transaction costs: The schemes under consideration are by nature voluntary and require beneficiaries to make a conscious choice to enroll, knowing that they will have to incur some transaction cost related to simply registering or also making contributions. Thus, it is very important

to consider the level of transaction costs involved and understand how they will influence people's incentives to enroll. If high transaction costs cannot be overcome or mitigated, noncontributory schemes may achieve higher coverage rates than contributory ones.

(3) Trust in government: People's trust in the government and its institutions can influence their decision to enroll and contribute to a scheme.

(4) Financial literacy: Contributory schemes require some financial understanding or computation from the individual to assess whether it would be cost effective to contribute. In this context, if financial literacy among the target population is low, it may be difficult to achieve high enrollment rates in contributory schemes.[33]

Examples of different schemes: Core and supplementary schemes are the two main types of noncontributory schemes that have emerged internationally. In the case of social pensions, core schemes can be found in developing countries such as South Africa, Bolivia, Botswana, Mauritius, Kosovo, and rural Brazil. In this context, social pensions are used as the main tool for addressing the coverage gap, in some cases covering up to 100 percent of the elderly. Larger core schemes are more likely to be found in countries with limited coverage of mandated contributory schemes or no such schemes at all. On the other hand, supplementary social pension schemes are intended to assist the elderly poor who are excluded from the formal system; these are more likely to exist in countries with moderate to large contributory schemes, such as Algeria, Egypt, Colombia, Turkey, Costa Rica, and Uruguay.

MDC schemes are emerging as a potentially viable option for expanding coverage to informal workers. Although MDCs exist in some developed countries such as the United States and Germany, laws establishing MDC schemes have been only recently passed in some middle- and low-income countries, including the Dominican Republic, Korea, China, India, Indonesia, Mexico, Vietnam, and Thailand. Yet only a few countries have recently launched implementation (see box 5.10 for a description of MDC schemes in India, Mexico, and China); thus little systematic evidence is available on their performance and impact. Robalino and Palacios (2009) argue that MDC schemes have numerous advantages for informal workers, namely, their portability across different jobs and their ability to accommodate flexible levels and frequency of contributions. Moreover, MDCs may be a more relevant tool to encourage enrollment among informal workers in middle- and low-income countries compared to other monetary incentives, such as tax

Box 5.10   The Design of MDC Schemes in India, Mexico, and China

MDC schemes in India, Mexico, and China exist as universal voluntary pension schemes. In the three countries, they are not stand-alone schemes but are instead plugged into existing umbrella schemes that leverage their infrastructure. The Indian Swavalamban[a] scheme is one of the most recent initiatives to motivate workers to enroll in pension systems. The scheme was rolled out nationwide in late 2010 and targets eligible informal sector workers who joined the national New Pension Scheme (NPS) in 2010 and 2011. The NPS is the country's mandatory DC pension scheme for central government employees and is voluntary for all others. Under Swavalamban, the government provides a yearly matching of Re 1,000 ($25) for three years to every new account, conditional upon members individually contributing between Re 1,000 and Re 12,000 yearly. Workers not employed by the government and not covered by any of the occupational provident funds in the country are eligible for the match. It is expected that the scheme will become permanent beyond the anticipated three years. The government has outsourced the management and administration of the scheme to private intermediaries, including microfinance institutions, NGOs, and others. The government plays a regulatory role and finances the match. It provides incentives to intermediaries based on performance, that is, the number of members they enroll.

The Mexican "Cuota Social" is an older scheme, introduced as a component of the Mexican Institute of Social Security reform package in 1997. A matching contribution is paid by the government at the rate of 1 peso per day, adjusted for inflation, disbursed on each day that an individual makes a contribution. Although the Cuota Social is not targeted, it is redistributive in nature because it is a flat rate.

While the Indian and Mexican examples entail governments subsidizing contributions of new members, the widely recognized New Rural Pension Scheme introduced in China in 2009 subsidizes pension benefits. The government provides a basic monthly contribution of Y 55 ($8) to retirees conditional upon having at least 15 years of contributions and a minimal annual contribution equivalent to 4–8 percent of the country's average personal income during the previous year. Additional contributions are matched by the government. Although the scheme is quite specific to the context of rural China, one interesting design feature relevant to coverage extension is that the scheme still offers the match to retirees who have not accumulated enough savings, on the condition that all family members above the age of 16 enroll in the new scheme and contribute on their behalf. Moreover, although the scheme is universal, in the sense that all rural populations of China are eligible, the design entails an implicit geographical targeting, because

box continues next page

Box 5.10   The Design of MDC Schemes in India, Mexico, and China *(continued)*
local governments in more affluent regions are encouraged to pay higher benefits and could require higher contributions on the part of their beneficiaries.[b]

Source: Robalino and Palacios 2009.
a. More information on the India New Pension Scheme and the Swavalamban scheme can be found at http://www.pfrda.org.in/.
b. For more on the Chinese New Rural Pension Scheme, see Shen and Williamson (2010) and Zhu (2009).

deductions or exemptions. First, lower-income informal workers are less likely to pay taxes in lower-income countries, and, second, tax incentives, if applied universally, may be regressive. When MDCs are structured as a flat co-contribution by governments, they cease to be regressive. Furthermore, evidence on the magnitude by which tax incentives affect enrollment and savings levels is mixed, and a debate exists around whether savings induced by tax incentives crowd out existing savings (Antolin and Ponton 2007).

The level of the matching contribution and the elasticities of the take-up and savings rate to the match are critical in determining the success of an MDC scheme in expanding coverage. The take-up rate is affected by both the level of the matching contribution and its magnitude relative to the individual's income level. Robalino and Palacios (2009) present a method to determine the parameters and costs of an MDC scheme. However, ex ante evidence on the take-up/match elasticity, a critical factor affecting the take-up of MDCs, is fairly limited, and the only evidence comes from U.S. experience in employer-matched 401(k) and individual retirement account (IRA) schemes. For example, a randomized field experiment offered matching incentives for IRA contributions in low- and middle-income neighborhoods in St. Louis, Missouri, at two levels (20 and 50 percent), while a control group was not offered any match. The higher match significantly affected both participation and contributions to the scheme. Take-up rates among the 20 percent match group (8 percent) were almost three times that of the control group (3 percent) and reached 20 percent in the 50 percent match group. Savings were also four and seven times higher in the 20 and 50 match groups, respectively, compared with the control group (Duflo and others 2005). Not all studies are conclusive about the power of matching with respect to increasing participation. Engelhart and Kumar (2006) used administrative data on 401(k)[34] participation and estimated that the elasticity of 401(k) participation with respect to the match rate ranged between 0.02 and 0.07; a 25 cent match per dollar of employee contribution resulted in an increase of 3.75 to 6 percent. The savings/match elasticity was also estimated to be modest.

Under contributory schemes, some design features can further improve incentives of target groups to enroll. Allowing flexible contributions and withdrawals are two potentially useful features to encourage take-up rates (Hu and Stewart 2009; Robalino and Palacios 2009). For types of work with volatile income (as in the agricultural sector or other seasonal sectors), it may be important to relax the rules on the regularity of contributions. In Chile, participation of seasonal and temporary workers is encouraged by allowing irregular frequencies of contributions. The Central Provident Fund in Singapore, a mandatory social insurance scheme originally designed to provide old-age income security, eventually allowed members to use their account funds for paying housing mortgages. As withdrawals to fund home ownership increased, concerns about the scheme's retirement objectives increased (Hu and Stewart 2009). Since liquidity of savings above a certain threshold may be a relevant issue for low- and middle-income countries, schemes could be designed to restrict withdrawals from specific portions of the account and for certain acceptable reasons.

Workers' preferences and perceptions: Preferences and perceptions of workers in Syria and Lebanon suggest a genuine demand for social insurance and a general willingness to pay for its services.[35] In Syria, about one-third of the surveyed workers are informal, 64 percent of which are interested in social insurance coverage. Similarly, 68 percent of informal workers in Lebanon are interested in being covered by social insurance. Figure 5.17 presents results from the survey. The majority of Syrian workers rank old-age benefits as the most important, whereas health insurance is the most important benefit for Lebanese workers, because the social insurance package there does not offer pension coverage. In both countries, preferences for different benefits are similar among formal workers and informal workers demanding coverage. The majority of formal workers in both countries consider the cost of social insurance to be reasonable, which indicates a general willingness to pay for coverage.[36] Further confirming a willingness to pay, cost is not identified as the most important reason for lack of interest in social insurance among groups of informal workers. In Syria, individuals' myopia (56 percent) and lack of knowledge about the system (55 percent) seem to be more important reasons than cost considerations.

Figure 5.17 Preferences and Perceptions of Informality among Workers in Lebanon and the Syrian Arab Republic

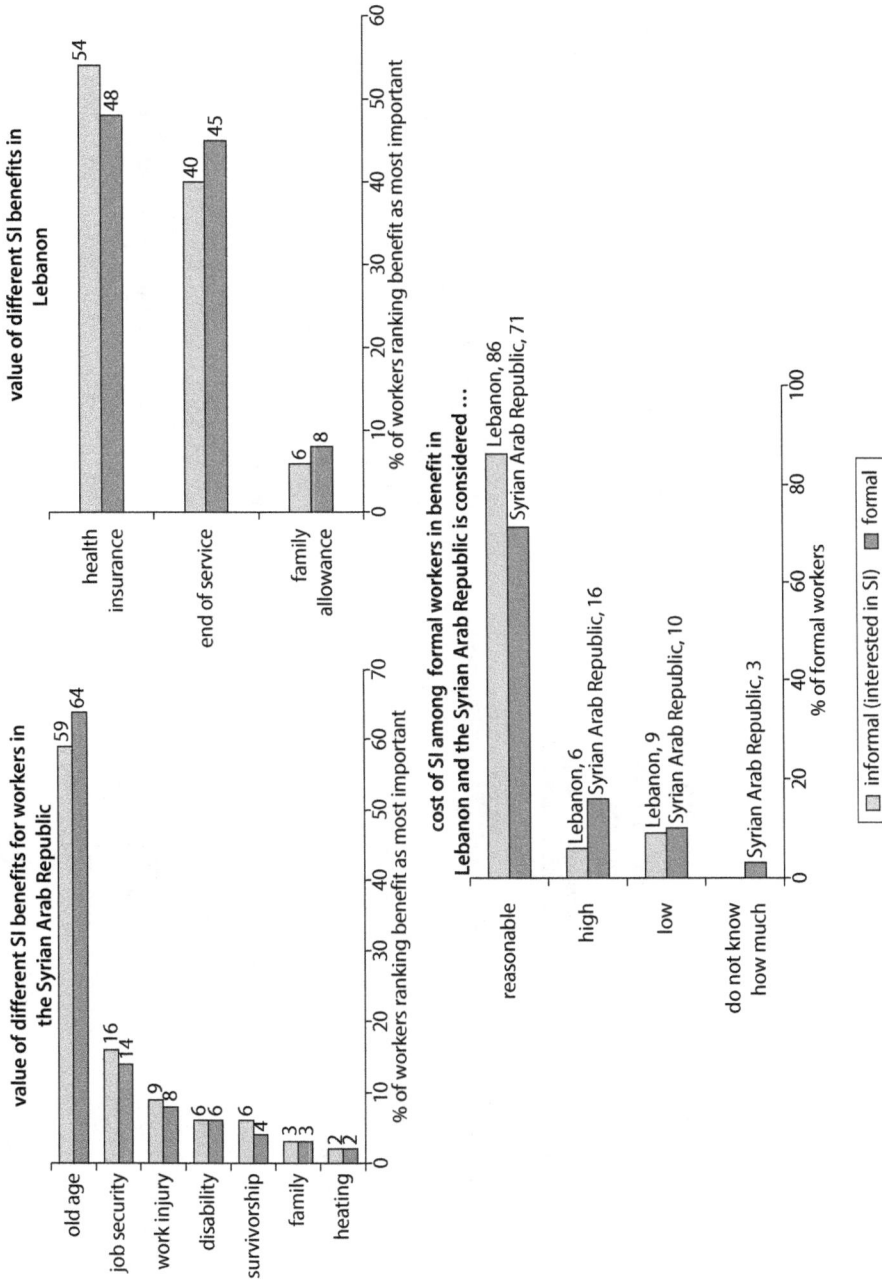

value of different SI benefits for workers in the Syrian Arab Republic

value of different SI benefits in Lebanon

cost of SI among formal workers in benefit in Lebanon and the Syrian Arab Republic is considered ...

☐ informal (interested in SI)   ■ formal

figure continues next page

Figure 5.17 Preferences and Perceptions of Informality among Workers in Lebanon and the Syrian Arab Republic *(continued)*

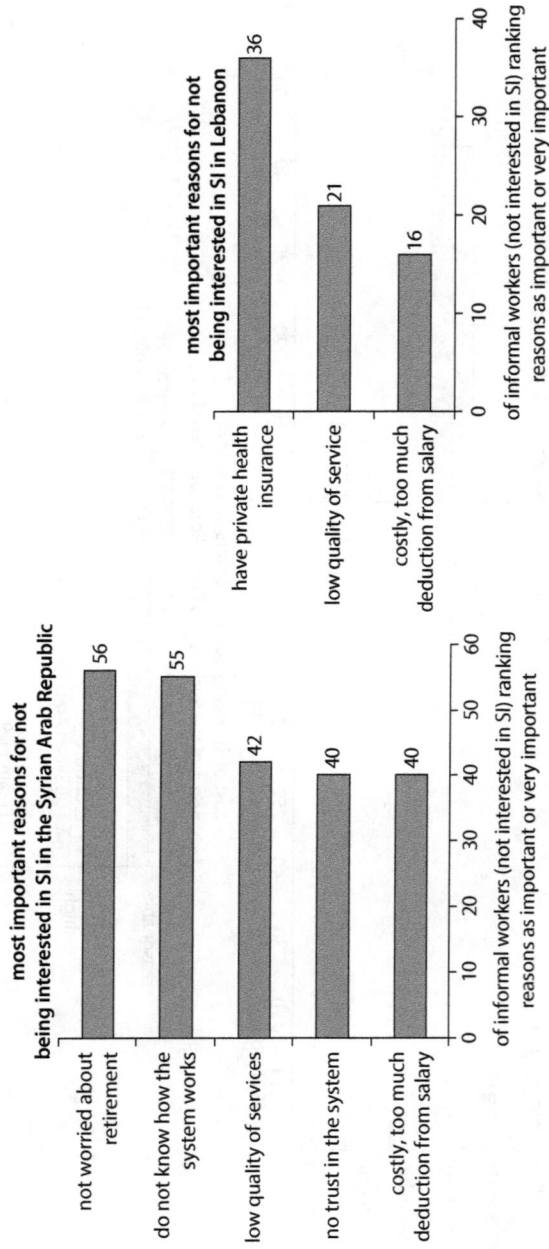

most important reasons for not
being interested in SI in the Syrian Arab Republic

most important reasons for not
being interested in SI in Lebanon

Sources: Syria Employee-Employer Survey (2011) and Lebanon Employee-Employer Survey (2011).
Note: SI = social insurance.

Cost considerations are also not the main reason in Lebanon either, where reliance on private health insurance as an alternative is most frequently cited.

Implications for MENA countries. Among MENA countries, the relevance of contributory and noncontributory schemes (whether targeted or universal) as coverage expansion strategies varies. In Lebanon and Jordan, the existing coverage rates and the development of proxy means testing systems indicate the viability of a targeted-contributory scheme. The countries' GDP rates, rural population rates, and poverty levels indicate a potential affordability of contributions, for at least some population groups (annex table 5A.1). Governments may consider fully subsidizing contributions of groups with no savings capacity, while matching contributions of groups with limited saving capacity, as determined by the proxy means test. The willingness to pay for social insurance, as implied by the survey results presented earlier, further confirms the potential relevance of a contributory scheme in Lebanon. In Syria, general country conditions (including lower levels of coverage and higher rural population rates) would guide policy choices away from introduction of a contributory scheme. However, the survey results indicate a certain level of demand and willingness to pay for social insurance among informal workers in registered firms. In this case, the government might consider introducing a contributory scheme targeting such workers.

Country conditions (especially high poverty rates) in Djibouti and the Republic of Yemen would point toward universal noncontributory schemes, while acknowledging that limited fiscal space is an important barrier. In Djibouti, although the share of the rural population is low, mobile and Internet penetration are also quite low, poverty is high among the elderly and the rest of the population, and no proxy means testing (PMT) system is in place (see box 5.9 for targeting methods). Although a PMT system exists in the Republic of Yemen, the high share of rural population, low mobile and Internet penetration rates, and high poverty levels favor the relevance of a universal strategy at this time. In Tunisia, coverage patterns and level of income make a contributory scheme viable for at least part of the population, but with no PMT in place, a contributory scheme in the short run may need to be based on a universal flat matching provided by the government.

Program implementation. Implementation arrangements and capacity differ widely in MENA. Some of the key elements for consideration include whether some of the tasks outlined in the pyramid in figure 5.16 can be contracted out to the private sector, while others remain under public management. Another important set of decisions involves how to best leverage existing infrastructure and institutions to implement new schemes. Box 5.11 describes the recent implementation of a new noncontributory health insurance scheme in India. Its implementation arrangements are continually being improved as the scheme evolves, a critical factor of its success so far.

Box 5.11   Implementation of the Indian Rashtriya Swasthya Bima Yojana

In 2008 the government of India introduced a noncontributory health insurance scheme. This is the first such scheme to cover the informal sector (95 percent of population) after earlier attempts to extend health insurance by the Ministry of Health failed. The new scheme, called "Rashtriya Swasthya Bima Yojana" (RSBY), was launched by the Ministry of Labor in April 2008 and targeted the 300 million individuals below the poverty line. RSBY provides hospitalization coverage of up to Re 30,000 for up to five members of each family. Individuals pay as little as Re 30 in registration fees yearly. The scheme recently expanded to households above the poverty line who are willing and able to pay a premium for the services provided. In only a few months, over 150,000 families enrolled. The government is now also considering gradual expansion of coverage to different categories of workers.

The arrangements through which the program is being implemented provide numerous lessons learned for other countries. A thorough investigation of the target group, poor informal workers, led to the realization that the scheme needed to be free, paperless, portable, independent of any identifiable employee-employer relationship, and impose minimal transaction cost on target groups. The government designed implementation arrangements in the shape of a pure business model for a social service where the scheme is funded publicly but operated privately. Administration of the scheme is contracted entirely to a third party insurer (TPI) selected on a competitive basis in each state. The TPI is responsible for enrolling persons and is paid a premium by the government for every person enrolled, creating an incentive for TPIs to expand coverage. Moreover, hospitals are paid based on each beneficiary treated. The government provides the list of eligible households to the insurer and a schedule for enrollment. The insurer is responsible for announcing the scheme and the enrollment procedure in the state and managing mobile enrollment stations

box continues next page

Box 5.11   Implementation of the Indian Rashtriya Swasthya Bima Yojana *(continued)*

and stations at frequently visited locations. The insurer also involves local grassroots entities including NGOs and micro-finance institutions. Members were provided with a unique "smart card," used for all transactions, on the spot when enrolling. In parallel, a unique national identification system in India is in the process of being developed.

Take-up of RSBY was initially quite slow, but today over 45 million people across 29 Indian states are covered by the scheme. Stakeholder ownership and extensive information campaigns were instrumental in increasing take-up rates. Another factor considered critical for the success of the program was having the right information technology systems to support the scheme in terms of operation and monitoring, as well as for fraud minimization. Today RSBY faces numerous challenges as well as promising opportunities. Increasing public awareness and information about the service and its benefits remains a huge challenge. Building capacity of all stakeholders and service providers is also a requirement. Another important challenge is improving the quality of services offered through this scheme. To address that, the government is attempting to create incentives for improved quality of services by rating the quality of hospitals. Corruption is another challenge: Fraud and collusion behavior between beneficiaries and hospitals have been detected in more than 50 hospitals.

Sources: Rashtriya Swasthya Bima Yojna, 2009; personal communication with Anil Swarup, Director General for Labour Welfare at the Ministry of Labor in India.

It is also worth mentioning that financial education and generally raising awareness about the value of social insurance can be a useful tool for supporting the implementation of social insurance programs and contributing to higher take-up rates. Evidence from developing countries shows that general awareness about social insurance can be improved. A survey in India shows that about 80 percent of the informal sector did not even know what pensions were. In Chile, the understanding of pensions among citizens is still very limited (rated at 2 on a scale of 2 to 7). Using data from Chile, Fajnzylber and Reyes (2010) show that an improvement in information provided by pension administrators increased the probability of making voluntary contributions by older workers but less so by younger workers. Women responded to the information significantly more than men. Even in developed countries such as the United Kingdom, research has shown that over 25 percent of pension credits remain unclaimed because people do not know they are eligible. Various initiatives can improve awareness and financial education, including training office staff in social insurance agencies (as in China) and community outreach and awareness through household visits to potential plan members (as in the United Kingdom). The recent Chilean pension reforms set up a "Pension Education Fund" to fund awareness-raising initiatives (Stewart 2006). The evidence from Lebanon and Syria also indicates low awareness about pension benefits and pension rights.

Lessons from behavioral economics. Findings from behavioral economics can complement rational economic models in understanding individuals' savings choices and behavior.[37] Behavioral research has shown that individuals procrastinate when making choices, especially important ones. This is known as "inertia" or "status quo" bias. When the choice involves selection among several options and the need to make complex computations, individuals are even more likely to behave passively. Such behaviors are incompatible with traditional models of economics based on the rationality of economic agents. Another finding is the concept of "loss aversion"; people are more active in avoiding losing something they already have rather than in acquiring new gains (Kahneman and others 1991). Furthermore, behavioral research has shown that altering the description of a certain problem or question (also called "framing") may result in different choices and judgments (Tversky and Kahneman 1981). To some extent, these findings explain certain savings behaviors, including, for example, the low take-up of voluntary retirement or other social insurance schemes. Figure 5.18 presents a notional framework for addressing individual saving behavior.

In the context of coverage expansion, auto-enrollment and default options in retirement savings schemes (or other types of social insurance schemes) can positively influence savings behavior. Under auto-enrollment, individuals are by default enrolled into a social insurance scheme unless (or until) they chose to opt out. In addition, saving rates are set at a default (usually conservative) rate with a choice to enroll in different saving options if desired. The idea is motivated by the philosophy of libertarian paternalism under which the government can influence an individual's choices without exerting coercion (Thaler and Sustein 2003). Auto-enrollment in social insurance schemes has been used in various developed countries, including Italy, New Zealand, the United Kingdom, and the United States. Some evidence from 401(k) plan experiments shows that auto-enrollment and default options are effective in increasing take-up of voluntary savings schemes and can

Figure 5.18 Implications of Rational and Behavioral Economics Theories Explaining an Individual's Savings Behavior

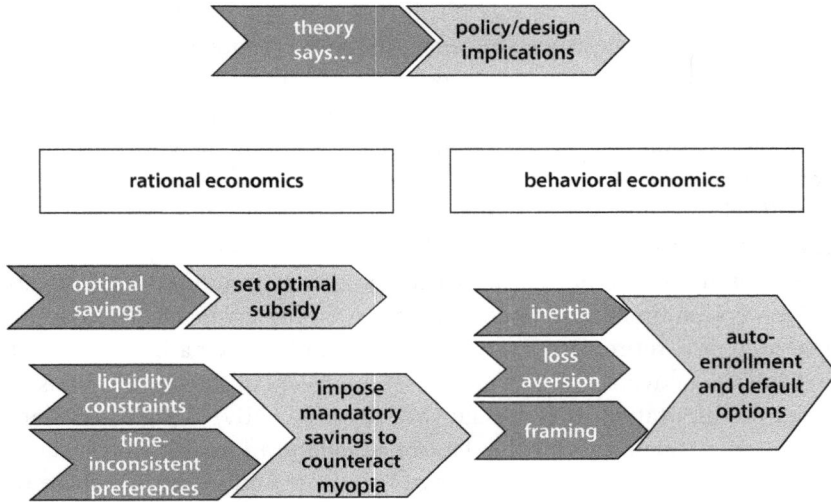

even be designed to increase savings. Using data from a large U.S. firm, Madrian and Shea (2001) found that automatic enrollment had a significant impact on enrollment and retirement savings behavior; an enrollment rate of 86 percent was achieved compared with 36 percent without auto-enrollment. Simply framing the question as "Check this box if you would *not* like to have 3 percent of your paycheck put into a 401(k)" instead of "Check this box if you would like to participate in a 401(k) and indicate how much you'd like to contribute" led to this difference. An interesting auto-enrollment default option scheme that does achieve increased savings is the experimental "Save More Tomorrow" scheme (Thaler and Benartzi 2004). Under this scheme, employees are invited to choose a target level of savings according to which they will automatically start contributing in one year at a low savings rate, with a gradually increasing rate until they reach their target. This feature is usually referred to as auto-escalation or auto-acceleration of savings. Note that it makes a difference if one needs to commit current earnings to saving in the present or commit to saving yet unearned future income.[38] Employees have the choice to opt out at any time. Evidence from four years of implementation shows a take-up rate of almost 80 percent; moreover, 80 percent of participants stayed through to the fourth year. Saving rates rose from 3.5 to 13.6 percent over the course of the program.

Conclusions to Part 2

Overall, coverage extension through the social insurance system is an important yet complex agenda in MENA. This part of the chapter first reviewed the link between the design of social insurance schemes, particularly pensions, and coverage outcomes. With the exception of the recently approved social insurance reform in Egypt, all MENA countries have DB pension systems with design features not in line with best international practices. Many of the existing substandard design characteristics of MENA DB pension schemes contribute to the low observed coverage rates beyond the already well-known concerns over financial sustainability. These flawed design features include limited legal coverage, short minimum vesting periods that promote gaming of the system, generous early retirement provisions that distort participation incentives, and the use of average wages in the last few years of service as a basis of benefit computation. It is crucial that these incentive design issues are addressed through reforms that ensure adequate, affordable, and sustainable benefits, while offering coverage to a large and increasing share of the population.

It is unlikely that in MENA coverage extension will be achieved effectively without special subsidized social insurance schemes targeted to informal workers, or even to those outside the labor force. Although this notion might be considered controversial, social insurance coverage, at least for certain social groups, should be separated from the formal employment relationship without compromising the unified overall logic (integration platform) of the social insurance system most easily established based on DC design features. Even if this is achieved, no homogeneous recipe for success can be offered; country conditions matter significantly. A decision tree approach that MENA governments could follow when deciding on the type of social insurance coverage extension programs was suggested. Once the incentive design of the existing formal sector social insurance scheme in MENA is improved, the key decisions with regard to coverage extension strategies are (1) whether contributory or noncontributory programs are more appropriate and (2) whether universal or targeted subsidies should be used. To support these critical decisions, a stylized set of indicators based on country conditions was developed to help governments assess the relevance of different schemes. Among targeted contributory interventions, piloting a MDC scheme with subsidies conditional to low saving capacity emerges as a viable option to expand coverage in some MENA countries, including Lebanon, Syria, and Jordan. In the short run, noncontributory schemes will still play an important supplementary role in these countries, particularly for those individuals who have already completed their working life and those with no savings capacity. Means-tested noncontributory strategies may have to be used as the main coverage extension strategy in poorer countries such as Djibouti and the Republic of Yemen where contributory schemes are not a strong option given current country conditions. In the case of new contributory schemes, design features and implementation arrangements geared at inducing voluntary participation that include auto-enrollment and auto-escalation of savings could be considered, in addition to complementary financial literacy and general awareness interventions.

It was also emphasized that the ex ante predictions of traditional, agent rationality–based, economic models are not sufficient for determining the subsidies needed to induce voluntary participation, critical in the informality context. The lessons learned from behavioral economics about observed behaviors being irreconcilable with rational agent assumptions should also be taken into account. Such lessons suggest the use of auto-enrollment arrangements and program features responding to loss aversion (as opposed to just risk aversion). The recent innovation of MDC program design for social insurance coverage expansion, especially if combined with a targeting mechanism that assigns subsidies conditioned on the income position of the individual or household, received special attention. Although little empirical evidence exists on the potential impact of such innovations (and virtually no evidence from MENA, other than inferences based on perception surveys), one could confidently argue that successful coverage extension programs would combine (1) a program design predicting subsidy needs based on ex ante predictor economic models of agent rationality with (2) lessons from observed behaviors reflecting bounded rationality put into an implementation environment, which (3) ensures low transactions costs from the perspective of the individual for enrollment and benefit delivery and (4) relies on investments in financial literacy and broader awareness building within the target group of the coverage extension effort.

Annex

Annex Table 5A.1 Country Conditions in MENA Countries

	Djibouti	Yemen, Rep.	Iraq	Morocco	Syrian Arab Republic	Jordan	Egypt, Arab Rep.	Algeria	Tunisia	Iran, Islamic Rep.	Lebanon
Rural population (% of population)[a]	12.3	68.78	33.5	43.64	45.44	21.54	57.24	34.14	33.1	31.02	12.92
GDP per capita, PPP ($ current)[a]	2,319	2,470	3,548	4,494	4,730	5,597	5,673	8,172	8,273	11,558	13,070
Coverage rate[a]		9	33	18	29		42	37	45		44
% employed with social security coverage[b]											
Poverty gap (elderly/nonelderly)[c]	43.52/45.09	34.57/41.75		13.2/18.98		9.81/14.18	4.09/8.62	—	—	—	—
Mobile cellular subscription (per 100 people)[d]	13	16	57	72	34	91	51	93	83	60	34
Internet users (per 100 people)[d]	2	2	1	33	17	27	17	12	27	32	23
Corruption Perception Index[e]	3.2	2.2	1.5	3.4	2.5	4.7	3.1	2.9	4.3	2.2	2.5
Existence of PMT	No	Yes	No	Yes	In preparation	In preparation	Yes	Yes	No		In preparation

Sources:

a. World Development Indicators, World Bank 2009.

b. Specific surveys for the Republic of Yemen, Iraq, Morocco , the Syrian Arab Republic, Egypt, and Lebanon as presented in chapter 2; coverage rates for the other countries are based on 2008 World Development Indicators, pension contributors as percent of labor force.

c. Robalino and others 2009.

d. World Development Indicators, World Bank 2008.

e. The Corruption Perception Index ranges from 0 to 10, 10 being for countries with no perceptions of corruption. From Transparency International 2010.

Note: GDP = gross domestic product; PPP = purchasing power parity; PMT = proxy means testing; — = not available.

Notes

1. Note that other taxes also contribute to the tax wedge. For detailed discussion, see below.

2. Note that as pointed out by Otonglo and Trumbic (2008), even in Turkey, the medium-run effect can be an increase in revenues, as the total amount of income declared increased, attributed to less understating of incomes. Importantly, evidence on the short-run effects of the Turkey case study should be interpreted with caution because this study is based on a before-and-after comparison, and many other changes might have occurred in the economy during the same period that also affected overall tax collection rates, making it hard to draw causal interpretations.

3. The fact that *Doing Business* rankings capture only a small part of the set of complementary reforms that are needed to effectively promote private sector growth can explain the apparent disconnect between the significant improvement in rankings recorded by some of the MENA countries and the continued perceived challenges to an inclusive growth process.

4. The EU15 was the number of member countries in the European Union prior to the accession of ten candidate countries on 1 May 2004 compromising Austria, Belgium, Denmark, Finland, France, Germany, Greece, Ireland, Italy, Luxembourg, the Netherlands, Portugal, Spain, Sweden, and the United Kingdom.

5. The term "fixed-term worker" means a person having an employment contract or relationship entered into directly with an employer where the end of the employment contract or relationship is determined by objective conditions, such as reaching a specific date, completing a specific task, or the occurrence of a specific event.

6. Wage data for Tunisia were not available to produce kernels similar to those depicted in figure 5.5.

7. The ILO, European Union, and OECD have embraced the concept of "flexicurity," combining flexible regulation, safety nets (such as unemployment insurance), and active social policies. One component of flexicurity policies is flexible and reliable contractual arrangements (from the perspective of the employer and the employee, of "insiders" and "outsiders") through modern labor laws, collective agreements, and work organization.

8. This is only an indicative data point that does not take into account, for example, the underlying educational attainment composition in the public and private employment sectors. The point is that public sector pay is relatively high even in Arab region countries, where public sector salaries are generally perceived to be low such as in Egypt.

9. Annual Employment and Unemployment Survey, Department of Statistics, 2008.

10. Data were collected from the Public Commission for Employment and Enterprise Development in Syria.

11. The Syrian example highlights distortions introduced by certain labor market institutions; the unintended contribution to the informality phenomenon is just one particular aspect. The public sector job queue consists of a self-selected group of job seekers with a preference for public sector employment; this preference drives their acceptance of informal and refusal of formal private jobs, at least temporarily. The government uses this queue to attempt to identify candidates for its training and private sector placement programs because the alternative registries are of little value; neither employers nor job seekers show up in other government registries because neither party believes in effective matches through such channels.

12. See MENA Education Flagship Report (World Bank 2008).

13. An apprenticeship is an arrangement that allows individuals to receive firm-specific training through a working relationship with an employer. Workers usually receive low wages during the apprenticeship period such that the training costs are shared among firms and workers during the period.

14. The expressions "social insurance system" and "pension system" are used somewhat interchangeably in this chapter. Pension systems are often thought of as a set of social insurance mechanisms, including old-age pension, disability pension, survivor benefit, and work injury benefit components. These are the social insurance components typically introduced at earlier stages of development. Pension systems in this sense are present in all the MENA countries, albeit with often limited coverage. A social insurance system is often thought of as one that incorporates some of the social insurance components typically introduced at higher levels of development, such as unemployment insurance, sickness and health insurance, and maternity benefits. These "second generation" social insurance benefits are typically introduced on top of the already existing pension system components.

15. See Holzmann and Hinz 2005; Holzmann and Palmer 2006.

16. In a funded DC scheme, savings are typically accumulated through investment in actual financial saving instruments.

17. See the discussion on the range of the cost of universal basic pensions later in this chapter based on Palacios and Sluchynsky (2006). A cost benchmark at 2 percent of GDP is what the World Bank projections suggest on universal flat pension expenditures in the case of Egypt.

18. Currently, $NZ318.12 (net, for single persons) is paid to those eligible, as determined by age (65) and residency. Benefits are adjusted annually based on the consumer price index and average wages. The main task of the pension administration is not really administering this simple payment mechanism, but rather building tools that improve financial literacy and communicating

to the public that the quality of life in retirement is heavily dependent on individual saving behavior.

19. For example, a claw-back with a basic pension reduction rate of 25 percent yields no reduction in the universal basic pension if no contributions were made during an individual's active life cycle (for example, this is the benefit for those who spent their entire career in the informal sector), whereas the top-up is completely phased out at an earnings-related pension level equivalent to four times the basic flat pension. The mathematical formula to calculate the pension benefit under the universal basic pension with a claw-back design is $p = \text{ERP}(y) - \max(0, a - b \times \text{ERP}(y))$, where p is the amount of the pension benefit, $ERP\ (y)$ is the pure earnings-related pension component benefit at life-cycle income measure y, a is the amount of the universal flat pension for those with no earnings-related pension, and b is a parameter reflecting the share of the earnings-related pension reducing the universal pension benefit.

20. For a detailed discussion on MDCs, see Robalino and Palacios (2009).

21. Notionally, participation requires a participation fee based on income, but as income is rarely observable outside of the formal sector, almost no one pays such a fee.

22. See Palacios and Whitehouse (2006) for more information on the evolution of civil service pension schemes worldwide.

23. See Pallares-Miralles and others (2011) for cross-country data on mandatory publicly and privately managed pension systems around the world.

24. Revalorization of past wages in the pension benefit formula means that past wages are taken into account with an adjustment equivalent to proportional changes in the general wage level between the time the pension contribution was paid and when the formula was applied to determine pension levels.

25. NDC schemes are DC schemes where contributions are not funded (that is, invested in financial instruments) and where individual earnings are based on individual contributions (PAYG). See Holzmann and Palmer (2006).

26. The lump-sum payments offered by MENA pension schemes to those who do not fulfill the minimum vesting requirement do not compare to the magnitude of pension payments received until death; contributions for these individuals would remain a sunk cost, for the most part, even with the lump-sum payment.

27. A simplified mathematical representation of the core of a defined benefit pension formula is $p = a \times T \times \bar{w}$, where T is the number of contributory years, $\bar{w}$ is some measure of the wage based on which contributions were made during at least a part of the active life cycle, and a is a parameter called the replacement rate referring to what share of earnings one year of contributions

replaced in old age by the DB pension system. Such a formula is calibrated (if at all) for a particular retirement age. Clearly *a* should be conditional on the actual age of retirement if sustainability matters.

28. In the case of Egypt, this features refers to the pension system before the recent legislated reform.

29. The internal rate of return (IRR) is a concept that creates an intuitive relationship between life-cycle contributions and the pension benefit flow. One can think about the internal rate of return as a real interest rate that, if applied to all career employee and employer contributions, would yield a savings amount by retirement equivalent to the (expected) value of the pension benefit flow until death. The IRR concept makes it easy to assess whether one should save inside or outside a pension system (provided that is a choice).

30. The accrual rate is a critical DB pension parameter. It is the rate by which pension benefits accumulate each year of contribution expressed as a percentage of the final salary.

31. World Bank employee-employer survey on workforce development (2001) conducted under the World Bank MILES program in Syria.

32. For a discussion of universal and targeted social pensions, see Holzmann and others (2009) and Palacios and Sluchynsky (2006).

33. OECD work on financial education and pensions can be found at http://www.oecd.org/document/37/0,3343,en_2649_15251491_25698341 _1_1_1_1,00.html.

34. 401(k) plans are widely used retirement savings plans among American workers, where employers often choose to match contributions that workers make into their individual accounts. IRA schemes are provided by an employer and are similar to a 401(k) but offer simpler and less costly administration rules. 401(k) and IRA schemes are DC schemes in design.

35. The firm-based survey in Syria is representative of workers in registered private sector firms in manufacturing and services sectors. The household-based survey in Lebanon is representative of private sector workers more generally.

36. It is worth mentioning that the Syrian Social Insurance system is an unsustainable one because contributions do not cover the cost of services. It is unknown whether workers' perceptions on the cost of social insurance would change if the contributions to be paid reflected the true cost of the services offered.

37. The field of behavioral economics brings together insights from psychology and economic theory in understanding individuals' economic choices and

decisions, with a focus on bounded rationality of economic actors. For recent experiments and writings on this topic, see Ariely (2008, 2010).

38. This behavior is consistent with the theory of time-inconsistent preferences, a formal and promising modeling attempt to explain certain behaviors in the rational agent environment.

References

Abowd, J., F. Kramarz, D. Margolis, and T. Phillippon. 2005. "Minimum Wages and Employment in France and the United States." Paris: CREST-INSEE.

Almeida, R., and P. Carneiro. 2005. "Enforcement of Labor Regulation, Informal Labor, and Firm Performance." Policy Research Working Paper 3756. Washington, DC: World Bank.

———. 2009. "Enforcement of Regulation, Informal Employment, Firm Size and Firm Performance." *Journal of Comparative Economics* 37 (1): 28–46.

Alterido, R., M. Hallward-Driemeier, and C. Pages. 2009. "Big Constraints to Small Firms' Growth? Business Environment and Employment Growth across Firms." Policy Research Working Paper 5032. Washington, DC: World Bank.

Angel-Urdinola, D., and A. Kuddo. 2010. "Key Characteristics of Employment Regulation in the Middle East and North Africa." World Bank SP Discussion Paper 1006. Washington, DC: World Bank.

Angel-Urdinola, D., and A. Semlali. 2010. "Labor Markets and School-to-Work Transition in Egypt: Diagnostics, Constraints, and Policy Framework." MPRA Paper 27674. Munich: University Library of Munich.

Angel-Urdinola, Diego F., Amina Semlali, and Stefanie Brodmann. 2010. "Non-Public Provision of Active Labor Market Programs in Arab-Mediterranean Countries: An Inventory of Youth Programs." Social Protection Discussion Papers No. 55673, World Bank, Washington, DC.

Antolin, P., and E. L. Ponton. 2007. "The Impact of Tax Incentives on Retirement Savings: A Literature Review." Conference Proceedings, OECD/IOPS Global Private Pensions Conference. Paris: OECD.

Ariely, D. 2008. *Predictably Irrational: The Hidden Forces That Shape Our Decisions.* London: HarperCollins.

———. 2010. *The Upside of Irrationality: The Unexpected Benefits of Defying Logic at Work and Home.* London: HarperCollins.

Auer, P. 2007. "In Search of Optimal Labor Market Institutions." In *Flexicurity and Beyond: Finding a New Agenda for the European Social Market*, ed. H. Jorgenson and P. K. Madsen, 67–98. Copenhagen: DJOF.

Auer, P., J. Berg, and I. Coulibaly. 2004. "Is a Stable Workforce Good for the Company? Insights into the Tenure-Productivity-Employment Relationship." Employment Strategy Papers 2004-15. Geneva: ILO.

Bartelsman, E., J. Haltiwanger, and S. Scarpetta. 2004. "Microeconomic Evidence of Creative Destruction in Industrial and Developing Countries." Tinbergen Institute Discussion Papers 04-114/3. Amsterdam: Tinbergen Institute.

Betcherman, G., and C. Pages. 2007. "Estimating the Impacts of Labor Taxes on Employment and Balances of the Social Insurance Funds in Turkey." Washington, DC: World Bank.

Bodor, A., D. Robalino, and M. Rutkowski. 2008. "How Mandatory Pensions Affect Labor Supply Decisions and Human Capital Accumulations? Options to Bridge the Gap between Economic Theory and Policy Analysis." Washington, DC: World Bank.

Bruhn, M. 2008. "License to Sell: The Effect License to Sell: The Effect of Business Registration Reform on Entrepreneurial Activity in Mexico." World Bank Policy Research Working Paper WP4538. Washington, DC: World Bank.

———. 2011. "License to Sell: The Effect of Business Registration Reform on Entrepreneurial Activity in Mexico." *Review of Economics and Statistics* 93 (1): 382–86.

di Filippo, M., and A. Bodor. Forthcoming. "Old-Age Pension System Induced Incentives as They Affect Participation in Informal Sector Employment in the Middle East and North Africa Region."

Draca, M., S. Machin, and J. Van Reenen. 2008. "Minimum Wages and Firm Profitability." Working Paper 13996. Cambridge, MA: National Bureau of Economic Research.

Duflo, E., W. Gale, J. Liebman, P. Orszag, and E. Saez. 2005. "Saving Incentives for Low- and Middle Income Families: Evidence from a Field Experiment with H&R Block." CEPR Discussion Paper 5332. Social Science Research Network.

Engelhardt, G. V., and A. Kumar. 2006. "Employer Matching and and 401 K Savings: Evidence from the Health and Retirement Study." Working Paper 12447. Cambridge, MA: National Bureau of Economic Research.

European Commission. 2006. *Employment in Europe 2006*. Brussels: European Commission.

———. 2010. "Employment in Europe 2010." Brussels: European Commission.

Fajnzylber, E., and G. Reyes. 2010. "How Much Saving Is Enough? Evaluation of a Large Scale Intervention on Retirement Saving Decisions." http://insr .wharton.upenn.edu/documents/seminars/F10-Fajnzylber.pdf.

Fialová, K., and O. Schneider. Forthcoming. "Labor Institutions and Their Impact on Shadow Economies in Europe." Background paper for "In from the Shadow: Integrating Europe's Informal Labor." Washington, DC: World Bank.

Grazier, B. 2007. "Making Transitions Pay: The Transitional Labor Market Approaches to Flexicurity." In *Flexicurity and Beyond: Finding a New Agenda for the European Social Model*, ed. H. Jorgenson and P. K Madsen, 99–130. Copenhagen: DJOF.

Grosh, M., C. del Ninno, E. Tesliuc, and A. Ouerghy. 2008. "For Protection and Promotion: The Design and Implementation of Effective Safety Nets." Washington, DC: World Bank.

Holzmann, R., and R. Hinz. 2005. "Old Age Income Support in the 21st Century." Washington, DC: World Bank.

Holzmann, R., and J. Koettl. 2010. "Portability of Pension, Health and Other Social Benefits." Washington, DC: World Bank.

Holzmann, R., and E. Palmer. 2006. "Pension Reform: Issues and Prospects for Non-Financial Defined Contributions (NDC) Schemes." Washington, DC: World Bank.

Holzmann, R., D. Robalino, and N. Takayama. 2009. "Closing the Coverage Gap: The Role of Social Pensions and Other Retirement Income Transfers." Washington, DC: World Bank.

Hu, Y., and F. Stewart. 2009. "Pension Coverage and Informal Sector Workers: International Experience." OECD Working Papers on Insurance and Private Pensions 31. Paris: OECD.

Johanson, R., and A. V. Adams. 2004. "Skills Development in Sub-Saharan Africa. Regional and Sectoral Studies." Washington, DC: World Bank.

Kahneman, D., J. Knetch, and R. Thaler. 1991. "Anomalies: The Endowment Effect, Loss Aversion and Status Quo Bias." *Journal of Economic Perspectives* 5 (1): 193–206.

Kaplan, D., E. Piedra, and E. Seira. 2007. "Entry Regulation and Business Start-Ups: Evidence from Mexico." Policy Research Working Paper 4322. Washington, DC: World Bank.

Kenyon, T., and E. Kapaz. 2005. "The Informality Trap." Viewpoint Series, Note 301. Private Sector Development Vice-Presidency. Washington, DC: World Bank.

Kugler, A., and M. Kugler. 2003. "The Labor Market Effects of Payroll Taxes in Middle Income Countries: Evidence from Columbia." Discussion Paper 0920. Bonn: IZA.

Lee, K. W. 2009. "Productivity Increases in SMEs: With Special Emphasis on In-Service Training of Workers in Korea." Social Protection Discussion Paper 0917. Washington, DC: World Bank.

Lemos, S. 2004. "The Effect of Minimum Wage on Prices." Bonn: IZA.

Levenson, A., and W. Maloney. 1998. "The Informal Sector, Firm Dynamics, and Institutional Participation." World Bank Policy Research Working Paper WPS1988. Washington, DC: World Bank.

Levy, S. 2006. "Social Security Reforms in Mexico: For Whom?" World Bank Conference on "Equity and Competitiveness in Mexico." Washington, DC: World Bank.

Loayza, N., A. M. Oviedo, and L. Serven. 2005. "The Impact of Regulation on Growth and Informality Cross-Country Evidence." Policy Research Working Paper 3623. Washington, DC: World Bank.

Madhu Singh, ed. 2005. "Meeting Basic Learning Needs in the Informal Sector." Technical and Vocational Education and Training, Vol. 2. Geneva: UNESCO-UNEVOC.

Madrian, B. C., and D. F. Shea. 2001. "The Power of Suggestion: Inertia in 401(K) Participation and Saving Behavior." *Quarterly Journal of Economics* 116 (4): 1149–87.

Maloney, W., and J. Medez. 2003. "Measuring the Impact of Minimum Wages: Evidence from Latin America." Working Paper 9800. Cambridge, MA: National Bureau of Economic Research.

McKenzie, D., and Y. S. Sakho. 2010. "Does It Pay Firms to Register for Taxes? The Impact of Formality on Firm Profitability." *Journal of Development Economics* 91 (1): 15–24.

OECD (Organisation for Economic Co-operation and Development). 2004. *Employment Outlook*. Paris: OECD.

———. 2008. *Employment Outlook*. Paris: OECD.

———. 2010. *Employment Outlook*. Paris: OECD.

Olivier, M. 2009. " Informality, Employment Contracts and Extension of Social Insurance Coverage." Geneva: International Social Security Association.

Otonglo, C., and T. Trumbic. 2008. "Doing Business. Case Study of Turkey." http://www.doingbusiness.org/~/media/FPDKM/Doing%20Business/Documents/Reforms/Case-Studies/2008/DB08-CS-Turkey.pdf.

Palacios, R. Forthcoming. "Framework for Implementing Social Programs (FISP)."

Palacios, R., and O. Sluchynsky. 2006. "Social Pensions Part I: Their Role in the Overall Pension System." Social Protection Discussion Paper 0601. Washington, DC: World Bank.

Palacios, R., and E. Whitehouse. 2006. "Civil-Service Pension Schemes around the World." Social Protection Discussion Paper 0602. Washington, DC: World Bank.

Pallares-Miralles, M., C. Romero, and E. Whitehouse. Forthcoming. "International Patterns of Pension Provision II: A Worldwide Overview of Facts and Figures."

Pierre, G., and S. Scarpetta. 2006. "How Labor Markets Can Combine Workers' Protection with Job Creation: A Partial Review of Some Key Issues and Policy Options." Social Protection Discussion Paper 0716. Washington, DC: World Bank.

Portugal, P., and A. Cardoso. 2006. "Disentangling the Minimum Wage Puzzle: An Analysis of Worker Accessions and Separations." *Journal of the European Economic Association* 4 (5): 988–1013.

Rashtriya Swasthya Bima Yojna. 2009. http://www.rsby.gov.in.

Razzaz, O. 2011. "The Political Economy of Social Security Reform: Lessons from the Jordan Experience." Mimeo. World Bank, Washington, DC.

Robalino, D. A. 2005. "Pensions in the Middle East and North Africa: Time for Change." Washington, DC: World Bank.

Robalino, D., V. Gudivada, and S. Oleksiy. 2009. "Preventing Poverty amongst the Elderly in MENA Countries: Role and Optimal Design of Old-Age Subsidies." Primer Pensions Series. Washington, DC: World Bank.

Robalino, D. A., and R. Palacios. 2009. "Matching Defined Contributions: A Way to Increase Pension Coverage." In *Closing the Coverage Gap: The Role of Social Pensions and Other Retirement Income Transfers,* ed. D. A. Robalino, N. Takayama, and R. Holzmann, 187–202. Washington, DC: World Bank.

Robalino, D. A., H. Ribe, and I. Walker. 2010. "Achieving Effective Social Protection for All in Latin America and the Caribbean: From Right to Reality." Washington, DC: World Bank.

Rutkowski, J. 2003. "The Minimum Wage: Curse of Cure?" Washington, DC: World Bank.

Semlali, A. 2008. "Youth Employability and Job Matching Challenges and Opportunities in the Middle East and North Africa Region." Washington DC: World Bank.

Shen, C., and J .B. Williamson. 2010. "China's New Rural Pension Scheme: Can It Be Improved?" *International Journal of Sociology and Social Policy* 30: 239–250.

Silva, J., V. Levin, and M. Morgandi. 2012. "Inclusion and Resilience: The Way Forward for Safety Nets in the Middle East and North Africa." World Bank, Washington, DC.

Singh, M., ed. 2005. "Meeting Basic Learning Needs in the Informal Sector— Integrating Education and Training for Decent Work, Empowerment and Citizenship." Hamburg: Institute for Education, UNESCO.

Smits, K. 2008. "Economic Aspects of the Minimum Wage Policy." Washington, DC: World Bank.

SSA. 2009. "Social Security Programs throughout the World: Africa, 2009." Washington, DC: Social Security Administration (SSA) and International Social Security Association (ISSA).

———. 2010. "Social Security Programs throughout the World: Asia and the Pacific, 2009." Washington, DC: Social Security Administration (SSA) and International Social Security Association (ISSA).

Steel, F. W., and D. Snodgrass. 2008. "Raising Productivity and Reducing Risks of Household Enterprises—Diagnostic Methodology Framework." WIEGO Network. Washington, DC: World Bank.

Stewart, F. 2006. "Financial Education and Pensions." Presentation at G8 International Conference on Improving Financial Literacy. Moscow: OECD.

Terrel, K., and T. H. Gindling. 2002. "The Effects of Minimum Wages on the Formal and Informal Sector: Evidence from Costa Rica." IZA Discussion Paper No. 1018.

Thaler, R. H., and S. Benartzi. 2004. "Save More Tomorrow: Using Behavioral Economics to Increase Employee Saving." *Journal of Political Economy* 112 (1): S164–S187.

Thaler, R. H., and C. R. Sustein. 2003. "Libertarian Paternalisms." *American Economy Review* 93 (2): 175–79.

Transparency International 2010 Corruption Perception Index (CPI). http://www.transparency.org/policy_research/surveys_indices/cpi/2010/results.

Tversky, A., and D. Kahneman. 1981. "The Framing of Decisions and the Psychology of Choice." *Science* 211 (4481): 453–58.

Van Adams, A. 2008. "A Framework for the Study of Skills Development in the Informal Sector of Sub-Saharan Africa." Washington, DC: World Bank.

Von Ginneken, W. 2009. *Extending Social Security Coverage: Concepts, Approaches and Knowledge Gaps.* Geneva: International Social Security Association.

World Bank. 2004. *Doing Business 2005.* Washington, DC: World Bank.

———. 2007. "Republic of Bolivia: Policies for Increasing Firms' Formality and Productivity." Report 40057-BO. Washington, DC: World Bank.

———. 2008. "Reducing Undeclared Employment in Hungary: Synthesis Report of the World Bank Study." Washington, DC: World Bank.

———. 2009. "From Privilege to Competition: Unlocking Private-Led Growth in Middle East and North Africa." Washington, DC: World Bank.

———. 2010. "Health Insurance in Lebanon: Improving Risk Pooling." Washington, DC: World Bank.

Yousef, T. 2004. "Development, Growth and Policy Reforms in Middle East and North Africa since 1950." *Journal of Economic Perspectives* 18 (3): 91–116.

Zavodny, M. 2000. "The Effect of the Minimum Wage on Employment and Hours." *Labour Economics* 7 (6): 729–50.

Zhu, Y. 2009. *A Case Study on Social Security Coverage Extension in China.* Geneva: International Social Security Association.

Ziderman, A. 2003. "Financing Vocational Training in Sub-Saharan Africa." Africa Region Human Development Series. Washington, DC: World Bank.

green press
INITIATIVE

www.ingramcontent.com/pod-product-compliance
Lightning Source LLC
Chambersburg PA
CBHW082135210326
41599CB00031B/5987